Atherosclerosis

A SCOPE® PUBLICATION

ISBN 0-89501-061-5

Copyright 1992, The Upjohn Company, Kalamazoo, Michigan 49001
Printed in The United States of America

UED4890.00

Authors:

Antonio M. Gotto, Jr, MD, DPhil *Editor-in-Chief*
Chairman, Department of Medicine
Baylor College of Medicine
Chief, Internal Medicine Service
The Methodist Hospital
Houston, Texas

Chapter 1

Antonio M. Gotto, Jr, MD, DPhil
Chairman, Department of Medicine
Baylor College of Medicine
Chief, Internal Medicine Service
The Methodist Hospital
Houston, Texas

Chapter 2

Robert W. Wissler, PhD, MD
Program Director
Multicenter Cooperative Study of the
Pathobiological Determinants of
Atherosclerosis in Youth
Distinguished Service Professor of Pathology
Department of Pathology
The University of Chicago
Pritzker School of Medicine
Chicago, Illinois

Chapter 3

David J. Skorton, MD
Professor and Associate Chair for
Clinical Programs
Department of Internal Medicine
College of Medicine
Professor, Department of Electrical and
Computer Engineering
College of Engineering
University of Iowa
Iowa City, Iowa
Thomas J. Ryan, MD
Professor of Medicine
Chief of Cardiology
Boston University School of Medicine
Boston, Massachusetts

Chapter 4

Stephen E. Epstein, MD
Chief, Cardiology Branch
National Heart, Lung, and Blood Institute
National Institutes of Health
Bethesda, Maryland

Chapter 5

Robert Roberts, MD
Chief of Cardiology
Professor of Medicine and Cell Biology
Baylor College of Medicine
Houston, Texas

Chapter 6

Michael E. DeBakey, MD
Chancellor and Chairman
Department of Surgery
Director, DeBakey Heart Center
Baylor College of Medicine
Houston, Texas
Gerald M. Lawrie, MD
Professor of Surgery
Department of Surgery
Baylor College of Medicine
Houston, Texas

Contents

Chapter 1
9 **Risk Factors for Atherosclerosis**
9 The Risk Factor Hypothesis
9 The Dyslipidemias
39 Hypertension
42 Cigarette Smoking
42 Seconday Risk Factors
45 Minor Risk Factors
46 Conclusion
46 Selected Readings

Chapter 2
51 **Important Points in the Pathogenesis of Atherosclerosis**
51 Introduction
56 Major Pathogenetic Processes in the Artery Wall
71 Risk Factors and Pathogenetic Processes
73 Points of Predilection of Severe Atherosclerosis
75 Other Modulating Factors That Influence the Pathogenesis of Atherosclerosis
83 How Does Knowledge of Pathogenesis Lead to the Concept That Atherosclerosis Is Preventable and Substantially Reversible?
84 The Spectrum of Intervention
86 Conclusion
86 Acknowledgements
87 Selected Readings

Chapter 3
89 **Diagnosis of Coronary Artery Disease**
89 Introduction
89 The History
94 The Physical Examination
95 An Overview of the Diagnostic Process
97 The Electrocardiogram (ECG)
105 Radiographic Techniques
112 Echocardiography
115 Radionuclide Techniques
122 Computed Tomography
124 Nuclear Magnetic Resonance Techniques
127 Selected Readings

Chapter 4
130 **Medical Treatment of Stable Angina Pectoris**
130 The Pathophysiologic Basis of Angina Pectoris
137 The Pharmacologic Treatment of Angina Pectoris
147 Physical Conditioning
148 Transcatheter Coronary Arterial Recanalization
151 Conclusion

Chapter 5
152 **Pathogenesis, Diagnosis, and Management of Acute Myocardial Infarction and Unstable Angina**
152 Pathogenesis
155 Classification
156 Diagnosis of Myocardial Infarction
165 Management of Myocardial Infarction
174 Complications of Myocardial Infarction
183 Prognosis of Q-Wave and Non–Q-Wave Infarction
186 Postinfarction Stratification and Investigation
188 Prophylactic Therapy Postinfarction
190 Unstable Angina
191 Conclusion
192 Selected Readings

Chapter 6
194 **Atherosclerotic Occlusive Disease of the Coronary Arteries: Surgical Considerations**
194 Introduction
195 Patterns of Atherosclerosis
195 Rates of Progression
204 Indications
205 Operative Technique
226 Results of Surgical Treatment
228 Selected Readings

229 **Index**

Preface

A remarkable reduction in the death rate from coronary heart disease has occurred since the middle of this century. The US age-adjusted mortality rate from myocardial infarction, which in 1950 was 226.4 per 100 000 people, declined to 124.1 per 100 000 in 1987. Similar reductions have occurred in age-adjusted mortality rates from strokes (88.8 in 1950 versus 30.7 in 1987) and hypertension (56.0 in 1950 versus 6.6 in 1987). These declining mortality rates can be attributed to three primary factors: preventive measures, earlier diagnosis, and improved treatment.

The success of preventive measures is founded on public education. Some researchers have calculated that the 20% decline in age-adjusted mortality from coronary heart disease that occurred between 1968 and 1976 was due largely to preventive efforts. Specifically, more than half was related to lifestyle changes, such as smoking cessation and dietary modification to reduce serum cholesterol. The antihypertension campaign initiated during the 1970s probably contributed to the decreased number of fatal cerebrovascular events. As a result of public education efforts, more Americans are choosing "heart-healthy" lifestyles that include eating less saturated fat and more polyunsaturated fat, exercising regularly, maintaining a healthy weight, and forgoing the use of tobacco.

The emphasis on earlier detection of risk factors (eg, elevated serum cholesterol, hypertension) and earlier diagnosis of coronary heart disease has often allowed the clinician to institute therapeutic interventions before the disease becomes clinically manifest. Such interventions may have the potential for significantly retarding or even reversing the disease process.

Finally, aggressive treatment has contributed to the reduced mortality rates. Improvements in emergency (prehospital) care, greater availability of coronary care units, the widespread use of thrombolytic therapy and percutaneous transluminal coronary angioplasty, advances in surgical techniques, and appropriate follow-up treatment after hospital discharge not only have prevented deaths but also have prevented a significant amount of morbidity.

However, much work lies ahead. We must not forget that, in spite of the progress we have made, coronary heart disease is still the leading cause of death in the United States. Statistics from the World Health Organization show the United States has the highest annual mortality rate from coronary heart disease of any industrialized country: 55 deaths among every 100 000 people, compared with 33 per 100 000 in Switzerland and 15 per 100 000 in Japan.

This book reviews our current knowledge about the pathogenesis, prevention, diagnosis, and treatment of coronary heart disease. We hope its readers will bring their own, fresh vision to the subject and will someday contribute new knowledge to combating this disease.

The importance of conquering this country's number one killer is reflected in the amount of time, the tremendous effort, and the stubborn dedication of the many people who made this book possible. Although it is impossible to thank each one, I am especially grateful to my colleagues and contributing authors, Drs Wissler, Skorton, Ryan, Epstein, Roberts, DeBakey, and Lawrie; to Suzanne Simpson, Shelley Overholt, and Daphna Gregg for their editorial work; and to The Upjohn Company for their continuing interest in medical education.

Antonio M. Gotto, Jr, MD, DPhil
Editor-in-Chief

Risk Factors for Atherosclerosis

The Risk Factor Hypothesis

Most of the people who die or are disabled because of atherosclerosis and subsequent coronary heart disease have one or more identifiable characteristics that predispose them to the development of these diseases. These characteristics, or risk factors, are classified as either primary or secondary, depending on the degree to which they affect the risk of developing coronary heart disease.

According to the risk factor hypothesis, a person who has a risk factor for coronary heart disease is more likely to develop clinical manifestations of the disease and is likely to do so earlier than a person with no risk factors. If the risk factors present are eliminated or their impact is reduced, then the subject's risk of developing coronary heart disease and its related complications will also be reduced.

Studies have identified three primary treatable risk factors, which are:
- Dyslipidemia, including elevated serum levels of total cholesterol, low-density lipoprotein (LDL) cholesterol, and triglyceride, and depressed serum levels of high-density lipoprotein (HDL) cholesterol;
- Elevated blood pressure; and
- Cigarette smoking.

Secondary risk factors, some of which are modifiable, are:
- Diabetes mellitus;
- Obesity;
- Lack of physical activity;
- Psychosocial and behavioral factors;
- Male gender;
- Estrogen depletion in women;
- Heavy use of alcohol; and
- A family history of premature coronary heart disease.

When the 1977 edition of this monograph was published, there was insufficient evidence to prove that eliminating a risk factor or lowering an abnormal biochemical risk factor to a "normal" level could decrease the occurrence of coronary heart disease. Since that time, several clinical trials have provided substantial proof that the risk of developing coronary heart disease can be reduced. Physicians now know that modifying risk factors, in particular, reducing elevated total serum cholesterol and LDL cholesterol levels, will lower a person's risk of developing coronary heart disease.

This chapter reviews in detail the correlation between lipid elevations and the development of coronary heart disease, the possible mechanisms involved in this relationship, and the management algorithms these relationships dictate for improved patient care. Also discussed is the evidence linking other risk factors to the development of coronary heart disease.

The Dyslipidemias

Cholesterol is a vital component of cell membranes in all tissues. Homeostasis of cholesterol is regulated by several mechanisms that deliver cholesterol to cells and remove it from cells. Disruption of these regulatory pathways can interfere with normal cell function and, in some cases, can lead to cholesterol accumulation in tissues.

To understand the link between lipid abnormalities and coronary heart disease, the reader must have a thorough grasp of the normal metabolism of lipoproteins and the relationship between lipid abnormalities and the pathogenesis of atherosclerosis.

Lipids, Lipoproteins, and Apolipoproteins

Cholesterol is one of the primary lipids of the human body, along with cholesteryl esters, triglycerides, phospholipids, and unesterified fatty acids. With the exception of unesterified fatty acid, these lipids are transported in the blood by emulsified, water-soluble complexes known as lipoproteins. The lipoproteins contain protein components known as *apolipoproteins (apo)*, which bind to the water-insoluble lipids to form water-soluble complexes. In their lipoprotein packaging, phospholipids are the most soluble of the lipid components, followed by (in decreasing order of solubility) cholesterol, cholesteryl esters, and triglycerides.

Figure 1
General structure of a lipoprotein

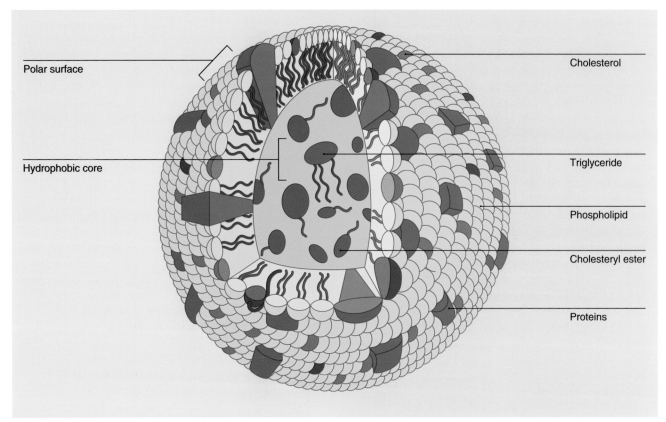

Polar surface

Hydrophobic core

Cholesterol

Triglyceride

Phospholipid

Cholesteryl ester

Proteins

The hydrophobic core is composed of cholesteryl ester and triglyceride packed at a much higher density than shown here. The polar surface is a monolayer of phospholipid. The amount of cholesterol on the surface varies according to the type of lipoprotein. The proteins here show the range of penetration that plasma apolipoproteins are believed to span.

The general structure of a lipoprotein is shown in Figure 1. In its mature form, a lipoprotein is a spherical particle consisting of a surface monolayer of apolipoproteins and phospholipids, an intermediate zone of cholesterol, and an inner core of triglyceride and cholesteryl ester.

The apolipoproteins serve a dual function. Not only do they bind and emulsify lipids, but they also contribute to the regulation of lipoprotein metabolism. Table 1 shows the distribution of apolipoproteins in plasma. Apolipoproteins contain amphipathic helical structures, β-pleated sheet structures, and disordered, random structures. The amphipathic helical structure is two-sided, consisting of inner and outer surfaces. The outer surface, which is exposed to the aqueous environment, contains alternating groups of water-soluble acidic and basic amino acids. The inner surface of the amphipathic helical structure contains the more hydrophobic amino acids. The primary forces holding the apoproteins and the lipid constituents of the lipoproteins together appear to be interactions between the hydrophobic surfaces of the amphipathic helices and the hydrophobic portions of lipids. How the lipoproteins are thermodynamically stabilized is unclear; it may involve a transfer of the hydrophobic surface of the amphipathic helices from the aqueous exterior to the more hydrophobic interior. The alternating acidic and basic groups and the hydrophilic outer surface of the amphipathic helices anchor the apoprotein to the lipoprotein surface.

There are five major families of plasma lipoproteins: the chylomicron, the very-low-density lipoprotein (VLDL), the intermediate-density lipoprotein (IDL), the low-density lipoprotein (LDL), and the high-density lipoprotein (HDL). They differ not only in density but also in size, ultracentrifugal properties, and electrophoretic characteristics (Table 2). The smaller the lipoprotein, the greater its protein content and density. There is also heterogeneity within each family.

Chylomicrons are the largest of the lipoproteins, ranging from 80 to 1000 nm in diameter, and have the highest sedimentation coefficient on ultracentrifugation (more than 400 Svedberg flotation units). These lipoproteins have the lowest density at an average of 0.95 g/mL. Chylomicrons do not migrate on paper or agarose gel electrophoresis, and normally they are absent from the blood after a 12-hour fast. Mature chylomicrons contain apo B_{48}, the apo As of intestinal origin, and the apo Cs and apo E produced in the liver.

VLDLs, the next-largest lipoproteins, range from 30 to 80 nm in diameter. On paper and agarose gel electrophoresis, VLDL particles migrate with pre-β mobility (that is, just ahead of the β-globulin fraction). The primary apoprotein constituents of VLDL are apo B_{100}, the apo Cs, and apo E, but they may also contain small amounts of apo A-I and apo A-II.

IDLs are 25 to 30 nm in diameter and have β mobility. They contain apo B_{100} and apo E. IDLs (also called VLDL remnants) are produced by the hydrolysis of VLDL triglycerides.

Like IDLs, the *LDLs* are a product of VLDL hydrolysis. Approximately 20 to 25 nm in diameter, LDLs demonstrate β mobility and they contain only apo B_{100}. From chylomicrons to VLDLs to IDLs to LDLs, there is a progressive decrease in triglyceride content and a progressive increase in cholesteryl ester content. In LDLs, the core is predominantly cholesteryl ester; in chylomicrons and VLDLs, it is predominantly triglyceride.

HDL particles are the smallest (5 to 12 nm in diameter) of the major lipoproteins. There are two primary fractions of HDL, the lipid-rich HDL_2 (1.061 to 1.210 g/mL, 9 to 12 nm) and the lipid-poor HDL_3 (1.125 to 1.210 g/mL, 5 to 9 nm). These two fractions can be further subdivided into HDL_{2a}, HDL_{2b}, HDL_{3a}, and HDL_{3b}; the last two are reduced

Table 1
Distribution of apolipoproteins in plasma

Apolipoprotein	Plasma concentration		Percentage distribution				Tissue source
	mg/mL	mol %	HDL	LDL	IDL	VLDL	
Apo A-I	130	43	100	–	–	–	Liver, intestine
Apo A-II	40	22	100	–	–	–	Liver
Apo A-IV	–	–	–	–	–	–	Intestine
Apo B$_{48}$	–	–	–	–	–	–	Intestine
Apo B$_{100}$	80	5	–	82	8	2	Liver
Apo C-I	6	9	97	–	1	2	Liver
Apo C-II	3	3	60	–	10	30	Liver
Apo C-III	12	13	60	10	10	20	Liver
Apo D	10	5	100	–	–	–	Liver
Apo E	5	2	50	10	20	20	Liver

Adapted with permission from Smith LC, Massey JB, Sparrow JT, Gotto AM Jr,
Pownall HJ. Structure and dynamics of human plasma lipoproteins. In: Pifat G,
Herak JN, eds. *Supramolecular Structure and Function.* New York, NY: Plenum
Press; 1983:205-244.

Table 2
Composition and properties of human lipoproteins

Properties	Chylomicrons	VLDL	IDL	LDL	HDL
Density (g/mL)	0.95	0.95-1.006	1.006-1.019	1.019-1.063	1.061-1.210
Size (nm)	80-1000	30-80	25-30	20-25	5-12
Flotation (Sf, 1.063)	400	20-100	12-20	1-12	–
Electrophoretic mobility	Origin	Pre-β	β	β	α
Major lipid constituents	Triglyceride (exogenous)	Triglyceride (endogenous), phospholipid	Esterified cholesterol, phospholipid	Triglyceride, esterified cholesterol	Phospholipid, cholesterol
Apoprotein constituents	Apo A-I Apo A-II Apo A-IV Apo B$_{48}$	Apo B$_{100}$ Apo C-I Apo C-II Apo C-III Apo E	Apo B$_{100}$ Apo E	Apo B$_{100}$	Apo A-I Apo A-II Apo C-II Apo E

in size and lipid content. The HDL particle contains nearly equal amounts of lipid and apoprotein in contrast to the LDL particle, which contains about 75% lipid and 25% apoprotein by weight. The lipid content of HDL is primarily cholesteryl ester and phosphatidylcholine (lecithin). HDL contains apo A-I, apo A-II, apo C, and apo E. On electrophoresis, HDLs migrate with the α-globulins; the terms α-*lipoproteins* and β-*lipoproteins* are sometimes used to refer to HDLs and LDLs, respectively.

A fascinating lipoprotein called *Lp[a]* has a density between LDL and HDL. It has been denoted by a variety of names, including "sinking" pre-β lipoprotein in reference to its VLDL-like pre-β migration but its inability, in distinction from VLDL, to float at a density of 1.006 g/mL. Lp[a] contains two apoproteins, apo B_{100} and a glycoprotein specific to Lp[a] called *apo[a]*, that are bound together by a disulfide bond. Human apo[a] has a high degree of homology with plasminogen, the precursor of plasmin. Elevated Lp[a] plasma levels are associated with increased risk of stroke and coronary heart disease and have been correlated with severe coronary heart disease in men who have elevated apo B concentrations. Lp[a] has been found in atherosclerotic plaques.

Lp[x], another unusual lipoprotein, has a high content of phosphatidylcholine and unesterified cholesterol. The presence of Lp[x] in plasma is usually diagnostic of obstructive liver disease.

Apolipoprotein A: Apoprotein A-I is synthesized in the intestinal wall and the liver. In all HDL species studied to date, apo A-I has been the apolipoprotein present in the greatest amount. The genes encoding apo A-I, apo C-III, and apo A-IV are located on chromosome 11; the apo A-I and apo C-III genes are located on opposite strands of DNA, and apo A-IV is positioned downstream from apo A-I. Thus, gene mutations in this region may disrupt the synthesis of all three apoproteins.

Apo A-I is an activator of lecithin:cholesterol acyltransferase (LCAT), a plasma enzyme essential in cholesterol metabolism and in transporting cholesterol from peripheral tissues into the plasma and back to the liver, a process called *reverse cholesterol transport* (see Transport of Cholesterol on page 22). Apo A-I is considered to be the prototype of the amphipathic helical structure. Typically, the amphipathic helical structure is formed by repeat units, each consisting of 22 amino acids, followed by proline, an amino acid that breaks the helical structure of protein. Apo A-I contains eight such repeat units. The messenger RNAs for apo A-I contain 33 and 66 base pairs, which code for 11 and 22 amino acid units, respectively.

Several laboratories have prepared synthetic peptide fragments homologous to apo A-I that also activate LCAT. The Segrest laboratory postulated that an acidic amino acid is required at residue 13 on the hydrophobic surface of the amphipathic helix for LCAT activation. Presumably, this acid residue helps to open up the lipid substrate to make it more accessible to LCAT.

Several apo A-I polymorphisms have been identified using the technique of restriction fragment length polymorphism (RFLP) mapping. (In RFLP mapping, restriction enzymes are used to cleave the DNA molecule into fragments of varying lengths at specific base sequences. A technique such as gel electrophoresis is used to separate the fragments by size, thus allowing the order of the DNA fragments to be determined and variant fragments to be identified.) Using RFLP techniques and the restriction enzyme *Pst*I, Ordovas et al identified a polymorphism at the noncoding 3′ end of the apo A-I gene that was reportedly linked to an increased risk of coronary heart disease. This variant allele (the P2 allele) was present in 3% to 4% of the general population and in 32% of subjects who had angiographic evidence of coronary heart disease before age 60. Other investigators reported that the S2 allele was associated with coronary heart disease and with hypertriglyceridemia. However, these findings have not been confirmed, and no consistent correlations have been established between apo A-I polymorphisms and dyslipidemia or coronary heart disease when different populations are compared.

Apo A-II, a 1600-dalton apoprotein synthesized by the liver, contains two identical peptide chains bound by a disulfide linkage. Although its function has not been clearly defined, some studies report that apo A-II is an activator of hepatic triglyceride lipase. Apo A-II is generally a minor constituent of HDL. One allele detected with the restriction endonuclease *MspI* may be associated with an increase in the concentration of apo A-II.

Apo A-IV is a large apoprotein (46 000 daltons) that is synthesized by the intestine and is found in chylomicrons and HDL. For reasons that are unclear, apo A-IV is dissociated more easily from lipoprotein particles into the nonlipoprotein fraction plasma than are other apolipoproteins. Apo A-IV has a high content of amphipathic helical structures and has been reported to be an activator of LCAT and a promoter of cholesterol transport from peripheral tissues. Dietary fat stimulates a transient increase in apo A-IV synthesis, but the precise contribution of apo A-IV to fat absorption remains to be defined.

Apo A-IV is polymorphic in humans; of the five different isoforms described, the most common variants are apo $A-IV_1$ and apo $A-IV_2$. The polymorphism results from a single point mutation that converts glutamine to histidine at residue 360. Studies of Tyrolean and Icelandic populations have shown different frequencies of these alleles. The apo $A-IV_2$ variant is associated with increased HDL cholesterol and decreased triglyceride levels.

The functions and disease associations of the apo As and the other apolipoproteins are summarized in Table 3.

Apolipoprotein B: Apo B is the primary apoprotein involved in serum cholesterol transport. It occurs in two forms: apo B_{100} and apo B_{48}. Apo B_{100} is thought to be a single polypeptide of approximately 550 000 daltons produced primarily in the liver. Apo B_{48} is 48% that size and is produced primarily in the small intestine in humans; the rat has been reported to make apo B_{48} in the liver as well.

Apo B_{100} is required for the formation of VLDL and is a major protein constituent not only of VLDL but also of IDL and LDL. Apo B_{100} accounts for about 25% of the weight of the LDL particle and contains a recognition site for the LDL receptor. (Because the LDL receptor recognizes both apo B_{100} and apo E, it is also called the B:E receptor.) Apo B_{48} does not contain a recognition site for the LDL receptor.

The molecular structure of apo B_{100} is somewhat different from other apoproteins. Apo B_{100} contains fewer amphipathic helical structures, which are located on the outer surface adjacent to the aqueous environment. This apoprotein has a higher number of β-pleated sheet structures, which contributes to its relative water insolubility once the lipid constituents of apo B_{100} are stripped away. Apo B_{100} has an extremely high affinity for the lipid components of lipoproteins.

The structure of apo B_{100} was identified by a combination of classic peptide sequencing and determining overlapping sequences of apo B_{100} complementary DNA from a library of known hepatic DNA sequences. The complementary DNA has 14.1 kilobases that code for 4563 amino acids and a 27 amino acid signal protein. The complete gene is 43 kilobases long, has 29 exons, and is located on the short arm of chromosome 2.

The ligand-binding region of apo B_{100} appears to be located between amino acid residues 3300 and 3600. A cluster of positively charged amino acids in this region is thought to bind to a negatively charged region of the LDL receptor on the cell surface. Yang et al prepared synthetic fragments of apo B_{100} consisting of amino acids from residues 3345 to 3381. A synthetic peptide from this region was able to recognize the LDL receptor and bind to it, suggesting that the region of apo B_{100} between residues 3345 and 3381 contains the ligand for recognition by the LDL receptor. A hypothetical model of LDL containing apo B_{100} is shown in Figure 2.

Table 3
Apolipoprotein functions and their association with human disease

Apolipoprotein	Function	Association with clinical disorders
A-I	Activates LCAT	Tangier disease; apo A-I/apo C-III deficiency; atherosclerosis
A-II	(? Activates hepatic lipase)	–
A-IV	(? Fat absorption)	–
B_{100}	Receptor-mediated catabolism of LDL	Abetalipoproteinemia; normotriglyceridemic abetalipoproteinemia (B_{100} deficiency); atherosclerosis
B_{48}	Chylomicron production	–
C-I	Activates (moderately) LCAT	–
C-II	Activates lipoprotein lipase	Familial type I hyperlipoproteinemia
C-III	Inhibits catabolism of triglyceride-rich lipoproteins	Apo A-I/apo C-III deficiency
E	Receptor-mediated catabolism of apo E-containing lipoproteins	Familial type III hyperlipoproteinemia

Adapted with permission from Breslow JL. Lipoprotein genetics and molecular biology. In: Gotto AM Jr, ed. *Plasma Lipoproteins*. New York, NY: Elsevier; 1987:359-397.

One of the fascinating stories of the molecular biology of apolipoproteins concerns the origin of apo B_{48}. Southern blot analysis indicates there is only one copy of the apo B gene in the human genome. The messenger RNAs (mRNA) for apo B in the liver and the intestine are approximately the same length. However, the mRNA in the intestine contains a single base substitution that results in a stop codon after amino acid residue 2152. Thus, there appears to be a unique editing process that leads to intestinal synthesis of apo B_{48}.

The functional significance of the intestine making apo B_{48} rather than B_{100} is not clear, although apo B_{48} may be instrumental in the intestinal secretion of chylomicrons. Chylomicrons incorporate B_{48} in the intestine, but because apo B_{48} par-

ticles do not contain the receptor-binding domain of apo B_{100} particles, chylomicron remnants require apo E to bind to receptors in the liver (see Transport of Cholesterol on page 22). In rats, the proportion of hepatic synthesis of apo B_{48} versus apo B_{100} is influenced by the activity of thyroid hormone, but the control mechanism in humans is not completely understood.

Several apo B polymorphisms have been described. A recent study suggested that *Eco*RI polymorphism is associated with an increased frequency of coronary heart disease and that the receptor-binding domain of apo B influences LDL metabolism. There are various associations between alleles of *Xba*I and *Eco*RI polymorphism with lipoprotein and apolipoprotein patterns and the occurrence of coronary heart disease. Huang et al described five polymorphisms that span the entire length of the apo B gene. Some apo B polymorphisms result in protein structure changes that can be demonstrated by antibodies, although

Figure 2
A model of low-density lipoprotein showing apo B$_{100}$ on the cell surface and penetrating the hydrophobic core

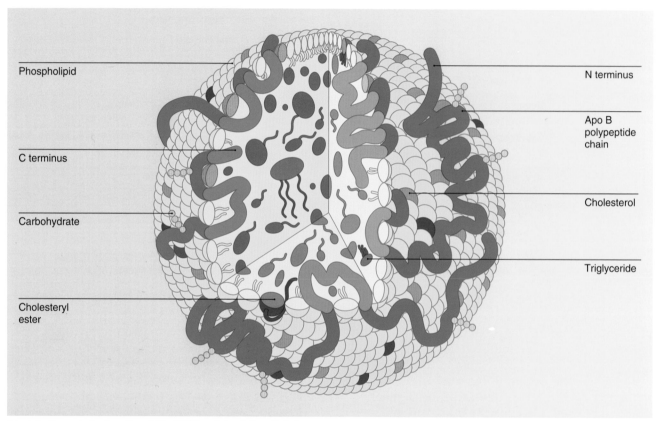

Phospholipid

N terminus

Apo B polypeptide chain

C terminus

Carbohydrate

Cholesterol

Cholesteryl ester

Triglyceride

Adapted with permission from Yang C, Kim TW, Weng S, Lee B, Yang M, Gotto AM Jr. Isolation and characterization of sulfhydryl and disulfide peptides of human apolipoprotein B-100. *Proc Natl Acad Sci USA*. 1990;87:5523-5527.

other polymorphisms, such as those in the 3′ flanking region, do not cause structural changes. The use of multiple RFLPs to construct haplotypes may be more helpful in finding correlations between coronary heart disease and isolated polymorphisms. Thus far, studies of isolated polymorphisms have not yielded results that are reproducible enough to be useful for predicting a person's risk of developing coronary heart disease.

Apolipoprotein C: Apo C-I, apo C-II, and apo C-III are synthesized in the liver and incorporated into nascent HDL particles. They can then be transferred to VLDLs and chylomicrons. Apo C-I can serve as an activator of LCAT, although apo A-I is likely the primary activator. Apo C-II activates lipoprotein lipase. Apo C-III (or the other apo Cs) may stabilize the surface of chylomicron remnants and VLDL remnants and perhaps prevent the premature uptake of these remnant particles by the liver.

Apolipoprotein E: Apo E is synthesized in macrophages and in the liver, brain, kidneys, adrenal glands, and muscles. The liver is thought to be the origin for most of the plasma apo E found in chylomicrons, VLDLs, IDLs, and HDLs. Apo E contains amino acid residues that are recognized by the LDL receptor, despite the lack of structural homology with apo B_{100}. Apo E also appears to modulate the uptake of chylomicron remnants by the liver through a mechanism that does not involve the LDL receptor, whereas IDL is thought to be removed through the interaction of apo E with the LDL receptor.

Three major alleles exist for apo E: E_2, E_3, and E_4. The most common isoform is apo E_3, which is found in approximately 76% of the US population and contains cysteine at residue 112 and arginine at residue 158. Apo E_2, found in approximately 13% of the US population, has cysteine at both of these residues. Apo E_4, found in about 11% of the US population, contains arginine at both residue sites. The receptor-binding domain of apo E has been localized to residues 140 through 160; amino acid substitutions in this domain and in other sites may affect apo E binding to LDL receptors.

The apo E_2 allele is associated with decreased binding affinity due to the substitution of cysteine for arginine at residue 158. Apo E_4 is thought to bind with a greater affinity than apo E_3, which, in turn, binds with a greater affinity than apo E_2. Remnants containing apo E_2 have defective binding to liver receptors and a delayed clearance from the circulation. A person can be homozygous for any one of these three alleles or can be heterozygous for any two of the three. The E_2/E_2 phenotype is associated with familial dysbetalipoproteinemia, although most people with this phenotype are normolipidemic or hypolipidemic.

Homozygosity for apo E_2 is associated with lower levels of total and LDL serum cholesterol, and homozygosity for apo E_4 is associated with higher levels. These correlations have been found in people both with and without coronary heart disease. Theoretically, an enhanced uptake of a chylomicron remnant containing only apo E_4 could lead to a secondary down-regulation of the LDL receptor, resulting in high circulating levels of LDL and total cholesterol.

Apolipoprotein and Lipoprotein Defects

Apo A-I mutations: Several mutations of apo A-I have been identified by electrophoresis and isoelectric focusing. Most of the mutants, which differ in charge, contain an additional acidic amino acid or two additional basic amino acids, and most do not affect the concentration of HDL or increase the likelihood of early development of coronary heart disease. A few of the mutants have been reported to be associated with a decrease in LCAT activation.

The Assmann laboratory in Muenster, Germany, has published extensively on apo A-I mutations (Table 4). Although the mutations are uncommon, more than 20 apo A-I isoforms with a single amino acid substitution have been identified. Many of these isoforms appear to be insignificant in terms of clinical consequences, but some mutations, such as a proline to arginine substitution at residue 165, are associated with decreased HDL concentrations. A proline to arginine substitution at residue 3 is associated with a variant type of pro-apo A-I (the precursor form), which may inhibit normal apo A-I synthesis. Apo A-I$_{Baltimore}$ has an arginine to leucine substitution at residue 10 but does not produce a decrease in apo A-I. In apo A-I$_{Milano}$, an arginine to cysteine substitution at residue 173 is associated with exceptionally low HDL concentrations but not with premature coronary heart disease. In fact, some individuals with apo A-I$_{Milano}$ live into their 80s without showing clinical manifestations of coronary heart disease.

Apo A-I/apo C-III deficiency: Some genetic mutations can produce an apolipoprotein deficiency that causes a marked reduction in or complete absence of HDL and results in severe premature atherosclerosis. In a documented case of two sisters with an apo A-I/apo C-III deficiency, each sister had a mutation in which a portion of the genetic material for apo C-III had been removed from its normal location, inverted, and placed upstream in the region coding for apo A-I. As a result, the sisters had a complete absence of apo A-I and apo C-III, as well as a marked deficiency of HDL. Both sisters experienced overwhelming atherosclerosis early in life, along with xanthomas in childhood and corneal opacification in young adulthood. Symptoms of heart failure developed at ages 25 and 31. The first-degree relatives of the sisters had one half of the normal quantities of apo A-I and apo C-III.

Table 4
Known single amino acid mutations in human apo A-I

Substitution	Number of known families	Functional implications
3:Pro → Arg	1	Impaired pro-apo A-I conversion
3:Pro → His	1	Impaired pro-apo A-I conversion
4:Pro → Arg	2	–
10:Arg → Leu	1	–
13:Asp → Tyr	1	–
26:Gly → Arg	1	Familial amyloidotic neuropathy
89:Asp → Glu	1	–
103:Asp → Asn	1	–
107:Lys → 0	9	Reduction of LCAT cofactor activity and lipid binding
107:Lys → Met	2	–
110:Glu → Lys	1	Low HDL cholesterol
136:Glu → Lys	1	–
139:Glu → Gly	2	–
143:Pro → Arg	1	Reduction in LCAT cofactor activity; relative deficiency in mutant isoform
147:Glu → Val	1	–
158:Ala → Glu	1	–
165:Pro → Arg	4	HDL deficiency; relative deficiency in mutant isoform
169:Glu → Gln	1	–
173:Arg → Cys	1	HDL deficiency; decreased cholesterol esterification rate; abnormal HDL particles; abnormal lipid binding
177:Arg → His	1	–
198:Glu → Lys	4	–
213:Asp → Gly	1	–

Reproduced with permission from Assmann G, Schmitz G, Funke H, von Eckardstein A. Apolipoprotein A-I and HDL deficiency. *Curr Opin Lipidol.* 1990;1:110-115.

LCAT deficiency: Some other apo A-I and HDL deficiencies are also associated with corneal opacification, but not all are accompanied by premature atherosclerosis. Familial LCAT deficiency is characterized by low levels of apo A-I and HDL, corneal opacities, and early coronary heart disease. However, in fish-eye disease, corneal opacification and apo A-I and HDL deficiences are not accompanied by premature coronary heart disease.

HDL deficiency: Perhaps the best understood of the HDL deficiencies is Tangier disease. Patients with this disorder have no normal HDL but do have very low concentrations of altered HDL. Abnormal amounts of cholesteryl ester are deposited in the reticuloendothelial system, and these patients have orange tonsils and neuropathy due to lipid deposition in the Schwann cells of the neurons. People with Tangier disease may develop coronary heart disease, but this does not usually occur until middle age. The exact defect in Tangier disease is not known but is thought to involve abnormal synthesis of HDL. The abnormal HDL may have an increased turnover rate and be able to function in reverse cholesterol transport to an adequate level, but the HDL may be unable to maintain the normal scavenger function of removing cholesteryl ester from the reticuloendothelial system.

Apo B mutations: Variations at the apo B gene locus were first described by Berg et al who identified 10 genetic variants of LDL that could be detected immunologically, deriving the antigenic-group (Ag) system of classification. At least 75 nucleotide changes in apo B have been reported; 54 are in the coding region of the protein.

Soria et al described the disorder familial defective apo B_{100} in which a mutation in exon 26 of the apo B gene results in a substitution of glutamine for arginine at residue 3500. Because the mutation occurs in the region that specifies binding to the LDL receptor, apo B_{100} affinity for the LDL receptor is apparently decreased. Familial defective apo B_{100} is characterized by mild to moderate elevations in circulating total cholesterol, apo B, and LDL.

Hypobetalipoproteinemia, characterized by reduced (40 to 180 g/dL) serum cholesterol levels, results from an autosomal dominant defect in apo B_{100}. In the heterozygous state, the clinical manifestations of hypobetalipoproteinemia are mild or completely absent, although mild neuropathy has been described in some patients. In homozygous patients, the clinical findings may be severe and indistinguishable from the manifestations of abetalipoproteinemia. The most common genetic basis appears to be a nonsense code or deletion mutation that results in synthesis of a truncated form of apo B_{100}. Apo $B_{Hopkins}$, a truncated form in which several carboxy-terminal amino acid residues are deleted, has been reported to result in an apo B with increased affinity to the LDL receptor.

In classic abetalipoproteinemia (originally called Bassen-Kornzweig syndrome) the clinical manifestations are malabsorption of fat, an atypical type of retinitis pigmentosa, acanthocytosis (abnormally shaped erythrocytes), and progressive neurologic disease. Abetalipoproteinemia was originally described as a complete absence of all apo B-containing serum lipoproteins (ie, chylomicrons, VLDL, IDL, and LDL); HDL was the only serum lipoprotein present in the patients. Recent studies suggest that in some (but not all) patients, apo B may be present in intestinal cells and produced by enterocytes. No defect has been found in the gene that codes for apo B, and investigators believe that the defect probably occurs in assembling the lipoprotein particle with apo B in the intestine and liver.

In normotriglyceridemic abetalipoproteinemia (a variant form of abetalipoproteinemia), serum LDL is absent, but apo B_{48} is formed and incorporated into chylomicrons in the intestine after ingestion of fat. Apo B_{100}, however, cannot be formed by the liver.

Apo C deficiency: Apo C-II deficiency is one of the best-studied apolipoprotein deficiencies. Because apo C-II is required for the activation of lipoprotein lipase, a deficiency of apo C-II causes a severe form of chylomicronemia characterized by extremely elevated fasting plasma triglyceride levels (500 to 10 000 mg/dL) and recurrent pancreatitis. Patients with apo C-II deficiency have severe fat intolerance and can exhibit all of the characteristics of familial lipoprotein lipase deficiency.

Apo E deficiency: Almost all patients with familial dysbetalipoproteinemia (also called type III hyperlipoproteinemia) are homozygous for the apo E_2 allele; rarely, the disease develops in persons heterozygous for apo E_3/E_2 or apo E_4/E_2. However, only a small percentage of E_2/E_2 subjects develop hyperlipidemia, suggesting that another factor (genetic or environmental) must be present in addition to the abnormal apo E.

Four different gene mutations have been found at the E_2 position. One of these, a substitution of glutamine for lysine at residue 146, is inherited as a dominant trait in contrast to normal apo E_2, which has a recessive mode of inheritance. The apo E_2/E_2 phenotype occurs in 1% to 2% of the population.

Cellular Lipoprotein Receptors

Brown and Goldstein shared the Nobel prize for Medicine or Physiology in 1985 for their landmark work on the role of LDL receptors in mediating lipoprotein metabolism. Two thirds of the body's excess LDL is removed by the hepatic LDL receptor. The LDL receptor is also abundant on lymphocytes and in numerous other tissues, including the adrenals and the ovaries.

Figure 3
The LDL receptor: a single protein of five domains. Each blue space denotes the site of a cysteine residue

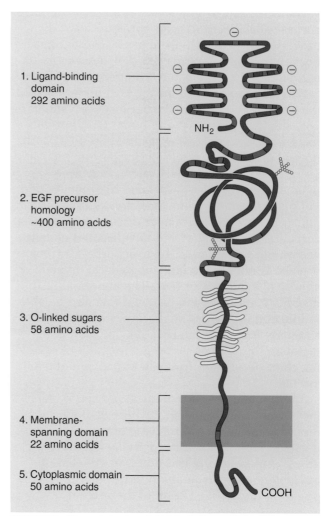

1. Ligand-binding domain
   292 amino acids

2. EGF precursor homology
   ~400 amino acids

3. O-linked sugars
   58 amino acids

4. Membrane-spanning domain
   22 amino acids

5. Cytoplasmic domain
   50 amino acids

NH_2

COOH

Reproduced with permission from Goldstein JL, Brown MS. Familial hypercholesterolemia. In: Scriver CR, Beaudet AL, Sly WS, Valle D, eds. *The Metabolic Basis of Inherited Disease.* 6th ed. New York, NY: McGraw-Hill; 1989:1215-1250.

The structure of the LDL receptor is shown in Figure 3. The outer portion of the receptor contains seven repeats with disulfide linkages and negatively charged amino acids. A point mutation in only one of these repeats may be sufficient to disrupt binding to apo B_{100}; however, disruption of binding to apo E may require more extensive changes. Negatively charged amino acids on the outer surface of the receptor bind to clusters of positively charged amino acids on apo B_{100} or apo E, both of which serve as ligands for the recognition of IDL and LDL.

Several other regions of the LDL receptor have been identified. One long segment is homologous to the epidermal growth factor precursor. Another region contains linkages with carbohydrate moieties. A small hydrophobic region spans the cell membrane, and a small area containing hydrophilic amino acids anchors the receptor within the cytoplasm of the cell.

The LDL receptor resides on the external surface of the cell in coated pits, which also house various other receptors, including the insulin receptor and the receptor for α_2-macroglobulin. Lipoproteins that contain apo B_{100} and apo E (primarily LDL and IDL) bind to the LDL receptors and are internalized by a process called receptor-mediated endocytosis. When an LDL or IDL particle binds to a receptor, the coated pit invaginates and internalizes the particle, forming a receptorsome. The receptorsome fuses with a lysosome within the cell, and the LDL is degraded to cholesterol, cholesteryl ester, apo B, and amino acids. This endocytic process results in the intracellular accumulation of cholesterol. Effects of intracellular cholesterol on the cell include:

- The down-regulation of the LDL receptor, which protects the cell from an overload of cholesterol;
- The suppression of 3-hydroxy-3-methylglutaryl coenzyme A (HMG-CoA) reductase, which turns off cholesterol synthesis within the cell; and
- The activation of acyl:cholesterol acyltransferase (ACAT), an enzyme that esterifies cholesterol, which allows excess cholesterol to be stored in the cell in the form of cholesteryl ester.

As a result, intracellular and extracellular cholesterol levels are regulated to maintain a constant level within the cell despite fluctuations in the supply of lipoproteins.

To a limited extent, cholesterol may be incorporated within the membranes of the cell or excreted from the cell, possibly through the mediation of HDL. The only way cholesterol is completely removed from the body is in bile acids. Cholesterol is incorporated into bile acids, which are either reabsorbed through the enterohepatic circulation or excreted in the stool. Approximately 1 g of cholesterol is removed from the body each day in stool.

Brown and Goldstein have studied the genetic regulation of LDL receptor activity. (See page 27 for a discussion of mutations that result in familial hypercholesterolemia.) Cholesterol or a more polar derivative, such as a hydroxylated sterol, is believed to bind to an intracellular protein that, in turn, binds to a region of the genes controlling the formation of mRNA for the LDL receptor. In this way, the cellular levels of cholesterol control the quantity of receptor protein made by the cell. A decrease in intracellular sterol increases the rate of synthesis of mRNA for the LDL receptor. The up- or down-regulation of four proteins—the LDL receptor, HMG-CoA reductase, HMG-CoA synthase, and prenyltransferase—appears to be coordinated by the quantity of intracellular cholesterol or sterol. As the cell receives an adequate supply of cholesterol from LDL, it suppresses its own (endogenous) cholesterol synthesis and also down-regulates the LDL receptor and the enzymes involved in cholesterol biosynthesis. Dietary cholesterol provided by the chylomicron remnants may also down-regulate the LDL receptor, entering the cell through a different receptor pathway. However, the details of this mechanism remain to be established.

In some animals (eg, the male hamster) and in those humans with a low rate of endogenous cholesterol synthesis in the liver, the LDL receptor is relatively suppressed by dietary cholesterol. In the rat, however, there is a much greater endogenous synthesis of cholesterol, and dietary cholesterol exerts a lesser effect on the LDL receptor. Also, hepatic LDL receptor activity is more resistant to modulation by HMG-CoA reductase inhibitors in rats than in humans.

Transport of Cholesterol

Exogenous cholesterol: Dietary cholesterol and triglyceride are transported by chylomicrons. The chylomicrons are released from the intestine into the lymph and proceed through the thoracic duct into the systemic circulation. Once they reach the capillaries, particularly those in adipose tissue and muscle, chylomicrons are exposed to lipoprotein lipase, an enzyme that is secreted by adipocytes and attaches to receptors located on the surfaces of endothelial cells. Insulin is required to maintain normal lipoprotein lipase activity. In diabetic ketoacidosis, lipoprotein lipase deficiency results in marked hypertriglyceridemia. An increase in lipoprotein lipase activity has been observed 3 to 6 hours after high-carbohydrate meals and after intravenous administration of heparin sulfate, dextran sulfate, or insulin. However, the precise mechanism governing lipoprotein lipase synthesis, processing, and secretion is unknown.

Lipoprotein lipase requires apo C-II for activation. This apoprotein is thought to be transferred to the surface of the chylomicron from circulating HDL particles. When activated, lipoprotein lipase acts on the large triglyceride component of the chylomicron, causing hydrolysis and releasing diglycerides and fatty acids. At this point, the chylomicron's surface components of apoproteins, phospholipids, and cholesterol are thought to be transferred to HDL particles. With this transfer of lipid and protein, HDL_3 particles are converted into the larger, more lipid-rich HDL_2 particles.

Newly formed chylomicrons incorporate apo A-I, apo A-IV, and apo B_{48} from the intestinal wall, and they acquire apo Cs and apo E while circulating in the lymph or blood. Although apo B_{48} is not recognized by any known cellular receptor, this apoprotein appears to be necessary for the incorporation of lipids into chylomicrons and for the secretion of chylomicrons by the cells of the intestinal wall.

Hydrolysis decreases the size and triglyceride content of the chylomicron, changing it to a remnant particle. Hui et al classified these chylomicron remnants as β-VLDL particles, because they exhibit some of the properties of VLDL particles and comigrate with the β-globulin fraction on paper and agarose gel electrophoresis. The chylomicron remnants are rapidly removed by the liver; the removal mechanism has not been elucidated but is mediated in some way by apo E. It may be that apo E and lipoprotein lipase are added to partially digested chylomicron particles as those particles reach the liver. The exact receptor for the chylomicron remnant is not known, but a candidate is the LDL receptor-related protein (LRP) discovered by Herz and colleagues. This large protein is structurally related to the LDL receptor but contains four times the number of amino acids. LRP exists as an approximately 600 000-dalton protein with a long external subunit (515 000 daltons) bound noncovalently to a short subunit (85 000 daltons) that spans the cell membrane and extends into the cytoplasm. LRP has recently been shown to be identical to the $α_2$-macroglobulin receptor, a very primitive structure whose function is unclear.

Removal of chylomicron remnants is the means for transferring dietary cholesterol from the intestine to the liver. A rapid uptake of these particles probably increases the intrahepatic supply of cholesterol and down-regulates the number of LDL receptors. Particles containing apo E_4 or apo E_3 are removed by the liver more rapidly than those containing only apo E_2. Thus, delayed clearance of chylomicron remnants containing only apo E_2 may have the effect of up-regulating the number of hepatic LDL receptors, leading to lower concentrations of LDL and total cholesterol in the blood. Particles containing only apo E_4 or apo E_3 would exert the opposite effect by causing a rapid increase of cholesterol in the liver cells. A delay in the clearance of chylomicron remnants may also cause postprandial lipemia, a phenomenon that is discussed on page 33.

Endogenous cholesterol: *Role of very-low-density lipoproteins*: Endogenous cholesterol and triglyceride are transported from the liver in VLDL particles. VLDL synthesis is stimulated by excessive consumption of calories, alcohol, or carbohydrates or by a high concentration of unesterified fatty acids reaching the liver. VLDL transports endogenous triglyceride to peripheral sites, where the triglyceride may be used for energy or stored.

Like chylomicrons, as VLDLs circulate through peripheral and adipose tissues, they are exposed to lipoprotein lipase and are hydrolyzed. During hydrolysis, the VLDL surface components of apoprotein, phospholipid, and cholesterol are transferred to HDL particles. The smaller, more dense VLDL remnants that remain are the IDLs. Most of the IDLs are rapidly removed from circulation by the hepatic LDL receptors, which recognize the apo E on the IDL surface. Some of the larger VLDL particles may be removed directly from the circulation by the liver, without proceeding through the IDL pathway.

In the rat and many other animal species, removal by the liver is the major fate of VLDLs and IDLs. In humans, however, a substantial proportion of IDL (perhaps 30%) is converted to LDL particles, a process thought to be mediated by hepatic triglyceride lipase. The proportion of

IDLs removed by the liver versus the proportion converted to LDLs is a major determinant of the quantity of LDLs circulating in the blood. In those animal species in which most of the IDL particles are removed by the liver, the circulating LDL concentration is relatively low. These species tend to be relatively resistant to atherosclerosis. In humans, the higher concentration of circulating LDL predisposes to atherosclerosis.

Role of low-density lipoproteins: The end product of VLDL catabolism is LDL, the preeminent atherogenic lipoprotein in humans. There is evidence that the atherogenicity of LDL may be increased by oxidation, which renders these particles cytotoxic. In support of this mechanism, deposits of oxidized LDL have been found in atherosclerotic plaques by several investigators, and physical and chemical changes consistent with advanced oxidative damage in the arterial wall have been documented. Recent studies in rabbits suggest that the drug probucol, acting as an antioxidant, can protect against atherosclerosis. In addition, reports from the Physicians' Health Study suggest that the antioxidant beta-carotene decreases the incidence of myocardial infarction.

Oxidation of the fatty acids or chemical modification of the free-lysine amino groups of apo B alters the LDL particle to the extent that it is no longer recognized by the LDL receptor. The modified LDL particle may be removed via another mechanism known as the *scavenger receptor pathway*. Recently, the structure of the macrophage scavenger receptor was elucidated in the laboratory of Krieger. The receptor (Figure 4) has a long, collagenlike neck, which may enable it to bind to modified or oxidized LDL, to polyanionic structures (eg, polyinosinic acid), and to various other substances (eg, endotoxin). The scavenger receptor would enable monocytes/macrophages to accumulate cholesterol and lipid from oxidized or modified lipoproteins in an unregulated way. Whether the scavenger receptor might also play a protective role in the vascular wall is not known.

A decrease in the number or the activity of hepatic LDL receptors may result in a higher circulating concentration of LDL. Brown and Goldstein have suggested that a lifetime of consuming foods

Figure 4
Schematic model of the predicted trimeric structure of the type I bovine scavenger receptor

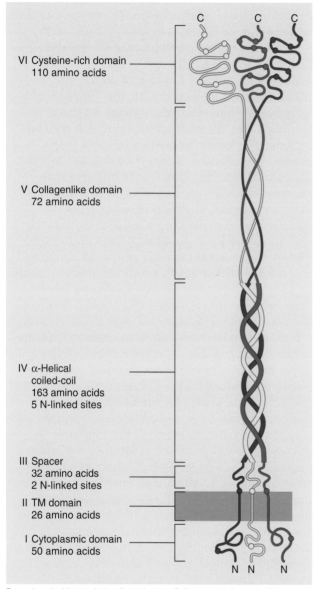

VI Cysteine-rich domain
110 amino acids

V Collagenlike domain
72 amino acids

IV α-Helical
coiled-coil
163 amino acids
5 N-linked sites

III Spacer
32 amino acids
2 N-linked sites

II TM domain
26 amino acids

I Cytoplasmic domain
50 amino acids

Reproduced with permission from Kodama T, Freeman M, Rohrer L, Zabrecky J, Matsudaira P, Krieger M. Type I macrophage scavenger receptor contains alpha-helical and collagenlike coiled coils. *Nature*. 1990;343:531-535.

rich in cholesterol and saturated fat could lead to chronic suppression of the LDL receptors. Some experimental evidence supports this hypothesis. Dietary cholesterol suppresses LDL receptor activity when chylomicron remnants are taken up by the liver. In animals, thyroid hormone injections increase LDL receptor activity; receptor activity decreases with aging. The Angelin laboratory has shown that in humans treatment with pravastatin (an inhibitor of HMG-CoA reductase activity and therefore of cholesterol synthesis) leads to an increase in the activity of hepatic LDL receptors.

Role of high-density lipoproteins: HDL is secreted in an incomplete form (called *nascent HDL*) and is assembled in the plasma. The components of HDL are derived from multiple sources, including the liver, intestine, and the surfaces of chylomicrons and VLDLs. HDL contains phospholipid and some apolipoproteins. The HDL synthesized in the liver contains apo A-I, apo A-II, and apo E. The HDL synthesized in the intestine contains apo A-I and apo A-IV. Castro and Fielding have suggested that a small fraction of HDL particles containing only apo A-I and exhibiting pre-β mobility may play a special role in the process of reverse cholesterol transport. Fruchart and colleagues linked the protective effect of HDL against atherosclerosis to particles that contain apo A-I but not apo A-II (Lp A-I); they found most HDL particles that contain both apo A-I and apo A-II (Lp A-I:A-II) have little or no protective effect.

HDL is derived from the surface components of chylomicrons and VLDLs during their lipolysis. The apolipoproteins of HDL may be transferred to chylomicrons and VLDLs and then perform functions specific to the chylomicrons and VLDLs. For example, apo E transferred from HDLs to chylomicrons mediates the uptake of chylomicron remnants in the liver. Apo C-II transferred from HDLs to chylomicrons and VLDLs helps to activate lipoprotein lipase. It has been suggested that the apo Cs prevent the premature uptake by the liver of chylomicron and VLDL remnants.

HDLs provide a reverse transport pathway for cholesterol from peripheral tissues to the liver, although this has not been proved as an anti-atherogenic mechanism. Reverse transport would be mediated by an HDL receptor that recognizes apo A-I, apo A-II, and apo A-IV. Graham and Oram described a 100 000-dalton protein that has such binding properties and is induced by loading cells with cholesterol. The protein contains several repeat units of amphipathic helices, thus resembling the apoprotein structure. It has been suggested that binding of apo A-I or A-IV to this protein on the cell surface promotes the translocation of cholesterol to the cell surface, where it may be transferred to HDL_3. Binding by the HDL receptor does not appear to involve the internalization of a lipoprotein particle, in contrast to the LDL receptor.

Cholesterol removed from the cells and incorporated into HDL is converted to cholesteryl ester through the action of LCAT. Once the HDL particle contains sufficient cholesteryl ester, it is referred to as a mature particle. Mature HDLs are spherical when viewed with the electron microscope, whereas nascent HDLs are discoid. Once the mature HDL particle is formed, a lipid exchange may occur between the HDL and the VLDL, IDL, or LDL. This process is mediated by cholesteryl ester transfer protein (CETP). Triglyceride from the less dense particles is transferred to LDL and HDL particles, while cholesteryl ester from the HDL particle is transferred to VLDL, IDL, or LDL. These cholesteryl ester–enriched particles can then be delivered to LDL receptors in the liver and removed from circulation.

While the chylomicron remnants and VLDLs become triglyceride poor as a result of the CETP-mediated exchange, LDLs and HDLs become triglyceride enriched. Thus, the process produces a larger class of LDL and HDL particles that are attacked by hepatic triglyceride lipase, an enzyme that catalyzes the hydrolysis of triglyceride and phospholipid. The end result is small, dense, protein-enriched LDL and HDL particles. The concentration of HDL_2 and the total concentration of HDL are reduced. This sequence of events could produce small, dense LDL particles and the dyslipidemic features of syndrome X described in the next section, Lipid Transport Disorders. The metabolic condition of small, dense LDL and reduced HDL levels is thought to predispose a person to atherosclerosis.

HDL can also transport cholesteryl ester from tissues to the liver through direct interaction with the apo E receptor. Thus, the fraction of HDL that contains apo E could transport cholesteryl ester directly to the liver without the CETP-mediated transfer to LDL, which presumably occurs when CETP is completely absent, as in rats. Evidence for an alternative mechanism in humans comes from a recent description of several Japanese families who have a deficiency of CETP and extremely high HDL_2 levels, but premature coronary heart disease does not develop in these families. The drug probucol, which lowers HDL serum levels, is reported to increase CETP activity. Since probucol induces regression of xanthomas, it may enhance cholesterol transport from peripheral tissues.

Concentrations of the subfraction HDL_2 are higher in females than in males and are increased by exercise and by the presence of estrogen; androgens decrease HDL levels. Concentrations of HDL_2 are also positively correlated with the activity of cellular lipoprotein lipase and inversely correlated with the activity of hepatic triglyceride lipase; HDL_2 may be the primary substrate for the latter enzyme. Ingestion of ethanol increases the circulating levels of both HDL subfractions, but it appears to exert the greater effect on HDL_3. Cigarette smoking decreases the concentration of HDL, especially HDL_2. Several drugs (including β-blockers) are known to decrease HDL concentrations.

HDL levels have an inverse relationship to serum triglyceride concentrations, as well as to the magnitude of postprandial lipemia (see page 33 for a discussion of postprandial lipemia).

Lipid transport disorders: Sniderman et al have described a condition called *hyperapobetalipoproteinemia (hyper-apo B)*, a familial disorder in which there is an increased proportion of apo B in VLDL, IDL, and LDL. These patients have concentrations of apo B_{100} that are as high as those found in patients with familial hypercholesterolemia. Hyper-apo B patients are at increased risk for coronary heart disease, although they may have fairly normal concentrations of total and LDL cholesterol.

It is thought that some hyper-apo B patients have familial combined hyperlipidemia, for which the basic defect has been postulated to be an overproduction of apo B_{100} in the liver. This excess production results in apo B_{100}-enriched VLDL, IDL, and LDL. Austin, Krauss, and colleagues have described two atherogenic lipoprotein phenotypes, apparently inherited as a single-gene trait: phenotype A is characterized by a predominance of large, bouyant LDL particles, and phenotype B is characterized by a major electrophoretic peak of small, dense, apo B-enriched LDL particles. Phenotype B is associated with a threefold-increased risk of myocardial infarction and increased levels of the triglyceride-rich lipoproteins and decreased levels of HDL cholesterol.

Reaven described a cluster of clinical findings, consisting of central obesity, glucose intolerance, increased VLDL triglyceride, low HDL, and hypertension. Reaven termed this constellation of findings *syndrome X* and postulated that the underlying basis is insulin resistance and hyperinsulinemia; however, the mechanism remains speculative at this time. Independently, Williams et al described the linked inheritance of hypertension and hyperlipidemia in Utah kindreds and called the disorder *dyslipidemic hypertension*.

In patients with persistent hypertriglyceridemia, there is an increased exchange of cholesteryl ester and triglyceride between the chylomicrons and VLDL particles and the LDL and HDL particles. The triglyceride-enriched LDL and HDL particles are larger than their unenriched forms and are believed to be enhanced substrates for hepatic triglyceride lipase. As a result, the triglyceride component is hydrolyzed, leading to small, dense LDL and HDL particles and a decrease in HDL concentration. Normal LDL patterns are reputedly restored by treating the patients with fibric acid derivatives.

Various mutations may affect the structure of apo B_{100} and the serum concentration of LDL. Additional mutations may be associated through gene disequilibrium with hyperlipidemia or with coronary heart disease, although the association with coronary heart disease has not been verified consistently from one population to another. Small, dense LDL particles in association with hypertriglyceridemia, dyslipidemic hypertension, syndrome X, hyper-apo B, or familial combined hyperlipidemia may predispose to early atherosclerosis. The basis for an increased atherogenesis with the small, dense LDL particles is unknown.

The presence of large lipoprotein complexes in plasma 10 to 12 hours after ingesting dietary fat is referred to as *chylomicronemia*. Fasting chylomicronemia may occur in patients with plasma triglyceride levels between 500 and 2000 mg/dL. Clinical manifestations of the chylomicronemia syndrome usually develop at triglyceride levels higher than 2000 mg/dL. Chylomicronemia syndrome is characterized by eruptive xanthomas, lipemia retinalis, abdominal pain, and pancreatitis.

Hyperlipidemias

Hyperlipidemias are disorders in which circulating levels of cholesterol, triglyceride, or both are elevated. Hyperlipidemias have traditionally been defined as total cholesterol levels and/or triglyceride levels that exceed the 95th percentile for patient age and sex (that is, a laboratory definition not in reference to specific genetic disorders). When hyperlipidemia is defined by a specific lipoprotein pattern, the diagnosis is called *hyperlipoproteinemia*. In fact, more than one type of hyperlipoproteinemia may be found in a given genetic disease. The different types of hyperlipoproteinemia are listed in Table 5. This typing system was originally based on the separation of the lipoproteins by preparative ultracentrifugation in conjunction with heparin-manganese precipitation and with identification of the lipoprotein patterns on paper electrophoresis.

Primary hypercholesterolemia: "Primary" indicates there is no known underlying disorder that would explain the elevated cholesterol. Of the genetic forms of hypercholesterolemia listed in Table 5, the most common is polygenic hypercholesterolemia.

Polygenic hypercholesterolemia: This disorder, which is also called primary moderate hypercholesterolemia, is characterized by an isolated elevation of LDL cholesterol. The specific causes and genetic abnormalities associated with polygenic hypercholesterolemia have not been defined, even though as many as 80% to 85% of individuals who have elevated serum cholesterol on routine screening have this disorder.

Polygenic hypercholesterolemia may have multiple causes, including increased absorption of dietary cholesterol, increased synthesis of lipoproteins by the liver, and a relative decrease in removal of LDL. There are usually no physical manifestations of polygenic hypercholesterolemia.

Familial hypercholesterolemia: Brown and Goldstein were the first to show that familial hypercholesterolemia is caused by depressed LDL receptor activity. This disorder is inherited as a dominant trait and is characterized by high serum levels of total cholesterol, elevated LDL cholesterol, and premature atherosclerosis.

The Brown and Goldstein laboratory has identified four classes of genetic mutations that result in familial hypercholesterolemia (Table 6). In one type, LDL receptors are not formed, such as in the deletion mutation seen in French Canadians in which the receptor mRNA is completely absent. A second type arises from a defective carbohydrate arrangement in the LDL receptor, producing an immature receptor that is unable to reach the cell surface. In still other types of familial hypercholesterolemia, binding capacity of the receptor is impaired, or the receptor is unable to internalize the bound LDL. All of these different genetic forms result in the phenotypic expression of familial hypercholesterolemia, with its characteristic clinical features.

Familial hypercholesterolemia is characterized by a high total cholesterol level, a normal triglyceride level, premature atherosclerosis, and xanthomas of the extension tendons of the hands, the achilles tendons, the eyelids, and the corneal arcus. Homozygotes (about 1 in 1 million people) are more severely affected than heterozygotes (about 1 in 500 people). In the homozygous state, severe hypercholesterolemia (650 to 1200 mg/dL total cholesterol) and xanthomas develop in early childhood; coronary heart disease often causes death before age 20. In the heterozygous state, total cholesterol concentrations are 350 to 550 mg/dL, and patients generally develop xanthomas and coronary heart disease after age 20. Heterozygous women usually develop coronary heart disease between the ages of 40 and 60, whereas coronary heart disease in men develops at an earlier age, typically between the ages of 30 and 50.

Table 5
Hyperlipoproteinemia phenotype definitions and their associations with genetic and other disorders

Phenotype	Laboratory definition	Associated genetic disorder	Conditions associated with secondary hyperlipoproteinemia
Type I	Hyperchylomicronemia and absolute deficiency of lipoprotein lipase Cholesterol normal Triglycerides greatly increased	Familial lipoprotein lipase deficiency Apo C-II deficiency	Dysglobulinemia, pancreatitis, poorly controlled diabetes mellitus
Type IIa	LDL increased Cholesterol increased Triglycerides normal	Familial hypercholesterolemia LDL receptor abnormal Polygenic hypercholesterolemia	Hypothyroidism, acute intermittent porphyria, nephrosis, idiopathic hypercalcemia, dysglobulinemia, anorexia nervosa
Type IIb	LDL increased VLDL increased Cholesterol increased Triglycerides increased	Familial hypercholesterolemia Familial combined hyperlipidemia	Hypothyroidism, nephrosis
Type III	Floating β-lipoproteins VLDL cholesterol/VLDL triglyceride > 0.35 Apo E_2 homozygote on isoelectric focusing Cholesterol increased Triglycerides increased	Familial dysbetalipoproteinemia	Diabetes mellitus, hypothyroidism, dysglobulinemia (monoclonal gammopathy)
Type IV	VLDL increased Cholesterol normal or increased Triglycerides increased	Familial hypertriglyceridemia Familial combined hyperlipidemia	Glycogen storage disease, hypothyroidism, disseminated lupus erythematosus, diabetes mellitus, nephrotic syndrome, renal failure, ethanol abuse
Type V	Chylomicrons and VLDL increased LDL present but reduced Cholesterol increased Triglycerides greatly increased	Familial type V hypertriglyceridemia Familial fasting chylomicronemia syndrome	Poorly controlled diabetes mellitus, glycogen storage disease, hypothyroidism nephrotic syndrome, dysglobulinemia, pregnancy, estrogen administration (either contraceptive or therapeutic) in women with familial hypertriglyceridemia

Adapted with permission from Havel RJ. Approach to the patient with hyperlipidemia. *Med Clin North Am*. 1982;66:319-333.

Table 6
Mutations at the LDL receptor locus that produce
familial hypercholesterolemia

Class of mutation	Location of LDL receptor	LDL binding to intact cells	Type of molecular lesion	Frequency among familial hypercholesterolemia patients
Class I Null alleles	Absent	None	Deletion	Common in French-Canadians
	Absent	None	Deletion	Rare
	Absent	None	Nondeletion	Common
Class II Transport-defective alleles	Intracellular	None	Nonsense	Common in Lebanese
	Intracellular	None	*	Common
	Intracellular	None	*	Rare
	Intracellular; a few in coated pits	Reduced	Deletion	Rare
	Intracellular; a few in coated pits	Reduced	Deletion	WHHL rabbits
	Intracellular; a few in coated pits	Reduced	*	Common in Afrikaaners
Class III Binding-defective alleles	Coated pits	None	Deletion	Rare
	Coated pits	None	Deletion	Rare
	Coated pits	Reduced	*	Common
	Coated pits	Reduced	Duplication	Rare
Class IV Internalization-defective alleles	Extracellular; a few in noncoated regions	Normal binding; defective internalization	Deletion	Rare
	Noncoated regions		Nonsense	Rare
	Noncoated regions		Insertion	Rare
	Noncoated regions		Missense	Rare

*Details of molecular lesion not known.

Adapted with permission from Goldstein JL, Brown MS. Familial hypercholesterolemia. In: Scriver CR, Beaudet AL, Sly WS, Valle D, eds. *The Metabolic Basis of Inherited Disease.* 6th ed. New York, NY: McGraw-Hill; 1989:1215-1250.

Treatment of patients with familial hypercholesterolemia is usually aimed at increasing LDL receptor activity. Factors that decrease the intrahepatic concentration of cholesterol are expected to increase LDL receptor activity, and factors that increase intrahepatic cholesterol concentration are expected to decrease the activity of the receptor. Dietary restriction of cholesterol and saturated fat may up-regulate LDL receptor activity, although diet alone does not sufficiently reduce cholesterol concentrations in familial hypercholesterolemia.

The effects of two types of drugs on LDL receptor activity have been studied extensively. Bile acid sequestrants bind the bile acids in the intestine for excretion in the stool. The net effect of these drugs is similar to that of a partial ileal bypass operation, namely, interruption of the enterohepatic circulation. (In the Program on the Surgical Control of the Hyperlipidemias [POSCH], bypass of the terminal 200 cm of the small intestine was successfully used to reduce cholesterol levels among hyperlipidemic survivors of myocardial infarction.) Ordinarily, bile acids are reabsorbed in the ileum, but when the enterohepatic circulation is interrupted, bile acids are excreted in the stool, and presumably the hepatic supply of cholesterol is drained as more cholesterol is converted to bile acid. The result is a presumed decrease in hepatic cholesterol and an increase in LDL receptor activity. Thus, the reduction of serum levels of LDL cholesterol by the administration of bile acid sequestrants is an indirect effect; the direct effect is to increase LDL receptor activity. Bile acid sequestrants in adequate doses generally lower LDL cholesterol levels by 15% to 20%.

Another method of decreasing intrahepatic cholesterol is to inhibit the rate-limiting step of cholesterol biosynthesis in the liver, namely, the conversion of HMG-CoA to mevalonic acid by the enzyme HMG-CoA reductase. A number of agents that are competitive inhibitors of HMG-CoA reductase activity have been developed, including compactin, lovastatin, simvastatin, pravastatin, and fluvastatin (Figure 5). It is thought that the enzyme inhibition by these drugs decreases intrahepatic cholesterol levels and thus increases LDL receptor activity. The end effect can be to lower serum levels of LDL cholesterol by 25% to 35%. Because bile acid sequestrants cause a compensatory increase in HMG-CoA reductase activity, using a reductase inhibitor in conjunction with a bile acid sequestrant may reduce LDL cholesterol levels by more than 50% and in some instances by as much as 70%.

Familial combined hyperlipidemia: This disorder can be difficult to distinguish from familial hypercholesterolemia. In isolated cases, LDL receptor activity is normal in familial combined hyperlipidemia, but there can be some overlap of receptor activity between persons who are heterozygous for familial hypercholesterolemia and normal individuals. Familial combined hyperlipidemia usually does not present until adulthood, whereas familial hypercholesterolemia can be diagnosed from a sample of umbilical cord blood. The xanthomas that are common in familial hypercholesterolemia are extremely rare in familial combined hyperlipidemia.

Because familial combined hyperlipidemia and familial hypercholesterolemia are both inherited as dominant traits, one of the patient's parents will be affected. One half of the siblings and more than half of the offspring would be expected to be affected.

As with familial hypercholesterolemia, familial combined hyperlipidemia is associated with premature coronary heart disease and often with carotid artery disease and peripheral arteriosclerosis. As the name implies, familial combined

Figure 5
Chemical structures of selected HMG-CoA reductase inhibitors

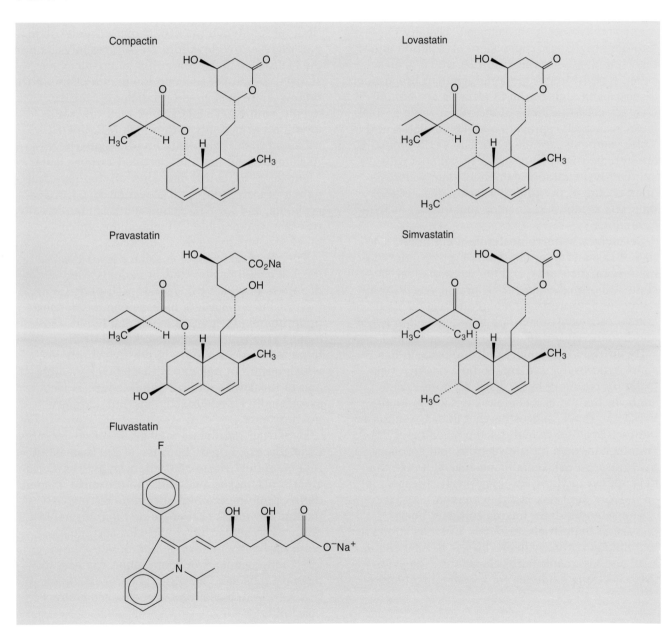

Compactin

Lovastatin

Pravastatin

Simvastatin

Fluvastatin

hyperlipidemia may produce one of several lipoprotein patterns, for example, an isolated elevation of either LDL or VLDL or an increase in both values.

Familial dysbetalipoproteinemia: Usually, cholesterol and triglyceride levels are elevated to about the same degree in this disorder, which is also called type III hyperlipoproteinemia or broad-beta disease. Although serum LDL levels are not increased, concentrations of the atherogenic β-VLDL particles, which represent both chylomicron and VLDL remnants, are elevated. The VLDL remnants are enriched with cholesterol. In patients with familial dysbetalipoproteinemia, atherosclerosis often occurs in peripheral arteries, and large tuberous xanthomas develop that are not attached to tendons.

Secondary hypercholesterolemia: About 5% to 10% of cases of hyperlipidemia are secondary to underlying disorders, and the workup must include a thorough medical history, physical examination, and appropriate laboratory testing. Well-known causes of secondary hypercholesterolemia and hypertriglyceridemia are listed in Table 5.

Hypertriglyceridemia: Epidemiologic studies show hypertriglyceridemia to be a positive risk factor for coronary heart disease on univariate analysis, but the association is weaker in multivariate analyses, suggesting that the association is indirect. Even on reanalysis, the meaning of the Framingham data on triglycerides and coronary heart disease risk remains unclear, although the data appear to show that hypertriglyceridemia is an independent risk factor in women.

The scientific base linking coronary heart disease to hypertriglyceridemia is not as strong as that linking coronary heart disease to total cholesterol and LDL cholesterol elevations. However, there is strong evidence from both animal and clinical studies for the atherogenic impact of triglyceride-rich lipoproteins. In the Helsinki Heart Study, the greatest benefit of hypolipidemic treatment (gemfibrozil) was among patients with type IIb hyperlipidemia (ie, LDL cholesterol elevation and triglyceride elevation). Recent reanalysis of the Helsinki data by Manninen and colleagues showed that in the placebo group, the LDL-to-HDL ratio was the best single predictor of cardiac events, with a particularly high-risk subgroup identified as patients with a high LDL-to-HDL ratio and high triglyceride levels. Similarly, Assmann found that Prospective Cardiovascular Muenster (PROCAM) data showed that the combination of LDL cholesterol elevation, hypertriglyceridemia, and low HDL cholesterol confers greater risk than comparable LDL elevations without these accompanying dyslipidemias.

The increased risk of coronary heart disease has been well established in patients with disorders in which triglyceride-rich particles are a feature. Such disorders include familial dysbetalipoproteinemia, familial combined hyperlipidemia, hyper-apo B, syndrome X, and dyslipidemic hypertension. Secondary hypertriglyceridemia, which occurs in patients with diabetes mellitus and in those with chronic renal failure, is also associated with atherosclerosis and coronary heart disease.

Hypertriglyceridemia may be linked to coronary heart disease, in part, because of the associated reduction in HDL concentration. Hypertriglyceridemia is also associated with the presence of small, dense, protein-enriched LDL particles that are thought to be more atherogenic than normal LDL particles. Whether these particles accumulate more easily in the arterial wall or whether they affect atherogenesis in some other way has not been established. The direct atherogenicity of triglyceride-rich remnant particles is a distinct possibility.

The character of VLDL particles is altered in hypertriglyceridemia. Except for the smallest particles, VLDL does not normally bind to the LDL receptor, possibly because the apo B_{100} present in the larger VLDL particle is not in the right configuration for binding or is not exposed to the LDL receptor. With successive hydrolysis of the VLDL particle, apo B_{100} assumes a recognizable config-uration, and the smaller VLDL particle is bound by the LDL receptor. VLDL particles in hypertriglycer-idemic subjects, however, bind to the LDL recep-tors, because triglyceride-rich VLDLs have a higher content of apo E. The physiologic signifi-cance of the apo E-rich VLDL particle is not known, but the increased content of apo E has the potential of diverting larger VLDL particles into cells with LDL receptors.

Type V (familial mixed) hyperlipidemia is asso-ciated with premature coronary heart disease in some (but not all) patients. The disorder is charac-terized by fasting chylomicronemia, increased VLDL, triglyceride concentrations greater than 500 mg/dL, measurable but diminished lipoprotein lipase activity, glucose intolerance, and hyperuri-cemia. Type V hyperlipidemia is a potentially lethal disorder, because pancreatitis can develop if the disease is not controlled. Physicians should be aware of this potential danger when a patient comes to the emergency room with abdominal pain and lipemic serum. Lipemia may also be caused by pancreatitis, but the severe hyperlipid-emia in patients with type V familial hyperlipid-emia actually causes pancreatitis, presumably because the large, lipid-rich particles impede pancreatic microcirculation.

Patsch et al have called attention to postpran-dial lipemia, an under-recognized form of hypertriglyceridemia. In case-control studies, patients with coronary heart disease had higher levels of diet-derived triglycerides 6 to 8 hours after a high-fat meal. Postprandial lipemia has been demonstrated to be positively correlated with fasting triglyceride levels and inversely correlated with lipoprotein lipase activity and HDL_2 concentrations.

There is no reported association between atherosclerosis and the fasting chylomicronemia in familial lipoprotein lipase deficiency and familial apo C-II deficiency. In these two rare disorders, severe chylomicronemia can appear during childhood as serum triglyceride levels in the thousands of mg/dL. The disorder can be life-threatening, because pancreatitis can occur if the chylomicronemia is not controlled by severe dietary fat restriction. Eruptive xanthomas devel-op on skin and mucous membranes and are characteristically distributed over the buttocks and elbows. Hepatosplenomegaly is present as a result of fatty infiltration of reticuloendothelial cells. There is no known drug therapy for either familial lipoprotein lipase deficiency or familial apo C-II deficiency.

Screening and Treatment
Cholesterol measurement: The National Choles-terol Education Program (NCEP) recommends that every adult American know his or her serum cholesterol level. Ideally, an adult's cholesterol level should be checked during routine health examinations. The NCEP also recommends that total cholesterol be measured in children (≥ 2 years of age) and adolescents who are at high risk because of a family history of premature coronary heart disease.

Plasma or blood cholesterol determinations can be made on nonfasting blood samples either in a clinical laboratory or with tabletop measuring devices. The latter have been used extensively for cholesterol screening and can be used outside physicians' offices, for example, at work sites, schools, and health clinics. A number of tabletop devices are available that yield results within the NCEP guidelines for accuracy and precision. However, the diagnosis of hypercholesterolemia should always be confirmed with values deter-mined by a clinical laboratory.

When a measurement of total cholesterol is 200 mg/dL or greater, it should be repeated at least once and the mean of the two measurements should be considered the person's serum cholesterol level. Serum cholesterol levels are dynamic because of instrument and methodologic variations and because of intraindividual biologic variability. Cholesterol measurements for a given person may fluctuate by about 10% as a result of these factors.

Evaluation of the clinical significance of a total cholesterol level that is elevated according to NCEP criteria requires a complete lipoprotein analysis of a fasting blood sample. Measuring triglycerides while a person is in a fasting state minimizes the distortion from biologic variability. Ideally, the person should be on his or her usual diet, neither gaining nor losing weight, and should not be acutely ill or taking drugs that affect lipid levels. Total and HDL cholesterol and triglyceride levels are measured, the HDL after precipitation of the other components. LDL cholesterol is calculated by the Friedewald formula:

LDL (mg/dL) =

total cholesterol − [HDL + 0.20 (triglycerides)]

National Cholesterol Education Program guidelines: The guidelines currently in use in the United States for diagnosing and managing hypercholesterolemia in adults are those published in 1988 by the NCEP (Tables 7 and 8). The initial cutoff points for total cholesterol levels are the same for men and women aged 20 years or older. Serum cholesterol levels are known to increase with age, and postmenopausal women have higher serum total cholesterol levels than men of the same age. It is not known whether the increase with age is a normal physiologic response. To encourage the detection and diagnosis of hypercholesterolemia, the NCEP guidelines embody some simplification.

A serum total cholesterol level less than 200 mg/dL is considered desirable. Individuals who have serum total cholesterol levels between 200 and 239 mg/dL are considered at borderline-high risk for coronary heart disease unless they have

coronary heart disease or two other risk factors, in which case they are considered at high risk. Any person with a total cholesterol level of 240 mg/dL or higher is considered to be at high risk for coronary heart disease.

By the NCEP treatment algorithm, persons with desirable serum cholesterol levels should follow a sensible diet and recheck their cholesterol within 5 years. However, recent studies have shown that a significant percentage of myocardial infarction patients before the infarction had total serum cholesterol levels less than 200 mg/dL, frequently with HDL levels less than 35 mg/dL. Data from the Framingham Heart Study have established that the risk of coronary heart disease is not only inversely but is also continuously related to serum HDL levels; that is, the suggested lower limit of normal (35 mg/dL) does not represent an all-or-nothing situation. For example, persons with an HDL level of 65 mg/dL have a lower risk of myocardial infarction than do persons with an HDL level of 45 mg/dL. The NCEP lists an HDL concentration of less than 35 mg/dL as a risk factor equivalent to the other major non-LDL risk factors to be considered in its algorithm, namely cigarette smoking, hypertension, diabetes mellitus, severe obesity, male gender, definite coronary heart disease, a family history of premature coronary heart disease, and a history of definite cerebrovascular or occlusive peripheral vascular disease (Table 9). However, the guidelines do not suggest that depressed HDL levels alone are cause for treatment.

According to the NCEP guidelines, persons at borderline-high risk should follow a diet aimed at lowering the total cholesterol level to within the desirable range and repeat cholesterol measurement within 1 year.

Treatment of persons in the high-risk category is based on the LDL cholesterol level and the presence of other risk factors or coronary heart disease. By the NCEP guidelines, a serum LDL level less than 130 mg/dL is considered to be desirable. An LDL level between 130 and 159 mg/dL confers borderline-high risk unless the patient has two additional risk factors or coronary heart disease, in which case the risk is high. An LDL level of 160 mg/dL or higher with no other risk factors is

Table 7
NCEP coronary heart disease (CHD) risk classifications for adults by total cholesterol level: 1988 guidelines

Total cholesterol (mg/dL)	Risk classification	Recommended follow-up
< 200	Desirable	Provide patient with general dietary and risk reduction educational materials. Repeat total cholesterol measurement within 5 years.
200-239	Borderline high	Determined by whether definite CHD or at least two other risk factors for CHD (Table 9) are present. If absent: provide dietary information and recheck annually. If present: treat as high risk.
≥ 240	High	Perform lipoprotein analysis; further action based on LDL cholesterol level (Table 8).

Adapted from The Expert Panel, National Cholesterol Education Program; 1988.

Table 8
NCEP coronary heart disease (CHD) risk classifications for adults by LDL cholesterol level: 1988 guidelines

LDL cholesterol (mg/dL)	Risk classification	Recommended follow-up*
< 130	Desirable	Provide patient with general dietary and risk reduction educational materials. Repeat total cholesterol level within 5 years.
130-159	Borderline high	If other risk is absent: Provide information on and instruction necessary to follow fat-modified diet. Recheck LDL cholesterol level annually.
		If other risk is present: Perform complete clinical evaluation and begin dietary therapy. Goal is < 130 mg/dL.
≥ 160	High	Perform complete clinical evaluation and begin cholesterol-lowering therapy.
		If other risk is absent: Goal is < 160 mg/dL. Institute dietary therapy. Drug therapy should be considered after trial of dietary therapy if LDL cholesterol level remains ≥ 190 mg/dL.
		If other risk is present: Goal is < 130 mg/dL. Institute dietary therapy. Drug therapy should be considered after trial of dietary therapy.

Adapted from The Expert Panel, National Cholesterol Education Program; 1988.
*Other risk is the presence of definite CHD or at least two other risk factors for CHD (Table 9).

Table 9
Risk factors for coronary heart disease (CHD), excluding existing heart disease, listed by the NCEP

Risk factor	Value
Elevated LDL cholesterol	≥ 160 mg/dL
Low HDL cholesterol	< 35 mg/dL
Smoking	> 10 cigarettes per day
Severe obesity	≥ 30% overweight
Male gender	
Hypertension	
Diabetes mellitus	
Family history of premature CHD	
History of cerebrovascular or occlusive peripheral vascular disease	

From The Expert Panel, National Cholesterol Education Program; 1988.

considered to confer high risk. The minimal treatment goal for persons without two additional risk factors or coronary heart disease is to lower the serum LDL level to less than 160 mg/dL. For individuals at high risk, the minimal goal is a serum LDL level less than 130 mg/dL.

Additional clinical research may allow us to define more precisely the critical total cholesterol and LDL cholesterol levels that predispose to atherosclerosis and to define serum levels that lead to stabilization or regression of atherosclerosis. Several angiographic clinical studies, including the Cholesterol-Lowering Atherosclerosis Study (CLAS), Familial Atherosclerosis Treatment Study (FATS), Lifestyle Heart Trial, POSCH, and the University of California, San Francisco, Arteriosclerosis Specialized Center of Research (UCSF-SCOR) Intervention Trial, have demonstrated a protective effect with vigorous therapy in which LDL was markedly decreased and HDL was generally increased.

Dietary and drug therapy for hypercholesterolemia: The principal treatment for patients with elevated LDL levels is to reduce the quantity of dietary saturated fat and cholesterol. According to the Keys and Hegsted equations, the proportion of total calories consumed as saturated fat is the single most important dietary determinant of serum cholesterol level. Population studies lend credence to this finding. In the Seven Countries Study, for example, the consumption of saturated fat was positively correlated with serum cholesterol levels, as well as with the prevalence of coronary heart disease.

In terms of lowering cholesterol levels, the Keys and Hegsted equations propose that the effect of removing 1 g of saturated fat from the diet is approximately the equivalent of adding 2 g of polyunsaturated fat. Monounsaturated fat is assumed in the formulas to have a neutral effect on serum cholesterol. However, there is recent evidence that the replacement of saturated fat with monounsaturated fat exerts a cholesterol-lowering action approximately equivalent to that of replacing saturated fat with polyunsaturated fat. Studies have indicated that monounsaturated fat does not appear to reduce levels of HDL, in contrast to the effect of a high quantity of polyunsaturated fat in the diet. Other investigators have found that monounsaturated fat has less cholesterol-lowering potential, so the monounsaturated versus polyunsaturated fat controversy remains unresolved. Removing saturated fat should be the primary dietary goal; cholesterol restriction and, when appropriate, weight reduction are also priorities.

Because of the concern over possible long-term effects of consuming large quantities of polyunsaturated fat, the American Heart Association (AHA) and the NCEP have recommended a balance of dietary fat calories in which polyunsaturated, monounsaturated, and saturated fat each make up approximately one third of the total daily fat intake. In the AHA Step One and Two Diets (Table 10), the proportion of total calories consumed as fat is 30%, compared with the 38% consumed by the average American.

There has been a great deal of interest in using dietary fish oil and omega-3 fatty acids to lower serum cholesterol levels. Cold-water fish (Table 11)

Table 10
American Heart Association Step One and Step Two Diets

Nutrient	Step one	Step two
Total fat	< 30% of calories	< 30% of calories
Saturated	< 10% of calories	< 7% of calories
Polyunsaturated	≤ 10% of calories	≤ 10% of calories
Monounsaturated	10% to 15% of calories	10% to 15% of calories
Carbohydrates	50% to 60% of calories	50% to 60% of calories
Protein	10% to 20% of calories	10% to 20% of calories
Cholesterol	< 300 mg/day	< 200 mg/day
Total calories	Amount to achieve and keep desirable weight	Amount to achieve and keep desirable weight

From The Expert Panel, National Cholesterol Education Program; 1988.

Table 11
Omega-3 fatty acid content (EPA and DHA) of 3 ounces of cooked (no fat added) fish

Herring, Atlantic	1.7 g
Mackerel, Atlantic	1.0 g
Salmon, sockeye	1.0 g
Mussels, blue	0.7 g
Whiting	0.7 g
Trout, rainbow	0.6 g
Tuna, white	0.6 g
Crab, Alaska king	0.4 g
Shrimp	0.3 g
Clams	0.2 g
Lobster, northern	0.1 g

Adapted from the *Composition of Foods: Finfish and Shellfish Products.* Washington, DC: US Department of Agriculture Handbook; 1987:8-15.

are rich in the two primary omega-3 fatty acids, eicosapentaenoic (EPA) and docosahexaenoic acid (DHA). In doses ranging from approximately 7 to 11 g/day, omega-3 fatty acids may decrease VLDL and triglyceride levels, but they have little effect on total cholesterol or LDL levels. Even at low doses (less than 2 g/day), omega-3 fatty acids decrease platelet aggregation and prolong bleeding time. The efficacy of fish oil is being tested in preventing restenosis after percutaneous transluminal angioplasty. Because omega-3 fatty acids are still being investigated, it is recommended that cold-water fish be added to the diet on a regular basis, but the use of fish-oil capsules is not advised at this time.

The specific role of dietary cholesterol in raising or lowering serum cholesterol levels is controversial. As discussed, Brown and Goldstein suggest that dietary cholesterol may suppress the activity of hepatic LDL receptors, an effect that has been demonstrated in animal studies but not in humans. Moreover, the effects of dietary cholesterol consumption vary widely among individuals. One variable might be the level of ACAT activity. Depressed ACAT activity may decrease absorption of dietary cholesterol by decreasing the quantity of cholesterol esterified in the wall of the intestine and thereby may decrease the amount of cholesteryl ester in the chylomicrons.

Shekelle et al found a relationship between the amount of cholesterol in the diet and the development of coronary heart disease that was independent of the effect of dietary cholesterol on the serum cholesterol level. The explanation for this observation is not immediately apparent, but it is hypothesized that increased consumption of cholesterol may stimulate the formation of atherogenic lipoproteins. Mahley and others have shown that cholesterol-enriched particles accumulate in animals fed high-cholesterol diets. These particles are analogous to β-VLDLs, which are remnant lipoproteins.

The serum cholesterol levels of most patients with polygenic hypercholesterolemia and familial combined hyperlipidemia respond to dietary changes. When drug therapy is needed, bile acid sequestrants, nicotinic acid, and HMG-CoA reductase inhibitors are useful in treating familial hypercholesterolemia. Probucol has been used in patients who are homozygous for familial hypercholesterolemia and may also be used in combination with one of the drugs mentioned above. Nicotinic acid and gemfibrozil are each extremely effective in conjunction with diet for patients with familial dysbetalipoproteinemia.

The addition of soluble fiber to the diet has been shown to exert a cholesterol-lowering effect of approximately 5% over and above the effect of other dietary modifications. Whether adding fiber to the diet exerts a cholesterol-lowering effect on its own, apart from its replacing dietary fat, remains controversial. While several earlier studies demonstrated such an effect, the exact mechanism is not known; it may be related to the inhibition of dietary absorption of bile acid and cholesterol, and β-glucans may be the active chemical substances responsible for this inhibition. Of the fibers, oat bran and guar gum seem to have the greatest effect in lowering cholesterol levels.

Hypertriglyceridemia screening and treatment guidelines: The physician should be aware that certain patients with elevated triglycerides are at increased risk for coronary heart disease. The National Institutes of Health Consensus Development Conference on Triglyceride, High-Density Lipoprotein, and Coronary Heart Disease, which convened in February 1992, stressed the relationship between elevated triglyceride and low HDL cholesterol levels in coronary heart disease risk. The panel defined borderline hypertriglyceridemia as triglyceride levels in the 250 to 500 mg/dL range and distinct hypertriglyceridemia as over 500 mg/dL. The definition of low HDL (ie, < 35 mg/dL) remains the same as proposed by the NCEP, although the NIH panel noted that this cut-off point may be too low for women and certain other patient populations. However, data were insufficient on this issue to alter the NCEP guidelines.

The panel issued the following recommendations for screening:
- HDL determinations should accompany measurements of total cholesterol (a nonfasting sample is acceptable) in all healthy subjects. The NIH panel cautioned that HDL measurements should be performed in locations where accuracy, appropriate counseling, and follow-up can be assured.
- HDL cholesterol and triglyceride levels should be determined, based on at least two fasting samples taken a minimum of 1 week apart, in the following subjects: (1) patients with known coronary heart disease (to assess for disease progression and development of additional cardiovascular complications); (2) subjects with increased total cholesterol levels (those with high HDL cholesterol and LDL cholesterol in the desirable range are considered to be at low or average risk); (3) patients with desirable total cholesterol levels who have two or more risk factors (those with low HDL cholesterol and/or elevated triglyceride levels are possibly at risk); (4) patients with disorders that are associated with elevated triglyceride and increased risk of coronary heart disease (eg, diabetes, central obesity, peripheral vascular disease, hypertension, and chronic renal disease); (5) patients with lactescent serum, lipidemia retinalis, xanthomas, or pancreatitis (to identify familial hyperlipidemic disorders and/or the likelihood of recurrent pancreatitis); and (6) patients currently on hygienic or drug therapy for elevated triglyceride and/or low HDL cholesterol (to evaluate the results of therapy).

The NIH consensus panel also issued treatment guidelines, stressing that hygienic measures should always be instituted in a patient with elevated triglyceride or HDL cholesterol, regardless of the total cholesterol level. Therapy must be individualized and include diet, weight control, exercise, and smoking cessation, as appropriate.

The American Heart Association Step One Diet is recommended for all patients with elevated triglyceride, although some patients require the Step Two Diet to achieve plasma lipid modification. Hygienic intervention alone is often sufficient to normalize triglyceride and HDL cholesterol levels. The NIH consensus panel urged that drug therapy be restricted to high-risk patients (ie, those who have multiple risk factors). The following treatment strategies were recommended:

- *LDL > 130 mg/dL:* If refractory to nonpharmacologic therapy, drug treatment may be required (however, drug therapy is not indicated if HDL cholesterol level is very high).
- *Triglyceride 250 to 500 mg/dL, HDL 35 mg/dL, and LDL ≤ 130 mg/dL:* Primary treatment is hygienic approach. No consensus was reached concerning pharmacologic treatment, but lipid-lowering drugs may be considered in unusual cases in which hygienic measures fail and the patient has existing coronary heart disease or a high-risk profile.
- *Triglyceride > 500 mg/dL:* Initial therapy consists of hygienic measures. If these fail, drug therapy is warranted to reduce the risk of pancreatitis. However, lipid-lowering drugs should be considered as initial therapy (in addition to hygienic measures) in patients with a history of pancreatitis.
- *HDL very low or absent, LDL ≤ 130 mg/dL, and triglyceride > 500 mg/dL:* This lipid profile probably represents one of various rare genetic disorders requiring expert evaluation; no specific therapy is available.
- *Primary hypoalphalipoproteinemia (HDL < 35 mg/dL, triglyceride and LDL levels usually normal):* Hygienic measures should be instituted and coexisting risk factors should be controlled. Drugs commonly used to raise HDL levels may be ineffectual.

There was no consensus for treating isolated mild, sporadic hypertriglyceridemia or low HDL levels in the general population. The panel also noted that data seem to be sufficient to merit considering postmenopausal status an additional risk factor for coronary heart disease.

Drug therapy for hypertriglyceridemia: Treatment with a fibric-acid derivative has been found to reverse the formation of small, protein-rich LDL particles, leading to the restoration of more normal-sized LDL particles, as well as to a reduction in triglyceride and VLDL concentrations. Fibric-acid derivatives are thought to increase the activity of lipoprotein lipase, although this effect has not been demonstrated conclusively. As noted in the Helsinki Heart Study, the use of gemfibrozil reduced coronary events most dramatically in patients with type IIb hyperlipidemia.

The rate of LDL catabolism or removal from the blood appears to be increased in hypertriglyceridemia. Some patients show an increase in LDL cholesterol levels when they are treated with a fibric-acid derivative, which may reflect an increased conversion of IDL to LDL. The significance of these findings is unknown, but patients should be monitored during treatment to avoid significant and prolonged increases in LDL cholesterol levels.

Drug therapy is clearly indicated for treatment of severe hypertriglyceridemia if diet fails. There is not yet any effective pharmacotherapy for lipoprotein lipase deficiency or for familial apo C-II deficiency.

Hypertension

Contribution to the Development of Atherosclerosis
The precise mechanism by which hypertension contributes to the development of atherosclerosis is unclear. There are a number of hypotheses, including endothelial cell damage, increased entry of lipoproteins into the arterial wall, and stimulation of smooth muscle cell growth.

The increased hydrodynamic pressure that accompanies hypertension might promote atherosclerosis by physically injuring endothelial cells. The injury would lead to smooth muscle cell proliferation and subsequent endothelial dysfunction, permitting increased adhesion of platelets and monocytes to the endothelial surface. Platelets, endothelial cells, and macrophages are all capable of producing growth factors that stimulate smooth muscle cell proliferation. Several investigators have described various abnormalities in the cell membrane of people with hypertension; for example, individuals from hypertensive families have an abnormality in the sodium-lithium countertransport mechanism. The cellular basis for these transport abnormalities is not known, but it may involve changes in the properties of the cell membranes of lymphocytes, macrophages, red cells, and platelets.

Just as diets rich in polyunsaturated fat are correlated with lower blood pressures than diets rich in saturated fat, changes in cell membranes may also be related to changes in diet. For example, a decrease in the linoleic acid content of the platelet cell membrane could decrease the membrane fluidity and lead to abnormalities of transport into and out of the cell. Diets with a high content of omega-3 fatty acids from cold-water fish lead to EPA replacing arachidonic acid in platelet cell membranes. These cell-membrane changes result in prolonged bleeding times and decreased platelet aggregation, which may reduce the adherence of platelets to the arterial wall. Platelet abnormalities may increase both platelet aggregation and the release of active substances that promote smooth cell proliferation. In patients with hypertension, a localized or generalized release of growth factors within the blood vessel wall may induce atherosclerosis by stimulating proliferation of smooth muscle cells.

The contractility of smooth muscle cells is related to the intracellular content of calcium. In theory, calcium antagonists may protect against atherosclerosis by causing a relaxation of smooth muscle cells and decreasing vascular tone. Conversely, an increase in intracellular calcium may increase vascular tone and promote cellular accumulation of cholesterol. In clinical trials, calcium channel blockers were found to decrease new plaque formation in coronary arteries but did not influence established plaques. Results from animal studies are conflicting, but in a number of experiments the use of calcium antagonists has decreased the severity of atherosclerosis in animals fed cholesterol-rich diets. Calcium antagonists may prevent the transformation of

vascular smooth cells from the contractile to the synthetic state and may promote cholesterol removal from macrophages.

Endocrinologic pathways are involved in regulating both blood pressure and lipoprotein metabolism. For example, the tone of the endothelial capillary walls supplying muscle and adipose tissue influences the activity of lipoprotein lipase. Vascular tone is increased by α-adrenergic agents and decreased by β-adrenergic agents. Therefore, α-blockers decrease capillary tone and increase blood flow, thereby increasing lipoprotein lipase activity and the clearance of triglyceride-rich lipoproteins. β-Blockers have the opposite effect.

Epidemiologic Studies and Clinical Trials

The Framingham Heart Study demonstrated a synergistic effect between hypertension and hypercholesterolemia in increasing coronary heart disease risk. When systolic blood pressure was plotted against coronary heart disease rates by different LDL-to-HDL ratios in this study, there was only a slight increase in the relative risk of developing coronary heart disease when the LDL-to-HDL ratio was 3:1. However, at an LDL-to-HDL ratio of 8:1, there was a significant increase in the relative risk of developing coronary heart disease at higher systolic blood pressures. Thus, at a given blood pressure, the LDL-to-HDL ratio was a determinant of the relative risk of developing coronary heart disease.

In investigations of kindreds from Utah, Williams et al found a familial association of hypertension and hyperlipidemia (which they called dyslipidemic hypertension) with a posited basis in hyperinsulinemia and insulin resistance (see Lipid Transport Disorders on page 26.)

Data from the small Oslo Hypertension Study suggested that the coronary heart disease mortality of mildly hypertensive patients may be greater when these patients are treated with propranolol and diuretics than when they remain untreated. A number of other studies have examined the relationship between antihypertensive therapy and the risk of developing coronary heart disease. In the Medical Research Council (MRC) trial, the treatment group received either a diuretic or a β-blocker. After 7 years of treatment, both the treated and placebo groups had experienced almost the same number of coronary events per 1000 patient-years. An interesting result from this trial was the difference between smokers' and nonsmokers' responses to β-blockers. β-Blockers did not affect the rate of coronary heart disease among smokers, but treatment with propranolol did reduce the rate of coronary events among nonsmokers (from 7.5 to 5.0 events per 1000 patient-years). The cardiac event rate for non-smokers receiving a β-blocker was also decreased in the International Prospective Primary Prevention Study in Hypertension (IPPPSH) from 11.6 to 5.4 per 1000 patient-years.

Based on an analysis of various trials, Rose concluded that the risk of coronary heart disease is reduced by antihypertensive therapy in non-smokers, and while lowering cholesterol may have a significant impact on reducing the risk for smokers, lowering blood pressure does not. Lowering cholesterol and blood pressure together significantly reduced coronary heart disease in the Göteborg Study, but antihypertensive therapy alone did not.

In the Multiple Risk Factor Intervention Trial (MRFIT) in the United States, hypertensive men with abnormal electrocardiographic patterns who were treated with diuretics had a higher mortality rate than hypertensive men in a control group. It was suspected that this difference may have been due to arrhythmias resulting from hypokalemia. Not all investigators support this hypothesis, however.

Although most of the trials of antihypertensive agents have shown a decrease in overall and cerebrovascular mortality, only the Hypertension Detection and Follow-up Program (HDFP) and the European Working Party on Hypertension in the Elderly (EWPHE) have reported a statistically significant decrease in coronary heart disease mortality. No such decrease was observed in the MRC trial, the Australian Therapeutic Trial in Mild Hypertension, or the Veterans Administration Cooperative Study, although a reduction in the rate of strokes was observed in all these studies.

Two lessons are to be learned from these studies. First, the physician should be aware of lipid and lipoprotein concentrations as well as blood pressure when devising a rational program of treatment for hypertension and hyperlipidemia. The second lesson is to use the lowest dose of diuretic necessary to control blood pressure. In general, diuretics have been used in elderly patients in whom β-blockers are less effective. Potential adverse effects of diuretics include increases in serum total cholesterol, LDL, triglyceride, and VLDL levels; hyperuricemia; decreased glucose tolerance; and hypokalemia.

The 1988 Report of the Joint National Committee on Detection, Evaluation, and Treatment of High Blood Pressure broadened the recommendations for first-line antihypertensive agents, adding angiotensin converting enzyme (ACE) inhibitors and calcium antagonists. Each type of agent appears to be effective, although different subsets of patients may respond better to a particular class of drugs. The action of a β-blocker, calcium antagonist, or ACE inhibitor may be enhanced by the addition of a diuretic.

More than 90% of hypertensive patients have primary hypertension, that is, hypertension not caused by a known underlying disorder, such as hyperthyroidism, pheochromocytoma, hyperaldosteronism, renovascular hypertension, or hyperadrenalism. Isolated systolic hypertension can accompany hyperthyroidism and is frequently seen in the elderly with this thyroid disorder. Severe episodic elevations of blood pressure suggest the possibility of pheochromocytoma, while persistent hypokalemia may be an indication of hyperaldosteronism. An abdominal bruit or a constriction of a renal artery may be an indication of renovascular hypertension, which can be diagnosed by measuring renal vein renin concentrations. Cushing's syndrome and hyperadrenalism have characteristic clinical manifestations.

Attention has recently been given to the non-pharmacologic treatment of borderline hypertension. Such therapy includes salt restriction, weight reduction for obese persons, a program of at least mild exercise, stress modification, relaxation techniques, and recognition of environmental or lifestyle factors that contribute to chronic elevations of blood pressure. One or more of these approaches may be appropriate for individuals whose systolic/diastolic blood pressure is in the range of 140/90 to 150/95 mm Hg.

Cigarette Smoking

According to the US Surgeon General, cigarette smoking is the most preventable risk factor for coronary heart disease. In a study of more than 18 000 British civil servants, coronary heart disease mortality was higher in smokers than in nonsmokers at any level of blood pressure or cholesterol. The British Regional Heart Study showed that in men aged 40 to 59, the risk of coronary heart disease was more than two times greater for smokers than for men who had never smoked. Approximately 50 million Americans smoke cigarettes, and although the number of adult smokers is falling, the number of teenaged girls who smoke is rising.

Numerous studies have shown that smoking is associated with peripheral atherosclerosis and with coronary heart disease in both men and women. In fact, it is unusual to see peripheral atherosclerosis in a woman who is neither a smoker nor a diabetic. Smoking also increases the risk for developing coronary heart disease by two- to threefold. Although some investigators suggest that smoking cigars, pipes, and low-tar cigarettes confers less risk than does smoking regular cigarettes, this has not been proved.

Kaufman et al reported that for young men the risk of developing coronary heart disease is approximately 2.8 times higher if they smoke. Moreover, the risk to smokers did not vary significantly in this study by the cigarette level of nicotine and carbon monoxide. These investigators concluded that low-tar, low-nicotine cigarettes do not provide protection against the development of coronary heart disease.

These findings were mirrored in the Framingham Heart Study. Members of the Framingham cohort who smoked filtered cigarettes still had an increased incidence of coronary heart disease. This association may reflect the practice smokers have of inhaling more deeply and more frequently when smoking low-tar, low-nicotine cigarettes than when smoking regular cigarettes. The

Framingham study also showed that the adverse effect smoking has on the incidence of coronary heart disease decreases by about half 1 year after a person stops smoking.

Potential mechanisms by which smoking may adversely affect the cardiovascular system include stimulation of the sympathetic nervous system by nicotine, replacement of oxygen by carbon monoxide, induced immunologic insult to the blood vessel wall, and increased platelet aggregation and adhesiveness.

Although breaking the cigarette-smoking habit is difficult, its positive correlation with decreased risks of cardiovascular disease, lung cancer, and chronic obstructive pulmonary disease justifies the goals of the US Surgeon General, the American Heart Association, the American Cancer Society, and the American Lung Association to obtain a smoke-free society by the year 2000.

Secondary Risk Factors

Diabetes Mellitus

Little evidence exists that controlling blood glucose plays a significant role in preventing macrovascular complications. At least one major clinical trial is under way to determine the efficacy of tight glucose control in decreasing damage to the microcirculation, particularly diabetic proliferative retinopathy. Conventional wisdom holds that tight glucose control will decrease the frequency or postpone the development of complications involving the eye, kidney, and nerves. However, evidence from controlled clinical trials is lacking. Aldose reductase inhibitors have been tested, but their beneficial effects on the development of diabetic neuropathy have not been established. The control of hypertension appears to be particularly important in preventing diabetic nephropathy and probably in controlling diabetic retinopathy. Careful attention to a program of diet, exercise, management of blood sugar, and treatment of hyperlipidemia (if present) is advisable for diabetics.

Population studies have shown hyperinsulinemia to be positively correlated with the presence of coronary heart disease. Hyperinsulinemia is measured in different ways, but the most frequently used measure is an excessive insulin response to glucose challenge. Hyperinsulinemia is an integral component of non–insulin-dependent diabetes and may occur in the absence of overt diabetes. Theoretically, an increased peripheral resistance to the action of insulin leads to hyperinsulinemia, which may stimulate hepatic triglyceride and VLDL synthesis. Hyperinsulinemia has been associated with hypertriglyceridemia and small, dense LDL particles in syndrome X and also with dyslipidemic hypertension. Insulin may play a primary role in the development of hypertension by increasing renal sodium reabsorption and in the development of atherosclerosis by acting as a growth factor and stimulating vascular smooth muscle cell proliferation.

There have been many different reports concerning lipoprotein patterns in insulin-dependent and non–insulin-dependent diabetes. Hypertriglyceridemia and increased levels of VLDL are common findings, as are low levels of HDL. In one recent study, an inverse relationship was found between the concentration of glycosylated hemoglobin and HDL level, implying that the poorer the degree of glucose control, the lower the HDL concentration. Levels of HDL in diabetics could be depressed for a number of reasons, including decreased HDL synthesis by the triglyceride-rich VLDLs and chylomicrons and increased HDL catabolism.

Diabetic ketoacidosis is often associated with type V hyperlipidemia, which is characterized by increased VLDL levels and chylomicrons in fasting serum. The association between diabetic ketoacidosis and type V hyperlipidemia reflects the fact that insulin is needed to activate lipoprotein lipase.

Recent studies have implicated oxidized lipoproteins in the development of atherosclerosis and diabetes. Oxidized LDL and chemically modified LDL (eg, glycated or glycosylated LDL) may be accumulated through scavenger receptor-mediated processes in macrophages, leading to the formation of foam cells. Oxidation of LDL appears to be inhibited by probucol, which associates with LDL apo B and protects the lipoprotein particle against oxidation. Findings by Morel and Chisholm suggest that probucol may also protect against the development of either genetically or chemically induced diabetes in experimental animals. These findings suggest that oxidized intermediates may play a role in the destruction of the islet cells that leads to the development of diabetes. Probucol treatment in animals delayed the onset of diabetes. Probucol also prevents activated macrophages from releasing interleukin-1, which may be toxic to endothelial cells and may also stimulate smooth muscle cell proliferation. Thus, a number of factors may increase the proliferation of smooth muscle cells or alter the properties of the endothelial cell in diabetes. Hyperinsulinemia and the glycosylation and oxidation of lipoproteins and other proteins are a few of the possibilities.

The proliferation of small blood vessels in the kidney and the retina may also be influenced by growth factors (eg, the angiogenesis growth factor) and by toxic metabolites. Clarification of normal and abnormal functioning of the arterial wall and endothelial cells should provide greater insight into the pathologic processes of macrovascular and microvascular changes in diabetic patients.

Obesity and Fat Distribution
Obesity is common in industrialized societies. Approximately 20% of men and 15% of women in the United States are obese. Obesity exacerbates hypertension, hypertriglyceridemia, and diabetes and insulin resistance. Data from the Framingham Heart Study show a strong positive relationship between weight gain and angina pectoris, myocardial infarction, and sudden death, especially among men.

Other studies suggest that obesity is an independent risk factor for coronary heart disease. Obesity is associated with higher levels of triglyceride and

VLDL and lower levels of HDL cholesterol. The relationship between obesity and coronary death has not been consistent, however.

A 12-year study of women in Göteborg, Sweden, indicated that so-called male-pattern (or "potbelly") obesity is more strongly associated with coronary heart disease than are other distributions of adipose tissue. Another study reported similar findings among men. Total obesity was not predictive for the risk of developing coronary heart disease; instead, the waist-to-hip ratio was the significant predictor of coronary heart disease.

Many approaches have been used to achieve weight loss, but despite an initial weight loss most people do not maintain the weight reduction over a 2-year period. The recommended rate of loss should not exceed 0.5 to 1 kg (about 1 to 2 pounds) per week. Crash diets are not advised. Patients who use crash diets to lose weight usually soon regain most of the weight. Behavior modification that reinforces new eating habits for maintaining a lower weight are more effective. The guidance of a dietitian is often important in successful weight reduction, and exercise and other physical activity can be useful adjuncts for weight control.

Physical Activity

Exercise is associated with higher serum levels of HDL, lower levels of blood pressure, a greater proportion of lean body mass, and less obesity. Studies with primates showed that aerobic exercise decreases the prevalence and severity of atherosclerosis in animals fed a high-fat, high-cholesterol diet. Aerobic exercise results in higher serum HDL levels and lower blood pressure in humans, but there has been no prospective clinical trial to establish the benefit of exercise in reducing the prevalence of coronary heart disease. In one ongoing study, however, physically fit men had a 50% lower risk of myocardial infarction than did men who were less well conditioned. Diastolic blood pressure is mildly reduced by regular aerobic exercise, and regular aerobic exercise increases HDL levels. Exercise can also improve glucose tolerance.

The amount of exercise required to decrease the risk of coronary heart disease has not been established. In one study, additional energy expenditure equivalent to 2000 kcal per week gave approximately the same degree of protection against coronary heart disease as did marathon running.

Although there is some increase in the risk of sudden death for a sedentary person who begins exercising, the risk of sudden death is decreased in persons who regularly exercise. Because of the potential risk for myocardial infarction or sudden cardiac death when sedentary persons age 35 and older begin exercising vigorously, it is advisable for them to have their cardiac status evaluated during an exercise test before beginning a new program of vigorous physical exercise. After evaluation, patients with no history of coronary heart disease who have a low risk of an adverse cardiac event during exercise do not require close monitoring or physician supervision. Similarly, the degree of supervision required for patients recovering from myocardial infarction depends on the risk stratification of the patient. For patients known to develop ischemic electrocardiographic changes either at rest or with exercise, close monitoring is advisable.

Although evidence from a definitive clinical trial is lacking, the American Heart Association, the British Joint Working Party, and the US Department of Health and Human Services have all recommended regular physical activity as part of a healthy lifestyle.

Psychosocial and Behavioral Factors

Considerable controversy has surrounded the question of whether personality type and stress affect coronary heart disease risk. A recent review of six prospective studies and many case-control reports leave little doubt that emotional distress often is a forerunner of coronary heart disease, particularly myocardial infarction.

A large study of Swedish construction workers showed a correlation between the prevalence of emotional factors and both fatal and nonfatal myocardial infarctions. In the Chicago Heart Association Detection Project and in the Western Electric Study, a graded inverse relationship existed between educational level and adjusted rates of coronary heart disease and death from all causes. The Western Electric Study suggested that less education and a lower socioeconomic level were associated with a greater risk of myocardial infarction. Similar observations have been made in other studies. This relationship may reflect, at least in part, the fact that more highly educated and affluent persons in the United States have adopted behavioral changes that improve health, including changes in exercise, diet, and smoking.

In 1980, a National Heart, Lung, and Blood Institute panel concluded that so-called type A people have an increased risk of developing coronary heart disease. Type A people are extremely time conscious, highly competitive, and constantly battling someone. In contrast, type B people tend to take life more casually. In the Framingham Heart Study, type A people had a higher rate of coronary heart disease. However, in the MRFIT and the Western Collaborative Group studies, no relationship was found between personality type (A or B) and the prevalence of coronary heart disease; the latter study did, however, report hostility as a risk factor. Some of the differences in these study results may reflect differences in the methods used to assess personality or differences in the populations studied.

Estrogens and Gender
It is well established that women experience coronary heart disease later in life than do men, although as many women as men die of coronary heart disease in the United States. In the United States, the average life span of a woman is 8 years longer than that of a man. Premenopausal women have higher serum HDL levels and lower LDL and total cholesterol levels. Premenopausal estrogen levels appear to be a strong protective factor against the early development of coronary heart disease. Estrogens decrease serum LDL, while raising serum triglyceride and HDL levels. With the decline of estrogen synthesis at menopause, LDL and total cholesterol levels in women exceed those of men, although HDL concentrations remain at higher levels.

A study at the Harvard School of Public Health reported a decrease in coronary heart disease in postmenopausal women who used estrogen replacement therapy. In this large survey of registered nurses, women who had received or were currently receiving estrogen therapy had approximately half the number of fatal or nonfatal myocardial infarctions than those who never received estrogen replacement. However, the Framingham Heart Study showed that postmenopausal women taking estrogen had an increased risk of cardiovascular mortality. The reason for this discrepancy is not clear, but the Framingham data are not consistent with most other studies.

The combination of estrogen and progestin in oral contraceptives may have various effects on serum lipid levels, depending on the relative strength of the estrogen and progestin components. Progestin tends to decrease both triglyceride and HDL cholesterol levels.

Alcohol
At least seven major clinical studies have linked an excessive consumption of alcohol to increased incidence of coronary heart disease and all-cause mortality. Moderate consumption of alcohol may increase both HDL_2 and HDL_3. Some studies have shown a decrease in the prevalence of coronary heart disease with moderate drinking, presumably due to a rise in HDL levels. However, alcohol is not currently recommended as a way of raising HDL or as a way of guarding against developing coronary heart disease. Alcohol intake is positively correlated with higher levels of blood pressure; also, alcohol depresses myocardial function and is toxic to the liver and nervous system.

Minor Risk Factors

There are several minor risk factors for coronary heart disease, one of which is variability in the level of trace metals. A relative deficiency of copper and an excess of zinc have been described as increasing the risk of developing coronary heart disease. In Italy, the degree of hardness of water had an inverse relationship to the rate of coronary heart disease mortality. Chronic hypercalcemia and excessive coffee consumption have also been listed as coronary heart disease risk factors. However, studies on these minor risk factors are not conclusive.

Conclusion

The US mortality rate for coronary heart disease has progressively declined over the past 4 decades, an improvement partly attributable to lifestyle changes. Increased public awareness of coronary heart disease risk factors has led many people to stop smoking, start exercising, and adopt "heart-healthy" diets consisting of less red meat and dairy products and a greater proportion of polyunsaturated fats. More people are being screened for hypertension and dyslipidemia and are making appropriate lifestyle modifications before these disorders can cause irreversible damage.

Although the decreased coronary heart disease mortality and the public's interest in prevention are encouraging signs, the fact remains that coronary heart disease mortality is higher in the United States than in most other industrialized countries. According to the World Health Organization, 55 in 100 000 Americans die of coronary heart disease annually, a rate that compares unfavorably with Switzerland (33 per 100 000) and Japan (15 per 100 000).

Clearly, efforts toward modifying coronary heart disease risk factors need to be increased on several fronts. Screening and prevention measures should become more widely available and more accessible at all socioeconomic levels. The goal should be early diagnosis before irreversible damage has occurred. Additional studies are needed to identify other potential risk factors for coronary heart disease. By increasing efforts to modify coronary heart disease risk factors, it should be possible to realize a 50% reduction in the present mortality rate and significantly reduce coronary heart disease morbidity.

Selected Readings

Lipids, Lipoproteins, and Apolipoproteins

Anantharamaiah GM, Venkatachalapathi YV, Brouillette CG, Segrest JP. Use of synthetic peptide analogues to localize lecithin:cholesterol acyltransferase activating domain in apolipoprotein A-I. **Arteriosclerosis.** 1990;10:95-105.

Assmann G, Schmitz G, Funke H, von Eckardstein A. Apolipoprotein A-I and HDL deficiency. **Curr Opin Lipidol.** 1990;1:110-115.

Assmann G, Schmitz G, Menzel HJ, Schulte H. Apolipoprotein E polymorphism and hyperlipidemia. **Clin Chem.** 1984;30:641-643.

Assmann G, Schulte H. Triglycerides and atherosclerosis: results from the Prospective Cardiovascular Muenster Study. **Atheroscleros Rev.** 1991;22:51-57.

Austin MA. Plasma triglyceride and coronary heart disease. **Arterioscleros Thromb.** 1991;11:2-14. Review.

Austin MA. Plasma triglyceride as a risk factor for coronary heart disease: the epidemiologic evidence and beyond. **Am J Epidemiol.** 1989;129:249-259.

Austin MA, Brunzell JD, Fitch WL, Krauss RM. Inheritance of low density lipoprotein subclass patterns in familial combined hyperlipidemia. **Arteriosclerosis.** 1990;10:520-530.

Baggio G, Manzato E, Gabelli C, et al. Apolipoprotein C-II deficiency syndrome: clinical features, lipoprotein characterization, lipase activity, and correction of hypertriglyceridemia after apolipoprotein C-II administration in two affected patients. **J Clin Invest.** 1986;77:520-527.

Berg K, Powell LM, Wallis SC, Pease R, Knott TJ, Scott J. Genetic linkage between the antigenic group (Ag) variation and the apolipoprotein B gene: assignment of the Ag locus. **Proc Natl Acad Sci USA.** 1986;83:7367-7370.

Breckenridge WC, Little JA, Steiner G, Chow A, Poapst M. Hypertriglyceridemia associated with deficiency of apolipoprotein C-II. **N Engl J Med.** 1978;298:1265-1273.

Breslow JL. Genetic basis of lipoprotein disorders. **J Clin Invest.** 1989;84:373-380.

Castro GR, Fielding CJ. Early incorporation of cell-derived cholesterol into pre-beta-migrating high-density lipoprotein. **Biochemistry.** 1988;27:25-29.

Fruchart JC. Lipoprotein heterogeneity and its effect on apolipoprotein assays. **Scand J Clin Lab Invest Suppl.** 1990;198:51-57.

Goldstein JL, Brown MS. Progress in understanding the LDL receptor and HMG-CoA reductase, two membrane proteins that regulate the plasma cholesterol. **J Lipid Res.** 1984;25:1450-1461.

Gotto AM. Cholesterol intake and serum cholesterol level. **N Engl J Med.** 1991;324:912-913. Editorial.

Graham DL, Oram JF. Identification and characterization of a high density lipoprotein-binding protein in cell membranes by ligand blotting. **J Biol Chem.** 1987;262:7439-7442.

Hennekens CH, Eberlein K. A randomized trial of aspirin and β-carotene among U.S. physicians. **Prev Med.** 1985;14:165-168.

Herz J, Hamann U, Rogne S, Myklebost O, Gausepohl H, Stanley KK. Surface location and high affinity for calcium of 500-kd liver membrane protein closely related to the LDL-receptor suggest a physiologic role as lipoprotein receptor. **EMBO J.** 1988;7:4119-4127.

Huang LS, Ripps ME, Breslow JL. Molecular basis of five apolipoprotein B gene polymorphisms in noncoding regions. **J Lipid Res.** 1990;31:71-77.

Hui DY, Innerarity TL, Milne RW, Marcel YL, Mahley RW. Binding of chylomicron remnants and beta-very low density lipoproteins to hepatic and extrahepatic lipoprotein receptors: a process independent of apolipoprotein B-48. **J Biol Chem.** 1984;259:15060-15068.

Inazu A, Brown ML, Hesler CB, et al. Increased high-density lipoprotein levels caused by a common cholesteryl-ester transfer protein gene mutation. **N Engl J Med.** 1990;323:1234-1238.

International Committee for the Evaluation of Hypertriglycerid-emia as a Vascular Risk Factor. The hypertriglyceridemias: risk and management. **Am J Cardiol.** 1991;68:1A-42A.

Kaplan NM. The deadly quartet: upper-body obesity, glucose intolerance, hypertriglyceridemia, and hypertension. **Arch Intern Med.** 1989;149:1514-1520.

Kodama T, Freeman M, Rohrer L, Zabrecky J, Matsudaira P, Krieger M. Type I macrophage scavenger receptor contains α-helical and collagen-like coiled coils. **Nature.** 1990;343:531-535.

Kowal RC, Herz J, Goldstein JL, Esser V, Brown MS. Low density lipoprotein receptor-related protein mediates uptake of cholesteryl esters derived from apoprotein E-enriched lipoproteins. **Proc Natl Acad Sci USA.** 1989;86:5810-5814.

Manninen V, Elo MO, Frick MH, et al. Lipid alterations and decline in the incidence of coronary heart disease in the Helsinki Heart Study. **JAMA.** 1988;260:641-651.

Manninen V, Tenkanen L, Koskinen P, et al. Joint effects of serum triglyceride and LDL cholesterol and HDL cholesterol concentrations on coronary heart disease risk in the Helsinki Heart Study: implications for treatment. **Circulation.** 1992;85:37-45.

Myant NB, Gallagher J, Barbir M, Thompson GR, Wile D, Humphries SE. Restriction fragment length polymorphisms in the apo B gene in relation to coronary artery disease. **Atherosclerosis.** 1989;77:193-201.

Oram JF. Cholesterol trafficking in cells. **Curr Opin Lipidiol.** 1990;1:416-421.

Ordovas JM, Schaefer EJ, Salem D, et al. Apolipoprotein A-I gene polymorphism associated with premature coronary artery disease and familial hypoalphalipoproteinemia. **N Engl J Med.** 1986;314:671-677.

Patsch JR, Prasad S, Gotto AM Jr, Patsch W. High density lipoprotein$_2$: relationship of the plasma levels of this lipoprotein species to its composition, to the magnitude of postprandial lipemia, and to the activities of lipoprotein lipase and hepatic lipase. **J Clin Invest.** 1987;80:341-347.

Reaven GM. Banting Lecture 1988. Role of insulin resistance in human disease. **Diabetes.** 1988;37:1595-1607.

Rohrer L, Freeman M, Kodama T, Penman M, Krieger M. Coiled-coil fibrous domains mediate ligand binding by macrophage scavenger receptor type II. **Nature.** 1990;343:570-572.

Sniderman A, Shapiro S, Marpole D, Skinner B, Teng B, Kwiterovich PO Jr. Association of coronary atherosclerosis with hyperapobetalipoproteinemia (increased protein but normal cholesterol levels in human plasma low density [beta] lipoproteins). **Proc Natl Acad Sci USA.** 1980;77:604-608.

Soria LF, Ludwig EH, Clarke HR, Vega GL, Grundy SM, McCarthy BJ. Association between a specific apolipoprotein B mutation and familial defective apolipoprotein B-100. **Proc Natl Acad Sci USA.** 1989;86:587-591.

Steinberg D, Parthasarathy S, Carew TE, Khoo JC, Witztum JL. Beyond cholesterol: modifications of low-density lipoprotein that increase its atherogenicity. **N Engl J Med.** 1989;320:915-924.

Strickland DK, Ashcom JD, Williams S, Burgess WH, Migliorini M, Argraves WS. Sequence identity between the alpha 2-macroglobulin receptor and low density lipoprotein receptor-related protein suggests that this molecule is a multifunctional receptor. **J Biol Chem.** 1990;265:17401-17404.

Utermann G. Lipoprotein (a): a genetic risk factor for premature coronary heart disease. **Curr Opin Lipidol.** 1990;1:404-410.

von Eckardstein A, Funke H, Henke A, Altland K, Benninghoven A, Assmann G. Apolipoprotein A-I variants: naturally occurring substitutions of proline residues affect plasma concentration of apolipoprotein A-I. **J Clin Invest.** 1989;84:1722-1730.

Williams RR, Hunt SC, Hopkins PN, et al. Familial dyslipidemic hypertension: evidence from 58 Utah families for a syndrome present in approximately 12% of patients with essential hypertension. **JAMA.** 1988;259:3579-3586.

Yang CY, Chen SH, Gianturco SH, et al. Sequence, structure, receptor-binding domains and internal repeats of human apolipoprotein B-100. **Nature.** 1986;323:738-742.

Yokode M, Hammer RE, Tshibashi S, Brown MS, Goldstein JL. Diet-induced hypercholesterolemia in mice: prevention by overexpression of LDL receptors. **Science.** 1990;250:1273-1275.

Diagnosis and Treatment of Dyslipidemia

American Heart Association. **Dietary Treatment of Hyper-cholesterolemia: A Manual for Patients.** Dallas, Tx: American Heart Association; 1988.

Blankenhorn DH, Nessim SA, Johnson RL, et al. Beneficial effects of combined colestipol-niacin therapy on coronary atherosclerosis and coronary venous bypass grafts. **JAMA.** 1987;257:3233-3240.

Brown G, Albers JJ, Fisher LD, et al. Regression of coronary artery disease as a result of intensive lipid-lowering therapy in men with high levels of apolipoprotein B. **N Engl J Med.** 1990;323:1337-1339.

Buchwald H, Varco RL, Matts JP, et al. Effect of partial ileal bypass surgery on mortality and morbidity from coronary heart disease in patients with hypercholesterolemia: report of the Program on the Surgical Control of the Hyperlipidemias (POSCH). **N Engl J Med.** 1990;323:946-955.

Cashin-Hemphill L, Mack WJ, Pogoda JM, Sanmarco ME, Azen SP, Blankenhorn DH. Beneficial effects of colestipol-niacin on coronary atherosclerosis: a 4-year follow-up. **JAMA.** 1990;264:3013-3017.

Connor SL, Connor WE. Coronary heart disease: prevention and treatment by nutritional change. In: Carroll KK, ed. **Diet, Nutrition, and Health.** Montreal, Canada: McGill-Queen's University Press; 1989:33.

The Expert Panel. Report of the National Cholesterol Education Program Expert Panel on detection, evaluation, and treatment of high blood cholesterol in adults. **Arch Intern Med.** 1988;148:36-69.

Fredrickson DS. **A Physician's Guide to Hyperlipidemia: Modern Concepts of Cardiovascular Disease.** New York, NY: American Heart Association; 1972.

Goldstein JL, Brown MS. Regulation of low-density lipoprotein receptors: implications for pathogenesis and therapy of hypercholesterolemia and atherosclerosis. **Circulation.** 1987;76:504-507.

Grande F, Anderson JT, Chlouverakis C, Proja M, Keys A. Effect of dietary cholesterol on man's serum lipids. **J Nutr.** 1965;87:52-62.

Grundy SM. Drug therapy: HMG-CoA reductase inhibitors for treatment of hypercholesterolemia. **N Engl J Med.** 1988;319:24-32.

Hegsted DM, McGandy RB, Myers ML, Stare FJ. Quantitative effects of dietary fat on serum cholesterol in man. **Am J Clin Nutr.** 1965;17:281-295.

Kane JP, Malloy MJ, Ports TA, Phillips NR, Diehl JC, Havel RJ. Regression of coronary atherosclerosis during treatment of familial hypercholesterolemia with combined drug regimens. **JAMA.** 1990;264:3007-3012.

Keys A, Menotti A, Karvonen MJ, et al. The diet and 15-year death rate in the Seven Countries Study. **Am J Epidemiol.** 1986;124:903-915.

LaRosa JC, Hunninghake D, Bush D, et al. The cholesterol facts: a summary of the evidence relating dietary fats, serum cholesterol, and coronary heart disease: a joint statement by the American Heart Association and the National Heart, Lung, and Blood Institute. **Circulation.** 1990;81:1721-1733.

Mattson FH, Grundy SM. Comparison of effects of dietary saturated, monounsaturated, and polyunsaturated fatty acids on plasma lipids and lipoproteins in man. **J Lipid Res.** 1985;26:194-202.

Multiple Risk Factor Intervention Trial Research Group. Multiple Risk Factor Intervention Trial: risk factor changes and mortality results. **JAMA.** 1982;248:1465-1477.

National Cholesterol Education Program. **Report of the Expert Panel on Blood Cholesterol Levels in Children and Adolescents.** Bethesda, Md: National Institutes of Health; 1991. NIH publication No. 91-2732.

Ornish D, Brown SE, Scherwitz LW, et al. Can lifestyle changes reverse coronary heart disease? The Lifestyle Heart Trial. **Lancet.** 1990;336:129-133.

Reihner E, Rudling M, Stahlberg D, et al. Influence of pravastatin, a specific inhibitor of HMG-CoA reductase, on hepatic metabolism of cholesterol. **N Engl J Med.** 1990;323:224-228.

Seven Countries Study. The diet and all-causes death rate in the Seven Countries Study. **Lancet.** 1981;2:58-61.

Stamler J, Shekelle R. Dietary cholesterol and human coronary heart disease: the epidemiologic evidence. **Arch Pathol Lab Med.** 1988;112:1032-1041.

Stampfer MJ, Sacks FM, Salvini S, Willett WC, Hennekens CH. A prospective study of cholesterol, apolipoproteins, and the risk of myocardial infarction. **N Engl J Med.** 1991;325:373-381.

Hypertension

British Hypertension Society. Treating mild hypertension: report of the British Hypertension Society Working Party. **BMJ.** 1989;298:694-698.

Castelli WP, Anderson K. A population at risk: prevalence of high cholesterol levels in hypertensive patients in the Framingham Study. **Am J Med.** 1986;80:23-32.

Hypertension Detection and Follow-up Program Cooperative Group. Five-year findings of the Hypertension Detection and Follow-up Program: I. Reduction in mortality of persons with high blood pressure, including mild hypertension. **JAMA.** 1979;242:2562-2571.

The International Prospective Primary Prevention Study in Hypertension Collaborative Group. Cardiovascular risk and risk factors in a randomized trial of treatment based on the β-blocker oxprenolol. **J Hypertens.** 1985;3:379-392.

Joint National Committee. The 1988 Report of the Joint National Committee on Detection, Evaluation, and Treatment of High Blood Pressure. **Arch Intern Med.** 1988;148:1023-1038.

Leren P, Foss PO, Helgeland A, Hjermann I, Holme I, Lund-Larsen PG. Effect of propranolol and prazosin in blood lipids: the Oslo Study. **Lancet.** 1980;II:4-6.

The Management Committee. The Australian Therapeutic Trial in Mild Hypertension. **Lancet.** 1980;1:1261-1267.

Multiple Risk Factor Intervention Trial Research Group. Mortality after 10½ years for hypertensive participants in the Multiple Risk Factor Intervention Trial. **Circulation.** 1990;82:1616-1628.

Paul O. The Medical Research Council Trial. **Hypertension.** 1986;8:733-736.

Rose G. Review of primary prevention trials. **Am Heart J.** 1987;114:1013-1017.

Staessen J, Bulpitt C, Clement D, et al. Relation between mortality and treated blood pressure in elderly patients with hypertension: report of the European Working Party on High Blood Pressure in the Elderly. **BMJ.** 1989;298:1552-1556.

Veterans Administration Cooperative Study Group on Antihypertensive Agents. Effects of treatment on morbidity in hypertension: results in patients with diastolic blood pressures averaging 115 through 129 mm Hg. **JAMA.** 1967;202:1028-1034.

Veterans Administration Cooperative Study Group on Antihypertensive Agents. Effects of treatment on morbidity in hypertension: II. Results in patients with diastolic blood pressure averaging 90 through 114 mm Hg. **JAMA.** 1970;213:1143-1152.

Cigarette Smoking

Castelli WP, Garrison RJ, Dawber TR, McNamara PM, Feinleib M, Kannel WB. The filter cigarette and coronary heart disease: the Framingham story. **Lancet.** 1981;2:109-113.

Cook DG, Shaper AG, Pocock SJ, Kussick SJ. Giving up smoking and the risk of heart attacks: a report from the British Regional Heart Study. **Lancet.** 1986;2:1376-1380.

Kannel WB, D'Agostino RB, Belanger AJ. Fibrinogen, cigarette smoking, and risk of cardiovascular disease: insights from the Framingham Study. **Am Heart J.** 1987;113:1006-1010.

Kaufman DW, Helmrich SP, Rosenberg L, Miettinen OS, Shapiro S. Nicotine and carbon monoxide content of cigarette smoke and the risk of myocardial infarction in young men. **N Engl J Med.** 1983;308:409-413.

Schaefer GJ, Michael RP. Task-specific effects of nicotine in rats: intracranial self-stimulation and locomotor activity. **Neuropharmacology.** 1986;25:125-131.

Physical Activity

Dannenberg AL, Keller JB, Wilson PWF, Castelli WP. Leisure time physical activity in the Framingham Offspring Study: description, seasonal variation, and risk factor correlates. **Am J Epidemiol.** 1989;129:76-87.

Jennings G, Nelson L, Nestel P, et al. The effects of changes in physical activity on major cardiovascular risk factors, hemodynamics, sympathetic function, and glucose utilization in man: a controlled study of four levels of activity. **Circulation.** 1986;73:30-40.

Kramsch DM, Aspen AJ, Abramowitz BM, Kreimendahl T, Hood WB Jr. Reduction of coronary atherosclerosis by moderate conditioning exercise in monkeys on an atherogenic diet. **N Engl J Med.** 1981;305:1483-1489.

Sellier P, Corona P, Audouin P, et al. Influence of training on blood lipids and coagulation. **Eur Heart J.** 1988;9: 32-36.

Shephard RJ. Exercise in the tertiary prevention of ischemic heart disease: experimental proof. **Can J Sport Sci.** 1989;14:74-84.

Obesity

Higgins M, Kannel W, Garrison R, Pinsky J, Stokes J. Hazards of obesity – the Framingham experience. **Acta Med Scand Suppl.** 1988;723:23-36.

Hunt SC, Wu LL, Hopkins PN, et al. Apolipoprotein, low density lipoprotein subfraction, and insulin associations with familial combined hyperlipidemia: study of Utah patients with familial dyslipidemic hypertension. **Arteriosclerosis.** 1989;9:335-344.

Kannel WB, Cupples LA, Ramaswami R, Stokes J, Kreger BE, Higgins M. Regional obesity and risk of cardiovascular disease: the Framingham Study. **J Clin Epidemiol.** 1991;44:183-190.

Lapidus L, Bengtsson C, Larsson B, Pennert K, Rybo E, Sjostrom L. Distribution of adipose tissue and risk of cardiovascular disease and death: a 12 year followup of participants in the population study of women in Gothenberg, Sweden. **BMJ.** 1984;289:1257-1261.

Larsson B, Svärdsudd K, Welin L, Wilhelmsen L, Björntorp P, Tibblin G. Abdominal adipose tissue distribution, obesity, and risk of cardiovascular disease and death: 13 year followup of participants in the study of men born in 1913. **BMJ.** 1984;288:1401-1404.

Wing RR, Bunker CH, Kuller LH, Matthews KA. Insulin, body mass index, and cardiovascular risk factors in premenopausal women. **Arteriosclerosis.** 1989;9:479-484.

Diabetes Mellitus

Black HR. The coronary artery disease paradox: the role of hyperinsulinemia and insulin resistance and implications for therapy. **J Cardiovasc Pharmacol.** 1990;15(suppl 5):S26-S38.

Howard BV. Lipoprotein metabolism in diabetes mellitus. **J Lipid Res.** 1987;28:613-628.

Kannel WB, D'Agostino RB, Wilson PWF, Belanger AJ, Gagnon DR. Diabetes, fibrinogen, and risk of cardiovascular disease: the Framingham experience. **Am Heart J.** 1990;120:672-676.

Kleinman JC, Donahue RP, Harris MI, et al. Mortality among diabetics in a national sample. **Am J Epidemiol.** 1988;128:389-401.

Morel DW, Chisholm GM. Antioxidant treatment of diabetic rats inhibits lipoprotein oxidation and cytotoxicity. **J Lipid Res.** 1989;30:1827-1834.

Psychosocial and Behavioral Factors

Clay CM, Dyer AR, Liu K, et al. Education, smoking, and non-cardiovascular mortality: findings in three Chicago epidemiological studies. **Int J Epidemiol.** 1988;17:341-347.

Dyer AR, Stamler J, Shekelle RB, Schoenberger J. The relationship of education to blood pressure: findings on 40,000 employed Chicagoans. **Circulation.** 1976;54:987-992.

Haynes SG, Feinleib M, Eaker ED. Type A behavior and the ten-year incidence of coronary heart disease in the Framingham Heart Study. **Acta Nerv Super (Praha).** 1982;(suppl 3):57-77.

Hecker MH, Chesney MA, Black GW, Frautschi N. Coronary-prone behaviors in the Western Collaborative Group Study. **Psychosom Med.** 1988;50:153-164.

Hollis JF, Connett JE, Stevens VJ, Greenlick MR. Stressful life events, type A behavior, and the prediction of cardiovascular and total mortality over six years: Multiple Risk Factor Intervention Trial Group. **J Behav Med.** 1990;13:263-280.

Ragland DR, Brand RJ. Coronary heart disease mortality in the Western Collaborative Group Study: follow-up experience of 22 years. **Am J Epidemiol.** 1988;127:462-475.

Rosenman RH, Chesney MA. The relationship of type A behavior pattern to coronary heart disease. **Acta Nerv Super (Praha).** 1980;22:1-45.

Shekelle RB, Gale M, Norusis M. Type A score (Jenkins Activity Survey) and risk of recurrent coronary heart disease in the Aspirin Myocardial Infarction Study. **Am J Cardiol.** 1985;56:221-225.

Gender

Campos H, McNamara JR, Wilson PWF, Ordovas JM, Schaefer EJ. Differences in low density lipoprotein subfractions and apolipoproteins in premenopausal and postmenopausal women. **J Clin Endocrinol Metab.** 1988;67:30-35.

Kannel WB. Metabolic risk factors for coronary heart disease in women: perspective from the Framingham Study. **Am Heart J.** 1987;114:413-419.

Stampfer MJ, Willett WC, Colditz GA, Speizer E, Hennekens CH. Past use of oral contraceptives and cardiovascular disease: a meta-analysis in the context of the Nurses' Health Study. **Am J Obstet Gynecol.** 1990;163:285-291.

Stampfer MJ, Colditz GA, Willett WC, et al. Postmenopausal estrogen therapy and cardiovascular disease: ten-year follow-up from the Nurses' Health Study. **N Engl J Med.** 1991;325:756-762.

Walsh BW, Schiff I, Rosner B, et al. Effect of postmenopausal estrogen replacement on the concentrations and metabolism of plasma lipoproteins. **N Engl J Med.** 1991;325:1196-1204.

Alcohol

Barboriak JJ, Anderson AJ, Hoffmann RG. Interrelationship between coronary artery occlusion, high-density lipoprotein cholesterol, and alcohol intake. **J Lab Clin Med.** 1979;94:348-353.

Cauley JA, Kuller LH, LaPorte RE, Dai WS, D'Antonio JA. Studies on the association between alcohol and high density lipoprotein cholesterol: possible benefits and risks. **Adv Alcohol Subst Abuse.** 1987;6:53-67.

Criqui MH. The roles of alcohol in the epidemiology of cardiovascular diseases. **Acta Med Scand Suppl.** 1987;717:73-85.

Ferrence RG, Truscott S, Whitehead PC. Drinking and the prevention of coronary heart disease: findings, issues, and public health policy. **J Stud Alcohol.** 1986;47:394-408.

Handa K, Sasaki J, Saku K, Kono S, Arakawa K. Alcohol consumption, serum lipids and severity of angiographically determined coronary artery disease. **Am J Cardiol.** 1990;65:287-289.

Hartung GH, Foreyt JP, Reeves RS, et al. Effect of alcohol dose on plasma lipoprotein subfractions and lipolytic enzyme activity in active and inactive men. **Metabolism.** 1990;39:81-86.

Minor Risk Factors

Leoni V, Fabiani L, Ticchiarelli L. Water hardness and cardiovascular mortality rate in Abruzzo, Italy. **Arch Environ Health.** 1985;40:274-278.

Manthey J, Stoeppler M, Morgenstern W, et al. Magnesium and trace metals: risk factors for coronary heart disease? Association between blood levels and angiographic findings. **Circulation.** 1981;64:722-729.

Rosmarin PC. Coffee and coronary heart disease: a review. **Prog Cardiovasc Dis.** 1989;32:239-245.

Shaper AG, Packham RF, Pocock SJ. The British Regional Heart Study: cardiovascular mortality and water quality. **J Environ Pathol Toxicol.** 1980;4:89-111.

Important Points in
the Pathogenesis
of Atherosclerosis

Introduction

This chapter is about the artery wall and how atherosclerotic plaques develop. It focuses on the interrelated cellular and chemical factors that are involved in this disease process. Fortunately, the fund of knowledge that helps explain atherogenesis in the most fundamental terms has been developing rapidly in the past few years. Unfortunately, there are many gaps remaining in that knowledge. Therefore, an attempt will be made to provide a matrix of the most important points on which additional knowledge can be arranged in an orderly way as it becomes available.

The atherosclerotic process primarily affects medium-sized (muscular) arteries and large (fibroelastic) arteries. The terms "muscular" and "fibroelastic" suggest some of the components of the artery wall, which is composed predominantly of smooth muscle cells but also contains collagen and elastin. These fiber proteins, which are so prominent in the artery and in the sclerotic part of atherosclerotic lesions, are synthesized by the smooth muscle cell.

Normal muscular (Figure 6a) and fibroelastic (Figure 6b) arteries have a smooth inner lining (intima) composed primarily of endothelial cells and a connective tissue layer. Between the endothelium and the internal elastic lamina, the normal intima may have an occasional monocyte or macrophage and an occasional or many smooth muscle cells.

Atherosclerotic plaques are made up of components that are reflected in the name of the disease process. *Athero* is derived from a Greek word meaning "soft, grumous, or porridgelike" and is used to describe the soft, cholesterol- and lipid-rich acellular parts of advanced plaques where much of the lipid is deposited. Sclerotic is derived from the Greek *skleros* meaning "hard" and is also descriptive, because the smooth muscle cells that proliferate to form a plaque also produce variable amounts of collagen and elastin, components that often give the plaque a firm, fibrous cap. Many analyses indicate that the atherosclerotic plaque is composed of about one-half lipid components and one-half protein, including cell protein and extracellular fibrous protein components (Figure 7a).

However, there are many deviations from this composition, depending on numerous factors that influence atherogenesis either in early life or during later years when the particular risk factors may have undergone remarkable alterations.

In addition to their space-occupying features, atherosclerotic plaques can produce other important effects that, in some instances, may ultimately produce severe stenosis of the lumen of the artery, especially in such muscular arteries as the coronary and carotid arteries. If the fibrous cap is fractured, ruptured, or ulcerated, or if the endothelial damage is sufficiently severe, acute thrombosis may be induced (Figure 7b). Thrombosis, in turn, may lead to rapid stenosis or to complete obstruction of the artery near the point where the atherosclerotic plaque is most severe. Sometimes, particularly in large arteries such as the abdominal aorta, the media under a large atherosclerotic plaque may be weakened enough to form an outwardly bulging thin-walled aneurysm that may rupture, causing sudden massive hemorrhage into the peritoneal cavity or elsewhere.

Investigations during the past decade elucidated the components of atherosclerotic plaques. For example, the form in which lipids and lipoproteins circulate in the blood is more important than the blood cholesterol level per se in determining whether an atherosclerotic plaque will develop. The principal pathways and processes by which cholesterol-carrying lipoproteins enter the artery wall and some of the factors that help to protect the artery from this infiltration and deposition of cholesterol-rich lipids will be described later in this chapter.

The principal cells in atherosclerotic plaques are not the ordinary contractile form of smooth muscle cells but are cells that have been modified phenotypically and thus constitute a new family of smooth muscle cells. These cells are much

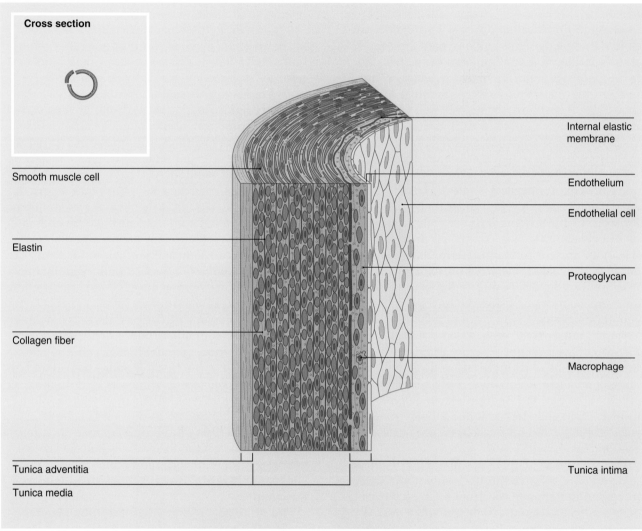

Cross section

Smooth muscle cell

Elastin

Collagen fiber

Tunica adventitia

Tunica media

Internal elastic membrane

Endothelium

Endothelial cell

Proteoglycan

Macrophage

Tunica intima

This artery (like all arteries) is composed primarily of smooth muscle cells with lamellae of elastin and collagen intervening. As the name implies, the muscular arteries have a greater proportion of smooth muscle cell components relative to the fiber proteins, which are extracellular products of the smooth muscle cells.

Figure 6b
The normal fibroelastic artery

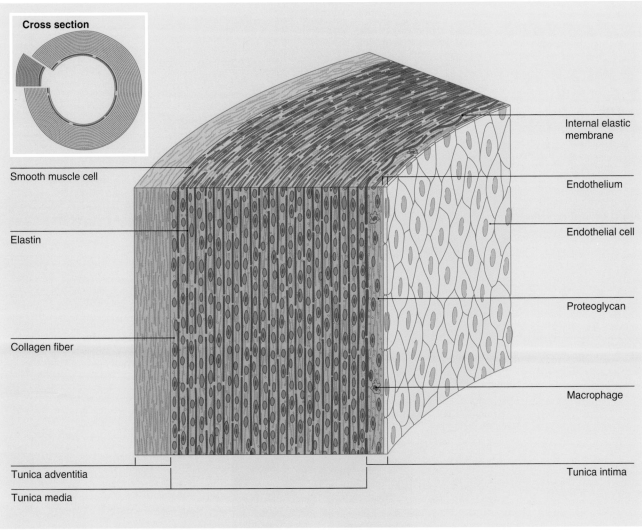

Cross section

Smooth muscle cell

Elastin

Collagen fiber

Tunica adventitia

Tunica media

Internal elastic membrane

Endothelium

Endothelial cell

Proteoglycan

Macrophage

Tunica intima

The fibroelastic artery is limited to the aorta and its largest primary branches. This artery differs from the muscular artery in having a larger component of collagen and elastin, even in its normal state.

Figure 7a
Advanced atherosclerotic plaque

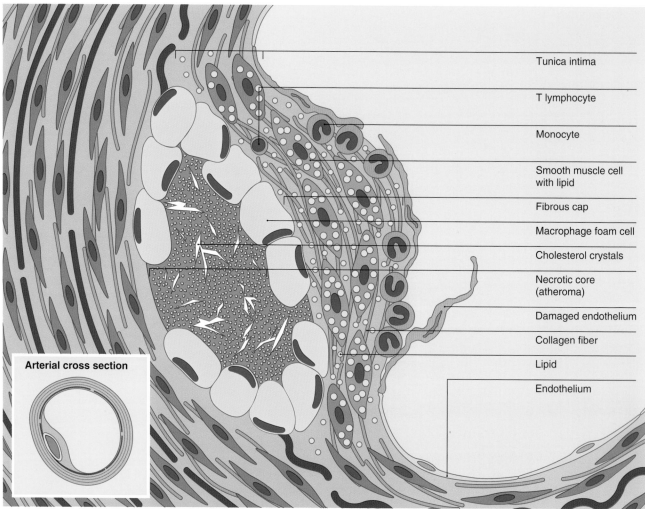

Tunica intima

T lymphocyte

Monocyte

Smooth muscle cell
with lipid

Fibrous cap

Macrophage foam cell

Cholesterol crystals

Necrotic core
(atheroma)

Damaged endothelium

Collagen fiber

Lipid

Endothelium

Arterial cross section

One of the major components of the advanced atherosclerotic plaque is the necrotic core, which is rich in cholesteryl esters. Frequently, the perimeter of this core shows many monocyte-derived macrophage foam cells. This core is sometimes referred to as an atheroma. The second major component is the fibrous cap, which is composed primarily of modified smooth muscle cells, some of which contain a substantial amount of lipid. The cap also contains large amounts of collagen, hence the term "fibrous."

Adapted with permission from Constantinides P. *Experimental Atherosclerosis*. Amsterdam, the Netherlands: Elsevier Publishing Co; 1965.

Figure 7b
An advanced atherosclerotic plaque with a fractured fibrous cap and the initiation of a thrombus

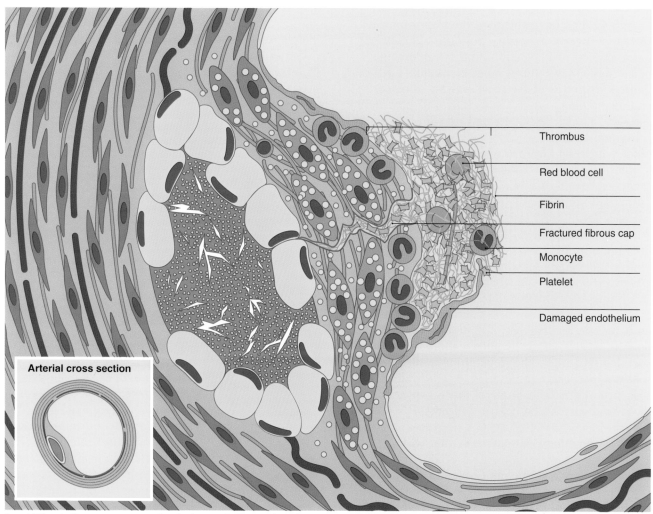

Thrombus

Red blood cell

Fibrin

Fractured fibrous cap

Monocyte

Platelet

Damaged endothelium

Arterial cross section

In addition to the space-occupying features of atherosclerotic plaques, they frequently produce their major clinical effect by inducing thrombosis. A thrombus is likely to form when the complicated plaque allows the components of the blood in the arterial lumen to be acted upon by thromboplastic substances in the plaque.

Adapted with permission from Constantinides P. *Experimental Atherosclerosis.* Amsterdam, the Netherlands: Elsevier Publishing Co; 1965.

more likely to continue to divide, synthesize collagen, and take up lipid than are the usual contractile cells in the media of the artery.

Today, the role of endothelial injury in atherosclerotic processes is much better understood. Recent studies have revealed the importance of cells that invade the artery from the bloodstream (namely monocytes and T and B lymphocytes) in the developing atherosclerotic plaque. Furthermore, knowledge of the biochemistry of elastin and of the many types of vascular wall proteoglycans and collagens has helped explain how these components influence atherogenesis. Even calcium, which generally has been considered to be a "tombstone" of the atherosclerotic process, is receiving renewed attention. Calcium metabolism in the cell membrane is essential in controlling cell proliferation. Therefore, calcium imbalance in the artery wall may be important in the early development of atherosclerotic plaque long before it becomes a visible component of the advanced lesion.

A framework has begun to emerge on which the major risk factors and their influences at the cellular level can be arranged and organized. There may be undiscovered or poorly evaluated risk factors that may affect the development of the atherosclerotic process, even though they are difficult to measure at this time. Some of these aspects of atherogenesis will be considered later.

Major Pathogenetic Processes in the Artery Wall

The Lipid, Lipoprotein, and Cholesterol Factors
For many years, the evidence has supported the concept that low-density lipoprotein (LDL), rich in apolipoprotein B (apo B), is the main form in which cholesterol is transported from the bloodstream into the arterial intima. In part, this understanding is based on the demonstration many years ago that apo B can be identified and quantitated in atherosclerotic lesions of all degrees of severity.

The pivotal role of LDL has been remarkably elucidated by the pioneering work of Goldstein and Brown. Their Nobel prize-winning work on the genetic defects in apo B (LDL) receptors has clarified the pathogenesis of familial hypercholesterolemia and the entire cellular control mechanisms of cholesterol metabolism.

Some forms of very-low-density lipoprotein (VLDL), especially those rich in apo B, may be at least as atherogenic under some circumstances as the LDLs. It is now known that LDLs are not a single chemical entity but are more accurately a family of particles that can be classified as subforms of LDL. The concentration levels of some of these LDLs (for example, LDL I) may be much more elevated in hyperlipidemia than others.

The 1980s brought not only an increased emphasis on the heterogeneity of VLDL and LDL but also a greater understanding of the various forms of high-density lipoproteins (HDL). The evidence supporting the protective role of HDL has become stronger. The HDL cholesterol level is not the only measure of how this lipoprotein fraction is expressed. Many investigations have indicated that some HDL fractions, particularly HDL_2 and HDL_3, can effectively block the entrance of cholesterol into cells and can expedite the export of cholesterol from the types of cells that are implicated in atherogenesis. The serum level of HDL cholesterol remains a widely used and convenient method of measurement. A more intensive look at HDL isoforms may elucidate their varying effectiveness as protectors against atherosclerosis. In time, the somewhat crude measurement of HDL cholesterol concentration may be replaced by much more informative measurements of the various high-density lipoproteins.

One of the major advances in knowledge regarding the effects of lipoproteins has been made recently. LDLs and perhaps some of the VLDLs undergo considerable changes when they enter the artery wall. Although the process by which these changes occur is still not completely understood, it is now recognized that oxidized LDL may become a predominant form of this lipoprotein fraction in the artery wall, and that oxidative changes dramatically alter the effects of LDL and the cells in which it is deposited (Figure 8).

Figure 8
Five mechanisms by which the oxidation of LDL may contribute to atherogenesis

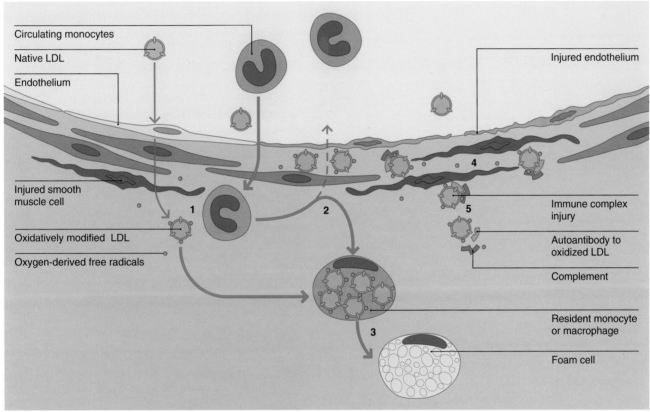

Circulating monocytes

Native LDL

Endothelium

Injured endothelium

Injured smooth muscle cell

Oxidatively modified LDL

Oxygen-derived free radicals

Immune complex injury

Autoantibody to oxidized LDL

Complement

Resident monocyte or macrophage

Foam cell

(1) Circulating monocytes are recruited by means of the chemotactic factor present in oxidized LDL but absent in native LDL. (2) Oxidized LDL inhibits the motility of resident macrophages and therefore their ability to leave the intima. (3) The enhanced rate of uptake of oxidized LDL by resident macrophages leads to the generation of foam cells. (4) Cytotoxicity of oxidized LDL leads to loss of endothelial integrity. (5) Epitopes of oxidized LDL may become antigenic and stimulate inflammatory autoimmune reactions.

Adapted with permission from Quinn MT, Parthasarathy S, Fong LG, Steinberg D. Oxidatively modified low density lipoproteins: a potential role in recruitment and retention of monocyte/macrophages during atherogenesis. *Proc Natl Acad Sci USA*. 1987;84:2995-2998.

Table 12
Mutations of apolipoprotein

Apolipoprotein defect	
A-I	Tangier disease
	Apo A-I$_{Milano}$
	Apo A-I$_{Marburg}$ and apo A-I$_{Giessen}$
	Apo A-I$_{Munster}$ 1-4
	HDL deficiency with planar xanthomas
	Familial deficiency of apo A-I and C-III
	Apo A-I absence
	Fish-eye disease
	Hypoalphalipoproteinemias
A-IV	Apo A-IV$_{Giessen}$
	Apo A-IV$_{Munster}$
B	Recessive abetalipoproteinemia
	Homozygous hypobetalipoproteinemia
	Normotriglyceridemic abetalipoproteinemia
	Chylomicron retention disease
	Familial hypobetalipoproteinemia with chylomicronemia
C	Apo C-II deficiency
	Apo C-II$_{Munster}$
	Apo C-III$_3$
E	Apo E$_2$ homozygosity Dysbetalipoproteinemia Familial type III hyperlipoproteinemia
	Type V hyperlipoproteinemia associated with the apo E$_4$ phenotype
	Apo E deficiency
	Other apo E variants

Oxidized LDL may be injurious to many of the cells that take part in the atherosclerotic process, thus implicating this form of low-density lipoprotein in many of the cell-injury phenomena associated with progressive atherosclerosis, including: endothelial cell death and desquamation, smooth muscle cell death, and the short life span of the lipid-laden macrophages (monocyte-derived foam cells). Whether these oxidized lipoproteins may also be important stimulators of the synthesis of platelet-derived growth factor (PDGF) and other related growth factors by injured endothelial cells and/or smooth muscle cells has not yet been extensively investigated. Nevertheless, the numerous observations indicating that some types of hyperlipidemic LDL may be of great importance in initiating the proliferation of contractile, resting smooth muscle cell populations make this a fruitful field for further study.

Hyperlipidemia and hypercholesterolemia are usually, but not always, clearly associated with atherogenesis. In a number of cases, atherosclerosis can be explained by various genetic deviations in apolipoprotein structure. Apolipoprotein genetic defects are presently being studied (Table 12). Some of these abnormalities are associated with increased risk, increased severity, and sometimes acceleration of the atherosclerotic process without accompanying hypercholesterolemia. In both Tangier disease and apo E dysbetalipoproteinemia, definite cellular metabolic malfunctions occur that permit accelerated atherogenesis without substantial hypercholesterolemia. The Tangier abnormality appears to be a multisystem defect of cholesterol and lipoprotein metabolism in monocyte-derived macrophages. It is characterized by severe deficiency or complete absence of normal HDL in plasma and probably increases the risk of accelerated atherogenesis in some of the victims. The known cellular interactions of HDL, some of which facilitate the understanding of Tangier disease, are summarized in Figure 9.

Many more apolipoprotein defects are likely to be discovered. These newly discovered genetic abnormalities will require new types of laboratory investigations in order to readily identify them in patients with accelerated or premature clinical manifestations of ischemic heart disease. In fact, much remains to be learned about many defects

Figure 9
Cellular interactions of HDL

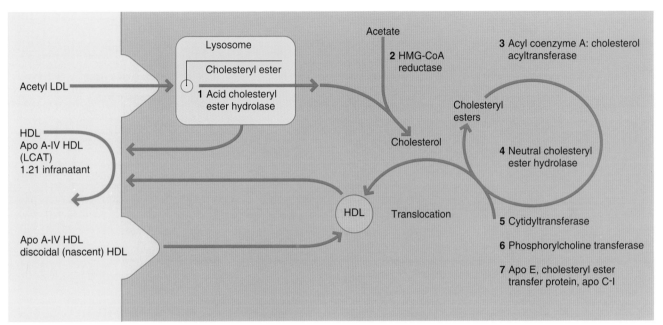

(1) ACEH (acid cholesteryl ester hydrolase) is a lysosomal enzyme that hydrolyzes cholesteryl esters. (2) HMG-CoA reductase is the key enzyme in cellular de novo synthesis of cholesterol. (3) ACAT (acyl coenzyme A:cholesterol acyltransferase) is a microsomal enzyme that re-esterifies cholesterol. (4) NCEH (neutral cholesteryl ester hydrolase) is a cytoplasmic cholesteryl ester hydrolyzing enzyme. Together with ACAT it controls the cellular cholesterol pool size. (5) and (6) Enzymes of phospholipid metabolism are important in lipoprotein particle assembly. (7) Apolipoprotein E, CETP (cholesteryl ester transfer protein), and apolipoprotein C-I are thought to be important for lipid translocation. LCAT is lecithin:cholesterol acyltransferase.

Adapted with permission from Assmann G. How an understanding of HDL's metabolism may help us discover new ways to evaluate atherosclerosis and its risk of progression in the living patient. In: Wissler RW, Bond MG, Mercuri M, Tanganelli P, Weber G, eds. *Atherosclerotic Plaques: Advances in Imaging for Sequential Quantitative Evaluation.* New York, NY: Plenum Publishing Co; 1991:163-170.

that have already been identified. Intensive study is still required of the role of apo E in relation both to the cellular pathogenesis of atherosclerosis and to protection against this disease. It is necessary to clearly delineate how apo E is involved in cell processes in the artery wall and how it functions in hepatic turnover and excretion of cholesterol via the bile ducts and the intestine.

For an overview of the ways in which abnormalities in lipoprotein particles are related to the development of atherosclerosis see Table 13. Undoubtedly, this table paints an incomplete picture that is likely to change as more knowledge is acquired. However, it offers a framework for understanding some lipoprotein trends that often correlate with development of or protection from atherosclerosis.

Lp[a] deserves a special comment because its presence appears to be strongly correlated, not only with the clinical effects of atherosclerosis

Table 13
Summary of the relationships of lipoproteins to atherogenesis

Current lipoprotein designations	Predominant apolipoprotein	Functions and presumed functions in atherogenesis
Chylomicrons	Apo B$_{48}$ Apo E	May furnish cholesterol and triglycerides for atherogenesis at the arterial cell surface due to action of lipoprotein lipase (Zilversmit) and via other remnants (Mahley, Getz).
VLDL	Apo B$_{100}$ Apo E Apo C-I to C-III	Little evidence of atherogenic effect except via lipoprotein lipase activity.
β-VLDL	Apo B$_{48}$ Apo E	Highly atherogenic remnant particles derived from chylomicrons in subjects (especially dogs) fed a high-cholesterol, high-fat ration (Mahley).
H-LDL*† LDL I†	Apo B$_{100}$	Perhaps the most consistently atherogenic fraction in human species (found in familial hypercholesterolemia) and lipogenic and mitogenic in other primates (Fless, Scanu, Fischer-Dzoga); when altered by endothelial cells or by malondialdehyde, it is avidly taken up by macrophages in vitro.
LDL II†		May support build-up of cholesterol in arterial smooth muscle cells.
LDL III†	Apo B$_{100}$	Little direct evidence of atherogenicity with the exception of mitogenic effect of particle after neuraminidase treatment (Fless, Scanu, et al).
Lp[a] (LDL IV)†		Epidemiologic evidence supports atherogenicity.
HDL$_c$	Apo E	Probably especially important in cholesterol excretions; ligand for the hepatic apo E receptor.
HDL$_1$	Apo A-I Apo A-II Apo E	Recognized by high-affinity receptors for hepatic apo E; may help in cholesterol excretion.
HDL$_2$	Apo E Apo A-I Apo A-II Apo Cs	Serum level correlates with protection against atherosclerosis in numerous species, including humans. Precursor to HDL$_1$.
HDL$_3$	Apo A-I Apo A-II Apo Cs	Precursor to HDL$_2$, but the level is not predictive; may also derive from HDL$_2$ by the action of hepatic lipase.

*LDL from hyperlipidemic serum (enlarged cholesterol-rich particle).
†LDL fractions as designated by Fless and Scanu.

Adapted with permission from Wissler RW. Principles of the pathogenesis of atherosclerosis. In: Braunwald E, ed. *Heart Disease: A Textbook of Cardiovascular Medicine.* 2nd ed. Philadelphia, Pa: WB Saunders Co; 1984:1183-1204.

(ie, coronary heart disease and stroke), but also with the effects of peripheral vascular disease, especially effects involving the carotid and femoral arteries. Studies are under way to gather quantitative evidence concerning the accumulation of this special low-density lipoprotein in developing plaques. Furthermore, practical ways of altering the levels of this fraction in the serum are being sought.

The Endothelium: The Role of Injury and Inflammation

Although arterial endothelium has not been studied as thoroughly as that in veins and capillaries, the common denominators of endothelial structure indicate that this cellular layer is an imperfect barrier to lipoprotein transport. In fact, LDLs, some of the remnants of both VLDLs and chylomicrons, and intact HDLs can gain entrance to the intima by means of endothelial cell transport vesicles. Although the factors regulating their permeability are not completely understood, evidence derived from in vivo studies indicates that as much as 10% of the circulating LDLs probably can pass freely through these transport vesicles (Figure 10). The endothelium also appears to receive its own cholesterol and fatty-acid supply from lipoproteins and lipoprotein fragments by means of pinocytosis and endocytosis. Whether there are also certain highly permeable spots in normal endothelium, as suggested by the studies reported by Björkerud et al and more recently by Stemerman et al, needs further study.

Most evidence from both human and experimental animal studies indicates that the endothelium is intact when fatty streaks and fatty plaques develop in the more vulnerable areas of the arterial tree. Nevertheless, there is increasing evidence that changes in the arterial cell surface accompanied by or independent of changes in the surface properties of monocytes, lymphocytes, and platelets may constitute an important part of the atherogenic process, especially when sustained low-grade immune complex or toxic injury is involved. After years of study, some investigators hold the view that some degree of endothelial injury and inflammation, not necessarily accompanied by noticeable endothelial cell loss, is an integral part of atherogenesis. They consider the initiation of atherosclerosis to involve a mild inflammatory process with all of the signs of subacute or chronic inflammation, ie, inflammatory cells (mainly monocytes and lymphocytes), edema, and fibrosis.

Some of the early theories about the role of PDGF in the development of atherosclerosis proposed that endothelial injury with endothelial cell loss, followed by platelet adhesion and platelet spreading, would turn out to be an important part of the early stimulation of smooth muscle cell proliferation. This sequence is probably a major pathogenetic process in obvious endothelial cell destruction by mechanical factors, such as balloon catheter injury, and in the advanced stages of the plaque. However, this process does not appear to be a dominant mechanism when atherogenesis begins primarily as a result of sustained hypercholesterolemia.

Atherogenesis can be regarded mainly as a reaction to injury or as a process caused primarily by oversupply and underutilization of lipoproteins in the artery wall. However, it is clear that two main components of the plaque are dominant. The lipid component, which in the early stages appears to be largely intracellular, seems to predominate in smooth muscle cells that have migrated into the intima and proliferated there. These smooth muscle cells make up the second major component of the developing plaque. Thus, in the early stages, lipid deposition and cell proliferation are the two major factors in the pathogenesis of atherosclerosis.

These two factors, lipid infiltration and smooth muscle cell proliferation, can be viewed as a synergistic reaction between the effects of a mild inflammatory process and prolonged hyperlipidemia, especially if the hyperlipidemia leads to the injurious action of oxidized LDL within the arterial intima (Figure 11). These two major contributors to the atherosclerotic process can reinforce each other to support the development of progressive atherosclerotic plaques. Plaques that appear

Figure 10
Endocytotic versus transcytotic vesicles as control mechanisms for LDL transport into and through endothelial cells

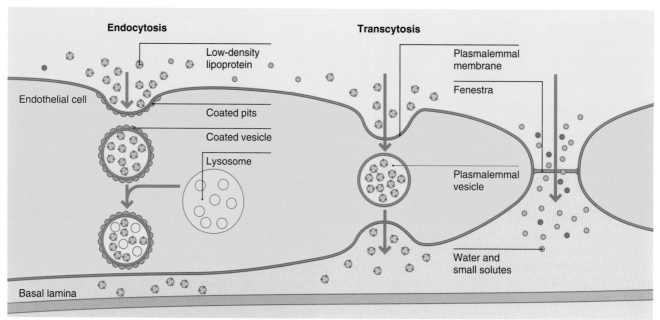

The uptake of LDL by LDL receptors in coated pits provides a more rapid mechanism for cholesterol transport than non-receptor transcytosis.

Adapted with permission from Simionescu N. Cellular aspects of transcapillary exhange. *Physiol Rev.* 1983;63:1536-1579.

Figure 11
The interactions between the two major mechanisms proposed for atherogenesis

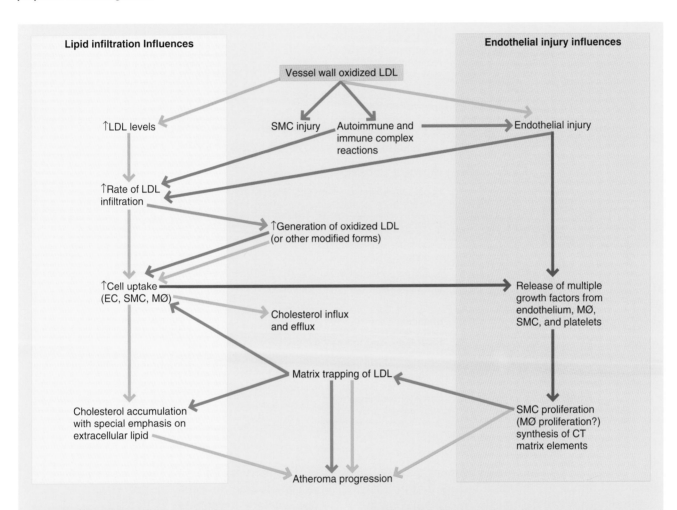

The steps involved according to the endothelial injury formulation are on the right, and those for the elevated blood-lipid cholesterol formulation are on the left.

■ LDL in high concentration induces endothelial cell (EC) injury, especially oxidized LDL, and increases the rate of LDL infiltration and cholesterol accumulation.

■ Endothelial injury increases the influx of LDL.

■ LDL is oxidized after it enters the arterial intima.

■ Oxidized LDL promotes autoimmunity and immune complexes, and injures smooth muscle cells (SMC) and endothelium.

■ Growth factors liberated from endothelial cells, SMC, and macro-phages (MØ) are triggered by elevated LDL levels. Smooth muscle cell-produced extracellular matrix binds and traps LDL molecules, which in turn may permit increased cellular uptake of LDL.

■ Conversion of intimal LDL to the oxidized form (or to other modified forms, such as glycated LDL, aggregated LDL, or LDL in immune complexes).

■ Synthetic products of connective tissue (CT) are active in forming a plaque matrix, which in turn contributes to cholesterol accumulation.

■ These combined influences contribute to the progression of atherosclerosis.

Adapted with permission from Steinberg D. Lipoproteins and atherosclerosis: a look back and a look ahead. *Arteriosclerosis*. 1983;3:283-301.

Table 14
Factors that injure arterial endothelium and produce increased permeability to macromolecules, including lipoproteins

Substance or physical condition	Mechanism involved	Clinical condition
Hemodynamic forces, tension, stretching, shearing, eddy currents	Separation or damage to endothelial cells, increased permeability, platelet sticking, stimulation of smooth muscle cell proliferation	Hypertension
Angiotensin II	"Trap-door" effect	Hypertension
Carbon monoxide or decreased oxygen saturation	Destruction of endothelial cells	Cigarette smoking
Oxidized or glycated LDL and VLDL	Free radicals and/or lipoxygenase or circulating glucose	Environmental pollution, cigarette smoking, diabetes
Catecholamines (epinephrine, norepinephrine, serotonin, bradykinin)	Hypercontraction, swelling and loss of endothelial cells, platelet agglutination	Stress, cigarette smoking
Metabolic products	Endothelial cell damage	Homocystinemia, uremia
Endotoxins and other similar bacterial products	Endothelial cell destruction, platelet sticking	Acute bacterial infections
Antigen-antibody complexes, immunologic defects	Platelet agglutination, cytotoxicity of immune complexes plus complement	Serum sickness, transplant rejection, immune complex diseases, systemic lupus erythematosus, cigarette smoking
Virus diseases	Endothelial cell infection and necrosis	Viremias
Mechanical trauma to endothelium	Platelet sticking, increased local permeability	Catheter injury
Hyperlipidemia with increase in circulating lipoproteins (cholesterol, triglycerides, phospholipids) and free fatty acids	Platelet agglutination usually over fatty plaques in areas of hemodynamic damage to endothelium	Chronic nutritional imbalance (high-fat and high-cholesterol diets), familial hypercholesterolemia, diabetes mellitus, nephrosis, hypothyroidism

to be accelerated in their development may be the result of a number of harmful factors that produce sustained endothelial damage. They often demonstrate a low-grade, nondestructive inflammatory reaction in which it may be difficult to identify the injurious or inflammatory agents.

The best-documented factors that promote atherogenesis by means of the synergism between hyperlipidemia and cell injury and help to produce increased permeability to macromolecules, including lipoproteins, are listed in Table 14. These factors are equated with a number of the dominant mechanisms by which endothelial damage is sustained and with the associated clinical conditions.

Monocyte Sticking and the Macrophage/Foam Cell Components of Developing Plaques

Many investigators studying animals fed athero-genic diets have called attention to an increased number of monocytes sticking to the endothelium, especially in those areas that are most likely to develop progressive atherosclerotic plaques. Recent studies aimed at learning more about the mechanisms of leukocyte sticking to the endo-thelium have led to the identification and charac-terization of endothelial leukocyte adhesion molecules (ELAMs) and their potential role in the early stages of atherogenesis.

The scavenger cells that are common in many types of subacute and chronic inflammatory processes are capable of being overloaded with cholesterol and fatty acids. These cells fit all the criteria of foam cells commonly seen in the lesions of animals that are highly susceptible to developing fatty streaks and fatty plaques when they are fed cholesterol. In other words, not only are they scavenger cells, but they also demon-strate the uptake of cholesterol by the scavenger pathway as originally proposed by Goldstein and Brown. In contrast to arterial smooth muscle cells, which are generally well regulated in terms of their lipid storage, Steinberg has emphasized that these monocyte-derived macrophages can take up very large amounts of modified lipoproteins, including those subjected to oxidation.

Although they are rarely the dominant cell in the developing atheromatous lesions in young people, the monocyte-derived cells frequently are present in small numbers and in small clusters just under the endothelium. There is evidence that they may transfer lipids to smooth muscle cells, which leads to overloading these cells and causing them to become foam cells. Under these circumstances, the macrophage can be regarded as a "nurse cell," because it may provide a major route by which cholesterol and cholesteryl ester accumulate in large quantities in the arterial intima, particularly within the cytoplasm of smooth muscle cells.

The macrophage and its functions are complex. Although there is no doubt concerning the macro-phage's role as a scavenger, at present it is diffi-cult to be certain whether its major net effect is to inhibit or promote atherogenesis. It may inhibit lesion progression by removing lipid from devel-oping plaques and by furnishing collagenases and elastases to counteract the sclerotic part of the plaque. The macrophage may also be a major force in promoting lipid accumulation both inside and around the smooth muscle cells and in producing growth factors that stimulate smooth muscle cell proliferation. To date, none of these functions have been well documented in human atherosclerotic lesions. Most animal models in which monocyte sticking has been documented also have an element of chronic endothelial damage that may not be present in many of the slowly developing atherosclerotic lesions in patients with sustained hypercholesterolemia.

Just as the smooth muscle cell fits the criteria of a multifunctional cell type in relation to athero-genesis, it is equally true that the monocyte-derived macrophage must be considered to be a highly multifunctional cell. Some reviews of its biology, detailed morphology, and cytochemistry have listed more than 100 possible functions of the macrophage.

Some of the functions of the macrophage that may particularly relate to the development of atherosclerosis are listed in Table 15. The macro-phage is extremely active as a secretory cell. The secretory products listed could be important in either atherogenesis or in the protective reactions against atherosclerotic lesions.

The first four classes of secretory products listed are lipoprotein lipase, apo E, angiogenesis factor, and macrophage-derived growth factor. These may be important in terms of both lipid deposition and smooth muscle cell proliferation, in addition to angiogenesis, which is often an important feature of the advanced plaque. The next four products (lysozyme, collagenase, elas-tase, and the hydrolases) may be considered elements of preventive, retarding, or regressive processes. The remaining secretory products may

Table 15
Macrophage functions related to atherogenesis and regression

Secretory products

Lipoprotein lipase

Apo E

Angiogenesis factor

Macrophage-derived growth factor

Lysozyme

Collagenase

Elastase

Lysosomal acid hydrolases

Superoxides and hydrogen peroxide

Complement factors

Prostaglandins

Prostacyclin (PGI$_2$)

Thromboxane

Leukotrienes

Platelet-activating factor

Interferons

Surface receptors

Acetyl LDL

Malondialdehyde LDL

Dextran sulfate LDL

β-VLDL

Apo B-containing lesion complexes

Chylomicron remnants

Fc fraction of immunoglobulins

Complement factor C3

Mannose

Insulin

Additional functions

Phagocytosis

Immunologic (antigen processing and presentation)

Cytolysis

Lipid metabolism (acid and neutral lipid hydrolases and synthetases)

either promote atherogenesis or plaque regression, depending on which functions are dominant at any given time.

The surface receptors are equally important in both atherogenesis and regression (Table 15). If modified LDL is an end product of LDL metabolism, then its vulnerability to digestion by macrophages could certainly be a step toward prevention or regression. Similarly, macrophage catabolism of modified LDL in the liver and spleen reticuloendothelial system may be a protective or beneficial process. This destruction of chylomicron or lipoprotein remnants, along with the presence of components of the immune system in lesions, might considerably retard the progression of plaques and decrease the severity of atherosclerotic lesions.

Other functions listed in Table 15 indicate the ambiguity of macrophage involvement in the atherosclerotic process. Phagocytosis and cytolysis, for example, might help to resolve an atherogenic lesion. Immunologic antigen processing and presentation and some phases of lipid metabolism might decrease the severity of the atherosclerotic plaque.

Smooth Muscle Cell Proliferation, Phenotypic Modulation, and Connective Tissue Synthesis

For many years there has been general agreement that the modified smooth muscle cell that is derived largely from the arterial media is the principal cell in atherosclerotic plaque at almost every stage of plaque development. It is true that some early fatty streaks, principally those found in infants and young children, show a predominance of monocyte-derived macrophages filled with lipid. It is also true that some animal models (notably the cholesterol-fed rabbit) have a large population of foam cells that are probably not derived from smooth muscle cells. However, most other lesions that have been studied extensively show a predominance of smooth muscle cells, many of them lipid laden and some of them converted to greatly overloaded lipophages that can be distinguished from monocyte-derived macrophage foam cells only by using suitable cell markers. As mentioned, some tantalizing evidence from in vitro studies shows that smooth muscle

Figure 12a
The genesis of plaque as proposed by the monoclonal hypothesis

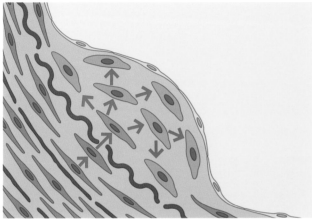

A single cell has a selective advantage. It migrates into the intima and divides (**left**). Progeny of the mutated cell is freed of some curb on proliferation and continues to multiply. By way

of contrast, the drawing (**right**) shows a polyclonal plaque that would arise from migration and proliferation of many cells of both types.

Adapted with permission from Benditt EP. The origin of atherosclerosis. *Sci Am.* 1977;236:74-85.

cells can be overloaded with lipid to become true foam cells by direct transfer of lipid from the neighboring macrophage foam cells.

There is general agreement that the smooth muscle cells (with or without lipid droplets) found in the intima of developing lesions are different metabolically from those found in the more or less quiescent underlying media. However, there is not yet agreement as to the cause, process of development, or the fundamental nature of the changes that occur in these modified smooth muscle cells in human and in experimental animal lesions. Some authorities view the change to modified smooth muscle cells as a fundamental

characteristic of the proliferating cells, which presumably pass on different synthetic and enzymatic properties to all other smooth muscle cells in the area (Figure 12a). This view of a somatic mutation (a virus- or carcinogen-induced, more or less irreversible shift in the cells' metabolic and genetic machinery) is strengthened by the recent identification of virus and viral products in atherosclerotic plaque cells and the presence of proto-oncogenes in some human plaques.

On the other hand, there is evidence that a potentially reversible shift occurs in cell metabolism, causing the smooth muscle cell to change from a contractile form to a more or less embryonic synthetic form (Figure 12b). This "phenotypic modulation" can be studied with some facility in vitro. Whether this change occurs in vitro or in vivo, the phenotypic shift should be regarded as a response to stimuli, such as from PDGF. The fundamental process by which the changes in smooth muscle cells occur is important because,

Figure 12b
**Contractile and synthetic forms of arterial
smooth muscle cells**

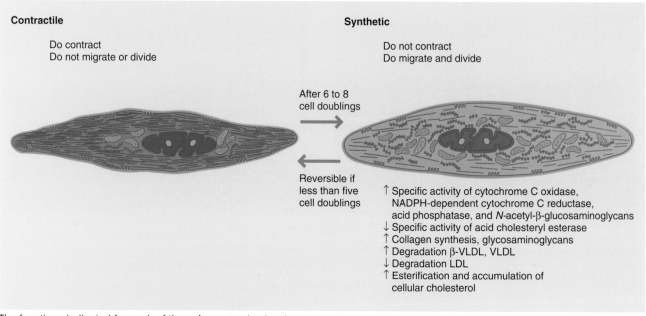

Contractile

Do contract
Do not migrate or divide

Synthetic

Do not contract
Do migrate and divide

After 6 to 8
cell doublings

Reversible if
less than five
cell doublings

↑ Specific activity of cytochrome C oxidase,
  NADPH-dependent cytochrome C reductase,
  acid phosphatase, and N-acetyl-β-glucosaminoglycans
↓ Specific activity of acid cholesteryl esterase
↑ Collagen synthesis, glycosaminoglycans
↑ Degradation β-VLDL, VLDL
↓ Degradation LDL
↑ Esterification and accumulation of
  cellular cholesterol

The functions indicated for each of these forms emphasize the
marked contrasts in the two cell phenotypes as they relate to
atherosclerosis.

Adapted with permission from Campbell GR, Campbell JH, Manderson JA, et al.
Arterial smooth muscle: a multifunctional mesenchymal cell. *Arch Pathol Lab
Med.* 1988;112:977-986. Copyright 1988, American Medical Association.

among other considerations, reversibility of the
atherosclerotic plaque may depend to some extent
on the reversibility of these cellular changes. The
modified smooth muscle cells in the lesions
appear to be more synthetic than those in the
contractile form; the synthetic forms take up lipid
more actively and proliferate readily in response
to stimuli.

What is it that stimulates the proliferation of the
smooth muscle cells in the lesion or in vitro? A
few years ago, the answer to this question might
have been much simpler than it is now. Evidence
from a number of laboratories suggested that a
narrow cut of the LDL fraction (the portion called

LDL I) was a potent stimulator of smooth muscle
cell proliferation in primary cultures after the
cells reached a quiescent phase of growth. Investigators have shown that this cell proliferation
could be successfully blocked by sufficient quantities of normal HDL from normolipidemic animals,
and that repeated stimulation by hyperlipidemic
serum would reinstitute cell proliferation.

Ross and coworkers discovered a PDGF that can be isolated from the platelet alpha granules. This PDGF appeared to be an essential growth factor for smooth muscle cells when they were in a growth phase. Continued investigation revealed this growth factor is synthesized by other cells as well, namely the monocyte-derived macrophage and the endothelial cell, particularly when the endothelial cell is proliferating or injured. Even the smooth muscle cell appears capable of synthesizing this PDGF by an autocrine mechanism. Many other growth factors have been discovered; at least three well-identified growth factors can be obtained from the monocyte-derived macrophage and at least two from the endothelial cell. At present, the mechanisms by which smooth muscle cells are stimulated in a sustained way to produce the cellular components of the atherosclerotic plaque can be related to one or more types of growth factors.

All that can be said with certainty is that the smooth muscle cell is likely to undergo sustained migration and proliferation under any one of a number of circumstances, including sustained hyperlipidemia, endothelial injury and regeneration, platelet adhesion, PDGF infiltration of an injured area of the artery, and monocyte infiltration into the artery wall, even when the endothelium is intact. The exact chain of events that might stimulate the smooth muscle cell to undergo an autocrine reaction to make its own stimulatory molecules of PDGFs remains to be determined.

The cells that make up the major population of atherosclerotic plaques are stimulated to synthesize more collagen, elastin, and probably more proteoglycans than they were synthesizing in the media of the artery. At present, not much is known about the factors by which these modified smooth muscle cells control the balance of fiber and matrix protein synthesis and other cell functions.

Why are some lesions in the human subject much more fibrous than others? There are only hints at present. For example, the lesions produced in at least three species of animals fed peanut oil as the only source of dietary fat are much more fibrous than the lesions that develop after prolonged butterfat or coconut oil feeding, even though the same amount of cholesterol and food

fat is present in each of the diets. To date, this increased fibroplasia induced by peanut oil has not been replicated by treating smooth muscle cells in vitro with lipoproteins or other serum fractions from animals fed peanut oil.

This brief summary indicates that much work remains before we can understand fully the stimuli and the responses of the smooth muscle cell in vivo or under in vitro conditions that stimulate atherogenesis in the whole organism.

Cell Necrosis in Advancing Atherosclerosis

Just as cell proliferation, lipid deposition, and the synthesis of many cell products are the hallmarks of developing atherosclerosis in many species (including the human), the process of cell necrosis is equally characteristic. Many investigators have linked necrosis in the atheroma to an ischemic or at least a cell nutrition problem of advanced atherosclerosis. When the arterial plaque becomes thick and rich in cholesterol and cholesteryl esters, it is assumed that many more cells die because the cell population cannot receive sufficient oxygen and food by diffusion. Cell proliferation is not able to keep up with cell death. Some of the in vivo and in vitro evidence supports this reasoning.

Oxidized LDL may be a major feature of the developing atherosclerotic plaque because oxidized LDL appears to be capable of producing necrosis of both the smooth muscle cell and the endothelium. Several other cell-damaging features are being investigated, and until the correlation of some of these substances with the presence or absence of cell breakdown becomes clear, the necrosis of cells in the severe atherosclerotic plaque will need additional investigation.

Microthrombi

For some time, many investigators have believed that a substantial part of the atherogenic process evolved from small mural thrombi collecting on

Figure 13
A scanning electron photomicrograph of thoracic aorta

Platelets

Mononuclear cells

Fibrin

The small area shown is part of a standard sample from a 32-year-old man who died of acute trauma; autopsy was performed 14½ hours postmortem. This photomicrograph shows a micro-thrombus consisting of platelets, fibrin, and mononuclear cells. Bar = 5 µm.

Reproduced with permission from Spurlock BO, Chandler AB. Adherent platelets and surface microthrombi of the human aorta and left coronary artery: a scanning electron microscopy feasibility study. *Scanning Microsc.* 1987;1:1359-1365.

almost normal artery walls, particularly in some areas of increased susceptibility to atherosclerosis. Most of the evidence for this type of pathogenesis is circumstantial, but if the right areas of developing lesions in human subjects and in animals are examined closely enough, microthrombi can be found (Figure 13). Usually, microthrombi are few in number, and the full transition to a lipid-containing small plaque has rarely been observed in the systemic arterial circulation.

Learning continues about the more susceptible areas in which plaques have the greatest propensity to develop. Studies now in progress on young human subjects both in the United States and worldwide should provide quantitative data that will help show how frequently microthrombi are found in young "healthy" individuals with various risk-factor profiles. Data linking the presence or absence of Lp[a] with this type of pathogenetic sequence should become available soon.

Risk Factors and Pathogenetic Processes

Almost all epidemiologic evidence indicates that risk factors, such as hyperlipidemia, cigarette smoking, hypertension, and diabetes, reinforce each other and have an additive effect on the development of lesions in humans. Similarly, data from a number of well-controlled experimental studies have demonstrated the same kind of interaction and reinforcement of one risk factor by another in relation to the types and the severity of lesions.

Hyperlipidemia and Immune Complexes
If the same type of additive association that occurs with risk factors also exists between circulating immune complexes and hyperlipidemia, perhaps it can explain the accelerated atherogenesis seen in young women with systemic lupus erythematosus (SLE), in heart transplant patients, or in the excellent animal model of serum sickness in the rabbit. The plaques seen in individuals who do not have circulating immune complexes are usually limited more or less to the intima and are eccentric with little evidence of inflammatory reaction (Figures 14A and 14C).

In contrast, recent reports indicate that atherosclerotic plaques in animals and in people who have circulating immune complexes are generally concentric, more or less transmural, and somewhat inflamed lipid-containing lesions (Figure 14B and 14D). This type of disease process is called *atheroarteritis*.

Cigarette Smoking
Cigarette smoking may promote atherogenesis in many ways. Several mechanisms involve the sustained stimulation of the adrenergic system, which results in excessive quantities of circulating epinephrine and norepinephrine. This adrenergic stimulation causes tachycardia, pressor effects, vasoconstriction, and direct damage to the endothelium, which is likely to result in increased permeability to lipoproteins.

Furthermore, it appears that hypersensitivity to tobacco products is widespread. Under these circumstances, cigarette smoking may augment the development of atherosclerosis by causing endothelial injury and inflammation due to delayed hypersensitivity. Such a chronic inflammatory response is also likely to increase endothelial permeability for lipoproteins.

Hypertension
Sustained, untreated hypertension is a major risk factor for augmenting and accelerating atherosclerosis. It might be possible to segregate and identify some of the arterial wall features that mark the influences of hypertension on the larger and medium-sized arteries, as well as the influences on arterial liposomes and connective tissue components. In addition, hypertension exacerbates the effects of the hemodynamic forces on the artery wall (see page 75).

Figure 14
**Eccentric and concentric coronary artery
lesions from young people**

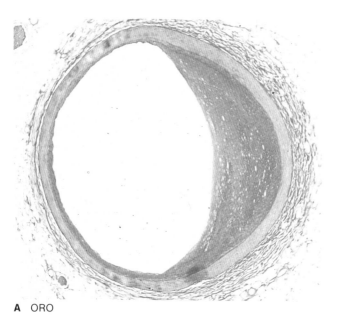

A ORO

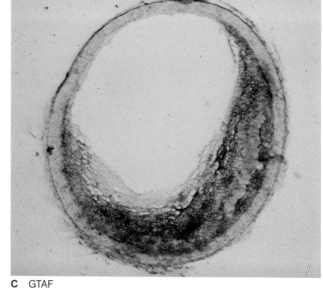

C GTAF

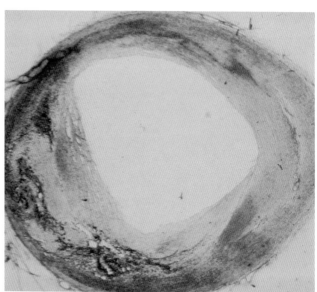

B ORO

D GTAF

(**A**) and (**B**) are both standard samples of the first 2 cm of the left anterior descending coronary artery that are stained with oil red O (ORO) to display the lipid. Cholesteryl esters are the darkest part of each lesion. Note the virtual absence of medial involvement in the eccentric intimal lesion from a 22-year-old white man (**A**) versus the remarkable involvement of intima and media in the concentric and largely transmural lesion in the artery from a 35-year-old white man (**B**). (**C**) and (**D**) demonstrate a similar contrast when the lesions are stained with the Gomori trichrome aldehyde fuchsin (GTAF) stain. (**B**) and (**D**) also suggest a more severe stenosis of the lumen produced by the concentric lesions, along with the increase in collagen (dark grey) present in this subject.

Figure 15
Typical aortic plaque in a diabetic Celebes monkey
(*Macaca nigra*)

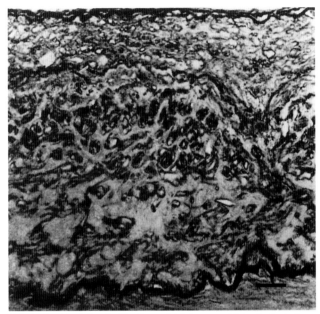

This lesion is stained with Gomori trichrome aldehyde fuchsin (GTAF) to demonstrate the abundant connective tissue elements accompanying the prominent intimal proliferation with superficial (subendothelial) concentration of elastin. Bar = 100 μm.

Reproduced with permission from Howard CF Jr, Vesselinovitch D, Wissler RW. Correlations of aortic histology with gross aortic atherosclerosis and metabolic measurements in diabetic and nondiabetic *Macaca nigra*. *Atherosclerosis*. 1984;52:85-100.

Diabetes Mellitus and Hyperlipidemia

The lesions in the arteries of patients with varying degrees of diabetes mellitus indicate that there is an interaction of diabetes, insulin resistance, and the hyperlipidemic state, especially with increases in the lower density, triglyceride-rich lipoproteins. The spontaneously diabetic monkey appears to show more cell proliferation for a given amount of lipid deposition (Figure 15). Further study of this animal model should help to explain the special effects of diabetes and its frequently associated hypertension with increased atherosclerosis. Hyperinsulinemia and insulin resistance have also been implicated in atherogenesis.

Another aspect of the pathogenesis of atherosclerosis in diabetes is the finding that glycated LDL and probably glycated VLDL are likely to increase the scavenger uptake of LDL by monocyte-derived macrophages. Furthermore, these altered molecules may be antigenic, thus producing a form of autoimmunity in the artery wall.

Points of Predilection of Severe Atherosclerosis

Certain areas of the vascular system are much more vulnerable to progressive atherosclerosis than others (Figure 16). These areas include the abdominal aorta, the proximal parts of the coronary tree, especially the left anterior descending artery, and an area near the bifurcation of the external and internal carotid arteries.

Hemodynamic Influences

It is almost certain that hemodynamic influences play an important role in determining points of special predilection for the development of atherosclerosis. Although possibly of little consequence when the blood lipid concentration is very low, particularly the LDL cholesterol and the β-VLDL cholesterol levels, these hemodynamic influences can achieve great importance when hyperlipidemia is present. Unfortunately, hyperlipidemia has been present in a large proportion of American adults for many years, and an epidemic is under way in which severe coronary, severe carotid, and severe iliac and aortic atherosclerosis are taking a large toll.

Figure 16
Sites of predilection for clinically significant atherosclerosis

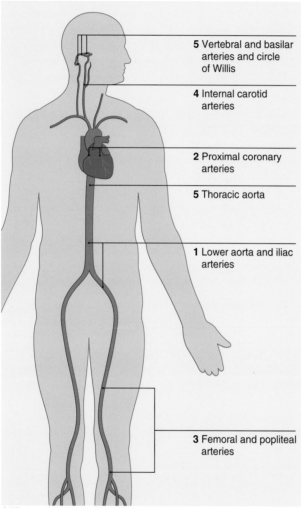

5 Vertebral and basilar arteries and circle of Willis

4 Internal carotid arteries

2 Proximal coronary arteries

5 Thoracic aorta

1 Lower aorta and iliac arteries

3 Femoral and popliteal arteries

Although substantial exceptions occur, the numbers indicate the usual order by rank of severity observed in these sites (with 1 being the most frequently involved with clinically advanced plaques). They also generally correspond to the order in which the disease process appears in these sites of predilection.

Adapted with permission from Wissler RW. Principles of the pathogenesis of atherosclerosis. In: Braunwald E, ed. *Heart Disease: A Textbook of Cardiovascular Medicine.* 2nd ed. Philadelphia, Pa: WB Saunders Co; 1984:1183-1204.

Figure 17
Blood-flow features at carotid bifurcation

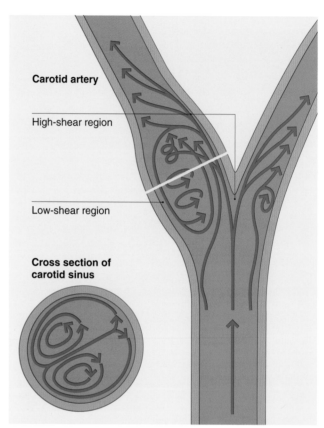

Carotid artery

High-shear region

Low-shear region

Cross section of carotid sinus

This figure depicts the region of flow separation with formation of secondary vortices. While flow remains laminar and mainly unidirectional in the high-shear flow-divider area, a very low-shear area is present on the lateral wall of the internal carotid artery. This area is where plaques are most likely to form and where blood flow accelerates with each cardiac cycle.

Adapted with permission from Glagov S, Zarins C, Giddens DP, Ku DN. Hemodynamics and atherosclerosis: insights and perspectives gained from studies of human arteries. *Arch Pathol Lab Med.* 1988;112:1018-1031. Copyright 1988, American Medical Association.

Current research reports are providing evidence that the most vulnerable areas for atherogenesis are not the places with the greatest shear stress, such as the flow dividers. In progressive disease, the most vulnerable areas are those where the blood is likely to move more slowly with some degree of eddying, turbulence, and a back-and-forth movement of the bloodstream during the cardiac cycle (Figure 17). In fact, the localization of many of the most prominent proximal coronary lesions, as well as lesions that have now been topographically plotted with great accuracy in numerous young human subjects, demonstrates that progressive plaques develop in these low-shear stress regions.

Alterations in the Hemodynamic Forces

Evidence seems to indicate that hypertension and tachycardia (ie, the tension on the vessel wall and the number of times per minute that the vessel wall is subject to hemodynamic stimuli) may be augmenting factors for the development of atherosclerotic plaques, all other stimuli (including hyperlipidemia) being equal. In contrast, increasing evidence suggests that retarding the pulse and lowering blood pressure may help to prevent the development of lesions in otherwise high-risk regions of the arterial system and in spite of elevated blood lipids.

These data indicate more clearly than before that hyperlipidemia and hemodynamic influences represent separate control mechanisms that can either reinforce or counteract each other to influence the prevention or the development and localization of the atherosclerotic process.

Other Modulating Factors That Influence the Pathogenesis of Atherosclerosis

Hyperresponders and Hyporesponders

One of the most interesting examples of the complexity of the pathogenesis of atherosclerosis is that some individuals are almost completely protected from developing this disease. As far as can be ascertained, they often ingest the same diet and receive the same hemodynamic stimuli as do most of the persons who develop atherosclerotic lesions.

Why is it that some animals can withstand a severely hypercholesterolemic diet and show little or no elevation of serum cholesterol or little lesion development, when in the same experiment the majority of the same species of animals develops severe atherosclerosis? Even more puzzling, why is it that some animals have elevated cholesterol and LDL levels throughout the course of a study but develop no lesions, whereas other animals that are housed and fed in the same way and obtained at the same time from the same source develop progressive atherosclerosis? At present, we do not have the complete answers to these questions, although these phenomena have been demonstrated many times in people and in many animal models.

Clearly, much more work needs to be done to determine the factors that can protect against the effects of atherosclerotic stimuli (ie, factors influencing endogenous cholesterol synthesis and factors controlling cholesterol deposition in the artery). It is hoped that humans will be able to capitalize on this natural protection that seems to exist in a small proportion of the currently at-risk population. Recent investigations indicate that the widely differing responses in individuals may be genetically determined.

The Influence of Circulating Immune Complexes and Their Effects on Atherogenesis

The discovery that serum sickness in humans and in the rabbit model is accompanied by severe necrotizing polyarteritis and that its pathogenesis is intimately linked to circulating immune complexes led to a detailed study of the combined effects of serum sickness and hyperlipidemia.

Recently it has been observed that some of the macaque species used in atherosclerosis studies have a high incidence of immune complex deposition in their kidneys. This realization occurred simultaneously with the recognition that the hyperlipidemic diet-induced atheromatous disease in the species with circulating immune complexes is characterized by a high incidence of concentric and transmural atherosclerosis, whereas those macaques with little or no evidence of circulating immune complexes demonstrate the usual eccentric and largely intimal atherosclerosis, which is similar to the usual disease process seen in humans.

Circumstantial evidence indicates that the atheromatous lesions described in patients with SLE have many of the features of atheroarteritis. These lesions have been described in relatively young patients with SLE who die of acute onset coronary disease and who often demonstrate few or no positive risk factors, such as hypercholesterolemia, cigarette smoking, or hypertension (Figure 18).

A correlation has been discovered recently between severe, concentric, transmural atheroarteritis in both old and young persons and the presence of circulating immune complexes. It is not yet clear how frequently this type of pathogenetic stimulus may occur, but current estimates indicate that it may be present in 10% to 20% of all cases of accelerated atherosclerosis, including young as well as older persons.

Although it seems likely that the sustained circulation of immune complexes contributes to atherogenesis through subtle damage to the endothelial cells, the mechanisms of action of circulating immune complexes during the process of atherogenesis require more study before they can be completely understood. Even now, there are indications that this modulating pathogenetic mechanism may represent a hidden and frequently unrecognized risk factor in accelerated atherogenesis in the young. The technology for performing quantitative tests to detect immune complexes in the blood and in the artery wall is rapidly improving. These tests should be included in studies of lesions and risk factors in both experimental animals and investigations of the pathogenesis of human atherosclerosis, when accelerated disease develops without major involvement by known risk factors.

The Effects of Various Food Fats on the Formation of Atherosclerotic Plaques

Controlled studies on the pathogenesis of atherosclerosis in experimental models have demonstrated that certain types of food fats may influence the types of atherosclerotic lesions produced. As extensively reported, coconut oil has an augmenting influence at the artery wall in rabbits, dogs, and monkeys. This characteristic, plus the fairly consistent dose- and time-related elevation of platelet factor-4 levels, indicates that strong endothelial injuring factors may be important in the accelerated and unusually severe atherosclerosis seen in these animals fed coconut oil who simultaneously receive a high-cholesterol diet.

Many laboratories have reported a paradoxical, severe atherogenicity in several species when peanut oil (a polyunsaturated fat) is fed as the sole source of dietary fat. The atheromatous plaques found in many of these experimental animals contain collagen-rich lesions. These results have been confirmed in successive experiments with identically treated animals. However, the mechanisms involved in the unexpectedly strong atherogenicity of peanut oil are not well understood.

The atherogenicity of peanut oil may be explained, in part, by the presence and the arrangement of two unusual fatty acids, behenic (docosanoic) acid and arachidic acid, on the triglyceride molecule. In addition, a profound decrease in HDL levels occurs in primates fed peanut oil. The mechanism that causes highly collagenous lesions to

Figure 18
Coronary atherosclerosis in systemic lupus erythematosus

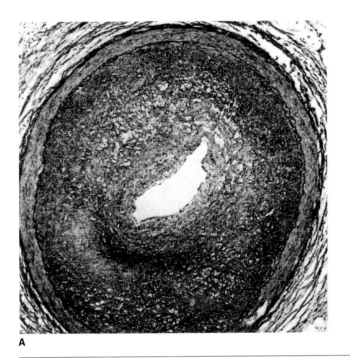

A

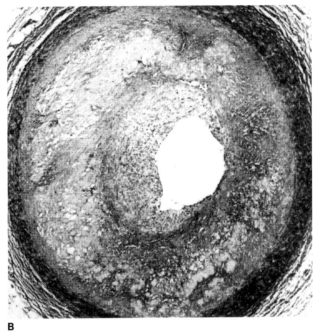

B

These two examples of severe atherosclerosis are from the left anterior descending (**A**) and the left marginal coronary arteries (**B**) of a 40-year-old woman who suffered from severe coronary disease complicating her SLE. These lesions are characterized by a concentric, highly stenosed, and markedly inflamed lipid-rich process that extends into the media.

Reproduced with permission from Bulkley BH, Roberts WC. The heart in systemic lupus erythematosus and the changes induced in it by corticosteroid therapy: a study of 36 necropsy patients. *Am J Med*. 1975;58:243-264.

develop has not been adequately explained. As further nutrition studies are performed, other food fats are likely to emerge that have characteristic atherogenic propensities in addition to those reported for coconut oil and peanut oil.

On the beneficial side of food fat influences are the remarkable effects of many of the marine oils that are rich in eicosapentaenoic acid and its closely related fatty acids. In numerous studies of experimental animals and people, these omega-3 fatty acids have been shown to decrease the concentrations and the toxic effects of prostaglandins (thromboxanes and related compounds) and to prevent many other atherogenic stimuli. Wheat germ oil fed to rhesus monkeys as the sole source of fat in an otherwise high-fat, high-cholesterol ration reportedly produces effects similar to those of marine oils. Reports of the effects of feeding rhesus monkeys marine oils and coconut oil in different proportions have clearly indicated that when menhaden fish oil replaces one third of the coconut oil in the ration, the blood lipid values are favorably influenced (ie, cholesterol, apo B, and LDL levels decrease). In spite of a comparable drop in HDL cholesterol concentrations, these animals had a remarkable decrease in atherosclerotic lesion formation in selected areas (eg, carotid arteries, aorta).

These omega-3 fatty acids, in the more concentrated and purified forms (with most of the cholesterol and other lipids removed), need more intensive study to determine their quantitative effect on atherogenesis when added to a more usual mixed-fat diet.

Viruses
Within the last decade, the results of a number of studies have been published indicating that certain common pathogenetic viruses or viral genomes are present in the developing human atherosclerotic plaque. So far, there has been no indication that these virus-laden atherosclerotic lesions are different from those in which viruses have not been isolated. At present, no definitive evidence has been collected to suggest that viruses play any part in the pathogenesis of the human disease. However, there is evidence that some of the atherosclerotic lesion components may be augmented in the virus-infected chicken.

Endotoxins
Experimental animal studies indicate that endotoxins may augment and accelerate atherogenesis. The study of endotoxins offers a splendid opportunity for evaluating acute and chronic endothelial injury, but there is little evidence that endotoxins are important in modifying the disease process in human arteries. As long as large amounts of endotoxins circulate in the blood because of the many gram-negative infections that are still a part of modern disease, further investigations of sustained endotoxemia and its effects on atherogenesis should be encouraged.

Homocystinemia and Uremia
Circulating homocystine and the presence of uremia may profoundly affect the development of atherosclerotic plaques in animals and humans, although no specific effects on lesion components have been reported. Elevated levels of circulating homocystine and the presence of uremia are two relatively common metabolic defects. The possible pathogenetic mechanisms by which these conditions may augment the severity and rate of development of atherosclerosis require further investigation.

Pulse Rate and Blood Pressure
It is now becoming clear from both epidemiologic and experimental studies that pulse rate and mean ambulatory blood pressure have a definite effect on the development of atherosclerotic lesions. When present as a sustained disease

Table 16
Probable mechanisms of action of risk factors at the cellular level

Hypercholesterolemia Whether due to high-cholesterol, calorie-saturated fat diet* or metabolically induced,* including inherited types	Increased levels of circulating low-density lipoproteins (LDL) damage endothelium and carry cholesterol into artery wall, especially if high-density lipoprotein (HDL) levels are low; lipid (cholesterol) is "trapped," accumulates in smooth muscle cells, or is bound to their extracellular products; leads to cell proliferation and/or necrosis, increased collagen formation, and cell injury due to oxidized LDL.
Hypertension	Increased endothelial permeability to LDL due to: 1. Increased artery wall tension. 2. "Trap-door effect" and endothelial damage produced by angiotensin. 3. Platelet sticking (norepinephrine-induced?) with release of vasoactive amines. 4. Especially bad when added to hypercholesterolemia. 5. Serum "factor" stimulates arterial smooth muscle cell proliferation.
Cigarette smoking	Damage to cells of artery wall due to: 1. Circulating carbon monoxide and oxidized LDL. 2. Platelet agglutination (norepinephrine-induced?). 3. Lipid mobilization (norepinephrine-induced?), leading to hyperlipidemia and increased lipid in artery wall. 4. Hypersensitivity to tobacco antigens.
Diabetes mellitus	Carbohydrate-induced hyperlipemia (VLDL) along with an increase of glycosaminoglycans in the intima that binds lipoproteins; factors in the serum of diabetics that are not related to lipoproteins, insulin, or sugar stimulate arterial smooth muscle cell proliferation, including circulating immune complexes to glycated lipoproteins.
Sedentary living and obesity	Appear to increase the tendency toward elevated serum LDL with relatively low serum levels of HDL, increased incidence of diabetes and hypertension, poor cardiac reserve, and increased work for the heart.

*May also stimulate platelet sticking and clotting tendency so that superimposed thrombosis is more likely to occur.

process, arterial hypertension affects both the media and the intima of the artery in ways that may help to accelerate atherogenesis. An overview of the classic risk factors and how they affect the atherosclerotic process at the cellular level is provided in Table 16.

From an optimistic point of view, it appears that both heart rate and blood pressure are likely to have a net protective effect when the heart rate is slower and the blood pressure lower than levels regarded as normal resting values (ie, pulse rate of 72 per minute and blood pressure 120/80 mm Hg). Conversely, tachycardia and hypertension apparently can be regarded as definite risk factors.

Sustained long-term systemic hypertension in humans has definite effects on the pathobiologic mechanisms of adaptation in both the intima and the media of the artery wall. These effects eventually result in clearly evident changes in both the components and topography of the atherosclerotic lesions.

von Willebrand's Disease
von Willebrand factor is synthesized in the endothelium. Theoretically, a congenital absence of the factor through a major genetic disorder such as von Willebrand's disease might be expected to have a strong protective effect against atherogenesis that develops from blood coagulation and

platelet-related stimuli. Thus far, little epidemiologic evidence has been gathered to support this theory, and the existing experimental data do not provide either clear supportive or contradictory evidence.

One early study of swine with von Willebrand's disease indicated that the absence of this factor does provide substantial protection against atherogenesis. Conversely, an ongoing and comprehensive study of this genetic defect at the University of North Carolina has failed to reveal much effect on either the hyperlipidemic swine's atherogenic responses to coronary artery injuries or on the severity and distribution of aortic lesions. Much more work needs to be done to explain the potential influence of this factor and other substances important in platelet sticking and platelet agglutination, such as liberation of vasoactive amines and/or PDGF from the platelet. The study of von Willebrand factor is receiving ongoing attention and support, which should ultimately clarify its role in atherogenesis.

Postprandial Lipids and Their Influence on Atherogenesis

Over the years, considerable emphasis has been placed on evaluating fasting blood lipid levels, with particular attention to fasting triglycerides and VLDL. However, it is becoming evident that studies of postprandial lipid values (similar to the studies of glucose tolerance in diabetes) are needed to evaluate the individual's fat tolerance and how it affects the pathogenesis of atherosclerosis.

One factor contributing to this shift of emphasis is the finding that chylomicron and VLDL fragments, which are broken down at the endothelium through the action of lipoprotein lipase, would have their major effect soon after fats are ingested. To date, no particular influence of these postprandial levels on the components of the atherosclerotic plaque has been revealed by serial pathogenetic studies. Although few investigations have been conducted, the data reported to date are tantalizing.

The study of the importance of postprandial lipid levels should be a fruitful area for further research. Many of the probes and markers that are now available for metabolic investigations in both experimental models and in the human subjects would be useful in such a study.

Thromboxane Influences

As the importance of prostaglandins has become better understood, especially the control of certain vascular phenomena, more attention has focused on prostacyclin-thromboxane balances. Thromboxane A_2 derived from platelets is one of the most active compounds in initiating arterial spasm and in the development of thrombotic phenomena. For this reason, studies were initiated to investigate the blood levels of thromboxane B_2 (the more stable metabolite of thromboxane A_2) following certain atherogenic stimuli. Ingesting certain marine oils or wheat germ oil will frequently prevent the elevation of thromboxane A_2 that occurs when coconut oil is the sole source or even a partial source of fats in the diet. This and many other observations indicate that thromboxane B_2 determinations may be of value in following atherogenic and thrombogenic tendencies.

In the meantime, it is likely that many new observations will elucidate the role of prostaglandins in the atherogenic process. The prostaglandin system as a series of modulating factors in the pathogenesis of atherosclerosis needs to be thoroughly evaluated, and it is important to understand the clinical effects of this system, especially with regard to arterial spasm and thrombosis.

Superoxides, Interleukins, and Other Active Compounds of Importance in Atherogenesis

As has been pointed out by cell biologists and pathobiologists studying the artery wall and its changes during atherogenesis, the cells of the artery wall exhibit many specialized functions that are highly regulated but can change as a result of certain types of stimulation. The functions in the endothelial cell can change from producing mainly anticoagulant substances (thrombomodulin, tissue fibrinogen activator, and prostacyclin) to producing procoagulent substances (tissue factor, plasminogen activator inhibitor, and von Willebrand factor).

Work in a number of laboratories has established that the cytokines interleukin-1 (IL-1) and tumor necrosis factor/cachectin can induce tissue factor–like procoagulant activity on the surface of human endothelial cells. These cytokines can trigger a coordinated change in most of the known endothelial-associated hemostatic mechanisms in a way that tips the balance toward activation of coagulation and promotion of thrombosis. Treatment with IL-1, for example, also increases the endothelial monolayer activity so that leukocytes adhere to intimal surfaces. Release of endogenous IL-1 as well as other interleukins may be part of the mechanism by which monocytes are recruited to sites of injury or inflammation on the endothelial surface. Cells in the blood vessel wall are known to be sources of these multipotential cytokines when they are stimulated by gram-negative bacterial endotoxin or IL-1. This stimulation can then induce the expression of IL-1 genes in human vascular endothelium and smooth muscle cells.

It can be surmised that under some circumstances the endogenous cytokines may initiate the cascade of alterations that characterizes the activated state of human endothelium. It is also clear that vascular wall cells have functions that play a part in the chronic aspects of atherogenesis; eg, they have a role in cell migration and proliferation. They are particularly important in the accumulation of extracellular matrix proteins, such as collagen and elastin, that characterizes the complicated atherosclerotic plaque.

The search has intensified to find the signals that stimulate the phenotypic modulation of smooth muscle cells, causing them to become

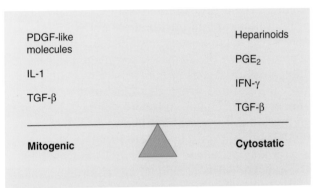

Figure 19
The balance between mitogenic and cytostatic factors in the proliferation of arterial smooth muscle cells in atherogenesis

A few of the major factors responsible for smooth muscle cell proliferation and the currently recognized major substances that apparently serve to inhibit the mitotic response. Abbreviations: PDGF, platelet-derived growth factor; IL-1, interleukin-1; TGF-β, transforming growth factor β; PGE₂, prostaglandin E₂; IFN-γ, interferon gamma.

Reproduced with permission from Libby P, Friedman GB, Salomon RN. Cytokines as modulators of cell proliferation in fibrotic diseases. *Am Rev Respir Dis.* 1989;140:1114-1117.

synthetic cells. Many investigators have been searching for new PDGF-initiated mechanisms by which the cells of the blood vessel wall or their infiltrating monocytes can provide autocrine or paracrine sources of mitogenic factors.

The work of Libby and others has been interpreted as indicating that IL-1 might be a major stimulator of smooth muscle cell proliferation. Investigators have shown that smooth muscle cells can produce IL-1, and that prolonged stimulation overcomes the inhibitory effects of prostaglandin E₂ on cell proliferation. Endothelial-derived IL-1 tends also to be a potential paracrine growth stimulator. More recent data have shown that smooth muscle cells cultured from human atherosclerotic lesions can secrete a product with PDGF-like mitogenic activity and can selectively transcribe the PDGF-α gene. Current observations indicate that all of the necessary components of autocrine growth-stimulatory loops appear to be present during human atherogenesis (Figure 19).

Endothelial and smooth muscle cells also appear to be able to express the genes for fibroblast growth factor, heparin-binding growth factor–like molecules, and transforming growth factor β, which can stimulate smooth muscle cell proliferation. In addition, there is growing evidence that some locally produced growth factors can antagonize the response to mitogens. This antagonism includes not only the effects of growth-inhibitory prostaglandins but also the effects of the cytokine interferon gamma (IFN-γ), an inhibitor of the proliferative response of human smooth muscle cells to PDGF or IL-1. INF-γ is probably produced by activated T cells, which are now known to constitute an important fraction of the infiltrating lymphocytes in many human atherosclerotic plaques (Figure 19).

While it has long been recognized that the endothelial cell in the artery wall is vital to maintain a hemostatic balance, there now also appears to be a similar paracrine balance in relation to smooth muscle cell proliferation. These controls on smooth muscle cell proliferation include growth inhibition produced by heparinlike molecules and the proteoglycans elaborated by smooth muscle cells as well as endothelial cells.

The main products of the endothelial cells that are considered to be anticoagulant are heparinlike glycosaminoglycans, prostacyclin, plasminogen activator, and thrombomodulin. The principal procoagulant products of these cells are von Willebrand factor, plasminogen activator inhibitor, thrombospondin, collagens, and tissue factor.

These and many other findings are interpreted as indicating that the vascular balance in the disease-free state reflects a multiplicity of functions of smooth muscle cells, inflammatory cells, and endothelial cells. The increased appreciation of the functional complexities of smooth muscle cells has made it possible to study many heretofore neglected aspects of the development of atherosclerosis and hypertension.

The role of LDL modified by free-radical oxidation and the altered interactions of vascular cells and oxidized lipoproteins has been discussed. Much current work is focused on demonstrating that endothelial cells, vascular smooth muscle cells, and activated monocyte-derived macrophages can oxidize LDL under certain circumstances, changing dramatically its chemical and physical properties. The oxidized lipoprotein exhibits an enhanced electrophoretic mobility and an increased density, and it contains a partially degraded apolipoprotein moiety. Oxidized LDL also carries dozens of products of lipid peroxidation not found in appreciable quantities on native LDL. Studies of vascular cells in culture have demonstrated that oxidized LDL exhibits a number of important differences from native LDL in the way it interacts with cells.

Oxidized LDL is recognized by the scavenger or acetyl LDL receptor on macrophages, is chemotactic for monocytes, and is cytotoxic due to one or more of the lipoprotein-borne products of lipid peroxidation. This toxicity appears to be particularly potent during DNA synthesis and may be correlated with the production of endothelial injury during atherogenesis. Oxidized LDL may also decrease the production of PDGF-like proteins by endothelial cells. Recent evidence indicates that oxidized LDL is present in atherosclerotic lesions in humans and in the Watanabe heritable hyperlipidemic rabbit. These findings are strengthened by the recent reports from a number of laboratories indicating that the administration of potent antioxidants will prevent the development of atherosclerosis in highly susceptible animals.

The work on oxidized LDL has provided a great deal of information and raised some important questions about this mechanism of cell injury and smooth muscle cell proliferation, the hallmarks of the reaction of the artery wall to hyperlipidemia. For example, does oxidized LDL that is transferred from macrophages to smooth muscle cells help to turn on PDGF synthesis? Further study should explain what turns on smooth muscle cells when they are placed in media containing LDL from hyperlipidemic serum. It might provide the link between hyperlipidemia and smooth muscle cell proliferation that has been demonstrated so well in in vitro studies but has never been completely understood as a pathobiologic mechanism (Figure 11).

How Does Knowledge of Pathogenesis Lead to the Concept That Atherosclerosis Is Preventable and Substantially Reversible?

There is increasing evidence that the lipid component of the atherosclerotic plaque, cell injury, and smooth muscle cell proliferation can be controlled by mechanisms that can be defined and manipulated. When these factors are sufficiently controlled, atherosclerosis should be amenable to effective intervention both by retarding or almost completely preventing lipid deposition and by inhibiting cell proliferation. It should also be possible to reverse a number of the most pathologic components of the plaque.

Plaque reversal has proved to be possible (Figure 20). Some of the strongest evidence of the regression of atherosclerotic plaques comes from studies using the rhesus monkey, one of the best models of human atherosclerosis available. In this model, when the blood lipid concentration levels are reduced to what might be considered basal levels, plaques undergo major changes that likely are beneficial. Basal levels are present in early adult life when metabolism is not perturbed and when the diet has been low in fat and cholesterol for a long period, as it is for much of the world's population.

At least seven different centers have performed more than a dozen studies of the regression of atherosclerosis in the rhesus monkey, all of which indicate that the lesions in this primate can be improved by therapy that lowers lipid levels. As far as can be ascertained, in every instance the more "humanoid" atherosclerotic plaques in the rhesus monkey and in certain breeds of swine have improved dramatically when the animals were subjected to rigorous lipid-lowering regimens. As Figure 20 indicates, the substantial changes that major components undergo are the healing of the damaged endothelium and the loss of most of the lipids, not only from in and around the cells in the developing parts of the lesion, but also from the necrotic centers of the lesions. In many of the studies, the majority of advanced plaques lost most of their necrotic centers.

Other important findings from these studies include the decreased mitotic rate of smooth muscle cells and the reorientation and condensation of fiber proteins within the plaque. Some of the more prolonged studies have demonstrated a decrease in the collagen, elastin, and calcium content of plaques as therapeutic intervention continued, especially when the results are expressed in relation to arterial segment rather than per unit of dry or wet weight.

The results of numerous studies have recently indicated that the advanced plaques of human atherosclerosis can be interrupted, retarded, and even reversed. The study that has received the most attention is the Cholesterol-Lowering Atherosclerosis Study (CLAS) led by Blankenhorn at the University of Southern California. The results of CLAS indicate that the combination of bile acid-sequestering agents and niacin is capable of retarding atherosclerosis and, in a sizable

Figure 20
Major changes in the components of advanced atherosclerotic plaques observed after therapy with cholesterol-lowering diet plus drugs

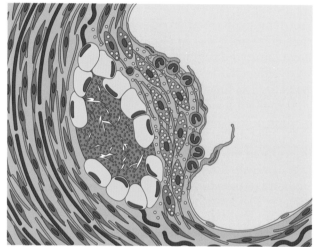

The changes depicted have been observed by numerous investigators during regression of advanced atherosclerotic lesions in rhesus monkeys and swine. The plaques become substantially smaller, both the fibrous cap and the necrotic center decrease in size, intracellular and extracellular lipid decrease remarkably, the collagen and elastin are condensed and remodeled to fit the smaller space, and the endothelial damage heals. According to some observers, the early period of the regression process is marked by an increase in the monocyte-derived macrophages at the edge of the necrotic center. At the later stages of regression, most of these cells disappear.

Adapted with permission from Wissler RW. Principles of the pathogenesis of arteriosclerosis. In: Braunwald E. ed. *Heart Disease: A Textbook of Cardiovascular Medicine*. 2nd ed. Philadelphia, Pa: WB Saunders Co; 1984:1183-1204.

number of patients, causing substantial lesion regression that is detectable by angiography.

It is apparent that as the number of these types of investigations increases, the results are becoming more definitive because of improved and less invasive methods for measuring the changes in atherosclerotic lesions on successive examinations. In fact, during 1990 the definitive results from five clinical trials of atherosclerosis regression have confirmed and amplified the reversibility of advanced coronary artery plaques.

These promising results have been obtained in substantial numbers of free-living patients treated with diet plus the combined use of suitable pharmaceutical agents. At present, the evidence indicates that atherosclerosis in humans is largely preventable, and that in some instances it is substantially reversible by using safe, relatively innocuous interventions.

The Spectrum of Intervention

There are several types of interventions that may be of value at different stages of life for persons in a society in which atherosclerosis is an almost universal problem (Figure 21). As long as nearly 50% of the US population has problems due to ischemic cardiovascular disease and ischemic

Figure 21
A spectrum of intervention into the atherosclerotic process

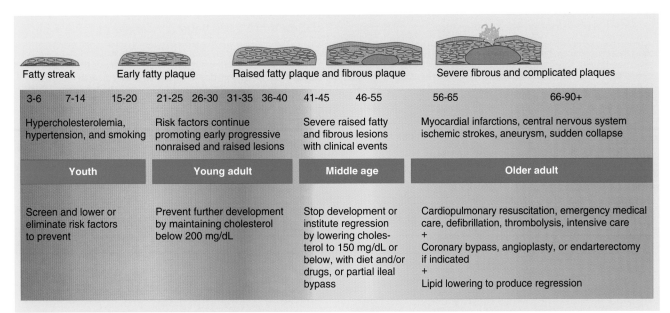

Fatty streak	Early fatty plaque	Raised fatty plaque and fibrous plaque	Severe fibrous and complicated plaques

3-6	7-14	15-20	21-25	26-30	31-35	36-40	41-45	46-55	56-65	66-90+

Hypercholesterolemia, hypertension, and smoking	Risk factors continue promoting early progressive nonraised and raised lesions	Severe raised fatty and fibrous lesions with clinical events	Myocardial infarctions, central nervous system ischemic strokes, aneurysm, sudden collapse
Youth	**Young adult**	**Middle age**	**Older adult**
Screen and lower or eliminate risk factors to prevent	Prevent further development by maintaining cholesterol below 200 mg/dL	Stop development or institute regression by lowering cholesterol to 150 mg/dL or below, with diet and/or drugs, or partial ileal bypass	Cardiopulmonary resuscitation, emergency medical care, defibrillation, thrombolysis, intensive care + Coronary bypass, angioplasty, or endarterectomy if indicated + Lipid lowering to produce regression

Preventive measures can be started early in life. Later in life, effective measures and careful monitoring can be instituted to decrease risk factors to the lowest possible levels. Measures designed to eliminate hypertension, encourage smoking cessation, and reduce the atherogenic blood lipids to the lowest possible (basal) levels need to be used in treating older adults who already suffer from the clinical effects of the atherosclerotic process.

Adapted with permission from Wissler RW. Principles of the pathogenesis of atherosclerosis. In: Braunwald E, ed. *Heart Disease: A Textbook of Cardio-vascular Medicine.* 2nd ed. Philadelphia, Pa: WB Saunders Co; 1984:1183-1204.

cerebrovascular disease, the majority of these disorders resulting from underlying atherosclerosis, all the possibilities for dealing with this national problem have to be considered.

Fortunately, many of the studies over the past 25 years have had a strong impact on preventing the development of atherosclerosis and its clinical effects, cerebrovascular and cardiovascular disease. An active and well-organized campaign has been instituted to encourage the US population to learn more about the causes and dangers of atherosclerosis and to do more to prevent the accumulation of cholesterol deposits in arterial walls. So far, most of the effort is nutritionally oriented and almost entirely aimed at lowering blood lipid levels, particularly the LDL and VLDL fractions.

The most urgent need in the near future is to identify those subjects in young adulthood and middle age who are definitely at high risk of developing the signs, symptoms, and laboratory indicators that mean they are particularly prone to severe atherosclerosis (Figure 21). Efforts must be made to teach these persons to practice active preventive medicine. Those patients who are already suffering from the effects of atheromatous disease will need to be treated rigorously. These individuals are likely to have continuing problems unless the disease is retarded or the lesions are reversed with modern therapy consisting of drugs and diet. Systems also need to be developed to identify persons in the younger age groups who most actively need to practice prevention.

As the cholesterol education program continues to help us to identify the most vulnerable individuals, one can anticipate that not only will the public become more involved, but also the healthcare community, the food industry, and the pharmaceutical companies will react in a favorable way. Their combined efforts will help those at risk prevent the life-threatening catastrophies caused by this number one killer, which often takes its toll in the prime of life.

Conclusion

This chapter has had as its main purpose the presentation, in as logical a way as possible, of some of the major factors and mechanisms responsible for the development of atherosclerotic plaques. It is written largely from the standpoint of what goes on in the artery wall and how these arterial events combine to produce the various components of the plaque.

The chapter has also dealt with some of the moderating factors not yet completely understood that probably contribute to the various reactions and interactions that result in the inhibition of the progressive development of atherosclerosis. Based on current knowledge of pathogenetic processes, the susceptibility of the plaque to prevention, retardation, and regression at the arterial wall level is evident.

Acknowledgements

This summary of current knowledge could not have been attempted without the years of association that I have been privileged to have with my colleagues and coworkers at the University, including Drs Godfrey Getz, Angelo Scanu, Seymour Glagov, Christopher Zarins, and most especially Dr Dragoslava Vesselinovitch. The manuscript could not have been produced without the diligent and talented help of Gertrud Friedman and the steadfast and skillful assistance of Alexander Arguelles, Megan Mok, and William Kransdorf. The illustrative material included in this chapter is the product of efforts by Dr Vesselinovitch and me, with the able assistance of Eunice Rivers and Chris Burke and the photographic skills of Gordon Bowie. I thank Dr Peter Libby for reading the manuscript and making constructive suggestions. I am indebted to Daphna Gregg and her colleagues for their editing of the completed manuscript. I am particularly grateful to Dr Tony Gotto for extending the invitation to prepare this chapter.

Selected Readings

Benditt EP. The origin of atherosclerosis. **Sci Am.** 1977;236(2):74-85.

Benditt EP, Barrett T, McDougall JK. Viruses in the etiology of atherosclerosis. **Proc Natl Acad Sci USA.** 1983;80:6386-6389.

Björkerud S, Hansson HA, Bondjers G. Subcellular valves and canaliculi in arterial endothelium and their equivalence to so-called stigmata. **Virchows Arch (B).** 1972;11:19-23.

Blankenhorn DH, Nessim SA, Johnson RL, Sanmarco ME, Azen SP, Cashin-Hemphill L. Beneficial effects of combined colestipol-niacin therapy on coronary atherosclerosis and coronary venous bypass grafts. **JAMA.** 1987;257:3233-3240.

Bulkley BH, Roberts WC. The heart in systemic lupus erythematosus and the changes induced in it by corticosteroid therapy: a study of 36 necropsy patients. **Am J Med.** 1975;58:243-264.

Campbell GR, Campbell JH, Manderson JA, Horrigan S, Rennick RE. Arterial smooth muscle: a multifunctional mesenchymal cell. **Arch Pathol Lab Med.** 1988;112:977-986.

Carew TE, Schwenke DC, Steinberg D. Antiatherogenic effect of probucol unrelated to its hypocholesterolemic effect: evidence that antioxidants in vivo can selectively inhibit low density lipoprotein degradation in macrophage-rich fatty streaks and slow the progression of atherosclerosis in the Watanabe heritable hyperlipidemic rabbit. **Proc Natl Acad Sci USA.** 1987;84:7725-7729.

Davis HR, Bridenstine RT, Vesselinovitch D, Wissler RW. Fish oil inhibits development of atherosclerosis in rhesus monkeys. **Arteriosclerosis.** 1987;7:441-449.

Fless GM, Kirchhausen T, Fischer-Dzoga K, Wissler RW, Scanu AM. Serum low density lipoproteins with mitogenic effect on cultured aortic smooth muscle cells. **Atherosclerosis.** 1982;41:171-183.

Francus T, Klein RF, Staiano-Coico L, Becker CG, Siskind GW. Effects of tobacco glycoprotein (TGP) on the immune system: II. TGP stimulates the proliferation of human T cells and the differentiation of human B cells into Ig secreting cells. **J Immunol.** 1988;140:1823-1829.

Getz GS, Mazzone T, Soltys P, Bates SR. Atherosclerosis and apoprotein E: an enigmatic relationship. **Arch Pathol Lab Med.** 1988;112:1048-1055.

Gimbrone MA Jr, Bevilacqua MP, Cybulsky MI. Endothelial-dependent mechanisms of leukocyte adhesion in inflammation and atherosclerosis. **Ann NY Acad Sci.** 1990;598:77-85.

Glagov S, Zarins C, Giddens DP, Ku DN. Hemodynamics and atherosclerosis: insights and perspectives gained from studies of human arteries. **Arch Pathol Lab Med.** 1988;112:1018-1031.

Goldstein JL, Brown MS. The low density lipoprotein pathway and its relation to atherosclerosis. **Ann Rev Biochem.** 1977;46:897-930.

Goldstein JL, Ho YK, Basu SK, Brown MS. Binding site on macrophages that mediates uptake and degradation of acetylated low density lipoprotein, producing massive cholesterol deposition. **Proc Natl Acad Sci USA.** 1979;76:333-337.

Griggs TR, Reddick RL, Sultzer D, Brinkhous KM. Susceptibility to atherosclerosis in aortas and coronary arteries of swine with von Willebrand's disease. **Am J Pathol.** 1981;102:137-145.

Howard CF Jr, Vesselinovitch D, Wissler RW. Correlations of aortic histology with gross aortic atherosclerosis and metabolic measurements in diabetic and nondiabetic Macaca nigra. **Atherosclerosis.** 1984;52:85-100.

Kritchevsky D, Tepper SA, Kim HK, Story JA, Vesselinovitch D, Wissler RW. Experimental atherosclerosis in rabbits fed cholesterol-free diets: 5. Comparison of peanut, corn, butter, and coconut oils. **Exp Mol Pathol.** 1976;24:375-391.

Libby P, Friedman GB, Salomon RN. Cytokines as modulators of cell proliferation in fibrotic diseases. **Am Rev Respir Dis.** 1989;4:1114-1117.

Libby P, Warner SJC, Friedman GB. Interleukin 1: a mitogen for human vascular smooth muscle cells that induces the release of growth-inhibitory prostanoids. **J Clin Invest.** 1988;81:487-498.

Mahley RW, Innerarity TL, Weisgraber KH, Fry DL. Canine hyperlipoproteinemia and atherosclerosis: accumulation of lipid by aortic medial cells in vivo and in vitro. **Am J Pathol.** 1977;87:205-226.

Malinow MR, Kang SS, Taylor LM, et al. Prevalence of hyperhomocyst(e)inemia in patients with peripheral arterial occlusive disease. **Circulation.** 1989;79:1180-1188.

Minick CR, Murphy GE, Campbell WG Jr. Experimental induction of athero-arteriosclerosis by the synergy of allergic injury to arteries and lipid-rich diet: I. Effect of repeated injections of horse serum in rabbits fed a dietary cholesterol supplement. **J Exp Med.** 1966;124:635-651.

Phillipson BE, Rothrock DW, Connor WE, Harris WS, Illingworth DR. Reduction of plasma lipids, lipoproteins, and apoproteins by dietary fish oils in patients with hypertriglyceridemia. **N Engl J Med.** 1985;312:1210-1216.

Poskitt TR, Fortwengler HP Jr, Bobrow JC, Roth GJ. Naturally occurring immune-complex glomerulonephritis in monkeys (Macaca irus): I. Light, immunofluorescence and electron microscopic studies. **Am J Pathol**. 1974;76:145-164.

Quinn MT, Parthasarathy S, Steinberg D. Endothelial cell-derived chemotactic activity for mouse peritoneal macrophages and the effects of modified forms of low density lipoprotein. **Proc Natl Acad Sci USA**. 1985;82:5949-5953.

Reidy MA, Schwartz SM. Endothelial injury and regeneration: IV. Endotoxin: a nondenuding injury to aortic endothelium. **Lab Invest**. 1983;48:25-34.

Ross R. The pathogenesis of atherosclerosis: an update. **N Engl J Med**. 1986;314:488-500.

Ross R, Glomset J, Kariya B, Harker L. A platelet-dependent serum factor that stimulates the proliferation of arterial smooth muscle cells in vitro. **Proc Natl Acad Sci USA**. 1974;71:1207-1210.

Simionescu N. Cellular aspects of transcapillary exchange. **Physiol Rev**. 1983;63:1536-1579.

Simionescu N, Vasile E, Lupu F, Popescu G, Simionescu M. Prelesional events in atherogenesis: accumulation of extracellular cholesterol-rich liposomes in the arterial intima and cardiac valves of the hyperlipidemic rabbit. **Am J Pathol**. 1986;123:109-125.

Spurlock BO, Chandler AB. Adherent platelets and surface microthrombi of the human aorta and left coronary artery: a scanning electron microscopy feasibility study. **Scanning Microsc**. 1987;1:1359-1365.

Steinberg D. Lipoproteins and atherosclerosis: a look back and a look ahead. **Arteriosclerosis**. 1983;3:283-301.

Steinbrecher UP, Parthasarathy S, Leake DS, Witztum JL, Steinberg D. Modification of low density lipoprotein by endothelial cells involves lipid peroxidation and degradation of low density lipoprotein phospholipids. **Proc Natl Acad Sci USA**. 1984;81:3883-3887.

Stemerman MB, Morrel EM, Burke KR, Colton CK, Smith KA, Lees RS. Local variation in arterial wall permeability to low density lipoprotein in normal rabbit aorta. **Arteriosclerosis**. 1986;6:64-69.

Thomas WA, Reiner JM, Florentin RA, Janakidevi K, Lee KJ. Arterial smooth muscle cells in atherogenesis: births, deaths and clonal phenomena. In: Schettler G, Goto Y, Hata Y, Klose G, eds. **Atherosclerosis IV: Proceedings of the Fourth International Symposium on Atherosclerosis**. New York, NY: Springer-Verlag; 1977:16-23.

Vesselinovitch D, Getz GS, Hughes RH, Wissler RW. Atherosclerosis in the rhesus monkey fed three food fats. **Atherosclerosis**. 1974;20:303-321.

Vesselinovitch D, Wissler RW, Fischer-Dzoga K, Hughes R, Dubien L. Regression of atherosclerosis in rabbits: Part 1. Treatment with low-fat diet, hyperoxia and hypolipidemic agents. **Atherosclerosis**. 1974;19:259-275.

Vesselinovitch D, Wissler RW, Schaffner TJ, Borensztajn J. The effect of various diets on atherogenesis in rhesus monkeys. **Atherosclerosis**. 1980;35:189-207.

Wissler RW, Vesselinovitch D. Interaction of therapeutic diets and cholesterol-lowering drugs in regression studies in animals. In: Malinow MR, Blaton VH, eds. **Regression of Atherosclerotic Lesions: Experimental Studies and Observations in Humans**. New York, NY: Plenum Press; 1984:21-41. NATO Advanced Study Institute, Series A, Life Sciences; vol 79.

Wissler RW, Vesselinovitch D, Bridenstine RT, Singh L. The effects of fish oil, wheat germ oil, and coconut oil in rhesus monkeys receiving a ration high in fat and cholesterol. **Arteriosclerosis**. 1988;8:603a. Abstract.

Wissler RW, Vesselinovitch D, Davis HR. Cellular components of the progressive atherosclerotic process. In: Olsson AG, ed. **Atherosclerosis: Biology and Clinical Science**. New York, NY: Churchill Livingstone; 1987:57-73.

Wissler RW, Vesselinovitch D, Davis HR, Lambert PH, Bekermeier M. A new way to look at atherosclerotic involvement of the artery wall and the functional effects. **Ann NY Acad Sci**. 1985;454:9-22.

Wolfbauer G, Glick JM, Minor LK, Rothblat GH. Development of the smooth muscle foam cell: uptake of macrophage lipid inclusions. **Proc Natl Acad Sci USA**. 1986;83:7760-7764.

Zilversmit DB. Atherogenesis: a postprandial phenomenon. **Circulation**. 1979;60:473-485.

Diagnosis of Coronary Artery Disease

Introduction

The diagnosis of coronary artery disease is a complex process that begins at the bedside and continues with a variety of diagnostic tests. The history and physical examination of the patient remain the cornerstones of making the initial diagnosis of coronary disease. For example, the clinician's decision to hospitalize and closely observe a patient with suspected acute ischemia is based primarily on the patient's history. Beyond taking the history and conducting the physical examination, the methods of confirming the diagnosis of coronary artery disease have undergone a revolutionary change. A variety of laboratory techniques, most of which are noninvasive, offer sophisticated insights into the structure, function, and physiologic state of the heart.

Management of the patient with coronary artery disease spans the range from preventive medicine and genetic studies to sophisticated diagnostic strategies and surgical and nonsurgical therapies. Dietary and pharmacologic interventions help reduce the degree of atherosclerosis in some patients. These and other effective interventions limit the acute ischemic damage caused by coronary artery disease.

However, to optimally deploy these therapeutic methods, extremely accurate diagnosis of the extent and consequences of coronary artery disease is necessary. Initially, it is important to determine if physiologically significant coronary artery disease is present. Next, an assessment of the anatomical extent of disease is often required, particularly for proper application of such therapeutic options as percutaneous transluminal coronary angioplasty (PTCA) and coronary artery bypass graft (CABG) surgery. Even when a precise anatomical assessment of the coronary arteries has been accomplished, additional information is required to ascertain if ischemic damage is present and its functional consequences. The assessment of ischemic damage commonly involves estimating global and regional left ventricular function. Investigators also try to evaluate myocardial perfusion, metabolism, and tissue characteristics to better assess the extent of salvageable myocardium. Finally, the patient's prognosis and thus decisions on the desirability of medical versus surgical treatment can then be made based on the anatomical extent of the coronary disease and on a detailed assessment of left ventricular function.

This chapter will review the highlights of diagnosing coronary artery disease, including evaluation of the patient's history and the results of the physical examination, the electrocardiogram (ECG), and several methods of cardiac imaging and cardiac catheterization. A wide array of choices is available for examining many aspects of cardiac structure and function. To guide the reader, the limitations and overlapping nature of many of these diagnostic techniques are noted, and the probabilistic approach to modeling the diagnostic process is introduced.

The History

A detailed history elicited thoughtfully and without haste remains the most important step in diagnosing coronary artery disease. The primary objective of this interview is to probe for the two pathognomonic features of coronary artery disease: angina pectoris or prior myocardial infarction. The finding of either one is diagnostic of coronary artery disease until proved otherwise. In all of medicine there are few other disorders that can be diagnosed with such a degree of certainty from the history alone. Because the description of angina pectoris constitutes prima facie evidence of the existence of significant coronary artery obstruction and because coronary artery disease is the leading cause of mortality in the United States, every physician, regardless of specialty, should become expert in recognizing this disorder.

Angina Pectoris

The characteristic features of angina pectoris are its oppressive nature, its usual retrosternal location, and its predictable provocation, which is usually some physical effort or emotional experience. Although clinicians have been describing the distinctive features of angina pectoris to students for more than two centuries, no descriptions have surpassed the clarity, conciseness, and color of the original description offered by William Heberden to the assembly of the Royal College of Physicians in 1772:

> There is a disorder of the breast marked with strong and peculiar symptoms, considerable for the kind of danger belonging to it, and not extremely rare, which deserves to be mentioned more at length. The seed of it, and sense of strangling, and anxiety with which it is attended, may make it not improperly be called angina pectoris. They who are afflicted with it, are seized while they are walking, (more especially if it be uphill, and soon after eating) with a painful and most disagreeable sensation in the breast, which seems as if it would extinguish life, if it were to increase or to continue; but the moment they stand still, all this uneasiness vanishes.

Quality of pain: Rather than being perceived by the patient as frank pain, angina pectoris is usually described as a feeling of heaviness, squeezing pressure, or an ache beneath the sternum. Often patients use the analogy, "like an elephant standing on my chest." To others it has features of indigestion and is often associated with a need to belch. For some, there is no association with pain or discomfort at all but, instead, sudden breathlessness while undertaking some customary activity. Because angina pectoris presents with many patterns, it is hazardous to inquire solely about the occurrence of "any chest pain." The patient may have angina, yet does not perceive the symptom as pain and thus responds negatively, leading the physician to an error in diagnosis.

Perhaps the most deceptive feature of angina pectoris is its short duration. Most patients are engaged in some physical activity at the time they first experience true angina; these patients usually stop the activity, often abruptly, and obtain relief in a matter of minutes. It is this fleeting quality that begets a false sense of security or at least suggests to the patient that the sensation just experienced cannot be serious. Indeed, the episode is often forgotten or denied. Typically, angina episodes last 1 to 5 minutes but can extend to 15 or 20 minutes. Characteristically, the episodes disappear within 1 to 2 minutes after sublingual administration of nitroglycerin. This rapid response can often be used to diagnostic advantage.

Location of pain: The classic location for angina pectoris is behind the middle or lower portion of the sternum, and frequently (but not invariably) angina radiates to the left shoulder and extends down the medial aspect of the left arm. Often the angina will radiate upward to the neck and throat region and is often perceived as intense jaw pain. Pain in the lower teeth or jaw is occasionally a manifestation of cardiac ischemia. This is rarely the case with pain in the upper teeth.

In identifying the location of chest discomfort associated with angina pectoris, the patient will often place a clenched fist over the sternum. The burning or aching sensation the patient may describe is actually the squeezing nature of the discomfort. This "clenched-fist" sign has come to be appreciated as a reliable indicator of true angina pectoris.

Because of the sensory innervation of the heart, pain or discomfort arising from an ischemic myocardium can be referred to any of the dermatomes that are in synaptic proximity to the dorsal nerve roots extending from C-8 to T-7. Thus, in addition to its classically described substernal location, angina pectoris may appear solely as a pain in either shoulder, the interscapular region, the back of the neck, or the forearms. Although the location of the pain in these instances may at first seem puzzling and atypical, the association of such pain with exertion should raise the examiner's suspicion that it is the equivalent of anginal pain. This type of pain is termed the *anginal equivalent*.

Precipitating factors: A key feature of classic angina pectoris is its precipitation by exercise or any other condition that increases myocardial oxygen consumption. This relationship directly reflects the underlying pathophysiology of coronary artery atherosclerotic obstruction and the resulting myocardial ischemia. Myocardial oxygen demand outstrips oxygen supply when coronary blood flow is limited because of an arterial lesion that causes significant obstruction. The resultant cellular ischemia unleashes a cascade of events that alter cell function at the molecular, biochemical, electrical, and mechanical levels. For the clinician at the bedside, these changes translate into the subjective symptoms of angina pectoris. The most common provocateurs of this supply-demand imbalance are physical exertion (including isometric stress), exposure to cold, emotional upset, excitement, fear, and frustration. These factors increase one or more of the major determinants of myocardial oxygen consumption: heart rate, contractile state of the myocardium, or ventricular wall tension (which is, in turn, related to ventricular pressure and volume).

Although the conditions causing angina pectoris vary widely from patient to patient, they tend to be reproducible in any given individual. No matter how characteristic of angina the description of discomfort may be or how classic its location, the failure to elicit a relationship between the symptom and a reproducible provocation is cause to question the diagnosis of underlying significant coronary artery disease. When a clear relationship exists, the term *classic angina pectoris* is commonly used. When no such relationship can be established with confidence, the somewhat nondescript term *atypical angina* is now customarily used. Surprisingly, such a distinction carries prognostic significance.

Variant angina: *Variant angina* is a comparatively rare and specific form of angina that occurs at rest or sometimes following exertion and must be distinguished from atypical angina. Variant angina was first recognized by Myron Prinzmetal and is often referred to as *Prinzmetal's angina*. Variant angina results from intense vasospasm of a coronary artery (either normal or partially diseased) that produces transmural ischemia and as a consequence is characterized by ST-segment elevation rather than ST depression on the electrocardiogram recorded during the ischemic episode. Because the vasospasm interrupts the myocardial supply of oxygen but does not alter oxygen demand, variant angina invariably occurs at rest. These vasospastic episodes are thought to represent transient neurohumoral imbalances and tend to be cyclical, often recurring at the same time of day in a given person. It is this temporal constancy of angina at rest, often occurring in a person who has few risk factors for coronary atherosclerosis, that should alert the clinician to the diagnosis of variant angina. Although responsive to coronary vasodilators, such as nitroglycerin or calcium channel blockers, the resulting myocardial ischemia can lead to very unstable syndromes including acute myocardial infarction.

Angina that is not angina: Several distinguishing features can help determine when a patient's chest pain is not angina. Nonanginal chest pain is rarely, if ever, reliably provoked or related to effort. Usually it is described as sharp, stabbing, influenced by respiration, and located laterally over the precordium. Often this nonanginal chest pain lasts for hours or even days and may be described as being worse at the "end of a hard day." Its origin is most likely related to underlying anxiety.

Differential diagnosis: Probably more important than the identification of nonanginal chest pain is the clinical challenge of recognizing anginalike chest pain caused by conditions other than underlying coronary artery disease. There are five clinical entities leading the list of thoracic conditions that should be considered as alternative explanations for apparent angina: (1) hypertrophic cardiomyopathy, (2) aortic valvular stenosis, (3) acute myocarditis, (4) acute pericarditis, and (5) costochondritis.

The first two conditions can indeed cause classic angina pectoris due to oxygen supply-demand imbalance consequent to cardiac hypertrophy, even without coronary obstruction. However, each has telltale physical findings that should surface during the physical examination. Acute myocarditis and pericarditis usually are associated with a recent viral infection, tend to have a pleuritic (respiration-related) component to the pain, and have electrocardiographic features that are often readily distinguished from those of transient ischemia. Acute and chronic costochondritis, also called Tietze's syndrome, will escape detection unless the clinician compresses the sternochondral junctions. Point tenderness over these joints is the distinguishing feature of Tietze's syndrome.

Because cardiac pain can be referred to the upper epigastrium as well as to the back, certain gastrointestinal disorders also enter into the differential diagnosis of coronary artery disease. Chief among these are peptic ulcer disease, esophageal disorders, and gallbladder disease.

Stratification of angina pectoris: Although angina pectoris may be pathognomonic of underlying coronary artery disease, it remains a subjective complaint limited by all the shortcomings of human communication. The patient may not describe the symptoms clearly or the examiner may not correctly understand all the nuances and subtleties of what the patient says. There is considerable wisdom in adopting the practice of stratifying one's opinion regarding the certainty of the diagnosis. After taking a history that suggests ischemic pain, it is helpful to grade one's interpretation according to the following: *definite angina* is reserved for those patients who give a description that is classic; *probable angina* describes patients in whom most but not all of the features of classic angina are present; *probably not angina* refers to chest pain complaints in which some but not many features of angina are present; or *definitely not angina* applies to patients in whom none of the features suggestive of angina are present.

In addition to having proved its prognostic significance in a recent large multicenter clinical trial, this stratagem is noteworthy because it precludes the category of "possible angina." Since all things are possible, this category serves as nothing more than a wastebasket for the indecisive. It has been established, for example, that a middle-aged man with definite angina has an 89% likelihood of having significant coronary artery narrowing (stenosis greater than 70% of the diameter) in at least one major epicardial artery at the time of coronary angiography. On the other hand, a middle-aged woman with probably not angina has only a 6% likelihood of having the same finding when evaluated with arteriography.

Functional Classification

In addition to using a grading scale for the likelihood of underlying coronary artery disease, a semiquantitative way of assessing the severity of angina is extremely practical. Although the severity of angina symptoms correlates poorly

Table 17
**Grade scale of angina according to activity
(Canadian Cardiovascular Society)**

I. "Ordinary physical activity does not cause ... angina."
Ordinary activity includes walking and climbing stairs.
Angina occurs with strenuous, rapid, or prolonged exertion
at work or recreation.

II. "Slight limitation of ordinary activity." Angina occurs from
walking or climbing stairs rapidly; walking uphill; walking
or stair climbing after meals, in cold, in wind, or under emotional stress, or only during the few hours after awakening.
Walking more than two blocks on the level and climbing
more than one flight of ordinary stairs at a normal pace
and in normal conditions causes angina.

III. "Marked limitation of ordinary physical activity." Walking
one to two blocks on the level and climbing one flight of
stairs in normal conditions and at normal pace causes
angina.

IV. "Inability to carry on any physical activity without discomfort – anginal syndrome may be present at rest."

Source: Campeau L. Grading of angina pectoris. *Circulation*. 1976;54:522.

with the extent of underlying coronary artery
disease in any individual patient, it is the severity
of symptoms that often dictates the therapeutic
options. The more incapacitated the patient, the
more expansive and aggressive the therapy
should be. The Canadian Cardiovascular Society
has devised a practical means of grading a
patient's angina according to the simple activity
scale outlined in Table 17. It is important to note
that the prognosis of a patient is influenced more
by the stability of the angina than its intensity.
Using this scale, it is evident that the patient with
grade IV intensity is in more urgent need of relief
than the patient with mild grade I or II symptoms.
However, the change in the frequency of the
anginal episodes, even though they are of grade I
or II intensity, is what predicts future adverse
events. When chronic stable angina develops a
crescendo pattern, becoming more frequent in
occurrence, occurring at rest, or characterized by
episodes that persist for longer than 20 minutes,
the term *unstable angina* is used. There is now
ample evidence that patients exhibiting the
characteristics of unstable angina are three times
more likely to have an adverse cardiovascular
event, such as acute myocardial infarction or even

death within the following 3 months, than patients
whose symptoms are more stable. For this reason,
patients with unstable angina are considered
prime candidates for urgent revascularization
procedures.

Reports of detailed angiographic and angios-
copic studies in which coronary artery lumens are
directly visualized (see the section on Cardiac
Catheterization, page 107) have suggested that the
coronary lesion in unstable angina is complex,
with platelet plugs superimposed on the atherosclerotic plaque. Particularly in patients with
angina at rest, the mechanism of unstable angina
is not always related to increases in myocardial
oxygen demand but may result from transiently
decreased oxygen supply due to platelet plugs,
coronary spasm, or both.

Perhaps the most serious form of unstable angina is that which develops in patients who have
just experienced an acute myocardial infarction.
The development of postinfarction angina during
the recovery phase carries an ominous prognosis.

Silent Ischemia
Some patients with functionally severe coronary
disease may have significant ischemia without
any pain. Most such patients are thought to have a
faulty warning system; this condition is more
common among diabetics. These patients are often
referred to as having *silent ischemia*, but it is still
uncommon for patients with repeated episodes of
ischemia not to experience angina during at least
some episodes. The converse situation is far more
common, ie, patients with known coronary disease
and angina have been documented to have ischemic episodes that are not always accompanied
by pain. In addition, nearly 50% of the ischemic
ST-segment depressions on ECG recorded during
exercise tests of patients with chronic angina
are not accompanied by pain. The significance
of these episodes of silent ischemia remains
to be established and is an area of intense
research interest.

Prior Myocardial Infarction

Although medical records continue to be the accepted means of establishing the occurrence of a prior myocardial infarction, the physician should not overlook the fact that as many as 80% of patients accurately recount myocardial infarction as part of their history. Because acute infarction rarely occurs in the absence of underlying coronary artery disease, a previous infarction becomes an important marker for the presence of coronary artery disease. In this subset of patients, questions relating to an assessment of ventricular function are of particular importance. The presence of exertional dyspnea in a patient who describes angina pectoris implies significant ventricular dysfunction. Because a prior myocardial infarction is likely to have resulted in a myocardial scar, significant congestive symptoms suggest a markedly reduced ejection fraction. The status of left ventricular function is the most important prognostic indicator in the patient with coronary artery disease. The presence of congestive symptoms and the absence of a history of infarction strongly suggest the occurrence of global ischemia in a patient with angina pectoris. This finding should alert the examiner to the presence of diffuse disease of all three major coronary arteries or left main coronary artery disease. In addition, exertion-induced congestive symptoms without chest discomfort may be another example of an anginal equivalent and indicate transient global ischemia.

The Physical Examination

The presence of coronary artery disease impacts little, and frequently not at all, on the results of a general physical examination; results of the physical examination may be entirely normal in a patient with coronary artery disease. It is important, however, to document abnormalities known to have an association with coronary disease, such as elevated blood pressure and diminished regional pulses and vascular bruits (suggestive of peripheral vascular disease), retinal abnormalities, premature arcus senilis, and the presence of xanthomata.

There are no cardiac findings specific for coronary artery disease, although the sequelae of a prior myocardial infarction may be in evidence. These sequelae can range from cardiomegaly to an ectopic precordial pulsation or the presence of a mid- or late-systolic murmur of mitral regurgitation that suggests the presence of papillary muscle dysfunction. A fourth heart sound (S_4), although common in coronary artery disease, is so ubiquitous in the adult population that its presence is of little value. Few data support the idea that the absence of a fourth heart sound makes the diagnosis of coronary disease unlikely.

The transient findings that surface during an episode of ischemia are potentially helpful in making the diagnosis. The most helpful of these is the appearance of a mid- or late-systolic murmur of mitral regurgitation during an episode of chest discomfort, indicating transient papillary muscle dysfunction. More subtle but common is the transient development of paradoxical splitting of the second heart sound during an episode of angina. This variation of second heart sound splitting is attributable to left ventricular dysfunction that results from the transient ischemic episode.

The physical examination of the patient suffering from an acute myocardial infarction is of critical importance for risk stratification and for choosing therapeutic options, but it is only of minor importance in making the diagnosis of coronary artery disease. Initially it is of great importance to establish the presence or absence of cardiogenic shock. Cardiogenic shock has various definitions, but its essential features are reduced blood pressure (often defined as less than 90 mm Hg systolic), decreased urinary output, and other evidence of organ hypoperfusion that reflects a seriously diminished cardiac output not attributable to hypovolemia. Cardiogenic shock is an indication that a critical mass of the left ventricle (usually more than 35%) has been damaged; the expected mortality rate is about 80%. Aside from this grave situation, any evidence of overt left ventricular failure with pulmonary rales in more than the lower third of the lung combined with acute infarction also indicates a poor prognosis. Elevated jugular venous pressure in the absence of other signs of overt congestive heart failure often indicates an associated right ventricular infarction. This finding has therapeutic implications, because such patients often require abundant amounts of intravenous fluids to maintain an adequate left ventricular output. Patients with right ventricular infarction are particularly sensitive to nitrates and other vasodilating drugs that are often given in the early stages of acute infarction; such agents may cause profound hypotension in these patients.

An Overview of the Diagnostic Process

Following a detailed history and physical examination, a variety of diagnostic laboratory tests may be used to confirm and extend the initial clinical diagnostic impression. In some cases, the information obtained from the different laboratory techniques overlaps to a substantial degree. For example, an ECG recorded during an episode of chest pain may reveal changes characteristic of myocardial ischemia, or an ECG recorded during the stress of treadmill exercise may reveal changes diagnostic of ischemia that were not present on the resting electrocardiogram. Additionally, global and regional left ventricular contractile function may be accurately assessed with echocardiography, angiography, radionuclide techniques, computed tomography (CT), and nuclear magnetic resonance (NMR) imaging. This redundancy of information requires the clinician to choose judiciously the appropriate diagnostic method for each particular clinical situation.

When choosing a diagnostic approach, several important factors must be considered:

- What is the specific clinical question to be answered? (Does the patient have coronary artery disease? How extensive is the disease? Has left ventricular function been affected?)
- What are the relative costs of the various techniques?
- What are the risks of morbidity and mortality associated with the diagnostic procedure?
- Will the results of the particular diagnostic test reduce the need for other potentially more risky or costly procedures?
- Will the information obtained from a particular diagnostic test alter subsequent management?

Certainly the answer to this last question must serve as the ultimate guide in choosing among the large number of tests available to the clinician caring for the patient with coronary artery disease. Diagnostic testing is difficult to justify without some certainty that the test results will alter the clinician's approach to the patient, whether this entails further diagnostic testing or deciding on a therapeutic option.

When choosing among a variety of somewhat redundant diagnostic tests, it is important to consider the positive and negative predictive values of these tests when used in different patient populations. For example, middle-aged men who have a variety of potent risk factors for coronary artery disease and symptoms strongly suggestive of ischemia have a high probability but not a certainty of having coronary artery disease. At the other end of the spectrum, young women who have no risk factors and whose symptoms are atypical of coronary artery disease have a low probability of having significant coronary atherosclerosis; however, on rare occasions even these patients have significant coronary disease. How can diagnostic testing help apply these probabilities and best serve the needs of patients? To choose an appropriate test for any patient, the clinician should understand the test's predictive values, which are calculated by applying Bayes' theorem to the prevalence of the disease and the sensitivity and specificity of the test.

Prevalence, Sensitivity, and Specificity

An estimate is needed of the number of people with coronary artery disease in a population with characteristics (sex, age, risk factors) similar to those of the particular patient under evaluation. These prevalence data are often referred to as the *prior* or *pretest probability of disease.*

Sensitivity is defined as the proportion of patients with a particular disease whose diagnostic test result is positive. Sensitivity is calculated by dividing the number of patients with a disease whose test result is positive (the true positives) by all patients with the disease (the true positives plus those who falsely had a negative test, ie, the false-negatives):

$$\text{sensitivity} = \frac{\text{true positives}}{\text{true positives} + \text{false-negatives}}$$

Specificity is defined as the proportion of patients without the disease whose test result is negative. Specificity is calculated by dividing the number of patients free of disease whose test result is negative (the true negatives) by all patients without the disease (the true negatives plus the false-positives):

$$\text{specificity} = \frac{\text{true negatives}}{\text{true negatives} + \text{false-positives}}$$

Given the sensitivity and specificity of the test as well as the prevalence of the disease, the probability of disease indicated by a positive or negative test result can be approximated. These are the positive and negative predictive values of the test, sometimes called the posttest probabilities. The positive predictive value is the probability that a patient who has a positive test result truly has the disease:

$$\text{positive predictive value} =$$

$$\frac{\text{true positives}}{\text{true positives} + \text{false-positives}}$$

The negative predictive value is the probability that a patient who has a negative test result is truly disease-free:

$$\text{negative predictive value} =$$

$$\frac{\text{true negatives}}{\text{true negatives} + \text{false-negatives}}$$

The importance of knowing the prevalence of disease in a population with characteristics similar to the patient in question cannot be over-emphasized. Table 18 lists the positive and negative predictive values for a diagnostic test that has 90% sensitivity and 90% specificity in three different patient populations: one with 5% prevalence of disease before the test is done (eg, young women with atypical symptoms), one with 90% prevalence (eg, middle-aged men with typical symptoms and multiple risk factors), and one with 50% prevalence. As Table 18 demonstrates, the predictive value of a positive or negative test result varies dramatically, according to the prevalence of disease in different populations. In the low-prevalence population, the predictive value of a negative test result is high, whereas the predictive value of a positive test result is low (ie, many false-positives occur). Conversely, in the high-prevalence population, the predictive value of a positive test result is high, whereas the predictive value of a negative result is low, because many negative results are false-negatives. It is in the population with intermediate prevalence that the discriminatory power of the test is greatest. Note that this variation in diagnostic value with variations in the prevalence of the disease occurs despite apparently excellent test sensitivity and specificity.

Although constructs such as Bayes' theorem are only as useful as the sensitivity, specificity, and prevalence data on which they are based, they do supply a structure for evaluating which diagnostic tests should be used for various patient populations.

Thus, evaluating the diagnostic utility of a particular test requires consideration of test sensitivity and specificity as well as the prevalence of the disease in a population with characteristics simi-

Table 18
The effect of prior probability (prevalence) of disease on predictive values of a positive or negative result of a test with 90% sensitivity and 90% specificity

	Population with 5% prevalence		Population with 50% prevalence		Population with 90% prevalence	
Total subjects	1000		1000		1000	
	50 with disease	950 without disease	500 with disease	500 without disease	900 with disease	100 without disease
Test results	TP:45 FN:5	FP:95 TN:855	TP:450 FN:50	FP:50 TN:450	TP:810 FN:90	FP:10 TN:90
Predictive value of a positive test	$\dfrac{45}{45+95}=32\%$		$\dfrac{450}{450+50}=90\%$		$\dfrac{810}{810+10}=99\%$	
Predictive value of a negative test	$\dfrac{855}{855+5}=99\%$		$\dfrac{450}{450+50}=90\%$		$\dfrac{90}{90+90}=50\%$	

Abbreviations: FN, false-negative result; FP, false-positive result; TN, true negative result; TP, true positive result.

lar to the patient under study. Without these minimal pieces of information, the diagnostic process can be difficult, redundant, needlessly costly, risky, and sometimes misleading.

The Electrocardiogram

The Resting ECG Tracing

The electrocardiogram tracing obtained at rest on a patient with coronary artery disease frequently demonstrates a normal pattern or manifests abnormalities that are not specific for ischemia. Therefore, the resting ECG tracing is an insensitive marker of coronary artery disease.

The most reliable ECG findings indicative of coronary artery disease are Q-wave abnormalities that appear as the result of a myocardial infarction. (A normal electrocardiogram pattern is shown in Figure 22.) Q-wave abnormalities represent the electrical death of cells across a variable width of myocardium extending outward from the subendocardial layer. Electrical silence in these areas produces alterations in the initial QRS forces. The early (first 0.04 second) QRS vectors tend to point away from the infarcted zone and toward the areas of muscle that are still viable. Thus, the characteristic pattern of an inferior wall myocardial infarction is the occurrence of Q waves in leads II, III, and aVF (Figure 23). An anterior wall infarction is characterized by Q waves in leads V_1, V_2, and V_3 (Figure 24), and an anterolateral wall infarction produces Q waves in leads I, aVL, and V_4 to V_6 (Figure 25). These "infarct patterns" cannot be considered pathognomonic for coronary artery disease, however, because they also occur in patients with certain cardiomyopathies.

It is well known that Q waves resulting from a prior myocardial infarction may disappear over time. This disappearance is particularly true of inferior infarctions; in as many as a third of patients, the diagnostic Q waves become less evident and disappear within a year or two after the infarction. Q waves indicative of a prior anterior infarction

Figure 22
Normal electrocardiogram pattern

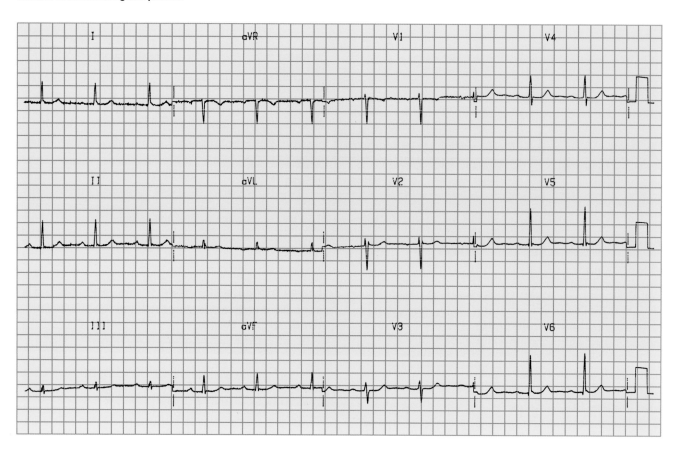

Figure 23
Typical electrocardiogram pattern in inferior myocardial infarction

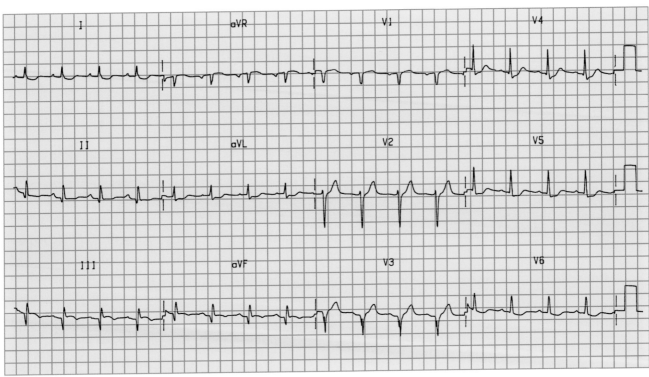

Deep 0.04-second Q waves are present in leads II, III, and aVF.
ST depressions also appear in leads I, aVL, V_4, V_5, and V_6 indicating ischemia in the anterolateral wall as well.

Figure 24
Typical electrocardiogram pattern in anterior myocardial infarction

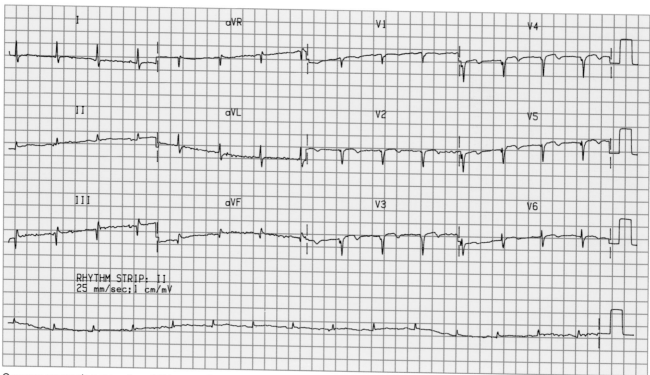

Q waves measuring more than 0.04 second are present in
leads V₁, V₂, V₃, and V₄, indicating an extensive area of anterior
wall infarction.

Figure 25
Typical electrocardiogram pattern in anterolateral myocardial infarction

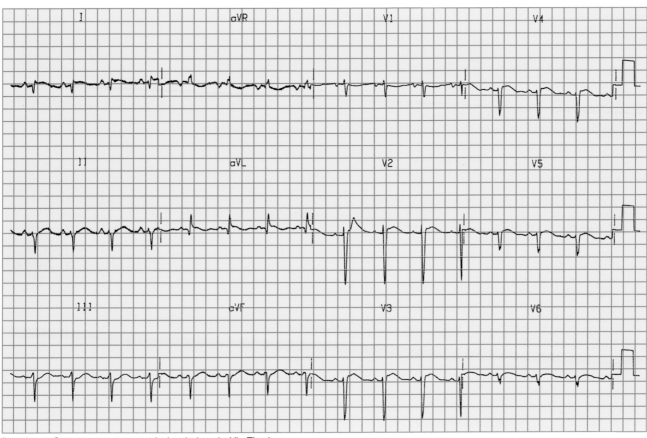

Prominent Q waves are present in leads I and aVL. The low-amplitude R waves in leads V_3, V_4, V_5, and V_6 are also characteristic of anterolateral infarction.

are less likely to disappear and usually remain until a second infarction occurs on the opposite (posterior) wall. This loss of the Q wave is attributed to opposing electrical forces that cancel each other on the ECG recording.

Coronary artery disease may also result in permanent T-wave inversions and ST-segment depressions that are not necessarily associated with QRS abnormalities. Because these findings occur under many other conditions, they are highly nonspecific. In contrast, ST-segment elevation suggests myocardial scar or aneurysm secondary to previous infarction.

The ECG During Angina

The recording of an ECG during an actual episode of anginal chest discomfort (typical of that which the patient has been experiencing) is one of the most expeditious and helpful noninvasive tests that can be performed. Ischemic changes may be manifested by abnormalities in the T wave or ST segment.

T-wave abnormalities: The subendocardial (innermost) layer of the myocardium is the area most vulnerable to ischemia, because it is farthest removed from the nutrient coronary vessels that lie on the epicardial surface of the heart. When mild to moderate ischemia occurs in the subendocardial region, the mean T-wave vector shifts away from the area of limited perfusion, and the ECG leads corresponding to this region show inverted T waves. When the ischemia is more severe, the T-wave vector points toward the area of limited perfusion, and the ECG leads corresponding to this region then show peaked T waves.

ST-segment abnormalities: ST segments may be similarly depressed or elevated in myocardial ischemia, depending on the severity and extent of the ischemia. ST segments become depressed when blood flow is reduced in the subendocardial region, whereas ST segments become elevated when blood flow is reduced across the full thickness of the myocardium (transmural reduction). Transient elevations of the ST segments at rest, which are usually but not invariably accompanied by anginal pain, indicate coronary vasospasm that can occur either alone or in combination with obstructive coronary artery disease.

ECG Exercise Testing

Just as acute changes occur in the ECG pattern during spontaneous attacks of angina pectoris while the patient is at rest, similar reversible changes can be precipitated by exercise that may or may not be associated with angina pectoris. The classic response to ischemia during the exercise test is ST-segment depression. The most commonly used definition for a positive finding on ECG exercise testing is a horizontal or downward ST-segment depression that is equal to or greater than 1 mm and lasts for at least 0.08 second, as compared with the resting value (TP or PQ segment) (Figure 26). When the resting ST segments are abnormal, an additional 1 mm of ST-segment depression or elevation is required during exercise testing for the result to be considered positive. Correlations between an abnormal (positive) test and the presence of coronary disease determined either angiographically or by clinical follow-up are best expressed by the sensitivity, specificity, and predictive value of the test.

It should be readily apparent that the sensitivity and specificity of the exercise ECG stress test can be altered by varying the criteria for what constitutes a positive finding. For example, if a positive response is defined as a 3-mm ST-segment depression rather than a 1-mm depression, the probability is high that all persons with positive responses will indeed have significant coronary artery disease. Although this approach greatly increases the specificity of the stress test, it substantially reduces the sensitivity because fewer patients with coronary disease will be detected. Conversely, the application of less stringent criteria would increase sensitivity but decrease specificity. Note that many other exercise test variables, such as total duration of exercise, the time to onset of ischemic ST-segment changes, the number of leads in which ischemic ST segments appear, the occurrence of chest pain, and exercise-induced decreases in blood pressure, have also

Figure 26
Characteristic ST-segment changes in response to exercise

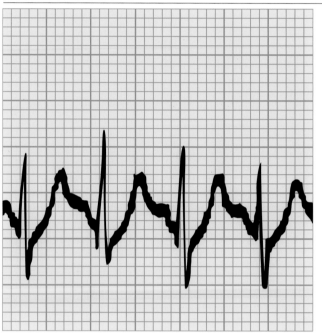

A

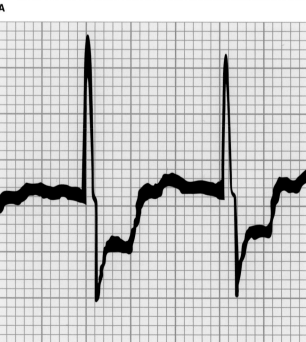

B

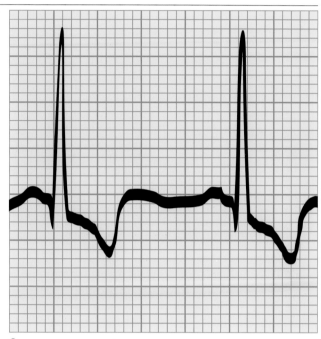

C

(A) This pattern shows the normal response associated with a heart rate of 170 beats per minute in a healthy subject.
(B) A 5-mm horizontal ST-segment depression indicates marked ischemia at a heart rate of 95 beats per minute.

(C) This downsloping ST-segment depression indicates persistent ischemia 6 minutes after exercise when the heart rate had returned to 72 beats per minute.

Table 19
Predictive value of positive and negative responses to exercise testing in a large population study

History	Sex	N	Prevalence of coronary artery disease (%)	Predictive value (%)	
				Positive ECG response	Negative ECG response
Definite angina	M	620	89	96	35
Definite angina	F	98	62	73	67
Probable angina	M	594	70	87	56
Probable angina	F	240	40	54	78
Nonischemic pain	M	251	22	39	86
Nonischemic pain	F	242	5	6	95

With increasing disease prevalence, the predictive value of a positive response to the exercise test increases and that of a negative response decreases. The opposite occurs as disease prevalence decreases.

For purposes of this analysis "probably not" and "definitely not" angina groups were pooled under the term "nonischemic pain" (see text).

been identified as indicators of disease and represent prognostic information. Nonetheless, the ST-segment response is still the most commonly accepted standard by which the significance of a diagnostic exercise test is judged.

The predictive value of any test that is *not* 100% sensitive and specific is influenced by the statistical laws of conditional probability (Bayes' theorem). This has been clearly illustrated in a large clinical trial involving 2045 subjects with chest pain who were categorized as having definite angina, probable angina, probably not angina, or definitely not angina. In this group of patients with bothersome chest pain, who are representative of patients a clinician would probably subject to stress testing for additional information, the prevalence of coronary disease was 67% among men and 28% among women. Although the predic-

tive value of a positive response was 88% for the men who had a high prevalence of coronary disease, it was only 46% for women, as might be predicted from their lower prevalence of coronary disease. Expressed in terms of risk, these data indicate that men were 2.4 times more likely than women to have coronary artery disease.

Among the men, a history of definite angina was highly predictive of coronary artery disease (89% prevalence), and a positive response to exercise testing had a high predictive value (96%) for coronary disease as confirmed by angiography. A negative response in these men was associated with a lower but still substantial likelihood of coronary artery disease (65%), which can also be expressed as a predictive value of a negative response of 35% (Table 19). In women with a history of definite angina, 62% had coronary artery disease, and the chance that coronary artery disease would be found increased to 73% when the exercise test response was positive. However, coronary artery disease was also found in 33% of women with a negative response and definite angina (a negative predictive value of 67%). In both men and women, the percentage of false-positive responses increased as the history of chest pain became more atypical (Table 19).

Studies such as this point out some of the limitations in the ability of exercise stress testing (and other noninvasive tests) to predict the presence or absence of coronary disease. As indicated in Table 18, when testing persons from a population in which the prevalence of the disease is high (eg, those with definite angina), a positive response is likely to indicate the presence of disease, whereas a negative response is more likely to be falsely negative. In contrast, when testing persons from a population in which the prevalence of disease is low (eg, those with probably not angina), a negative response is likely to indicate the absence of disease, and a positive response is more likely to be falsely positive.

In addition to disease prevalence, other factors influence the rates of false-positive and false-negative responses when exercise testing is used to diagnose coronary artery disease. False-positive responses may be caused by heart disease, hypertension, administration of digitalis and antiarrhythmic agents, hypokalemia, bundle branch block, left ventricular hypertrophy, mitral valve prolapse, and the preexcitation syndrome. Patients with these conditions seem ideally suited for exercise radionuclide studies or other methods of noninvasive testing.

Patients with prior myocardial infarctions may have false-negative responses (ie, the presence of coronary disease is not detected) because healed infarctions leave residual scars in which there is no remaining viable myocardium that can become ischemic. However, the most common cause for a false-negative response to exercise testing is failure to achieve adequate stress (aerobic demand). In healthy subjects, a false-negative response can be avoided by requiring the heart rate to increase to 85% of its maximum predicted value. A helpful rule of thumb for calculating the maximum predicted heart rate is to subtract the patient's age from 220, an empirical constant. For most patients, the duration of exercise is determined by the development of adverse symptoms, such as the onset of severe angina, significant shortness of breath, a fall in systolic blood pressure, or muscle fatigue. A workload equivalent to 6.5 METs provides adequate stress for most patients. (1 MET = energy expenditure at rest, equivalent to an oxygen uptake of approximately 3.5 mL O_2 per kg body weight per minute.) If such levels of stress are not attained during exercise testing and objective evidence of ischemia is not seen, the test is probably inadequate.

Ambulatory ECG Monitoring

Continuous ECG monitoring in ambulatory patients for 48 hours or longer is now commonplace. Although initially devised to quantitate the frequency and nature of cardiac arrhythmias, this technology has now developed to the point where ischemic ST-segment changes can be recorded reliably. Ambulatory monitoring has shown that patients with known coronary artery disease and typical angina pectoris have a surprising number of episodes of ischemic ST-segment changes not associated with symptoms of angina. These episodes of silent ischemia may account for as many as 75% of all ischemic episodes recorded in patients with known disease. The long-term significance of ischemic ST-segment depressions recorded by ambulatory ECG monitoring has not been clinically established and clearly will be influenced by whether data are recorded from symptomatic or asymptomatic populations.

Radiographic Techniques

Chest Roentgenography

The chest roentgenogram is the oldest and continues to be the most widely available method of cardiac imaging. Although to some extent superseded by the powerful noninvasive techniques of echocardiography, radionuclide imaging, computed tomography (CT), and nuclear magnetic resonance

(NMR) imaging, routine chest radiography can still offer substantial insights into the management of patients with coronary artery disease. Although routine chest roentgenography is not useful in the diagnosis of coronary artery disease, it may offer important information on chronic ischemia-related left ventricular dysfunction and the state of the pulmonary vasculature.

Cardiac evaluation by chest roentgenography is usually based on posteroanterior (Figure 27) and lateral images. By combining information gained from these views, the size and configuration of all four cardiac chambers can be estimated. Other imaging techniques, particularly echocardiography, CT, and NMR, offer more reliable information on the sizes of the individual chambers than chest roentgenography. Nonetheless, cardiomegaly detected from chest roentgenograms is a potent predictor of poor outcome in patients with coronary artery disease.

Chest roentgenograms in patients with chronic stable angina frequently demonstrate completely normal heart size and pulmonary vasculature. Acute severe myocardial ischemia may produce roentgenographic evidence of heart failure (ie, congestion of the lungs caused by elevated pulmonary venous pressure from elevated left atrial and left ventricular diastolic pressures) with or without cardiomegaly. Acute ischemia of lesser severity usually causes no abnormalities detectable on standard chest roentgenograms.

Abnormal deposition of calcium in regions of old myocardial infarction may occasionally appear as radiopaque areas on chest roentgenograms. Occasionally, calcification of atherosclerotic plaque in a diseased coronary artery may be seen on plain film; however, cardiac fluoroscopy is usually required to visualize coronary calcifications. Even when detected on cardiac fluoroscopy,

Figure 27
Appearance of a normal heart on posteroanterior chest roentgenogram

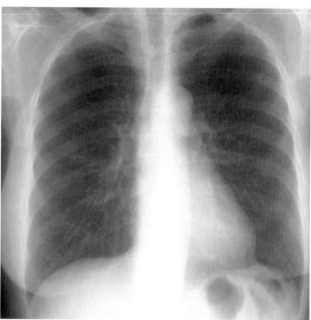

Courtesy of Dr William Stanford, Department of Radiology, The University of Iowa.

coronary artery calcification may not predict significant coronary obstruction; thus, coronary calcification is not useful as a screening procedure for coronary artery disease.

Two chest roentgenographic patterns in chronic ischemic left ventricular dysfunction are noteworthy. An abnormal configuration of the left ventricular border on the posteroanterior chest film implies the presence of an aneurysm that formed as a result of prior myocardial infarction (Figure 28). A dilated left ventricle associated with chronic abnormalities of pulmonary vasculature indicates previous massive myocardial infarction or repeated smaller infarctions.

In addition to being useful in the situations just cited, chest roentgenography serves an important purpose in identifying coexistent pulmonary disease from a variety of causes in patients with coronary artery disease.

Cardiac Catheterization

Coronary angiography: The current gold standard for the diagnosis of coronary artery disease is its angiographic demonstration following the selective injection of radiopaque contrast medium into the ostia of the left and right coronary arteries via cardiac catheterization. The technique was pioneered in the late 1950s and early 1960s, most notably by Sones and by Judkins, and stands as one of the most important advances in diagnostic cardiology over the past half century.

High-energy fields intensify the sharply focused fluoroscopic images produced by heat-protected x-ray tubes and powerful generators, which makes it possible to adequately visualize coronary vessels as small as 200 µm in diameter. These images are recorded simultaneously on high-resolution video screens and fine-grain 35-mm cinefilm, allowing the physician to study the basic recordings in a variety of ways. Inspection of a coronary artery on instant replay often provides a reasonable estimate of the patency of a major epicardial

Figure 28
Posteroanterior chest roentgenogram of a patient with a left ventricular aneurysm

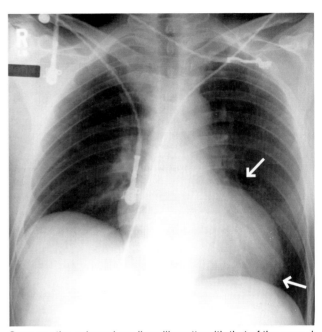

Compare the enlarged cardiac silhouette with that of the normal heart in Figure 27. Also note the prominent bulge along the left heart border (between the arrows); this is the roentgenographic appearance of the aneurysm.

Courtesy of Dr William Stanford, Department of Radiology, The University of Iowa.

Figure 29
Angiogram of the left coronary artery in a normal subject, right anterior oblique projection

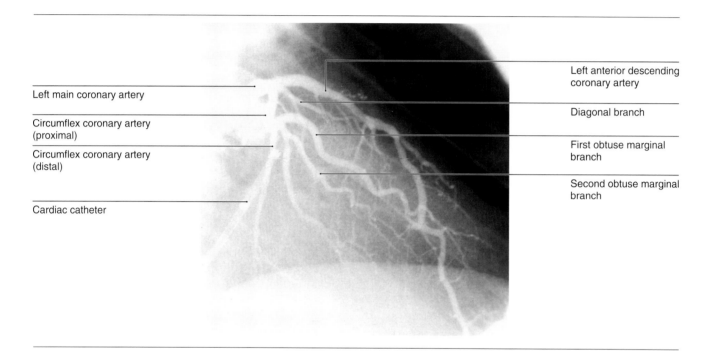

Left main coronary artery

Circumflex coronary artery (proximal)

Circumflex coronary artery (distal)

Cardiac catheter

Left anterior descending coronary artery

Diagonal branch

First obtuse marginal branch

Second obtuse marginal branch

artery (Figure 29) and the degree of obstruction of any of its major segments (Figure 30), as well as the presence of coronary collaterals. This capability has created the entirely new field of therapeutic or interventional cardiology. This field involves balloon dilatation (or PTCA) of obstructive lesions and other techniques for managing obstructive coronary disease. On repeated viewings of the cinefilm images taken in multiple views, it is possible to define the precise anatomic location of lesions obstructing the major coronary arteries and their important branches.

Simple visual estimates of the severity of stenotic lesions in terms of percent diameter stenosis (ie, the percent reduction of the arterial lumen at its narrowest point compared with a presumably normal segment) exhibit considerable intra- and interobserver variability. In addition, evidence from experimental animal studies and clinical trials in humans suggests that visual estimates of percent diameter stenosis may not reliably indicate the actual functional significance of a lesion. This finding has led to the required practice of using at least some caliper method of quantitating lesion severity. Digital computer image enhancement and analysis are now widely available, and quantitative angiography is becoming more common. Quantitative angiographic methods use such techniques as automated deter-

Figure 30
Angiogram of the left coronary artery in a patient with a discrete high-grade narrowing in the proximal left anterior descending coronary artery

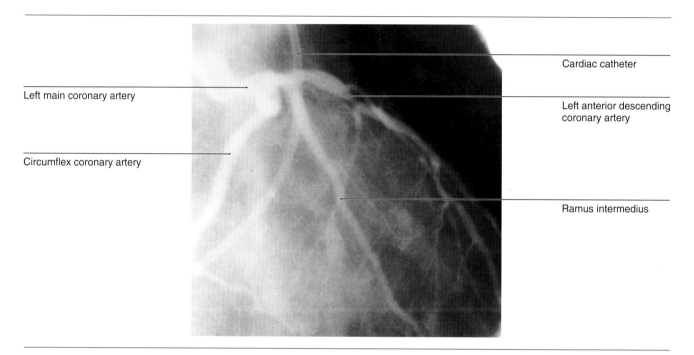

Left main coronary artery

Circumflex coronary artery

Cardiac catheter

Left anterior descending coronary artery

Ramus intermedius

mination of arterial contours and the principles of fluid dynamics to more precisely and accurately determine the hydraulic significance of a given stenosis. Invasive and noninvasive estimates of physiologic (not merely anatomic) severity of coronary stenoses are also being more widely used. For example, estimates of regional decrements in myocardial perfusion or coronary flow reserve offer important information concerning the functional significance of a lesion, information not apparent from angiographic anatomic analysis alone.

The success of coronary revascularization, whether with bypass surgery or with interventional catheter techniques, depends on accurate anatomic information that, in turn, is directly related to the skills of the angiographer performing the catheterization, the skills of the physician interpreting the angiograms, and the quality of the equipment used to record and process the images.

It is only with a comprehensive knowledge of the normal coronary anatomy that the physician can identify a missing vessel, ie, one that is not visualized because of a total occlusion or high-grade lesion at the origin of a branch of one of the major epicardial arteries. Because the number of diseased vessels is a major determinant of a patient's "natural history" and the prognosis often relates to lesion location (such as the left main coronary artery), it is crucial that a severe lesion not be overlooked.

Coronary angiography provides the physician with an extraordinarily powerful diagnostic tool. However, the problems and limitations inherent in this technique must be completely understood.

There are risks associated with the procedure, and the magnitude of those risks is related to the experience and skill of the person performing the angiography. Overall, coronary angiography is (and should be) safe. The risk to life should average less than 0.2%, and the risk of major adverse effects (for example, stroke, myocardial infarction, or major bleeding) should be less than 0.5%. However, certain patients are at higher risk and can be identified before catheterization or during visualization of the coronary arteries. The elderly are at highest risk, especially elderly women and patients who have decompensated congestive heart failure. Other patients at increased risk for complications during coronary angiography include patients with critical left main coronary stenosis, severe three-vessel disease (> 90% stenosis in each of the three major coronary arteries), multivessel disease with left ventricular dysfunction (ejection fraction < 35%), or critical aortic valve stenosis. Despite a higher risk of complications in these patients, the risk-benefit ratio may be favorable if angiography is required to make an appropriate therapeutic decision.

It is important to emphasize that coronary angiography does not provide direct information about the patient's functional capacity and symptoms (ie, the functional significance of a particular coronary lesion). Thus, the demonstration of significant coronary stenosis should be viewed as an anatomical finding to be correlated with the clinical features and coronary physiology of the individual patient. Measurements of coronary flow and flow reserve (the ratio of coronary flow during maximal dilation to flow at rest) in animal studies suggest that a diameter narrowing of at least 50% is required for a lesion to have functional significance (Figure 31). However, the presence of 50% diameter stenosis serves as only a rough guideline for the clinical interpretation of

Figure 31
The relationship of resting and maximal coronary flow in animal models of coronary stenosis

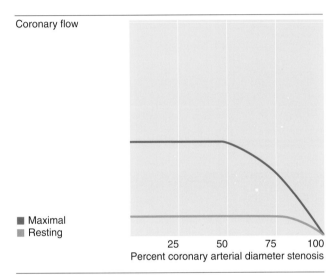

The difference between resting and maximal flow (which may be obtained by exercise or pharmacologic vasodilation) is termed coronary flow reserve. Note that maximal flow (and thus flow reserve) begins to decrease at approximately 50% diameter stenosis, while resting flow is maintained until the stenosis produces greater than 75% diameter reduction.

Adapted with permission from Gould KL, Lipscomb K, Hamilton GW. Physiologic basis for assessing critical coronary stenosis: instantaneous flow response and regional distribution during coronary hyperemia as measures of coronary flow reserve. *Am J Cardiol.* 1974;33:87-94.

angiograms. Some patients with apparently less severe stenoses have decreased coronary flow reserve. Some studies in which the degree of obstruction assessed by coronary angiography was compared with that found at postmortem examination have suggested that significant underestimation of atherosclerosis by coronary angiography can occur. However, quantitative study of coronary obstructions when postmortem coronary angiography is performed with the arteries fixed at physiologic intraluminal pressures shows excellent agreement with direct postmortem measurements. It should be noted that postmortem studies, in contrast to coronary angiography, do not detect changes in coronary caliber due to altered coronary vascular smooth muscle tone or to a thrombus that has undergone spontaneous lysis.

Left ventricular angiography: Left ventricular angiography (ventriculography) is normally a part of the integrated procedure of cardiac catheterization and coronary angiography. However, because it requires the rapid injection of 30 to 50 mL of contrast medium directly into the left ventricle, left ventricular angiography may be excluded from the diagnostic evaluation of certain high-risk patients if reliable noninvasive methods are available for assessing left ventricular function (eg, echocardiography, radionuclide blood pool scanning). When viewed in the right anterior oblique projection, the left ventricle takes on the geometric appearance of a prolate ellipsoid, and standard mathematical formulas can be applied to calculate the volumetric measurements of the left ventricular chamber. These calculations, however, are less accurate for chambers with abnormal shapes due to coronary disease, because such ventricles do not fit the geometric model. Comparing the estimated ventricular volume at the end of diastole to the volume at the end of systole provides an accurate estimate of the stroke volume. The fraction of blood ejected during systole (the ejection fraction) is derived by dividing the stroke volume by the end-diastolic volume; the ejection fraction is one of the most reliable means of assessing overall ventricular function. In normal individuals, the ejection fraction usually ranges from 60% to 70%. Ventricular function is considered impaired when the ejection fraction is less than 50%, and severe ventricular dysfunction is considered present when the ejection fraction is less than 35%. The major determinant of survival for any patient with significant coronary artery disease is global left ventricular function, and the prognosis worsens with a lower ejection fraction.

Because coronary artery disease affects regional vascular beds and thus the blood supply to particular regions of the myocardium, the left ventriculogram should be carefully assessed for evidence of regional wall motion abnormalities. A specific region of the myocardium, such as the anterior wall, the apical segment, or the inferior wall, can be qualitatively assessed for vigor and completeness of contraction during systole. Conventionally, the Greek terms *hypokinesis*, *akinesis*, and *dyskinesis* are used to distinguish segments that contract poorly, do not contract at all, or paradoxically bulge, respectively. Automated techniques that use manual or computerized border detection or video densitometry are helping to quantify the assessment of these abnormalities in regional wall motion. An akinetic, noncontracting segment of the ventricular wall is characteristic of a myocardial scar caused by a prior myocardial infarction. Not infrequently, an area of infarcted myocardium bulges outward during systole and represents a dyskinetic segment.

A left ventricular thrombus can often be identified as a filling defect in the opacified left ventricle, although echocardiography and CT are more sensitive in identifying a thrombus. Similarly, the presence of mitral regurgitation or an associated interruption of the ventricular septum (ventricular septal defect) can be detected by ventriculography. For the patient with coronary artery disease, all of these features affect the prognosis and the risk of undertaking revascularization procedures. In general, the worse the ventricular function, the higher the risk of any given procedure.

Other tests performed at catheterization: Hemodynamic assessment is a routine part of coronary angiography and includes recording pressures in the left ventricle and the aorta. Depending on the requirements of the individual patient, cardiac output may be determined, and a separate catheterization of the right heart may be performed to measure pressures in the pulmonary artery and right ventricle. Ventricular pressure measurements obtained simultaneously with volume measurements during ventriculography make it possible to calculate pressure-volume loops. This method provides a graphic demonstration of ventricular systolic function, as might be predicted from the Frank-Starling principle.

In recent years, there has been a growing appreciation of the influence myocardial ischemia has on the diastolic function of the left ventricle. Decreased ventricular compliance is one of the earliest manifestations of the ischemia, and this effect on diastolic function can best be detected by a pressure-volume loop analysis. Abnormalities in hemodynamic function, particularly heart rate and ventricular diastolic pressure, precede the electrical changes or the symptoms of angina during transient ischemic episodes.

Catheterization of the coronary sinus is sometimes undertaken to assess the products of myocardial metabolism. The measurement of lactic acid in the coronary sinus effluent has been used to assess whether the myocardium is consuming or producing lactate as it shifts from aerobic to anaerobic metabolism.

Newer technologies: A number of new techniques now in the developmental stage offer considerable promise for evaluating the patient with coronary disease during cardiac catheterization.

Coronary angioscopy performed with fiberoptic catheter systems permits direct visualization of the intravascular wall. As an investigative tool, this method has already provided valuable information relating the specific morphology of lesions to various clinical conditions. For example, it has confirmed the central role of plaque fissuring and rupture in the pathogenesis of acute myocardial infarction and the dynamic role of platelet plugs in the evolution of unstable angina.

Digital angiographic methods may be used to quantify contrast dye appearance time, which provides an estimate of coronary flow reserve that is valuable in assessing the functional significance of a lesion.

Doppler flow probes and scanning ultrasound devices have now been miniaturized and can be inserted directly into coronary vessels. This technology not only allows more accurate estimates of regional coronary flow and flow reserve, but it also provides the opportunity for intraluminal imaging of the atherosclerotic process. Intraluminal sonography has the potential for being the most precise quantitative method for measuring lumen diameters, vessel wall thicknesses, and cross-sectional areas. Further developments anticipated in this area will greatly enhance the capabilities of interventional procedures that rely on balloons, lasers, and atherectomy devices.

Echocardiography

Ultrasound examination of the heart is a commonly used diagnostic technique that has its greatest usefulness in defining cardiac morphology and, with Doppler ultrasound techniques, cardiac and great vessel blood flow patterns. The high spatial resolution and frequent image acquisition rate of echocardiography permit excellent definition of cardiac chamber size, wall thickness, and valve anatomy and mobility. Through the use of the Doppler principle, the velocity and pattern of intracardiac blood flow may be measured quantitatively. The portable nature of echocardiographic equipment permits these studies to be carried out in a variety of clinical settings, including the intensive care unit and emergency department. A disadvantage of echocardiography is the difficulty in obtaining adequate images in patients who have narrow intercostal spaces (through which the examination must be done because ultrasound does not readily penetrate bone); who have excessive lung tissue between the chest wall and the heart (especially common in chronic lung disease); or who are extremely obese.

Nonetheless, echocardiographic data of good quality can be obtained in most patients, permitting noninvasive, painless, safe, and relatively inexpensive imaging of cardiac structure and function. Recent additions to the technologic capabilities of ultrasound include transesophageal imaging that may be used in patients for whom transthoracic images of adequate quality cannot be obtained. The transesophageal approach has also proved to be of great value in obtaining intraoperative recordings, allowing cardiac function to be evaluated during surgical procedures.

Echocardiography can be used to diagnose the presence of coronary artery disease by identifying stress-induced regional wall motion abnormalities. By obtaining a baseline echocardiogram under resting conditions and another echocardiogram during or immediately after maximal exercise stress or pharmacologic vasodilation, areas of new wall motion defects can be identified. If a particular myocardial region is noted to exhibit hypokinesis, akinesis, or dyskinesis during stress, but resting wall motion is normal, the clinician can assume that this segment of myocardium was rendered ischemic during the period of stress. The mechanism of this induced ischemia is similar to that seen in exercise ECG testing and relates to the inability of blood flow in a narrowed coronary artery to increase sufficiently to meet local myocardial oxygen demands. Thus, stress echocardiography identifies the functional mechanical consequences of coronary stenosis when resting flow is sufficient to permit normal contraction, but stress-induced increases in myocardial oxygen consumption are not matched by adequate increases in blood flow. This method of identifying relative hypoperfusion of certain regions during stress is a strategy common to radionuclide imaging and to ventriculography. Stress echocardiography (when adequate quality images can be obtained) appears to be a reasonably sensitive and specific method of identifying regions of hypoperfused myocardium and, by inference, significantly narrowed coronary arteries.

In the setting of established acute infarction, regional wall motion disturbances may persist indefinitely, particularly if the region of myocardium is eventually replaced by noncontractile scar tissue. The extent of abnormal cardiac motion identified by echocardiography and, conversely, the amount of myocardium retaining normal contractile function can be helpful in assessing the patient's prognosis after myocardial infarction. It is important to note that wall motion abnormalities identified by echocardiography (or by other imaging techniques) are somewhat nonspecific within the spectrum of coronary artery disease. Acute ischemia, acute infarction, and chronic infarction with scarring may all produce similar abnormalities of regional wall motion and thickening. Thus, unless echocardiographic wall motion abnormalities are known to be transient, it may be difficult to distinguish acute ischemia from acute or chronic infarction through assessment of wall motion.

An important role of echocardiography in coronary artery disease is the identification of some of the functional consequences and complications of ischemic injury. Doppler techniques can be used to accurately identify mitral valve regurgitation, caused by either ischemic papillary muscle dysfunction or papillary muscle rupture. Similarly, Doppler techniques can be used to identify an infarction-induced ventricular septal defect. Differentiating a ventricular septal defect from acute rupture of a papillary muscle can be difficult, and echocardiography can be significantly helpful in this clinical circumstance. Left ventricular aneurysm, left ventricular intracavitary thrombus (Figure 32), and cardiac rupture with formation of a pseudoaneurysm (a region of sealed-over rupture) can be identified from echocardiographic data.

Although echocardiography cannot presently image coronary artery anatomy with precision, this technique may someday be helpful in localizing areas of anatomic obstruction, particularly with transesophageal methods. High-frequency epicardial imaging techniques can be used to

Figure 32
Left ventricular thrombus in a two-dimensional echocardiogram

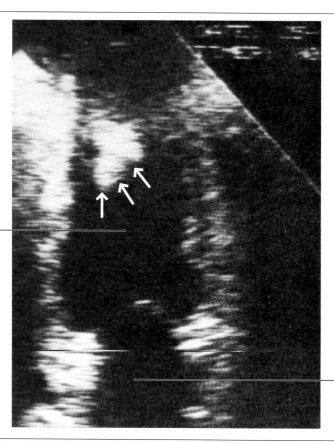

Left ventricle

Left atrium

The image is an apical two-chamber view in which the left ventricle and left atrium are visible. In the left ventricular apex, the arrows indicate a bright, protuberant mass, the echocardiographic appearance of left ventricular thrombus.

Reproduced with permission from Visser CA, Kan G, Meltzer RS, et al. Embolic potential of left ventricular thrombus after myocardial infarction: a two-dimensional echocardiographic study of 119 patients. *J Am Coll Cardiol.* 1985;5:1276-1280.

investigate coronary artery anatomy in the operating room. As mentioned, a new generation of catheter-mounted imaging probes may also permit detection of the presence and degree of coronary stenosis in the catheterization laboratory by direct imaging of the coronary arterial lumen and wall.

Another important use of echocardiography for patients with coronary artery disease is to identify coexisting abnormalities that may mimic certain features or alter the management of ischemic heart disease. For example, the identification of hypertrophic cardiomyopathy, aortic stenosis, mitral valve prolapse, dissecting aortic aneurysm, and other abnormalities helps to clarify certain symptoms or to detect coexisting abnormalities, and can greatly affect how the physician manages the patient with coronary artery disease.

Radionuclide Techniques

Radionuclide techniques are among the oldest and most widely used noninvasive diagnostic imaging techniques for assessing patients with coronary artery disease. Radionuclide methods use emission imaging to create pictures of the heart. In emission imaging, a radioactive compound is injected into the vascular system or sometimes is inhaled. The photons emitted from radioactive decay traverse the body tissues and are detected by an external detector or camera. The information obtained from a radionuclide image depends on several factors, including:

- The biologic behavior of the molecule or compound that is labeled;
- The nature of the radionuclide used for labeling; and
- The nature of the photon detection and image formation processes.

Evaluation of Cardiac Function
Several classes of compounds can be radioactively labeled and used for radionuclide imaging studies. One important category of these radiotracers includes compounds that provide an image of the intravascular blood pool. For example, red blood cells can be labeled using sodium pertechnetate Tc 99m. Because the red cells remain within the

vascular space, ^{99m}Tc provides a blood pool image. Studying the ebb and flow of radioactive counts from the intrathoracic blood pool, which consists predominantly of blood within the heart and great vessels, gives important information on global and regional function of the left and right ventricles. Thus, measurements of right and left ventricular ejection fractions and recognition of regional abnormalities of wall motion due to ischemia may be accomplished using blood pool scans obtained throughout the heart cycle (Figures 33 and 34). Because the radioactive emissions of the blood pool at any given point in the heart cycle bear a direct relationship to ventricular volume, the curve describing radioactive counts versus time appears similar to a ventricular volume curve. From this time-activity curve, the ejection fraction as well as parameters related to global ventricular filling (diastolic function) can be calculated. If appropriate corrections are made for radioactivity in a known volume of the patient's blood and for attenuation of radioactive emissions as they pass through the body, absolute ventricular volumes can also be estimated.

Evaluating global and regional left ventricular function before and during exercise or with pharmacologic stress may identify regions of hypoperfusion based on physiologic principles similar to those described for stress echocardiography. That is, myocardial regions that receive blood from a severely narrowed coronary artery may become ischemic during stress when increased oxygen demands cannot be met by increased coronary flow. Widespread experience with cardiac blood pool scans performed at rest and during exercise has shown that the development of regional wall motion disturbances with

Figure 33
Radionuclide (^{99m}Tc) blood pool scan in a patient with normal left ventricular function

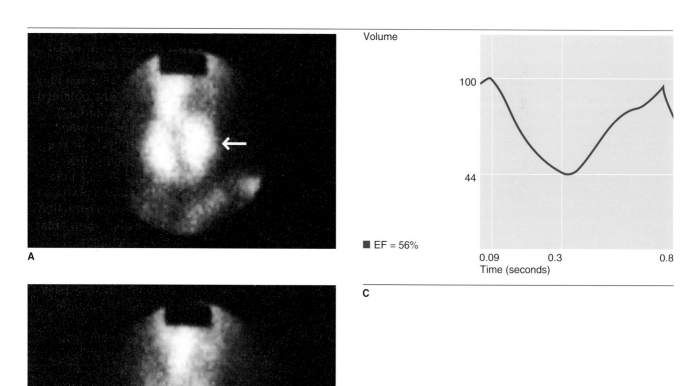

Volume

100

44

■ EF = 56%

0.09   0.3   0.8
Time (seconds)

A

B

C

Left anterior oblique view of the heart at end diastole (**A**) and end systole (**B**). Note the left ventricle (arrows) decreases in size with contraction. (**C**) Left ventricular time-activity curve, a plot of radioactive counts (within the left ventricular cavity) versus time in the heart cycle. Total counts within the left ventricular chamber at end diastole are normalized to "100" on the vertical axis. The ejection fraction (EF) of the left ventricle is calculated as the difference between end-diastolic and end-systolic counts, divided by the end-diastolic counts, giving the percent of radioactive counts (proportional to ventricular volume) ejected during left ventricular contraction.

Courtesy of Dr Peter Kirchner, Department of Radiology, The University of Iowa.

Figure 34
**Radionuclide blood pool scan in a patient with reduced left
ventricular systolic function and an inferoapical wall motion
abnormality**

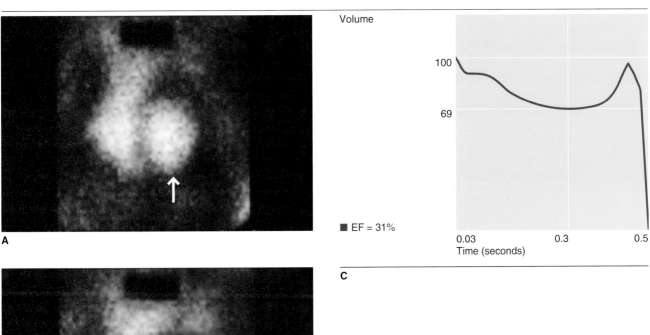

Left anterior oblique view of the heart at end diastole (**A**) and
end systole (**B**). Note that there is very little change in the size
and brightness of the left ventricle with contraction, particularly
in the inferoapical region (arrows). (**C**) Time-activity curve over
the left ventricle, showing a reduced ejection fraction (EF) of
31%.

Courtesy of Dr Peter Kirchner, Department of Radiology, The University of Iowa.

stress or the failure to appropriately increase left ventricular ejection fraction with exercise can identify patients with significant coronary artery disease. The ability to increase the ejection fraction with exercise has important prognostic implications.

In addition to providing information on how coronary artery disease affects the left ventricle, radionuclide techniques offer some of the most reliable noninvasive information on right ventricular global function. Because right ventricular infarction also occurs as a result of coronary disease (eg, it occurs in conjunction with one third of the infarctions of the inferoposterior portion of the left ventricle), radionuclide techniques are important in assessing the patient with right ventricular infarction.

As mentioned, assessment of the diastolic portion of the left ventricular time-activity curve permits delineation of some attributes of global left ventricular filling related to ventricular compliance. Because patients with coronary disease may exhibit abnormal filling performance at a time when global systolic performance is normal (that is, when the ejection fraction is normal), evaluating diastolic performance may enhance the sensitivity of the detection of coronary disease.

Evaluation of Myocardial Perfusion

A second important class of compounds used in radionuclide imaging includes those that provide information on myocardial perfusion. The most widely used at present is thallium-201, a monovalent cation with properties somewhat similar to those of potassium. The concentration of thallium-201 in the myocardium after intravenous injection is related to several factors, including regional myocardial blood flow and regional myocyte membrane function. The relatively poor physical characteristics of thallium-201 as an imaging agent,

along with many other technical and biologic factors, preclude the use of this tracer to determine absolute regional myocardial blood flow. Thallium scintigraphy is useful, however, as an indicator of relative regional differences in myocardial blood flow. Thallium is extracted efficiently by the normal myocardium; therefore, the distribution of thallium deposition within the myocardium is roughly proportional to regional myocardial blood flow.

Diagnosis of coronary artery disease with thallium-201 is based on one of two strategies that maximizes the differences in perfusion between myocardium served by normal coronary arteries and myocardium supplied by significantly narrowed vessels. First, as in the case of stress echocardiography and stress radionuclide blood pool scanning, thallium scintigraphy offers useful information by comparing images taken during exercise and at rest. If thallium-201 is injected intravenously during peak exercise, images obtained soon thereafter will depict the regional distribution of perfusion at the time of injection. Regional defects in thallium uptake during physical stress indicate relative regional decrements in blood flow (Figures 35 and 36). As the method is commonly used, if any regional decreases in thallium uptake are noted on the stress image, then a later "redistribution" image is obtained. If thallium distribution appears more homogeneous in the subsequent redistribution scan, then it can be inferred that the hypoperfusion was transient and due to stress-induced ischemia related to a hemodynamically significant coronary arterial stenosis. If the thallium defect does not reverse ("fill in") in the redistribution scan, in the majority of cases the area of decreased uptake represents nonviable myocardium, either acutely infarcted or replaced with scar. In a sizable minority of patients, however, even "fixed" (ie, nonreversible) thallium defects are associated with severely ischemic but potentially viable myocardium. Thallium scintigraphy is somewhat more sensitive and specific in the diagnosis of coronary artery disease than exercise ECG. Furthermore, the appearance of multiple or large defects in perfusion identifies patients likely to have relatively poor outcomes.

Figure 35
Thallium-201 scintigram at peak exercise in a patient without evidence of myocardial ischemia

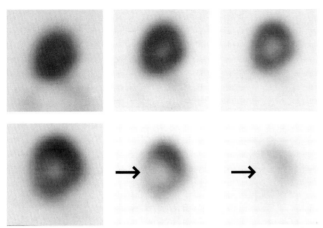

The images obtained using single photon emission computed tomography (SPECT) represent transverse "cucumber" slices through the left ventricle in mutually parallel sections from apex (upper left) to base (lower right). Note the homogeneous distribution of the tracer in all sections except the most basal (lower right), in which the membranous ventricular septum commonly appears as an area of decreased uptake (arrows).

Courtesy of Dr Karim Rezai, Department of Radiology, The University of Iowa.

Figure 36
Thallium-201 scintigram at peak exercise in a patient with evidence of myocardial ischemia

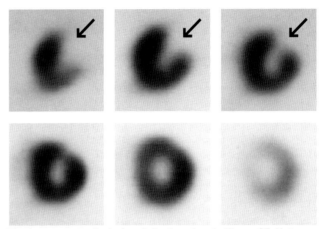

The images are oriented and displayed as in Figure 35. Note the defect (reduced tracer uptake) in the anterolateral left ventricular wall (arrows). On later "redistribution" (rest) scans this defect "filled in," suggesting that the exercise-induced defect was due to relatively reduced perfusion of the anterolateral wall.

Courtesy of Dr Karim Rezai, Department of Radiology, The University of Iowa.

The second strategy used to maximize regional differences in myocardial perfusion is pharmacologic vasodilation. As shown in Figure 31, coronary flow reserve is one useful measure of the significance of coronary stenosis. After intravenous injection of a vasodilator such as dipyridamole, flow in normal coronary arteries is greatly increased, whereas significantly narrowed vessels exhibit a much smaller increase, producing a heterogeneous appearance on a subsequent thallium-201 scan. Radionuclide perfusion imaging after pharmacologic vasodilation may become a common alternative to exercise stress testing for patients who cannot perform exercise.

Either exercise stress or pharmacologic vasodilation can be used to detect the presence and extent of transient thallium defects, which are useful indicators of the extent of coronary artery disease and its prognosis.

Identification of Acute Infarction
A third use for radionuclide methods in evaluating the patient with coronary artery disease is to identify acutely necrotic myocardium resulting from infarction. As opposed to the thallium technique, which identifies hypoperfused myocardium as a "cold spot" or area of deficient tracer uptake,

infarct-avid agents are taken up only by necrotic tissue, producing a "hot spot" scan. The most commonly used agent for illuminating infarcts is ^{99m}Tc pyrophosphate, which is also used as a bone imaging agent. Calcium accumulation in the peripheral zones of myocardial infarction, especially 24 to 72 hours after coronary occlusion, is associated with uptake of pyrophosphate. The technique of ^{99m}Tc pyrophosphate scintigraphy is most useful in the patient presenting 2 to 3 days after the onset of acute chest pain. By this time, cardiac enzyme levels (creatine kinase) that were probably above normal some hours after the onset of pain are no longer elevated. Infarction is demonstrated by the abnormal uptake of pyrophosphate in a region of myocardium. Radiolabeled antimyosin antibody developed from monoclonal antibody technology supplies another radioisotopic marker for acute necrosis.

Recent Technical Improvements in Emission Imaging

Some technical factors should be considered in radionuclide imaging of coronary artery disease. Experience with relatively low-energy radionuclides, such as thallium-201, has underscored the substantial problems that result from the attenuation of photons as they pass through body tissues on the way to the gamma camera. Because the amount of attenuation varies when the photons traverse different paths through the body, certain anatomic regions may be more difficult to evaluate by thallium-201 scintigraphy than other regions. For example, because photons traverse a longer path from the posterobasal left ventricular wall than from the anterior left ventricular wall, a substantial decrease in apparent count density (image intensity) is visible when posterobasal regions are evaluated, strictly because of attenuation effects; this effect can confound identification of regional hypoperfusion. At least two solutions to this problem have been implemented. First is the development of imaging agents with better physical characteristics, such as those labeled with ^{99m}Tc. Second is the development of a computer-based method of improving the representation of regional radiotracer tissue distribution. Emission computed tomography is similar in principle to computed tomography. Photon emissions are detected at various angles around the patient, usually by moving the gamma camera through a 180° arc. The information on photon emission from these various angles is combined by computer to produce a cross-sectional or tomographic (slicelike) image of the distribution of the radionuclide in the plane in which the various measurements were obtained (Figures 35 and 36). Because thallium-201 and ^{99m}Tc each release a single photon as they decay, computerized tomographic techniques applied to these radionuclides are termed *single photon emission computed tomography (SPECT)*. Initial experience with SPECT techniques suggests some increase in the accuracy of identification of myocardial perfusion defects.

Positron emission tomography: Another fundamentally different class of radionuclides is characterized by the simultaneous release of two photons with radionuclide decay. The physical process leading to this event is the release of a positron (positive electron) as certain radionuclides decay. When the positive electron encounters a negative electron, their combined mass is converted to energy, producing the emission of two photons traveling at high speeds in opposite directions. A detector system surrounding the patient detects the two photons as they arrive approximately simultaneously on opposite sides of the detector ring. Based on this detection scheme (coincidence detection), high-quality computerized reconstruction of the distribution of positron-emitting tracers has become possible with positron emission tomography (PET).

Radioactive isotopes of several biologically essential atoms are positron emitters. Oxygen 15, carbon 11, nitrogen 13, fluorine 18, and other isotopes can be incorporated into physiologically important compounds and used to perform unique imaging studies. For example, oxygen 15 can be incorporated into water to study the distribution of water for measuring regional myocardial perfusion. Similarly, nitrogen 13 (incorporated into ammonia) or rubidium 82 is extracted by myocardium in proportion to blood flow. The images are of higher resolution, in part, because positron-emitting radionuclides emit photons of much higher energy (511 keV, as opposed to 80 keV for thallium-201).

In addition to improvements in the assessment of regional myocardial perfusion, positron-emitting radionuclides incorporated into substrates important in myocardial energy production permit the study of certain aspects of intermediary metabolism. This technique makes it possible to study the biochemistry of the myocardium in both health and disease. For example, deoxyglucose labeled with fluorine 18 can be used to study glucose uptake by myocytes. With PET, the evaluation of combined myocardial substrate uptake and myocardial perfusion offers a unique strategy for assessing the patient with acute ischemia. Normally, fatty acids constitute the preferred energy substrate for myocardium, although glucose is also used. Imaging of normal myocardium with a flow-dependent tracer, such as nitrogen 13 ammonia, and a glucose-labeled compound, such as fluoro-deoxyglucose, reveals relatively homogeneous distribution of both of these tracers. In acutely ischemic but salvageable myocardium, PET shows a decreased blood flow with nitrogen 13 ammonia, producing a cold spot in the blood flow image, but PET does not show a decrease of radiotracer uptake when the glucose imaging agent is used. In fact, ischemia produces an increase in anaerobic glycolysis, actually increasing the regional uptake of glucose. Therefore, the combination of decreased perfusion and preserved or increased glucose uptake identifies ischemic but viable myocardium. Concordant decreases in the uptake of a flow tracer and substrate indicate irreversibly damaged or scarred myocardium (Figure 37).

Figure 37
Positron emission tomographic images of the left ventricle

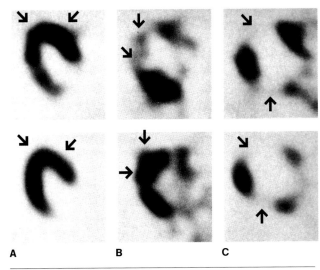

A   B   C

The images are cross-sectional views of the left ventricle "sliced" through its long axis, so that the apex is at the upper left of each image. The images in the top row were acquired using nitrogen 13 ammonia as an indicator of myocardial perfusion. The images in the bottom row were acquired using fluorine 18 deoxyglucose as an indicator of glucose uptake by the myocardium.
(A) Normal perfusion and glucose uptake are apparent in the apical region (arrows).
(B) In a patient with ischemia, reduced perfusion to the apex is indicated by a defect in the nitrogen 13 ammonia image (arrows), whereas glucose uptake is preserved.
(C) In a patient with infarction, concordant decreases in perfusion and glucose uptake are noted in apical and posterior regions (arrows).

Reproduced with permission from Tillisch J, Brunken R, Marshall R, et al. Reversibility of cardiac wall-motion abnormalities predicted by positron tomography. *N Engl J Med*. 1986;314:884-888.

The substantial expense of PET has limited its use in cardiovascular practice. A significant part of this expense is the on-site cyclotron needed to produce the short-lived isotopes. Less expensive cyclotrons and generator-produced isotopes, such as rubidium 82, may lower the cost and eventually lead to wider use of PET.

Although the precise role of the various new radionuclide imaging methods of evaluating patients with coronary artery disease has yet to be determined, radioisotopic techniques will certainly continue to be of major importance in evaluating the presence, severity, and regional metabolic consequences of coronary artery disease.

Computed Tomography

Computed tomography (CT) is an imaging technique based on measurements of x-ray attenuation from various angles. Computer techniques blend these x-ray attenuation measurements into a composite image resembling a slice through the imaged organ at a particular level. CT images are exquisitely detailed and present a strikingly realistic depiction of anatomy. These systems are widely used for medical diagnoses, especially for disorders of the central nervous system, chest, and abdomen. Despite the excellent quality of images obtained with modern scanners, evaluation of the heart with CT techniques until recently has been a difficult challenge, because most scanners require more than 1 second to complete the acquisition of data for an image. Although fast enough for high-quality images of nonmoving organs, a 1-second scan produces a blurred image of the heart, which goes through its entire cycle of filling and emptying at least once during this time. However, CT systems have been developed that permit very rapid scanning, completing images in 10 to 60 milliseconds. These rapid scans effectively freeze cardiac motion and permit delineation of cardiac anatomy with the high resolution and excellent detail CT scans provide of other parts of the body.

Although its clinical use has only recently begun, rapid cardiac CT scanning already appears to be potentially useful in analyzing global and regional left ventricular function. Excellent information can be provided, for example, about patients in whom high-quality echocardiograms cannot be obtained. CT-based estimates of right and left ventricular volumes, ejection fractions, and cardiac mass correlate closely with actual anatomic values. The superb anatomic detail in ultrafast images permits identification of cardiac thrombi and the thin walls of left ventricular aneurysms.

In addition to the analysis of cardiac structure and function, CT may be used to determine whether a coronary artery bypass graft is patent or occluded (Figure 38). Differentiation between patent and occluded grafts is important in evaluating patients with recurrent chest discomfort or other problems months to years after coronary artery bypass graft. Because the only alternative method of defining patency of bypass grafts is to perform selective coronary angiography, CT scanning may become an excellent noninvasive alternative for diagnosing the presence of occlusion in coronary artery bypass grafts. In addition, attempts are under way to use CT data for estimating regional myocardial perfusion. By applying techniques of indicator-dilution theory, the kinetics of myocardial arrival and washout of an iodinated radiographic contrast agent may be useful in identifying myocardial perfusion defects. Although investigative at present, this work may supply clinicians with an additional method of identifying relative changes in myocardial perfusion and potentially measuring absolute perfusion.

Figure 38
Ultrafast computed tomographic scans of patent coronary artery bypass grafts

Ascending aorta

Descending aorta

A

Ascending aorta

Descending aorta

B

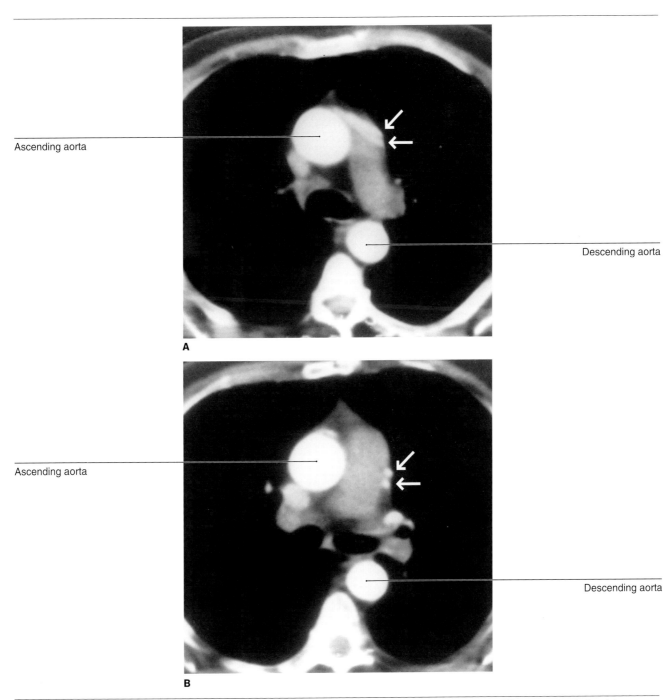

(A) Transaxial (transverse) scan shows the ascending aorta and descending aorta, as well as longitudinal views of two bypass grafts (arrows) arising from the ascending aorta.

(B) In this transaxial scan at a different anatomic level, two grafts are visualized in cross section (arrows).

Courtesy of Dr William Stanford, Department of Radiology, The University of Iowa.

Nuclear Magnetic Resonance Techniques

Nuclear magnetic resonance (NMR) techniques are the newest additions to the diagnostic capabilities of clinicians caring for patients with coronary artery disease. Although comparatively early in their development and clinical applications, some potentially unique contributions of NMR imaging and spectroscopy merit discussion.

The basis of NMR imaging and spectroscopy is the nuclear magnetic resonance phenomenon. Certain atomic nuclei (essentially those with an odd number of nucleons, ie, protons or neutrons) have the characteristic of angular momentum or "spin." The spinning motion of these charged nuclei creates a small magnetic field. Such nuclear magnetic dipoles are normally oriented in varying, random directions and produce no net magnetic field for the entire sample or subject of interest. However, if the subject is placed in a strong magnetic field, sufficient numbers of the individual atomic nuclear magnetic dipoles will align with the field to produce a small net magnetization oriented along the external magnetic field. This net magnetic vector can then be perturbed by introducing an additional oscillating (radio frequency) magnetic field that "flips" or changes some of the individual nuclear magnetic moments to a higher energy level. When the additional oscillating magnetic field is discontinued, the individual magnetic dipoles realign with the strong static field, thus returning the net magnetization to its position of equilibrium. The return of the temporarily excited magnetic dipoles to their lower energy "relaxed" state after the oscillating magnetic field is removed causes emission of a small amount of electromagnetic energy. The detection and study of this energy produce the rich variety of information available from NMR techniques.

At least three types of NMR information may be of use in the diagnosis of the presence and consequences of coronary artery disease. First, the rate of return of the net magnetization to its equilibrium state after removal of the oscillating magnetic field is described by two time constants: $T1$ (spin-lattice) and $T2$ (spin-spin) relaxation times. The $T1$ phenomenon is referred to as spin-lattice relaxation because energy is exchanged between the spins of excited nuclei and their surrounding molecular framework (the lattice). The $T2$ phenomenon is referred to as spin-spin relaxation because energy is exchanged among neighboring spinning nuclei themselves, not with the lattice. Because the biologic and physical mechanisms responsible for $T1$ and $T2$ relaxation phenomena differ, these relaxation times may be used independently to offer insight into certain aspects of the physical and physiologic state of the tissue. Investigations have demonstrated that these relaxation time values are altered by acute ischemia, reperfusion, and acute and chronic myocardial infarction.

Second, the NMR signals can be used to construct images of the heart that bear some resemblance to CT images. These high-resolution data can be used to assess global and regional left ventricular function and thus demonstrate regional contractile abnormalities consistent with segmental ischemic disease. The relatively long acquisition time of NMR imaging, however, may make it difficult to identify regional ischemia through detection of stress-induced wall motion abnormalities. Nonetheless, established wall motion abnormalities (such as those due to acute or chronic infarction) demonstrated on NMR may still be useful in diagnosing coronary artery disease and its complications.

The $T1$ and $T2$ values of a tissue are important determinants of regional intensity in an NMR image. Alterations in these relaxation times may cause regional changes in image brightness. For example, $T2$ is prolonged in acute infarction. Thus, acutely infarcted myocardium is sometimes recognized as a bright area (Figure 39) in a type of NMR image in which increased intensity indicates prolonged $T2$ values (called $T2$-weighted image).

Figure 39
Nuclear magnetic resonance image of a patient with a recent anteroseptal myocardial infarction

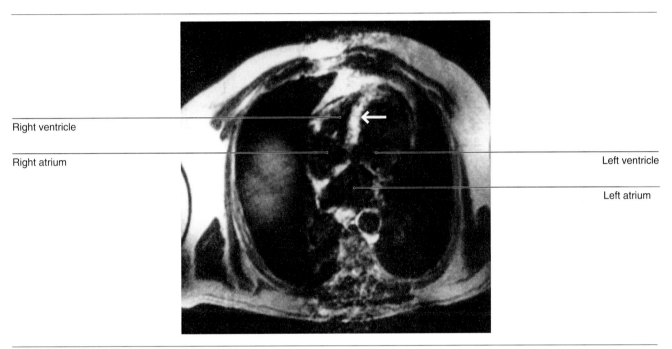

Right ventricle

Right atrium

Left ventricle

Left atrium

The image is oriented to depict a four-chamber view of the left and right ventricles and atria. Regions of myocardium with prolonged T2 relaxation time values will appear brighter than surrounding myocardium (a T2-weighted image). In this scan, the ventricular septum (arrow) appears brighter than the surrounding myocardium, corresponding to the patient's known anteroseptal infarction.

Courtesy of Dr John E. Stuhlmuller, Department of Internal Medicine, and Dr William Stanford, Department of Radiology, The University of Iowa.

The T2-weighted image appears to be a promising approach to identifying acute infarction and estimating infarction size, particularly with image enhancement by NMR contrast pharmaceuticals.

Third, NMR spectroscopy is potentially useful in evaluating patients with coronary artery disease. By studying the precise characteristics of the signal, information can be obtained on the molecular environment of the atomic nuclei under study. The use of NMR spectra to indicate the molecular environment of specific atomic nuclei has been the most common application of this technology in analytical chemistry during the last 30 years. In fact, NMR has been one of the frequently used quantitative analytic techniques in organic chemistry.

Recent advances in computer image processing techniques have permitted the acquisition of in vivo NMR spectroscopy data from localized tissue regions. The vast potential of this technique lies in its ability to examine certain aspects of in vivo myocardial biochemistry. For example, myocardial bioenergetics, such as the metabolism of high-energy phosphate compounds, may be studied with NMR spectroscopy (Figure 40). In addition, aspects of enzyme kinetics and other features of intermediary metabolism may also be evaluated from NMR spectra. At this time, the eventual role of nuclear magnetic resonance techniques in coronary artery disease diagnosis and management is unclear. However, the potential for obtaining information on structure, function, and metabolism in the same examination suggests an important future role for these techniques in clinical cardiology.

Figure 40
Nuclear magnetic resonance phosphorus 31 spectra from animal subject (A) before, (B) during, and (C) after release of a coronary artery occlusion

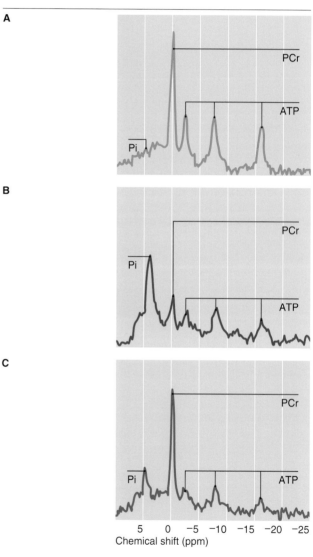

The spectrum shows the amount of inorganic phosphate (Pi), phosphocreatine (PCr), and the three phosphate groups of adenosine triphosphate (ATP) plotted along an axis labeled ppm (parts per million), an indication of the relative NMR frequency at which the resonance phenomenon occurs for each compound. Note that with coronary occlusion there is a decrease in PCr and ATP and an increase in Pi.

Reproduced with permission from Rehr RB, Tatum JL, Hirsch JI, Wetstein L, Clarke G. Effective separation of normal, acutely ischemic, and reperfused myocardium with P-31 spectroscopy. *Radiology.* 1988;168:81-89.

Conclusion

As the 20th century draws to a close, life expectancy from birth has extended from an average of 42 years in 1900 to approximately 75 years in 1988. Although this does not indicate that the actual life span of humans has been extended, it is clear that more people are living to advanced ages because fewer are dying in infancy or early childhood of the once common infectious disorders. As more people live longer, it is inevitable that more and more persons will experience the degenerative disorders associated with aging, one of the most prevalent of which is atherosclerosis. The truly great advances in the field of cardiology will be made in the area of disease prevention. The diagnosis and management of atherosclerosis will be with us, however, until disease prevention becomes totally effective and feasible.

Today's physician is armed with extremely powerful tools with which to make a precise diagnosis of the extent and significance of underlying coronary artery disease. This improved ability to evaluate patients is clearly related to the rapid advances in technology made during the past three decades.

There is every indication that this technologic explosion will continue well into the next century. As the technical sophistication of cardiology practice grows, there is an almost equal sense of urgency to apply the technology. It is critically important that these forces do not outstrip the information base that should guide the use of advanced technology. As life expectancy approaches the life span of our species, clinicians in the field of cardiology will increasingly be faced with the diagnostic and therapeutic dilemma of knowing, "We can ... but should we?"

Selected Readings

General Considerations/Diagnostic Process

Borer JS, Rosing DR, Miller RH, et al. Natural history of left ventricular function during 1 year after acute myocardial infarction: comparison with clinical, electrocardiographic and biochemical determinations. **Am J Cardiol**. 1980;46:1-12.

Cohn PF. Total ischemic burden: definition, mechanisms and therapeutic implications. **Am J Med**. 1986;81:2-6.

Collins SM, Skorton DJ, eds. **Cardiac Imaging and Image Processing**. New York, NY: McGraw-Hill Book Co;1986.

Diamond GA, Forrester JS. Analysis of probability as an aid in the clinical diagnosis of coronary-artery disease. **N Engl J Med**. 1979;300:1350-1358.

Epstein SE, Quyyumi AA, Bonow RO. Medical intelligence current concepts: myocardial ischemia – silent or symptomatic. **N Engl J Med**. 1988;318:1038-1043.

Goldman L. Cost-effective strategies in cardiology. In: Braunwald E, ed. **Heart Disease: A Textbook of Cardiovascular Medicine**. 3rd ed. Philadelphia, Pa: WB Saunders Co; 1988:1680-1692.

Gould KL, Lipscomb K, Hamilton GW. Physiologic basis for assessing critical coronary stenosis: instantaneous flow response and regional distribution during coronary hyperemia as measures of coronary flow reserve. **Am J Cardiol**. 1974;33:87-94.

Hoffman JI. Maximal coronary flow and the concept of coronary vascular reserve. **Circulation**. 1984;70:153-159.

Ladenheim ML, Kotler TS, Pollock BH, Berman DS, Diamond GA. Incremental prognostic power of clinical history, exercise electrocardiography and myocardial perfusion scintigraphy in suspected coronary artery disease. **Am J Cardiol**. 1987;59:270-277.

Marcus ML, White CW, Kirchner PT. Isn't it time to reevaluate the sensitivity of noninvasive approaches for the diagnosis of coronary artery disease? **J Am Coll Cardiol**. 1986;8:1033-1034. Editorial.

Marcus ML, Wilson RF, White CW. Methods of measurement of myocardial blood flow in patients: a critical review. **Circulation**. 1987;76,245-253.

Rutherford JD, Braunwald E, Cohn PF. Chronic ischemic heart disease. In: Braunwald E, ed. **Heart Disease: A Textbook of Cardiovascular Medicine**. 3rd ed. Philadelphia, Pa: WB Saunders Co; 1988:1314-1378.

Ryan TJ. An internist's view of coronary artery surgery. **Adv Intern Med**. 1987;32:69-86.

Weiner DA, Ryan TJ, McCabe CH, et al. Significance of silent myocardial ischemia during exercise testing in patients with coronary artery disease. **Am J Cardiol**. 1987;59:725-729.

Electrocardiography/Stress Testing

Ellestad MH. **Stress Testing: Principles and Practice**. 3rd ed. Philadelphia, Pa: FA Davis; 1986.

McNeer JF, Margolis JR, Lee KL, et al. The role of the exercise test in the evaluation of patients for ischemic heart disease. **Circulation**. 1978;57:64-70.

Schlant RC, Blomqvist CG, Brandenberg RO, et al. Guidelines for exercise testing: a report of the American College of Cardiology/American Heart Association Task Force on assessment of cardiovascular procedures (Subcommittee on Exercise Testing). **J Am Coll Cardiol**. 1986;8:725-738.

Weiner DA, Ryan TJ, McCabe CH, et al. Exercise stress testing: correlations among history of angina, ST-segment response and prevalence of coronary-artery disease in the Coronary Artery Surgery Study (CASS). **N Engl J Med**. 1979;301:230-235.

Weiner DA, Ryan TJ, McCabe CH, et al. Prognostic importance of a clinical profile and exercise test in medically treated patients with coronary artery disease. **J Am Coll Cardiol**. 1984;3:772-779.

Angiography/Catheterization

Davis K, Kennedy JW, Kemp HG Jr, Judkins MP, Gosselin AJ, Killip T. Complications of coronary arteriography from the Collaborative Study of Coronary Artery Surgery (CASS). **Circulation**. 1979;59:1105-1112.

Levin DC, Gardiner GA. Coronary arteriography. In Braunwald E, ed. **Heart Disease: A Textbook of Cardiovascular Medicine**. 3rd ed. Philadelphia, Pa: WB Saunders Co; 1988:268-310.

Wilson RF, Marcus ML, White CW. Prediction of the physiologic significance of coronary arterial lesions by quantitative lesion geometry in patients with limited coronary artery disease. **Circulation**. 1987;75:723-732.

Zijlstra F, Fioretti P, Reiber JHC, Serruys PW. Which cineangio-graphically assessed anatomic variable correlates best with functional measurements of stenosis severity? A comparison of quantitative analysis of the coronary cineangiogram with measured coronary flow reserve and exercise/redistribution thallium-201 scintigraphy. **J Am Coll Cardiol**. 1988;12:686-691.

Echocardiography

Kerber RE, ed. **Echocardiography in Coronary Artery Disease**. Mount Kisco, NY: Futura Publishing Co; 1988.

Ryan T, Vasey CG, Presti CF, O'Donnell JA, Feigenbaum H, Armstrong WF. Exercise echocardiography: detection of coronary artery disease in patients with normal left ventricular wall motion at rest. **J Am Coll Cardiol**. 1988;11:993-999.

Visser CA, Kan G, Meltzer RS, et al. Embolic potential of left ventricular thrombus after myocardial infarction: a two-dimensional echocardiographic study of 119 patients. **J Am Coll Cardiol**. 1985;5:1276-1280.

Radionuclide Techniques

Eagle KA, Strauss HW, Boucher CA. Dipyridamole myocardial perfusion imaging for coronary heart disease. **Am J Cardiac Imag**. 1988;2:292-303.

Gould KL. Identifying and measuring severity of coronary artery stenosis: quantitative coronary arteriography and positron emission tomography. **Circulation**. 1988;78:237-245.

Johnson LL, Seldin DW, Becker LC, et al. Antimyosin imaging in acute transmural myocardial infarctions: results of a multicenter clinical trial. **J Am Coll Cardiol**. 1989;13:27-35.

Tillisch J, Brunken R, Marshall R, et al. Reversibility of cardiac wall-motion abnormalities predicted by positron tomography. **N Engl J Med**. 1986;314:884-888.

Schelbert HR, Buxton D. Insights into coronary artery disease gained from metabolic imaging. **Circulation**. 1988;78:496-505.

Strauss HW, Boucher CA. Myocardial perfusion studies: lessons from a decade of clinical use. **Radiology**. 1986;160:577-584.

Wallis DE, O'Connell JB, Henkin RE, Costanzo-Nordin MR, Scanlon PJ. Segmental wall motion abnormalities in dilated cardiomyopathy: a common finding and good prognostic sign. **J Am Coll Cardiol**. 1984;4:674-679.

Computed Tomography

Brundage BH, Rich S, Spigos D. Computed tomography of the heart and great vessels: present and future. **Ann Intern Med**. 1984;101:801-809.

Steiner RM, Flicker S, Eldredge WJ, et al. The functional and anatomic evaluation of the cardiovascular system with rapid-acquisition computed tomography (cine CT). **Radiol Clin North Am**. 1986;24:503-520.

Nuclear Magnetic Resonance Imaging

Gibson RS, Beller GA. Should exercise electrocardiographic testing be replaced by radioisotope methods? In: Rahimtoola SH, ed. **Controversies in Coronary Artery Disease: Cardiovascular Clinics**. Philadelphia, Pa: FA Davis; 1983:1-31.

Kaufman L, Crooks L, Sheldon P, Hricak H, Herfkens R, Bank W. The potential impact of nuclear magnetic resonance imaging on cardiovascular diagnosis. **Circulation**. 1983;67:251-257.

McNamara MT, Higgins CB, Schechtmann N, et al. Detection and characterization of acute myocardial infarction in man with use of gated magnetic resonance. **Circulation**. 1985;71:717-724.

Pykett IL, Newhouse JH, Buonanno FS, et al. Principles of nuclear magnetic resonance imaging. **Radiology**. 1982;143:157-168.

Rehr RB, Tatum JL, Hirsch JI, Wetstein L, Clarke G. Effective separation of normal, acutely ischemic, and reperfused myocardium with P-31 MR spectroscopy. **Radiology**. 1988;168:81-89.

Schaefer S, Gober J, Valenza M, et al. Nuclear magnetic resonance imaging-guided phosphorus-31 spectroscopy of the human heart. **J Am Coll Cardiol**. 1988;12:1449-1455.

Medical Treatment of Stable Angina Pectoris

Figure 41
The determinants of myocardial oxygen supply and myocardial oxygen demand

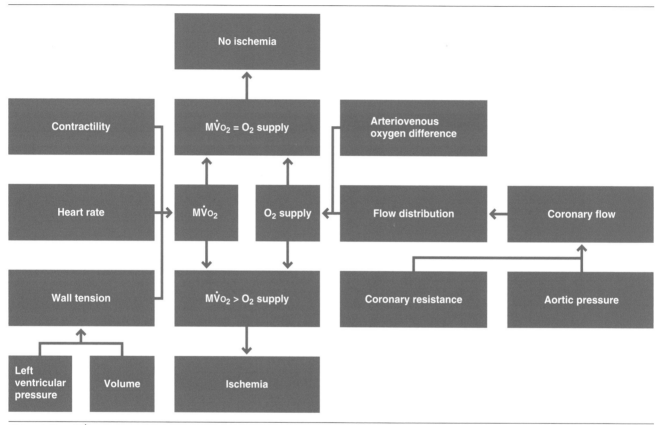

Abbreviation: MV̇o₂, myocardial oxygen demand.

The Pathophysiologic Basis of Angina Pectoris

Introduction

When developing a rational strategy for medical treatment of angina pectoris, it is critical that the physician has an intimate knowledge of the pathophysiologic mechanisms leading to myocardial ischemia. These mechanisms can be understood best by considering the relative balance between the delivery of oxygen to the myocardium and the myocardial demand for oxygen. Because myocardial ischemia occurs when myocardial oxygen demand (MV̇o₂) exceeds the capacity of the diseased coronary vessels to deliver

oxygen, ischemia can be precipitated by either an excessive increase in oxygen demand or a decrease in oxygen delivery. Therapeutic success depends on a favorable alteration of this imbalance. Either the capacity of the coronary arteries for delivering blood to the ischemic regions of myocardium must be augmented or myocardial oxygen demands must be reduced. If the major factors of this equation are unbalanced, myocardial ischemia will result.

The views expressed in this chapter represent Dr Epstein's personal views and are not necessarily the official views of NHLBI, NIH.

Factors Altering $M\dot{V}_{O_2}$

Left ventricular wall stress, an important determinant of $M\dot{V}_{O_2}$, is calculated using the Laplace relationship. Wall stress is directly proportional to intraventricular pressure and radius of the chamber (which reflects intravascular volume), and it is inversely proportional to wall thickness. Thus, an increase in left ventricular pressure or volume will augment wall stress and predispose to angina by increasing $M\dot{V}_{O_2}$. Likewise, a faster heart rate or an increase in myocardial contractility predisposes to ischemic pain because of the greater oxygen demands that result from these changes. Left ventricular failure is the only exception to the rule that an increase in myocardial contractility raises $M\dot{V}_{O_2}$. In this situation, pharmacologic therapy that increases contractility will decrease left ventricular volume and end-diastolic pressure. These changes will favorably affect the myocardial oxygen supply-demand ratio by reducing $M\dot{V}_{O_2}$ and, as a consequence of reducing left ventricular wall tension, will enhance blood flow to the ischemic myocardium.

The Control of Coronary Blood Flow

The autoregulatory system: The normal coronary system consists of large epicardial vessels offering little resistance (R_1 in Figure 42) to myocardial flow and small intramyocardial arteries and arterioles that, because of their small diameter, are the major source of coronary vascular resistance (R_2 in Figure 42). Myocardial flow can, in simplified terms, be thought of as inversely related to coronary resistance and directly related to coronary driving pressure, a relationship that is expressed by the equation:

$$Q = \Delta P / R$$

where Q is blood flow, ΔP is the driving pressure across the coronary bed, and R is the coronary resistance.

The media of coronary arterioles contains well-developed smooth muscle that has the capacity to dynamically alter its intrinsic tone in response to the oxygen demands of the myocardium. In effect, this ability constitutes an autoregulatory system that results in a tightly coupled relationship between myocardial oxygen demand and myocardial oxygen delivery: as demand increases, the arterioles dilate, thereby decreasing resistance

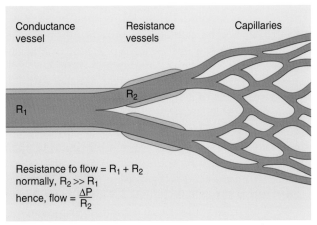

Figure 42
A representation of a coronary artery

Conductance vessel Resistance vessels Capillaries

R_1 R_2

Resistance fo flow = $R_1 + R_2$
normally, $R_2 \gg R_1$
hence, flow = $\dfrac{\Delta P}{R_2}$

R_1 represents resistance to flow caused by large conductance (epicardial) vessels, and R_2 represents resistance to flow caused by small resistance vessels or arterioles. ΔP is the driving pressure across the coronary bed.

Reproduced with permission from Epstein SE, Talbot TL. Dynamic coronary tone in precipitation, exacerbation and relief of angina pectoris. *Am J Cardiol.* 1981;48:797-803.

and causing blood flow to increase in proportion to the increased oxygen demand; as demand decreases, the arterioles constrict, thereby increasing resistance and causing an appropriate decrease in flow.

The impact of a fixed coronary stenosis on coronary flow reserve: Any coronary atherosclerotic lesion transforms the epicardial vessel that originally had a low resistance to flow into one that offers considerable resistance to flow. Flow is maintained, however, by compensatory changes induced by the autoregulatory mechanisms; the increase in R_1 is offset by arteriolar dilatation, which decreases R_2. The resistance of the atherosclerotic vessel becomes flow limiting when the ceiling of the vasodilator reserve capacity of the arterioles is exceeded. When this occurs, further requirements for vasodilatation to prevent an increase in resistance to flow can no longer be met; therefore, the capacity for flow to increase during any metabolic stress, such as exercise, is exhausted. When the critical level of myocardial oxygen demand cannot be met by increases in oxygen delivery, myocardial ischemia ensues (Figure 43). Thus, in a normal person, myocardial blood flow increases as a result of progressive arteriolar dilatation in proportion to the increase in myocardial oxygen demand. In a patient with a fixed obstruction due to coronary artery disease, the arterioles use their limited dilator reserve, and blood flow increases in response to increased oxygen demand until the vasodilator reserve is exhausted. Then blood flow can no longer increase, even though myocardial oxygen demand increases and a flow deficit results, leading to myocardial ischemia and angina pectoris.

Dynamic alterations in coronary resistance: Dynamic alterations in both large- and small-vessel coronary vascular resistance play an important role in altering coronary flow and coronary flow reserve, changes that have important clinical consequences.

Large-vessel constriction: The demonstration in the 1970s that spasm of the large coronary arteries could occur spontaneously and could result in sufficient decreases in blood flow to cause myocardial ischemia profoundly changed our thinking about the mechanisms responsible for ischemic pain. For the first time, it was proved that angina pectoris is not caused solely by a fixed obstruction that limits the maximal capacity of coronary flow; dynamic alterations in the degree of coronary obstruction could also play a contributory role.

Large-vessel spasm initially was thought to occur either in vessels with atherosclerotic lesions or in "normal vessels." However, it is now believed that most instances of large-vessel spasm are caused by vessel disease that impairs endothelial function, even if the disease is not morphologically evident in angiographic studies. Thus, the affected endothelium no longer acts as a barrier that prevents circulating vasoactive substances from diffusing into the smooth muscle located in the media.

Normal endothelium plays a primary and active role in modulating vessel tone by secreting a substance or substances called *endothelial-derived relaxing factor* (EDRF, most likely nitric oxide), a potent vasodilator. Thus, the vasodilation normally caused by certain substances (acetylcholine, serotonin, histamine, etc) is modulated by endothelial release of EDRF. When endothelial function is impaired, these same substances lead to vasoconstriction through direct actions on smooth muscle.

This impaired endothelial function predisposing to vasoconstriction could occur in coronary vessels in which the endothelium is damaged by atherosclerotic lesions. However, studies have demonstrated that hypertension, nicotine, and elevated levels of blood cholesterol can cause endothelial dysfunction even in the absence of morphologically evident endothelial injury. Such endothelial dysfunction probably accounts for many cases of variant, or Prinzmetal's, angina (angina developing at rest and usually associated with ST-segment elevations) in patients whose coronary arteries appear normal when evaluated by angiography. Although the recognition of large-vessel vasospasm as the cause of Prinzmetal's angina led to seminal changes in our concepts of the mechanisms responsible for myocardial ischemia, true variant angina is relatively uncommon, and if true variant angina were the only clinical result of coronary vasospasm, it would not be so important.

More recent studies have identified a larger role in anginal syndromes for dynamic changes in coronary vascular resistance. Thus, angina occurring during exercise can be caused by exercise-induced coronary vasoconstriction as a result of either passive coronary collapse or active coronary vasoconstriction. The mechanism of vessel

Figure 43
The relationship between myocardial oxygen demand and myocardial oxygen supply

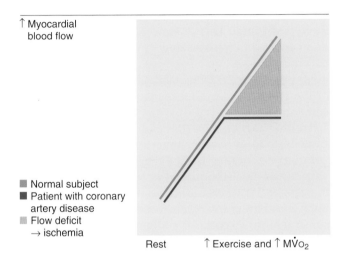

↑ Myocardial
blood flow

■ Normal subject
■ Patient with coronary
artery disease
▨ Flow deficit
→ ischemia

Rest   ↑ Exercise and ↑ M$\dot{V}O_2$

In a normal person, myocardial blood flow increases in proportion to the increase in myocardial oxygen demand. In a patient with a fixed obstruction (R_1 in Figure 42) due to coronary artery disease, blood flow increases in response to increased oxygen demand until the ceiling for arteriolar dilatation (R_2 in Figure 42) is reached. At this time, flow can no longer increase despite the continued increase in myocardial oxygen demand. A flow deficit results, thereby leading to myocardial ischemia and angina pectoris. Abbreviation: M$\dot{V}O_2$, myocardial oxygen demand.

Reproduced with permission from Epstein SE, Talbot TL. Dynamic coronary tone in precipitation, exacerbation and relief of angina pectoris. *Am J Cardiol.* 1981;48:797-803.

Figure 44
Vessel collapse with increased myocardial blood flow

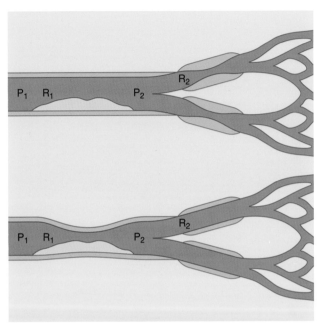

Top: Under baseline conditions, flow across the area of stenosis is modest, and no large pressure gradient develops.
Bottom: With vasodilator intervention, the pressure gradient across the area of stenosis increases. The resulting fall in intraluminal pressure may lead to collapse of the vessel, thereby increasing the degree of stenosis. Abbreviations: P, pressure; R, coronary resistance.

Reproduced with permission from Epstein SE, Cannon RO III, Talbot TL. Hemodynamic principles in the control of coronary blood flow. *Am J Cardiol.* 1985;56:4E-10E.

collapse is depicted in Figure 44, which shows a large coronary artery narrowed by an atherosclerotic lesion.

During exercise, the rate of flow across the stenotic lesion increases. Any increase in the rate of flow across an area of resistance will lead to a pressure drop due to kinetic energy losses; the magnitude of the pressure drop is related to the

severity of the stenosis and the magnitude of the increase in flow. The resulting decreased intraluminal pressure predisposes the artery to collapse, thereby increasing the severity of stenosis and accounting for the exercise-induced large-vessel constriction. Alternatively, coronary constriction during exercise could be the result of an active vasoconstrictor stimulus, such as exercise-induced α-adrenergic stimulation of the coronary vessels by neurogenic stimulation or circulating catecholamines, or production of other circulating vasoconstrictor substances.

Figure 45
The role of vascular tone in angina

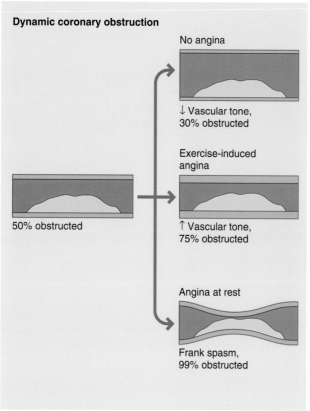

Dynamic coronary obstruction

No angina

↓ Vascular tone,
30% obstructed

Exercise-induced
angina

50% obstructed

↑ Vascular tone,
75% obstructed

Angina at rest

Frank spasm,
99% obstructed

An atherosclerotic lesion can cause angina at rest, exercise-induced angina, or no angina, depending on the underlying tone of the coronary vessel.

Adapted with permission from Epstein SE, Talbot TL. Dynamic coronary tone in precipitation, exacerbation and relief of angina pectoris. *Am J Cardiol.* 1981;48:797-803.

The exercise-induced coronary flow changes could also lead to coronary constriction, if the endothelium is damaged and its dilating mechanisms are impaired. Normal endothelium reacts to the shear forces caused by increasing flow velocity by secreting EDRF. When the endothelium is damaged, an increased flow velocity can lead to coronary constriction, because either the mechanism by which EDRF causes dilation is impaired or the endothelium releases vasoconstrictor substances.

Another mechanism that could potentially contribute to dynamic changes in large-vessel coronary resistance is an exaggeration of the vasoconstrictor stimuli that normally play upon the epicardial vessels and determine vessel tone. Such alterations in coronary tone, if profound, could lead to Prinzmetal's angina or, if less severe, could interfere with the normal augmentation of flow that occurs with exercise.

This concept suggests there may be a spectrum of effects resulting from various degrees of coronary vascular tone (Figure 45). If constrictor influences are sufficiently severe to cause total or near-total coronary obstruction, angina occurs at rest; if they are of intermediate degree, angina is induced by low-level exercise; or, if basal tone actually diminishes and the vessel dilates, exercise capacity might improve. Such variable coronary resistance can lead to variable anginal thresholds (Figure 46).

Small-vessel constriction: The results of various studies now support the concept that dynamic changes of vasoconstrictor influences exerted on the small intramural coronary arteries also play an important role in the precipitation of anginal pain. This mechanism is largely responsible for the anginal pain in patients with normal epicardial coronary vessels and no evidence of large-vessel spasm.

These patients are characterized by several clinical and coronary hemodynamic features. Their angina may be indistinguishable from that of patients with angina pectoris due to coronary atherosclerosis. However, the pain often has atypical features; the most common instance of

Figure 46
The relationship between myocardial oxygen demand and myocardial oxygen supply in a patient with both fixed and dynamic components to coronary arterial obstruction

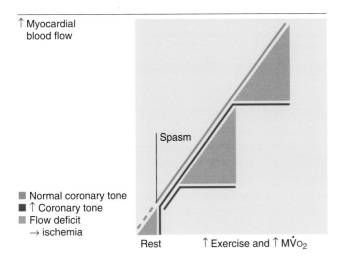

↑ Myocardial blood flow

Spasm

■ Normal coronary tone
■ ↑ Coronary tone
■ Flow deficit
  → ischemia

Rest   ↑ Exercise and ↑ M$\dot{V}$o$_2$

Depending on the magnitude of vessel tone, flow deficits resulting in ischemia could occur under the following conditions: at rest, leading to angina at rest; at relatively low levels of exercise, leading to poor exercise capacity; or only at high levels of exercise, leading to good exercise capacity. Abbreviation: M$\dot{V}$o$_2$, myocardial oxygen demand.

Reproduced with permission from Epstein SE, Talbot TL. Dynamic coronary tone in precipitation, exacerbation and relief of angina pectoris. *Am J Cardiol.* 1981;48:797-803.

this is *variable threshold angina.* In this type of angina, at times the patient has severe, incapacitating angina at rest; at other times only moderate or strenuous exercise precipitates angina; and at still other times even strenuous exercise does not produce pain. These characteristics suggest a dynamic and changing magnitude of coronary resistance rather than a fixed stenosis, which would be expected to be associated with a relatively constant anginal threshold.

Coronary hemodynamic studies have demonstrated that patients with this syndrome have an abnormal coronary vasodilator response to the metabolic stress of cardiac pacing. When the heart is paced to rates of 150 beats per minute, these patients exhibit a blunted response (less of a decrease in coronary resistance and less of an increase in coronary flow) compared with patients without this problem. The small coronary arteries also seem to be more sensitive to the vasoconstrictor effects of ergonovine and cannot dilate normally in response to dipyridamole, a potent dilator of coronary arterioles.

The diameters of the large coronary arteries in these patients remain normal during pacing and ergonovine administration, indicating that the site of increased resistance limiting vasodilator reserve is located in coronary arteries too small to be imaged angiographically. Because the abnormality appears to lie in the small intramural coronary arteries, this syndrome is now referred to as *microvascular angina.*

Silent myocardial ischemia: Silent myocardial ischemia documented by ST-segment depressions on electrocardiographic (ECG) monitoring of an ambulatory patient has emerged as a topic of intense interest. This interest has developed because a high percentage of ischemic episodes that occur in patients with severe symptomatic coronary disease are not associated with angina; approximately 10% to 15% of acute myocardial infarctions are silent, and some asymptomatic patients successfully resuscitated after cardiac arrest subsequently have exercise-induced silent ischemia as the only manifestation of underlying coronary artery disease.

Investigations have indicated that the patho-physiologic basis of silent ischemia is exactly the same as symptomatic ischemia. That is, the silent episodes can occur either because of an excessive increase in myocardial oxygen demand or because of an increase in coronary resistance. The ischemic episode is not perceived by the patient as being painful, because either the patient has a higher pain threshold than normal (referred to as a "defective anginal warning system") or the ischemic episode is mild or of short duration.

The clinical importance of silent ischemia in the patient with symptomatic coronary artery disease, in particular, the relationship of silent ischemia to prognosis, appears to be similar to that of ischemia associated with angina. In other words, it is the occurrence and severity of the ischemia that are of prognostic importance, not whether they are or are not associated with anginal pain.

Common situations precipitating ischemia and their contributing mechanisms: An understanding of the factors responsible for maintaining the balance between myocardial oxygen supply and oxygen demand facilitates a more rational interpretation of the mechanisms responsible for precipitating angina pectoris under varying circumstances. For example, exercise precipitates angina in a patient with coronary artery disease mainly because the increase in myocardial oxygen demand exceeds the capacity of the diseased coronary vessels to accommodate increased blood flow. However, as discussed, exercise-induced coronary constriction with resulting impairment of blood flow may also play a role in the imbalance between oxygen demand and oxygen supply.

Exercise capacity frequently decreases in patients with coronary artery disease after they eat a meal. This occurs because of an excessive increase in $M\dot{V}o_2$. Studies have shown that exercise performed after consuming a 1000-calorie meal is associated with a faster heart rate and higher mean arterial pressure than occur when the same level of exercise is performed under fasting conditions. (However, it may also be possible that a vasoconstrictor substance is released into the bloodstream by the gut during digestion, causing coronary vasoconstriction and a decrease in coronary flow.)

Similarly, when exposed to low environmental temperatures, patients with coronary artery disease commonly experience angina while performing tasks that are well tolerated at more moderate temperatures. Exercise performed in the cold has been shown to cause a greater increase in arterial pressure than an identical level of exercise performed at a more comfortable temperature. Thus, the same intensity of exercise causes a higher $M\dot{V}o_2$ in the cold than in moderate temperatures, a factor that undoubtedly contributes to the ease with which angina is precipitated in a cold environment. Marked elevations in blood pressure are also observed even with localized exposure to cold, such as eating iced foods or immersing a hand in ice water.

An increase in $M\dot{V}o_2$ is not the only mechanism by which cold exposure contributes to the precipitation of angina, as suggested by studies demonstrating that immersion of the hand in ice water can lead to coronary vasoconstriction, thereby impairing myocardial flow delivery. Thus, the reflex causing constriction of the systemic arteries may also cause constriction of the coronary arteries and establish a second contributory mechanism for the development of angina. Hemodynamic changes leading to an increase in $M\dot{V}o_2$ and, likely, to coronary vasoconstriction may also be precipitated by anger, fear, and pain.

Anginal pain often occurs in the patient with hypertension. Although the increase in $M\dot{V}o_2$ induced by hypertension can account for worsening angina in a hypertensive patient with coronary artery disease, a large percentage of hypertensive patients with angina actually have perfectly normal epicardial vessels. It has now been demonstrated that one of the mechanisms responsible for the anginal pain in such patients is an impairment of the vasodilator reserve of the small intramural coronary vessels. These hypertensive patients have microvascular angina.

Any situation that might lead to hypotension, such as hemorrhage or the administration of vasoactive agents, could cause myocardial ischemia, particularly if there is underlying coronary atherosclerosis. Myocardial ischemia can also be caused by any factor that diminishes oxygen availability at a given rate of blood flow, such as anemia or an unfavorable shift in the oxyhemoglobin dissociation curve.

Unfavorable shifts in the oxyhemoglobin dissociation occur, for example, in response to exposure to carbon monoxide, an effect that may partially explain the deleterious actions of cigarette smoking on exercise capacity in patients with coronary artery disease. Favorable shifts in the oxyhemoglobin dissociation curve that make more oxygen available for any given level of oxygen tension (Po_2) occur in patients with cyanotic heart disease, myocardial ischemia, or congestive failure.

Finally, nonhomogeneous distribution of blood flow normally occurs across the myocardial wall, so that endocardial flow is less than epicardial flow. This nonhomogeneous blood flow is largely the result of the greater myocardial wall tension at the endocardial surface than at the epicardial surface. This difference results in greater compression of subendocardial coronary arterioles and collaterals, thereby increasing their resistance to flow. Although this difference in blood flow is normal, during acute episodes of myocardial ischemia or during any situation that elevates left ventricular filling pressures, such as congestive heart failure or aortic stenosis, this difference is increased, and inadequate amounts of blood are provided to the endocardium. These changes help to explain the observation that the endocardium is particularly vulnerable to the effects of ischemia.

The Pharmacologic Treatment of Angina Pectoris

The mechanisms that determine oxygen supply and demand are shown in Figure 41. By modifying these mechanisms, a pharmacologic approach to therapy can relieve anginal pain. An agent can relieve angina by decreasing myocardial oxygen demand, by improving myocardial flow, or by a combination of these effects.

An agent that works by decreasing myocardial oxygen demand achieves the clinical benefit by lowering $M\dot{V}o_2$ for any given level of external stress, such as exercise. Hence, following treatment, the ceiling for myocardial oxygen delivery is reached at a higher level of exercise intensity than would be the case without such treatment. Angina, however, still occurs at the same ceiling of myocardial oxygen delivery.

Agents that relieve angina by increasing myocardial oxygen delivery actually allow the patient to tolerate a higher level of myocardial oxygen demand before the onset of angina. Consequently, the myocardium can attain a higher work load before ischemia occurs because peak myocardial blood flow and oxygen supply have increased.

Although most antianginal agents have a predominant mechanism of action, probably no agent acts by only lowering $M\dot{V}o_2$ or only increasing blood flow.

Nitroglycerin
Clinical efficacy: One of the best known and most effective agents for relieving angina due to coronary artery disease is nitroglycerin. Nitroglycerin administered 0.3 mg to 0.4 mg sublingually consistently ends the usual attack of angina pectoris. A useful treatment that is often neglected is the prophylactic administration of nitroglycerin a few

minutes before the patient begins an activity that usually provokes an anginal attack. For some patients, the prophylactic administration of nitroglycerin is particularly useful before entering into emotionally tense situations; before undergoing physical stresses, such as sexual intercourse and athletic activities; or before physical activity that usually does not result in angina but is undertaken on a cold day.

Since the introduction of nitroglycerin over a century ago, alternative forms of nitrate therapy that would extend the duration of the antianginal effects have been sought. Nitrates with different molecular structures and different routes of administration are available. An alternative to changing the molecular structure of nitroglycerin to achieve longer duration of action is to alter its mode of administration.

Cutaneous application of nitroglycerin (available in a lanolin-base ointment and in transcutaneous patches designed for slow release) has been shown to protect against the development of angina and to enhance exercise capacity for prolonged periods of time. Cutaneous delivery systems increase blood levels of nitrates for as long as 24 hours and are particularly effective in preventing nocturnal angina when applied just prior to retiring. Long-acting preparations are also effective in preventing angina during extended activities, such as golfing and hiking.

A problem inherent in taking long-acting preparations, however, is the possible development of nitrate tolerance. This potential problem is discussed in the section on side effects on page 140.

The mechanisms of action of nitrates: The beneficial effects of nitrates on myocardial ischemia are due to their complex influences on both oxygen requirements and oxygen delivery (Figure 41), resulting in decreased $M\dot{V}o_2$ and increased oxygen delivery.

A decrease in $M\dot{V}o_2$: Nitroglycerin diminishes left ventricular filling pressure and volume, thereby decreasing myocardial wall tension and reducing $M\dot{V}o_2$ for any given level of systolic intraventricular pressure. Nitroglycerin also reduces myocardial wall tension by diminishing systolic arterial pressure.

An increase in oxygen delivery: Nitroglycerin reduces resistance to coronary collateral flow, in part, because it decreases ventricular volume and pressure. The associated decrease in myocardial wall tension reduces the compressive forces on intramural arteries and collateral channels, thereby reducing resistance and enhancing flow to ischemic capillary beds.

In addition, nitroglycerin produces a decrease in $M\dot{V}o_2$ in the nonischemic myocardium that probably results in metabolically mediated constriction of the arterioles supplying this part of the myocardium. Because the arterioles supplying ischemic myocardium remain dilated, perfusion pressure at the origin of collateral channels increases, causing preferential shunting of blood from nonischemic to ischemic regions (Figure 47). Nitroglycerin probably also causes direct dilation of coronary collateral channels. A direct enhancement of coronary collateral function has been demonstrated following intracoronary injection of nitroglycerin in patients with coronary artery disease who are undergoing coronary artery bypass and in experimental animals.

In coronary stenoses that are eccentric (ie, do not affect the entire circumference of the vessel), the smooth muscle of the intact segment of artery can constrict or dilate. Nitroglycerin is capable of dilating many of these segments, thereby reducing resistance due to stenosis and increasing the capacity of the diseased coronary artery to supply blood to the myocardium.

Figure 47
Potential mechanisms that may lead to "benign" vasoconstriction

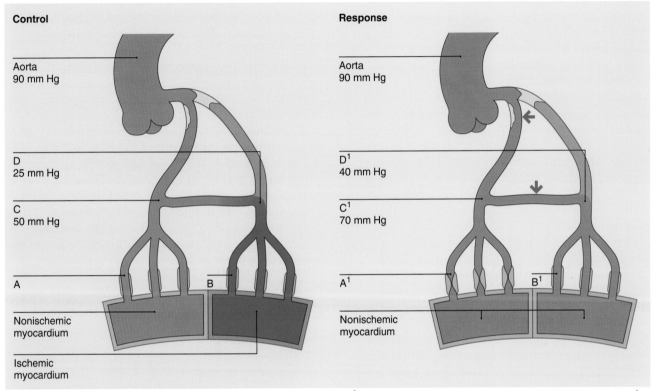

Control

Aorta
90 mm Hg

D
25 mm Hg

C
50 mm Hg

A

B

Nonischemic
myocardium

Ischemic
myocardium

Response

Aorta
90 mm Hg

D^1
40 mm Hg

C^1
70 mm Hg

A^1

B^1

Nonischemic
myocardium

The yellow areas show total occlusion of one coronary artery and partial occlusion of a second coronary artery. The two coronary arteries are connected by a collateral channel. Muscles surrounding the coronary arterioles are depicted in pink. In the control condition shown on the left, myocardial oxygen demand ($M\dot{V}o_2$) is normal; because of the obstruction, perfusion pressure at the origin of the collateral vessel (C) is low, resulting in greatly decreased collateral flow (D). Nitroglycerin administration, shown on the right, causes a decrease in

$M\dot{V}o_2$ that leads to a constriction of the coronary arterioles (A^1) supplying nonischemic myocardium; the arterioles (B^1) supplying the ischemic area remain dilated. This causes an increase in the perfusion pressure at the origin of the collateral vessel (C^1), leading to an increase in collateral flow (D^1) with a subsequent increased flow to the ischemic myocardium. Nitroglycerin can also improve ischemia in some patients by dilating eccentric stenoses and the collateral channels (arrows).

Side effects: The favorable effects of nitroglycerin on $M\dot{V}o_2$ and myocardial blood flow are somewhat offset by its unfavorable hemodynamic actions. Although the decrease in systolic pressure favorably alters $M\dot{V}o_2$, the concomitant decrease in coronary perfusion pressure tends to reduce myocardial blood flow and thus oxygen delivery. The reflex increase in heart rate, in response to the reduction in arterial pressure, increases myocardial oxygen consumption. The decrease in diastolic filling time associated with the more rapid heart rate also unfavorably influences myocardial blood flow. The effect of nitroglycerin on myocardial ischemia is the result of the net effect of its many influences on myocardial oxygen consumption and delivery. Given the clinical efficacy of nitroglycerin, its deleterious effects are clearly outweighed by its beneficial effects.

There are also two potentially important complications inherent in the administration of long-acting nitrate preparations: drug *dependence* and drug *tolerance*. Dependence develops when the body needs the drug to maintain physiologic homeostasis. That nitrate dependence occurs is suggested by the experience of nitrate workers who developed headaches and other withdrawal symptoms during weekend holidays when they were not exposed to nitrate. It also has been suggested that nitrate workers had an increased incidence of acute myocardial infarction. The postulated cause of acute myocardial infarction is that the coronary arteries become dependent on nitrate to maintain normal tone; when nitrate is absent, spasm ensues, resulting in diminished myocardial blood flow.

Studies of patients taking long-acting nitrates have shown that nitrate tolerance often develops; the body becomes resistant to its pharmacologic actions. This resistance can occur as early as 6 to 12 hours after starting therapy. It appears that tolerance is caused by nitrate-induced depletion of sulfhydryl groups in vascular smooth muscle cells. This explanation has been suggested by studies demonstrating that sulfhydryl donors, such as N-acetylcysteine and methionine, prevent the development of nitrate tolerance in patients, and that this is achieved by replenishing depleted vascular sulfhydryl groups. This mechanism is further suggested by the fact that captopril, a sulfhydryl-rich angiotensin converting enzyme (ACE) inhibitor, attenuates the production of nitrate tolerance, whereas enalapril, an ACE inhibitor without sulfhydryl-donating sites, has no such effect.

The development of nitrate tolerance has important therapeutic implications, because patients no longer respond to the beneficial effects at plasma drug levels that previously relieved angina. This problem can be resolved by providing the patient with a drug-free period. Thus, a patient who experiences angina mainly during the morning and afternoon can be given a long-acting preparation during these hours, but not in the evening, which results in a 12-hour nitrate-free period. This approach usually prevents the development of nitrate tolerance.

β-Receptor Blocking Agents

Clinical efficacy: Stimulation of the cardiac sympathetic nerves and increased levels of circulating catecholamines augment heart rate and myocardial contractility. These changes predispose the patient with coronary artery disease to angina pectoris. Modulation of adrenergic stimulation of the heart by agents capable of blocking β-adrenergic receptors represents an important component of the physician's armamentarium in the medical management of patients with angina pectoris. The efficacy of this approach has been demonstrated by many studies showing that β-blockers reduce the frequency of anginal episodes, decrease the consumption of nitroglycerin tablets, and enhance exercise capacity.

The mechanisms of action of β-blocking agents: The β-blockers are thought to exert their salutary effects by decreasing $M\dot{V}o_2$ and by increasing oxygen delivery.

A decrease in $M\dot{V}o_2$: Reducing $M\dot{V}o_2$ for any given level of activity increases the amount of exertion a patient can sustain before reaching the critical value of $M\dot{V}o_2$ associated with the onset of ischemic chest pain. β-Receptor blockade directly decreases the sympathetically mediated augmentation of heart rate and myocardial contractility that accompanies exercise. By diminishing myocardial contractility, the β-blocker also attenuates the exercise-induced increase in cardiac output, thereby modestly reducing the normal rise in blood pressure that occurs with exercise. Reductions in heart rate, contractility, and blood pressure all tend to lower $M\dot{V}o_2$. However, β-receptor blockade also increases ventricular volume, which tends to augment $M\dot{V}o_2$. Clinical benefit from β-blockers probably occurs because the oxygen-sparing effects of reduced heart rate, contractility, and blood pressure more than offset the additional oxygen demands imposed by an increase in ventricular volume.

An increase in oxygen delivery: Theoretically, β-blockers selectively augment blood flow to ischemic regions. By reducing $M\dot{V}o_2$, β-blockers cause a metabolically mediated "benign vasoconstriction" in nonischemic regions, while producing little change in the areas that are ischemic (Figure 47). Reduction in $M\dot{V}o_2$ benefits the ischemic myocardium by helping to restore the balance between oxygen demands and limited oxygen supply. However, benign vasoconstriction also raises the perfusion pressure of the collaterals supplying nonischemic myocardium. A favorable redistribution of blood flow from nonischemic to ischemic regions could result if sufficient collateral channels are available.

Side effects: Although β-blockers are effective in treating angina pectoris, they have the potential for causing serious side effects. When a β-blocker reduces sympathetic inotropic support to a severely impaired myocardium, congestive heart failure can be precipitated or exacerbated. Therefore, β-blockers must be used with considerable caution in patients with severe myocardial dysfunction because not only can they develop symptoms of congestive heart failure, but they also are the group least likely to experience relief of angina pectoris.

Virtually no patients with coronary artery disease, but without overt evidence of congestive failure, develop failure when given β-blockers. In the occasional patient who experiences congestive symptoms, however, the symptoms almost always can be controlled by concomitant administration of diuretics and, if necessary, digitalis. β-Blockers should be used with caution in patients with asthma, because the loss of β-receptor–induced bronchodilatation could lead to severe respiratory insufficiency.

An interesting and potentially serious side effect of abrupt discontinuance of the shorter acting β-blockers has been noted. Some patients develop more easily precipitated angina, angina at rest, and even myocardial infarction and death upon abrupt withdrawal of the drug. It is possible that such side effects are the result of an up-regulation (increase in number) of the β-receptors following prolonged inhibition of the receptors. After abrupt withdrawal of the blocking agent, the same concentration of catecholamines at the neuroeffector junction, either released neurally or present in the blood, may cause excessive adrenergic stimulation by interacting with the increased number of receptors, thereby increasing $M\dot{V}o_2$ and predisposing to angina.

Another potential cause for the observed complications following abrupt withdrawal is the considerable increase in patients' exercise limits when they are taking β-blockers. Continued participation in these more demanding activities exposes the patient to many more situations requiring higher levels of $M\dot{V}o_2$ (and thus predisposing to the development of angina) than was the case before the patient experienced the $M\dot{V}o_2$-lowering effects of the β-blocker. Therefore, when a β-blocker is discontinued outside the hospital, it should be gradually decreased rather than abruptly withdrawn. This precaution is not necessary with long-acting preparations, because their slower rate of removal from the body presumably is sufficient to avoid the abrupt withdrawal syndrome.

To ensure that β-blockers will be used in the safest and most effective way, it is important to explain carefully to the patient the expected benefits and the potentially dangerous side effects. The latter include the development of shortness of breath, decreased exercise capacity, or more overt evidence of left ventricular failure. The patient should be instructed to stop taking the drug and call his or her physician if such side effects occur. β-Blockers are administered initially in relatively small doses, and the dosage is gradually increased every few days until symptomatic improvement or mild side effects occur.

The Combined Use of Nitroglycerin and β-Blockers

Both β-blockers and nitrates have some circulatory effects that lower $M\dot{V}o_2$ and some that raise $M\dot{V}o_2$. Increasing $M\dot{V}o_2$ diminishes the beneficial effects of these agents on angina. It is therefore of considerable therapeutic importance that β-blockers and nitrates have opposing circulatory influences

Table 20
Complementary actions of nitroglycerin and propranolol on some of the determinants of myocardial oxygen demand

	Nitroglycerin	Propranolol
Ventricular volume	↓	↑
Diastolic wall tension	↓	↑
Systolic wall tension	↓	±
Heart rate	↑	↓
Contractility	↑	↓

that cancel each other's oxygen-wasting properties (Table 20). For example, the increase in ventricular volume produced by a β-blocker that augments $M\dot{V}o_2$ is opposed by the reduction in ventricular volume accompanying nitrate administration. Conversely, the sympathetically mediated increases in heart rate and contractility reflexively induced by nitroglycerin are attenuated by propranolol. Thus, the combined administration of these two agents has a particularly favorable effect on exercise capacity.

Calcium Channel Blockers
Clinical efficacy: The development of calcium channel blockers represents a major advance in the treatment of angina pectoris. The results of numerous clinical trials have demonstrated the efficacy of calcium channel blockers in relieving angina pectoris in patients with coronary atherosclerosis. Exercise capacity is increased, the number of spontaneously occurring episodes of angina is reduced, and the number of ischemic episodes occurring over 24 hours (as assessed by ambulatory ECG monitoring) is decreased.

An important advantage of calcium channel blockers is that they have been shown to be therapeutically effective in patients with angina who are not responsive to either nitrate or β-blocker therapy. Thus, by exerting their salutary effect through different mechanisms of action, calcium channel blockers can add to the effects of nitrates and β-blockers or actually improve symptoms in patients refractory to these forms of therapy.

The mechanisms of action of calcium channel blockers: Discovered in 1962 by a German chemist, calcium channel blockers have diverse molecular structures. Verapamil is a phenylethylamine derivative, nifedipine is a dihydropyridine derivative, and diltiazem belongs to the class of drugs called benzothiazepines. Since the Food and Drug Administration approved these drugs, other calcium channel blockers have been approved for use in the United States, and newer agents will soon be available. Currently, they all fall into one of the three original categories. It is possible, however, that other types of calcium antagonists that affect calcium transport sites other than the voltage-sensitive calcium channel will be developed, which would expand the therapeutic uses of pharmacologic agents affecting cytosolic calcium levels.

Verapamil, nifedipine, and diltiazem share the common effect of inhibiting the entry of calcium into cells via the voltage-sensitive calcium channel. However, because of their different molecular structures, each agent works at a different site of the channel and has effects not shared by the others. In addition, although newer calcium channel blockers also affect the voltage-sensitive calcium channel, there is evidence that some of these agents have different tissue specificity, suggesting that calcium channels in different tissues have different binding characteristics. These properties probably account for the difference in the myocardial, electrophysiologic, and vascular actions of the various calcium antagonists.

The primary mechanism by which currently available calcium channel blockers exert their beneficial effects in patients with angina pectoris is based on their capacity to block the entry of calcium into the cell via the voltage-sensitive calcium channel, thereby decreasing cytosolic calcium levels. This action relaxes the vascular smooth muscle cell, thereby causing vasodilatation, and diminishes cardiac myocyte tension, thereby causing decreased myocardial contractility. Decreasing the cytosolic calcium of cells within the sinoatrial node slows the heart rate, and decreasing the cytosolic calcium of cells within the atrioventricular node slows conduction. Therefore, this single cellular action (lowering cytosolic calcium levels) leads to a complex array of physiologic effects, many of which alter the relationship between myocardial oxygen supply and demand.

A decrease in $M\dot{V}o_2$: All three of the available categories of calcium channel blockers decrease $M\dot{V}o_2$ by diminishing arterial resistance, which decreases blood pressure. However, reduction in arterial pressure causes reflex sympathetic responses that may be deleterious. For example, the bolus effect of the original preparation of nifedipine could sometimes lead to hypotension and reflex tachycardia, changes that could precipitate angina. The new formulation of the drug, which has a slower absorption rate and longer duration of action, is free of such effects. If other calcium antagonists developed in the future are rapidly absorbed, they might exhibit similar deleterious actions.

Verapamil and diltiazem not only reduce arterial resistance, they also directly slow the heart rate by depressing the sinoatrial node. In addition to the decrease in $M\dot{V}o_2$ that results from lowering arterial resistance, slowing the heart rate also decreases $M\dot{V}o_2$, thereby reducing anginal symptoms. Nifedipine has little effect on sinoatrial node function. Verapamil also decreases contractility to some extent, an effect that undoubtedly contributes to its antianginal actions. Diltiazem has significantly less negative inotropic effect, and nifedipine, when used clinically, has almost none.

An increase in myocardial oxygen delivery: The calcium channel blockers relax vascular smooth muscle located not only in the systemic arteries but also in the coronary arteries. Therefore, these agents reduce both systemic and coronary vascular resistance. The coronary vasodilating actions of these drugs significantly enhance their beneficial symptomatic effects, especially in patients with a dynamic vasoconstrictor component contributing to elevated coronary resistance. Thus, when nifedipine improves exercise capacity in patients with coronary artery disease, some of this improvement is the result of increased myocardial blood flow during peak exercise. It therefore appears that the coronary vasodilator actions of calcium channel blockers, at least in certain patients, improve exercise capacity by increasing the peak capacity of the coronary circulation to deliver blood to areas of the myocardium that are potentially ischemic.

Verapamil can also increase the rate of myocardial relaxation in diastole, thereby facilitating diastolic filling in patients who have impaired relaxation of the left ventricle. By accelerating the rate of left ventricular relaxation, myocardial tension in early diastole falls more rapidly. This leads to a more rapid decrease in the compressive forces exerted by the myocardium on the intramural coronary vessels, an action that facilitates filling of the coronary vessels in early diastole and presumably leads to an improvement in blood flow to the myocardium. Nifedipine and diltiazem have only minor effects on diastolic function. Table 21 lists the major mechanisms responsible for the antianginal effects of nifedipine, verapamil, and diltiazem.

Side effects: Being structurally dissimilar, each of the calcium channel blockers has a different side-effect profile (Table 22). Seen frequently with nifedipine capsules, reflex tachycardia and hypotension have been eliminated by a new delivery system providing slow release of the drug. The compensatory reflex mechanisms that are stimulated when calcium channel blockers are administered are demonstrated in Figure 48. Although the potent vasodilating actions of these agents could lead to clinically important hypotension, this potentially serious side effect is unusual in the patient given only a calcium channel blocker. However, concomitant administration of drugs that interfere with the compensatory reflex sympathetic responses could cause hypotension. This is particularly true if a vasodilator with α-adrenergic blocking actions (ie, prazosin or quinidine) is given along with a calcium channel blocker; patients can develop hypotension and even syncope. α-Adrenergic blocking agents should therefore be used only with extreme caution in conjunction with any of the calcium channel blockers.

Although verapamil can cause a deterioration in left ventricular function that can lead to pulmonary congestion, this side effect is almost invariably seen only in patients with prior evidence of left ventricular dysfunction. Moreover, in most instances verapamil can be administered safely to patients with mildly impaired left ventricular function, provided diuretics are administered concomitantly.

Noncardiac side effects of calcium channel blockers include headache, flushing, peripheral edema, constipation, postural dizziness, and gastrointestinal complaints. The most common side effects are constipation in patients taking verapamil and peripheral edema in patients taking nifedipine.

The Combined Use of Calcium Channel Blockers With β-Blockers and Nitroglycerin

The results of numerous studies have demonstrated that the combination of a calcium channel blocker with either a β-blocker or a nitrate preparation improves exercise capacity to levels beyond those achieved with only a β-blocker or a

Table 21
Mechanism of action leading to antianginal effects of the calcium channel blockers

	Nifedipine	Verapamil	Diltiazem
↓O$_2$ demand			
Systemic vascular resistance	+++	++	++
Heart rate	↑±	↓	↓
Contractility	±	↓	±
↑O$_2$ supply			
Improved diastolic function	±	+	±
Coronary vascular resistance	+++	++	++

Symbols: +, mild effect; ++, moderate effect; +++, marked effect; ±, no or minimal effect.

Table 22
Cardiac side effects of calcium channel blockers

	Nifedipine	Verapamil	Diltiazem
Congestive heart failure	0	+	0
Hypotension	++	+	0
Reflex tachycardia	++	0	0
SA-node depression	0	+	++
AV-node depression	0	++	+

Symbols: 0, none; +, minimal likelihood; ++, more likely.

Figure 48
Intrinsic and reflex actions of calcium channel blockers

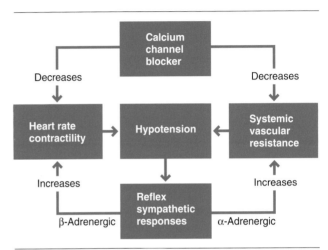

All of the clinically available calcium channel blockers are potent vasodilators and therefore have the capacity to increase systemic vascular resistance. Verapamil decreases heart rate and contractility, whereas diltiazem has little effect on contractility. These actions lead to varying degrees of arterial hypotension, which then evokes baroreceptor-mediated reflex sympathetic responses that oppose the primary hypotensive action of the drug. Thus, the net physiologic effect of calcium channel blockers is a composite of the direct actions and reflex-sympathetic responses that are evoked.

nitrate preparation. Exercise capacity can be further improved in certain patients by triple therapy (a calcium channel blocker, β-blocker, and nitrate preparation). However, the improved efficacy is associated with a greater likelihood of precipitating an important hemodynamic side effect, such as hypotension, left ventricular failure, or excessive bradycardia. Hence, although triple therapy has been and should be used, the physician should use care when combining these three classes of agents.

The most commonly used combination of β-blocker and calcium antagonist (and probably the combination causing the fewest important cardiac side effects) is any of the β-blockers with

nifedipine. Because nifedipine has essentially no depressant effects on the sinoatrial or atrioventricular nodes and has little negative inotropic activity, the addition of a β-blocker to nifedipine therapy is reasonably safe. In contrast, β-blockers must be used very carefully with either diltiazem or verapamil, primarily because these agents can have additive depressant effects on both the sinoatrial and atrioventricular nodes and, in the case of verapamil, on myocardial contractility.

A Strategy for Choosing Antianginal Agents for the Individual Patient

A general statement cannot be made as to which calcium antagonist is most efficacious or whether calcium antagonists, as a group, are better than β-blockers. Some patients seem to respond best to one calcium channel blocker, other patients to another calcium channel blocker. Likewise, some patients appear to experience most benefit from β-blockers, whereas other patients respond better to a calcium channel blocker. The physician treating angina pectoris, therefore, must be familiar with the use of nitrates, β-blockers, and all three classes of calcium channel blockers, because it cannot be predicted which class of agents or which drug within a class would be the best for an individual patient. Moreover, it is frequently necessary to use combination therapy to achieve optimal symptomatic benefit.

To devise the optimal treatment strategy for the individual patient with coronary artery disease, it is helpful to determine which mechanism leading to angina most likely predominates in that patient: does the patient primarily have a fixed obstruction caused by an atherosclerotic plaque, or is there an important dynamic component to the elevated coronary resistance involving vasoconstriction of the large or small coronary vessels? Although a simple clinical assessment cannot definitively determine the dominant mechanism, it can provide the beginning of a rational approach to choosing the most appropriate antianginal agent or agents.

If a patient has angina at rest only, it can be inferred that there is a dynamic component to the obstruction that involves vasoconstriction of either the large or small coronary vessels. Patients who have reproducible effort-related angina without much variability in frequency or severity and no

Table 23

Choice of antianginal agent according to mechanism responsible for angina

Pathophysiologic mechanism	$\downarrow M\dot{V}o_2$ $\uparrow MBF$		
	Nitrates	Calcium antagonists	β-blockers
Dynamic	1	1	3
Fixed	1	2	1
Mixed	1	1	2

Definitions: 1, first preference; 2, second preference; 3, not indicated. Abbreviations: $M\dot{V}o_2$, myocardial oxygen demand; MBF, myocardial blood flow.

episodes of rest pain (fixed threshold angina) can be assumed to suffer from a fixed coronary artery obstruction that constitutes the predominant underlying mechanism leading to ischemia. Patients with variable threshold angina may have either a dynamic coronary obstruction without coronary artery disease (more likely small-vessel than large-vessel vasoconstriction) or they may have a mixed mechanism, consisting of a flow-limiting atherosclerotic plaque plus superimposed dynamic alterations in coronary resistance.

Table 23 lists the therapeutic approaches implicit in the concept that the choice of a pharmacologic agent for treatment should depend on the predominant pathophysiologic mechanism responsible for precipitating angina. In a patient with angina occurring predominantly at rest, it can be inferred that coronary flow is limited mainly by dynamic factors. Therefore, therapy is selected that decreases coronary resistance and increases blood flow; this therapy is best achieved by administering nitrates, calcium channel blockers, or a combination of the two. The β-blockers would be largely ineffective and might even lead to worsening of the symptoms.

In patients with documented coronary artery disease and a history of exertional angina with no variable threshold component (including no pain at rest), it can be assumed that the major cause of symptoms is a fixed coronary stenosis. Therapy should be directed toward reducing $M\dot{V}o_2$. These patients would derive benefit from the $M\dot{V}o_2$-lowering effects of nitrates, β-blockers, or calcium channel blockers. The specific agent or combination to be used for the individual patient would have to be determined on an empirical basis.

Variable threshold angina due to both dynamic and fixed mechanisms (mixed angina) requires therapy with agents that favorably influence both myocardial blood flow and myocardial oxygen consumption. Such patients would probably experience maximal benefit from a combination of nitrates and calcium channel blockers, nitrates and β-blockers, or all three.

Digitalis Glycosides and Diuretics

Digitalis glycosides do not have a direct influence on a patient's angina in the absence of left ventricular failure. In the absence of left ventricular failure, the added myocardial oxygen demand caused by the digitalis-induced increase in inotropic activity may actually cause more severe angina. In the presence of left ventricular failure, however, the decrease in ventricular volume accompanying digitalis treatment may, by decreasing myocardial wall tension, cause a net decrease in $M\dot{V}o_2$.

Diuretics given to the patient with left ventricular failure would also reduce ventricular volume and wall tension and thereby diminish $M\dot{V}o_2$. The reduction in left ventricular wall tension may be sufficient to reduce the forces compressing coronary vessels and actually increase blood flow to the ischemic myocardium. Thus, digitalis and diuretics are important in the treatment of angina when the patient manifests signs or symptoms of left ventricular failure. In the absence of such symptoms, these agents are ineffective and in the case of digitalis may actually prove deleterious.

Physical Conditioning

The patient's physical condition significantly influences the circulatory response to exercise and therefore the patient's exercise capacity. Physical deconditioning causes a faster heart rate and higher blood pressure response to a given level of exercise, whereas physical conditioning results in the opposite response. The patient with coronary artery disease who follows a conditioning program can perform at a more intensive level of exercise before the critical $M\dot{V}o_2$ is reached that precipitates angina. It has been postulated (although not proved) that exercise conditioning also enhances oxygen delivery to ischemic regions of the myocardium by stimulating the growth of collateral vessels.

Regardless of the precise mechanisms involved, it is clear that physical training substantially increases the exercise capacity of patients whose angina pectoris is the result of coronary artery disease. The opposite of the conditioning process (a progressive reduction in activity level) leads to a diminution of exercise capacity. Thus, a timid patient (or physician) may initiate a vicious cycle: extreme limitation of activity is prescribed because of angina, leading to a reduction in exercise capacity that, in turn, ensures even greater limitation of activity. This cycle can be broken only by restoring the patient's confidence that engaging in moderate activity (relative to his or her own maximum capacity) is beneficial.

Before undertaking any conditioning program, the patient with coronary artery disease should exercise under the observation of a physician and with continuous ECG monitoring. If serious arrhythmias develop at the exercise loads that the patient would perform during the conditioning program, appropriate therapeutic measures should be initiated before the program is started.

The best method for promoting good physical conditioning is somewhat controversial. A structured physical activity class in a neighborhood gymnasium, administered by trained personnel, and with resuscitation equipment available is probably the optimal situation. However, most patients do not have access to or cannot afford such a facility. Although a regular program of jogging is an excellent conditioning technique, it has some drawbacks. Excessively hot or cold weather may impose undue stress on patients; in addition, minor and not-so-minor orthopedic complications are common. A good alternative is for the patient to purchase a stationary bicycle, which permits exercise to be performed at home in a comfortable environment. Bicycle exercise also eliminates the excessive stress that jogging imposes on the musculoskeletal system.

An additional benefit of a regular exercise program is the general feeling of well-being experienced by persons in good physical condition. This sense of well-being often reduces background levels of anxiety, which, in turn, tends to reduce the frequency of anginal episodes. It should be emphasized, however, that imposition of an exercise program on a person who has not exercised before and who dislikes exercise may lead to adverse psychological and physical effects.

Finally, some patients do die suddenly or experience a cardiac arrest during jogging or in an exercise class. Whether these events are causally related to the physical exertion is not definitely known. However, there is evidence indicating that sudden death can occur (although uncommonly) as a result of exercise. Thus, the physician should be aware of the potential benefits as well as of the risks (however small) before prescribing an exercise program for an individual patient.

It must also be emphasized that the beneficial effects of an exercise program do not necessarily apply to patients with severe left ventricular dysfunction (ejection fraction less than 25%). There is some evidence suggesting that exercise conditioning in these patients could actually cause further deterioration in left ventricular function.

Transcatheter Coronary Arterial Recanalization

Percutaneous Transluminal Angioplasty
Balloon angioplasty: The development of percutaneous transluminal coronary angioplasty (PTCA) was a major breakthrough in the treatment of coronary artery disease. Transcatheter techniques made it possible to dilate a markedly narrowed segment of coronary artery, and ischemic symptoms that severely limited activity could be relieved without the need for open heart surgery. The procedure involves passing a specially designed angioplasty catheter containing a deflated balloon at its distal end to the site of coronary artery stenosis. The balloon is then inflated, which compresses, fractures, and remodels the atheroma, thereby opening the stenosis. The procedure is usually associated with the development of plaque fissures and dissection. This injury, however, may contribute to the ultimate beneficial effect of PTCA, because the further reduction in the severity of stenosis that occurs over a period of months after the procedure may be the result of healing and retraction of the traumatized atheroma.

With current sophisticated catheter delivery systems, stenoses are successfully opened in over 90% of patients, provided that patients are properly selected and that physicians experienced in angioplasty carry out the procedure. Acute closure of dilated vessels requiring emergency coronary bypass occurs in about 2% to 3% of procedures. Surgical treatment undertaken because of acute closure carries a higher risk than when performed in patients with stable symptoms, undoubtedly because of the rapidly evolving ischemia. The overall mortality rate of PTCA is somewhat less than 1%.

Late closure of a dilated vessel (restenosis) occurring within the first 3 to 6 months after PTCA is a serious problem, because it develops in 25% to 50% of patients whose PTCA was initially successful. The restenosis seems to be, in part, due to a proliferative process involving medial smooth muscle cells rather than to late acute thrombotic occlusion, which in the natural history of coronary artery disease is usually the event that precipitates acute myocardial infarction. The difference between these two mechanisms probably explains why late restenosis almost invariably presents as recurrent angina rather than as acute myocardial infarction or sudden death.

Most patients experiencing restenosis can be dilated successfully by repeating PTCA, although the reocclusion rate after the second procedure is slightly higher than the first. Patients who subsequently experience restenosis can have a third and fourth dilatation, but restenosis rates continue to increase because certain patients seem to be "reoccluders." Ultimately, with repeated angioplasty procedures as many as 80% to 90% of patients undergoing PTCA experience long-lasting salutary effects. Angioplasty sites that remain open for 6 months have a high probability of remaining open for at least the next 3 to 5 years.

As catheter technology has advanced, it has become feasible to dilate increasing numbers of lesions once considered to be out of the domain of angioplasty, and even patients with complex three-vessel disease may experience excellent results with angioplasty. There are, however, subgroups of patients in whom angioplasty is contraindicated. With rare exceptions, PTCA is not attempted in patients with left main coronary artery disease that is unprotected by bypass grafts supplying the left anterior descending or circumflex coronary arteries. Neither is PTCA attempted in patients with a severely narrowed major coronary artery that supplies collaterals to one or more totally occluded major vessels. In these situations, acute occlusion of the artery being dilated would almost inevitably lead to a catastrophic outcome.

Stents: New technologies now in clinical use have expanded the application of transcatheter arterial recanalization. Thus, expandable metallic endovascular prosthetic devices are being placed in coronary arteries that have occluded multiple times following PTCA. These stents serve as a scaffold to maintain vessel patency after PTCA.

Lasers and atherectomy devices: Additional technologies have been developed for treating patients who are not candidates for balloon angioplasty or in whom a prior attempt has failed. Two newer transcatheter techniques have been specifically designed to deal with these problems. PTCA is rarely successful in opening a totally occluded artery, because the guide wire and catheter cannot be advanced through the occlusion. However, high-energy laser light can be directed, through a fiberoptic catheter, to the site of obstruction. The laser is capable of carving a narrow channel through the obstruction, which then permits insertion of a balloon catheter to open the vessel completely.

The early versions of laser catheter systems were unable to debulk lesions; they were used solely to create a channel large enough to allow guide wires and balloons to be advanced to the lesion. However, the newer multifiber lasers can debulk lesions and thus can successfully open arteries. These laser devices may be especially effective in recanalizing arteries with diffuse or long lesions.

Directional atherectomy, in which catheter-based rotating devices have been designed to either cut or pulverize occluding atheroma, has also proved effective in removing large portions of an occluding atheroma. These systems are particularly well-suited to treating discrete, noncalcified lesions.

Data are being obtained to determine the success rate of these newer technologies in opening lesions, the type of lesions best suited to their actions, and their risk profiles. However, we may be moving toward a time when there is no single definitive angioplasty device. It seems likely that therapy will be individualized and that the device selected will depend on the particular characteristics of the lesion.

Indications for Transcatheter Coronary Recanalization

Despite the increasing sophistication of the technology, transcatheter coronary recanalization still carries a definite risk to the patient and undoubtedly will continue to do so in the future. These risks are approximately comparable to the risks of coronary artery bypass, although the inconvenience and cost to the patient are considerably less.

Because of this definite risk, these procedures should (with occasional exceptions) be offered only to patients who, from risk-benefit considerations, are thought to be candidates for bypass surgery. (The exception would be the patient who, for one reason or another, cannot be operated upon but is so symptomatically limited it would be appropriate to proceed with transcatheter recanalization.)

A detailed discussion of the indications for surgical treatment and therefore for angioplasty is beyond the scope of this chapter. However, there are two basic indications for surgical treatment: to relieve symptoms and to improve chances for survival. Coronary artery bypass would be indicated in the following instances:

- All physicians would agree that patients whose symptoms seriously interfere with the quality of life despite medical therapy are candidates for coronary artery bypass. If their anatomy is appropriate, such patients could also be considered for transcatheter recanalization.
- Coronary artery bypass improves survival in patients with moderately depressed left ventricular function who have three-vessel coronary disease. A strong case has also been made that surgical treatment improves survival in patients with normal left ventricular function who have three-vessel coronary disease and myocardial ischemia induced by low levels of exercise. Data also indicate that patients with two-vessel disease who have depressed left ventricular function at rest and inducible ischemia with exercise testing do not do well with medical therapy. These patients may be better candidates for surgical treatment.

- Patients with proximal left anterior descending artery disease who have inducible ischemia upon exercise testing appear to be at risk of developing severe myocardial injury if acute total occlusion at the site of stenosis should occur. Although data are lacking, many physicians consider these patients to be suitable for coronary artery bypass.

Because successful PTCA appears to do the same thing as coronary artery bypass (eg, improve blood flow to the ischemic myocardium), it seems reasonable to assume that the enhanced survival demonstrated in certain subgroups of patients treated with coronary bypass would also occur following PTCA. This may be true. However, in a patient judged to have high-risk anatomy prior to a revascularization procedure, an acute occlusion of a native coronary artery that has been bypassed would have no important sequelae, whereas an acute occlusion of a vessel that has been opened by angioplasty might have a catastrophic outcome. Hence, definitive statements regarding the role of PTCA and other transcatheter recanalization procedures in high-risk patients must await the results of randomized studies.

Patients with single- or double-vessel disease or patients with triple-vessel disease without inducible ischemia during exercise testing appear to have an excellent prognosis with nonsurgical therapy. Thus, if their symptoms are minimal or well-controlled by medical therapy, it appears reasonable not to subject them to the risks of surgical treatment. It seems unwise to apply transcatheter recanalization techniques to these patients, because the risk of these procedures would likely outweigh the small risks experienced during the natural course of their disease.

The therapeutic strategy outlined in this section is based on a patient assessment performed at a specific time. Because coronary artery disease is continually evolving, implicit in this strategy is the requirement that these patients be continually re-evaluated. Most patients judged to be at low risk of sudden death or acute myocardial infarction at one time in the course of their disease will ultimately develop more severe or extensive coronary disease.

Conclusion

An Approach to Medical Treatment
The patient with angina pectoris should be evaluated for coexisting medical problems that might unfavorably influence his or her overall status and, if identified, these problems should be treated. In particular, hyperthyroidism, anemia, and tachyarrhythmias tend to augment myocardial oxygen consumption, thereby predisposing the patient to the development of angina pectoris. If a patient is overweight, $M\dot{V}o_2$ at any given level of exercise will be higher, contributing to impaired exercise capacity. Hypertension predisposes to angina in the patient with coronary artery disease, not only by increasing $M\dot{V}o_2$, but sometimes by increasing the vascular resistance of the coronary microcirculation.

Anxiety and tension should also be dealt with, not by routine administration of psychotropic agents, but as part of a total approach to the patient's disease. The physician's approach should include the following:

- Provide a careful and complete explanation of why angina occurs and how it can be avoided.
- Discuss various risk factors and the control of factors, such as hypertension and hyperlipidemia.
- Give a reassuring (but honest) opinion concerning the possibilities of the patient leading a reasonably normal life for many years.
- Describe the comprehensive medical approach planned and the chances of substantially reducing the frequency of angina.
- Discuss the availability and advisability of PTCA, newer percutaneous techniques that can open stenotic coronary arteries (eg, lasers or atherectomy devices), or coronary artery bypass.

Finally, the physician should be aware of the possibility that he or she may not have had the time to elicit a comprehensive history of emotional difficulties experienced by the patient or the patient's spouse in response to a potentially life-threatening illness. If important emotional problems are suspected, the busy physician might best refer the patient and the patient's spouse to a psychotherapist to ensure that any emotional problems are identified and dealt with. An approach in which the problems of the whole patient are evaluated and the patient becomes a participant (not just a passive recipient) in the planning of his or her therapy almost invariably results in an improved psychological and therefore symptomatic response to the disease.

Pathogenesis, Diagnosis, and Management of Acute Myocardial Infarction and Unstable Angina

Pathogenesis

In most industrialized countries, the most common cause of death in adults is ischemic heart disease, which is almost always due to obstructive coronary artery disease resulting from atherosclerosis. Although many other causes of coronary artery obstruction may lead to ischemic heart disease, these disorders are so rare that for practical purposes ischemic heart disease can be considered to reflect coronary atherosclerosis. (The etiology and pathogenesis of coronary atherosclerosis are presented in more detail in chapter 2.)

There are two theories of the pathogenesis of atherosclerosis: the insudation theory proposed by Virchow and the encrustation theory proposed by Rotansky. In the insudation theory, uptake of lipid from the blood into the arterial wall is central to the etiology and pathogenesis of atherosclerosis. Proponents of the encrustation theory believe repeated formation of thrombi followed by reorganization (spontaneous lysis, healing, and endothelialization of the clot) is the main culprit, with lipid being an innocent bystander.

These two theories will be described briefly, as will the atherosclerotic lesion, because features of both theories are now thought to be relevant to the pathogenesis, diagnosis, and treatment of atherosclerosis. These proposed mechanisms of the development of atherosclerosis are particularly important because myocardial infarction, the most serious manifestation of ischemic heart disease, is associated with a thrombus superimposed on an atherosclerotic plaque. The understanding of both thrombus and plaque formation and the prevention of their development are probably necessary if ischemic heart disease is to be conquered.

Regardless of which theory is correct, there is universal agreement that the atherosclerotic plaque starts early in life, probably as a fatty streak in children. The atherosclerotic plaque increases gradually or intermittently throughout life, leading to symptomatic cardiovascular disease, usually in the sixth or seventh decade. The predominant cells of the atherosclerotic plaque are monocytes, some platelets, red blood cells, and smooth muscle cells from the media that have migrated into the intima. There is a large extracellular accumulation of cholesterol esters in the plaque matrix. With the passage of time, the atherosclerotic plaque generates more and more collagen, presumably secreted by the smooth muscle cells, and may ultimately undergo calcification. Cell cultures have demonstrated that platelets release platelet-derived growth factor (PDGF) that can stimulate smooth muscle cell proliferation and their migration from the media into the intimal layer. Some evidence indicates that serum lipids may induce proliferation of smooth muscle cells, as well as stimulate production of secretory products from monocytes and other cells present in the atherosclerotic plaque.

There is increasing evidence that endothelial damage (whether induced by smoking, hypertension, or physical trauma) can pave the way for the adhesion of platelets and other blood components. This adhesion leads to thrombosis and the simultaneous insudation (accumulation) of lipoproteins from the blood, resulting in the development of the atherosclerotic plaque. Currently, the most widely accepted theory of atherogenesis is the response to injury theory. Smooth muscle cells are known to secrete collagen, elastin, and other glycosaminoglycans. Normally the synthesis and turnover of collagen and elastin are properly coordinated to give the vessel the appropriate tensile strength in response to various stimuli, such as the coordination of vasomotion, which, in turn, is responsible for autoregulation of coronary flow. There is little doubt that endothelial damage, believed to be present early in the initiation of the atherosclerotic lesion, and proliferation of smooth muscle cells stimulated by a variety of growth factors released from various blood components play a significant role in the pathogenesis of the atherosclerotic lesion. Atherosclerosis of the coronary arteries occurs primarily within 2 to 3 cm of the ostia. The clinical manifestations of ischemic heart disease are a result of coronary obstruction induced by the space-occupying atherosclerotic plaque and the functional impairment of the endothelium caused by the plaque.

Coronary thrombosis (originally described by Herrick in 1912) was downplayed for several decades but now has been properly documented. Herrick stated that myocardial infarction almost always is associated with a coronary thrombus superimposed on an atheromatous plaque. The initiating factor for the coronary thrombus remains unknown, however, and considerable experimental and clinical data implicate several different mechanisms:

- Endothelial damage exposes the underlying connective tissue, predisposing to thrombosis.
- Rupture of an atheromatous plaque causes hemorrhage.
- The plaque ulcerates.
- Vasoconstriction causes subsequent stasis and possible endothelial injury.

In addition to these potential mechanisms, considerable data indicate that an atheromatous plaque significantly impairs the ability of the coronary artery to dilate or constrict in response to appropriate stimuli. The atheromatous plaque also impairs the ability of the endothelium to secrete products that normally maintain fluidity of the blood. In the atheromatous vessel, acetyl-choline, which normally induces coronary vasodilatation, may induce vasoconstriction, because the endothelial relaxing factor (possibly nitric oxide) is no longer synthesized. It is also likely that synthesis of several other factors important in preventing thrombosis (eg, the thrombomodulin receptor, tissue plasminogen activator, glycosaminoglycans, and protein C) is impaired. Although it may not interrupt blood flow, it appears that an advanced atherosclerotic lesion of the coronary artery can induce thrombosis by inhibiting the mechanisms that normally protect against thrombosis.

For some time, thrombus formation was thought to be incidental and secondary, whereas vasoconstriction was thought to be the primary cause of myocardial infarction. Vasoconstriction may indeed be primary, initiating thrombosis through either rupture of the plaque, damage to the endothelium, or induced stasis. Just as the two theories of the development of atherosclerosis are being unified, so are the roles of vasoconstriction and thrombosis in the development of acute myocardial infarction, because vasoconstriction is an essential part of the clotting process. Once activated, platelets secrete a variety of agents, such as thromboxane A_2 and serotonin, that stimulate constriction of the coronary artery and cause further aggregation of platelets. Therefore, vasoconstriction and clotting occur simultaneously. It may be that one or the other of these processes predominates in initiating the thrombus, but it is more likely that both play a necessary role in initiating and maintaining coronary obstruction. Because myocardial infarction is associated with complete coronary obstruction from a thrombus superimposed on an atherosclerotic plaque, and because restoration of flow is necessary to salvage myocardium, therapy almost always involves some therapeutic means of clot lysis and inhibition of vasoconstriction, no matter whether vasoconstriction or thrombosis is the initial event.

The following pathogenetic features are important in considering the diagnosis and management of acute myocardial infarction:

- Acute myocardial infarction is almost always associated with complete coronary obstruction due to a thrombus superimposed on coronary atherosclerosis. Before thrombosis, the atherosclerotic plaque usually obstructs the lumen by 50% to 80%.
- Myocardial necrosis secondary to ischemia is almost always initiated in the subendocardium and spreads to the epicardium. If the coronary occlusion is complete and sustained as in Q-wave infarction, 70% to 90% of the involved myocardium distal to the lesion will undergo ischemia and subsequent necrosis.
- Based on direct experimental and indirect clinical evidence, ischemia for 15 to 20 minutes produces irreversible injury. Therefore, angina, which involves ischemia without irreversible injury, is associated with briefer intervals of ischemia.
- Necrosis usually begins 30 minutes after the onset of ischemia. However, the extent of the necrosis and the duration of its evolution (usually 4 to 6 hours) are influenced by collateral flow and other factors that alter myocardial oxygen supply and demand. Decreasing myocardial oxygen demand may limit infarct size or delay the development of necrosis, but it appears that increasing coronary flow is much more effective and definitive in limiting infarct size.
- Recent studies indicate that acute myocardial infarction (at least Q-wave infarction) is usually initiated in the morning and corresponds to the time of decreased sympathetic drive, increased plasma fibrinogen levels, and increased platelet adhesiveness. The potential causative role of each of these factors remains to be elucidated.
- Myocardial infarction is a regional disease limited to the area supplied by the obstructed vessel, and the degree of damage that occurs depends, in part, on the extent and duration of the coronary obstruction and the existing collateral flow. Thus, myocardial infarction is restricted to the vascular territory of one of the three major coronary vessels or their branches.

- Lack of coronary flow deprives the myocardium of oxygen. Therefore, myocardial metabolism, which is normally aerobic and utilizes primarily fatty acids, becomes anaerobic and utilizes glucose in the glycolytic pathway rather than in the Krebs cycle. Anaerobic metabolism provides much less adenosine triphosphate (ATP), 2 mol rather than 32 mol per molecule of glucose metabolized, resulting in decreased force and velocity of contractions in the affected segment of the myocardium. The myocardium almost immediately becomes stiffer or noncompliant. The mechanism of this change is unknown but is believed to be the result of impaired muscle relaxation due to impaired calcium sequestration and uptake by the sarcoplasmic reticulum.
- The hemodynamic sequelae to myocardial infarction, which are more severe and more sustained than those of ischemia, consist of increased end-diastolic pressure in the ventricle and related atrium and a tendency for the cardiac output to decrease.
- More than 50% of patients experiencing their first episode of myocardial infarction have significant obstructive atherosclerosis in only one vessel, thereby emphasizing the need for secondary prevention.
- Right ventricular infarction due to obstruction of the right coronary artery once was considered a rare event but now is known to occur in conjunction with left ventricular damage in the majority of patients with inferior infarction.
- Atrial infarction occurs in association with ventricular infarction and is more common in the right atrium. However, significant damage is rare, and atrial infarction is a cause of clinical manifestations in no more than 8% to 10% of patients.

- Recent documentation has shown that Q-wave and non–Q-wave infarction have distinctly different natural histories. Patients recovering from Q-wave infarction have a high mortality rate during the first 6 to 12 weeks after the infarction, followed by a low rate of mortality in subsequent years. In contrast, patients recovering from non–Q-wave infarction have a low rate of mortality during the first few weeks, followed by a prolonged period (1 to 2 years postinfarction) of high mortality. The cumulative mortality 2 years postinfarction is similar for patients with Q-wave and non–Q-wave infarction.

Classification

Traditionally, myocardial infarction has been classified as transmural or subendocardial (nontransmural). Transmural infarction associated with a Q wave on the electrocardiogram (ECG) implies that the myocardial injury extends from the endocardium to the epicardial surface. Subendocardial infarction implies that the injury is restricted to the subendocardium. However, it has become clear that a transmural infarction does not always involve an injury that extends to the epicardium, and that a subendocardial infarction is not always restricted to the subendocardium. It now is considered more appropriate to classify myocardial infarction on the basis of ECG patterns. Accordingly, patients exhibiting a Q wave are referred to as having a Q-wave infarction, and patients exhibiting changes restricted to the ST-T segments are referred to as having a non–Q-wave infarction. It is estimated that about 30% to 40% of patients have non–Q-wave infarctions. This classification is important in terms of clinical manifestations, prognosis, and treatment.

Clinical Features
Patients most commonly present with chest discomfort, which they may describe as chest pain, shortness of breath, chest tightness, or simply discomfort. Cardiac pain commonly radiates to the arm, neck, and (less commonly) to the jaw. The most consistent feature of cardiac chest pain is the presence of a retrosternal component. Pain restricted to the left inframammary region is seldom cardiac, and rarely does cardiac pain originate below the rib cage. Nausea and vomiting may accompany chest pain, particularly in association with an inferior infarction. Esophageal pain is almost identical with cardiac pain and may also be relieved by nitroglycerin, although relief is not immediate as it often is with angina. However, the duration of pain, its character, and its distribution are extremely unreliable for differentiating reversible and irreversible cardiac injury. This unreliability is confirmed by the fact that only one third of patients admitted to coronary care units are subsequently found to have acute myocardial infarctions.

The patient should be examined in the supine and left lateral decubitus positions. The physician should pay particular attention to the patient's overall physical appearance, the jugular venous pulses, the peripheral arterial pulses, and the palpation of the precordium. Typically, the patient is extremely anxious and has a pale face, beaded with perspiration, accompanied by the sensation of difficulty in breathing while lying still and propped up with pillows. The patient with severe chest pain may clench his or her fist and motion toward the sternum, the so-called Levine sign. The patient's appearance, posture, and gestures will, in large part, be dictated by the severity and duration of the chest pain.

The peripheral arterial pulse, although frequently normal, may be either slower or faster than normal. A slower than normal pulse (60% of patients with inferior infarction have bradycardia during the first hours postinfarction) may gradually increase over the next few hours. A rapid pulse often occurs with extensive anterior infarction. Persistent sinus tachycardia beyond the initial 24 hours is associated with very high mortality. The pulse volume may be diminished, reflecting decreased contractility. The blood pressure is usually normal but may be elevated as a result of anxiety or diminished due to cardiac failure. Patients with inferior infarction may develop bradycardia and hypotension secondary to the so-called von Bejold-Jarish reflex.

The majority of patients have an irregular pulse due to ventricular or supraventricular arrhythmias. Most patients with inferior infarction have a concomitant right and left ventricular injury that may be manifested by increased jugular venous pressure and accentuated A wave. Patients with inferior infarction may or may not exhibit distention of the jugular veins upon inspiration (Kussmaul's sign) as a result of the decreased compliance of the right ventricle, even in the absence of right-sided failure. The jugular venous pressure may be elevated due to right ventricular or biventricular failure. An estimated 60% to 70% of patients with inferior infarction manifest Kussmaul's sign in the initial hours. Ventricular or supraventricular ectopic beats can be distinguished by timing the jugular venous pulse with that of the ectopic beat. If the dysrhythmia is ventricular, a large A wave occurs due to contraction of the atrium against the closed atrioventricular valve. A normal A wave appears if the dysrhythmia is supraventricular.

The examination of a patient with possible myocardial infarction is never complete until the precordium has been palpated in the left lateral decubitus position. Within the first 24 hours postinfarction, some abnormality of the precordial pulsations can be palpated in most patients, either the lack of a point of maximal impulse or the presence of diffuse contraction. The area of involvement of infarction is usually hypokinetic, akinetic, or actually bulges in the opposite direction during systolic contraction. Atrial contraction is palpable in about 30% to 40% of patients.

The intensity of the first heart sound may be diminished because of decreased contractility. A fourth sound is heard in practically all patients and, in fact, in many normal individuals older than 45. A third heart sound is heard in about 20% to 30% of patients, reflecting left ventricular dysfunction, and is regarded as an early sign of cardiac failure. The third heart sound may be the only manifestation of cardiac decompensation. When there is extensive damage and the left ventricular ejection is markedly delayed because of prolonged ventricular contraction, the second heart sound may be single; however, a rare paradoxical split reflects severe ventricular decompensation. On occasion, a unique diastolic murmur occurs due to obstructed flow through a partially stenosed coronary artery. The murmur is distinctive, producing a crescendo-decrescendo ejection-like sound in diastole. The presence of a systolic murmur from papillary muscle dysfunction, although transient, is common in the initial hours after onset of myocardial infarction. A pericardial friction rub is heard 2 to 3 days postinfarction in about 10% of patients.

Diagnosis of Myocardial Infarction

Electrocardiographic Assessment

In an attempt to standardize the diagnostic criteria for acute myocardial infarction, the World Health Organization (WHO) in 1959 proposed a classification (now referred to as the two-out-of-three criteria) based on the presence of two or more of the following: chest pain, elevated plasma enzymes, or new Q waves on the ECG tracing. The criteria served the important function of standardizing diagnosis and rapidly became the standard throughout the world. Since the WHO criteria were developed, diagnostic techniques with greater sensitivity and specificity have been developed. In 1959, the lactic dehydrogenase (LDH) isoenzymes assay had just been introduced as a diagnostic marker of myocardial infarction, but the data were too scanty to be incorporated into the WHO classification. By 1970, tests for plasma creatine kinase (CK) and its isoenzymes had been introduced, and the use of isoenzymes in the diagnosis of myocardial infarction became widespread. Today, absolute confirmation of the diagnosis of myocardial infarction is based primarily on finding an elevated level of the plasma creatine kinase isoenzyme CK-MB. Despite widespread use of CK-MB levels, the WHO has not revised its classification.

In about two thirds of the patients with myocardial infarction, analysis of serial ECG tracings shows a characteristic profile of ST-segment elevation followed by the development of new Q waves. Other patients have only minor changes or have marked changes consisting of ST-T segment elevation or depression. When the changes are restricted to the ST-T segment, confirmation by enzymatic or radiographic assessment is essential, because these ECG patterns are also associated with myocardial ischemia with reversible injury. When the changes are restricted to the ST-T segment, the diagnosis of non–Q-wave infarction is made, providing elevated CK-MB levels or some other objective evidence of infarction is found. Previous myocardial infarction and residual Q waves or left bundle-branch block may mask the development of new Q waves, making diagnosis by ECG tracing more difficult.

On the basis of the ECG pattern, patients are divided into those with Q wave and those with non–Q-wave infarction, a distinction with significant prognostic implications.

In patients with posterior infarction, a more specific manifestation is a large R wave in the V_1 lead that is equal to or exceeds the S wave and new ST changes. In fewer than half the patients, the only manifestation of lateral infarction is an ST-segment depression (and no Q wave) in ECG recordings from the lateral leads. Right precordial leads should be used to evaluate inferior infarction in patients with concomitant right ventricular involvement. An ST-segment elevation in recordings from these leads is very suggestive of right ventricular infarction; if ST-segment elevation is not found, it is difficult to diagnose right ventricular infarction with the electrocardiogram. Atrial infarction should be suspected if the PQ segment is elevated or depressed, the morphology of the P-wave changes, or atrial arrhythmia is present, such as frequent premature atrial beats, atrial flutter, or fibrillation.

Isoenzymes

In general, the diagnosis of myocardial infarction is confirmed by measuring serial elevations of plasma CK-MB, with LDH isoenzyme determination reserved for the patient who presents late (more than 72 hours after infarction). In addition to their greater specificity, CK isoenzyme measurements have several advantages over LDH measurements: CK isoenzymes are more rapidly released from tissues and more rapidly cleared from the plasma, and sensitive, rapid, and easy-to-use quantitative assays are now available. One of these sensitive assays can detect a significant elevation of plasma CK-MB within 4 hours after onset of infarction; peak plasma values are reached within an average of 24 hours. Because patients frequently reach the hospital 2 to 4 hours after the onset of symptoms, most patients have a significantly elevated plasma CK-MB at the time of hospital admission. Plasma CK-MB levels return to normal within 72 to 96 hours (Figure 49).

Other enzymes, such as aspartate aminotransferase (AST, previously SGOT), hydroxybutyric dehydrogenase (HBD), or alanine aminotransferase (ALT, previously SGPT), in the past were measured on a daily basis; however, these laboratory studies are no longer necessary and are an unnecessary expense. With the current widespread use of thrombolysis and the resulting early restoration of perfusion, plasma CK-MB levels become markedly elevated usually within 30 to 60 minutes after thrombolysis.

Figure 49
Serial changes in serum CK-MB and total CK activity in a patient with acute myocardial infarction

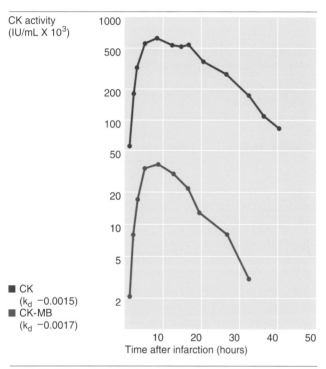

CK activity
(IU/mL X 10^3)

■ CK
  (k$_d$ −0.0015)
■ CK-MB
  (k$_d$ −0.0017)

Time after infarction (hours)

Note that CK-MB activity declined more rapidly than total CK activity, although in this case the difference in disappearance rates (k$_d$) was small. The changes in total CK and CK-MB shown in this figure generally follow the same pattern observed in patients with uncomplicated myocardial infarction.

Reproduced with permission of the American Heart Association, Inc. from Roberts R, Henry PD, Sobel BE. An improved basis for enzymatic estimation of infarct size. *Circulation*. 1975;52:743-754.

Figure 50
Serial changes in CK-MB and total CK activity in a patient with acute myocardial infarction complicated by frequent intramuscular injections

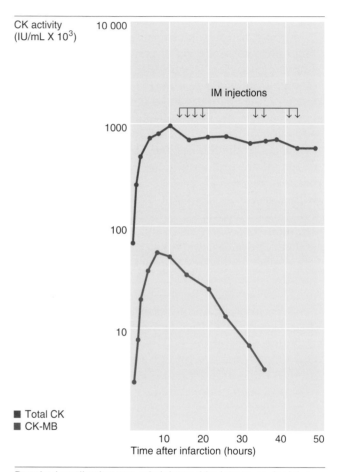

CK activity
(IU/mL X 10^3)

IM injections

■ Total CK
■ CK-MB

Time after infarction (hours)

Required medication was administered by intramuscular injection at the times indicated by the arrows. This intervention led to a persistent elevation of total CK activity. CK-MB activity declined in the pattern typically seen in patients with uncomplicated myocardial infarction.

Reproduced with permission of the American Heart Association, Inc. from Roberts R, Henry PD, Sobel BE. An improved basis for enzymatic estimation of infarct size. *Circulation*. 1975;52:743-754.

Although total plasma CK activity is a highly sensitive index of infarction, it is nonspecific and may be elevated by a variety of conditions, including intramuscular injection (Figure 50), trauma, cardiac catheterization, surgery, cerebrovascular accident, and thyroid disease. Electrical cardioversion causes significant elevation of the total plasma CK, but unless repeated several times, it does not induce an elevation in plasma CK-MB. In patients who undergo early reperfusion (within 4 to 6 hours after the onset of myocardial infarction), CK-MB should be assessed hourly for the first few hours. Because there is a more rapid release of enzymes with successful thrombolysis, the diagnosis of myocardial infarction with CK-MB analysis is possible within 30 to 60 minutes. Enzyme plasma activity reaches a maximum within 10 to 15 hours. Early diagnosis of myocardial infarction may be important to determine which patients should be treated with angioplasty or surgery after thrombolytic therapy.

Patients admitted for possible myocardial infarction should have a blood sample drawn for CK-MB analysis on admission and every 4 to 6 hours during the first 24 to 48 hours. However, if the patient undergoes thrombolytic therapy, samples should be obtained every hour for the first 6 to 8 hours, then every 4 to 6 hours for 48 hours, and then every 12 hours throughout the hospital stay. If the plasma CK-MB level is not elevated within 24 hours of the onset of symptoms, myocardial infarction can be excluded, and the patient can be transferred out of the coronary care unit. However, if the patient has unstable angina, is in cardiac failure, or has other abnormalities, he or she may require further monitoring for myocardial infarction.

Plasma CK-MB levels are more reliable for diagnosing myocardial infarction when a change in enzymatic activity (either an increase or a decrease) is observed in two or more samples. If only one sample is available, then a significant elevation of the CK-MB level (twofold above the normal level) strongly supports the diagnosis of myocardial infarction in an appropriate clinical setting. Infrequent sampling (once or twice a day) in patients with minimal injury, such as patients with non–Q-wave infarction, may lead to a false-negative diagnosis. Myocardial infarction after noncardiac surgery is also reliably determined from serial analysis of plasma CK-MB levels every 4 to 6 hours. Other enzymes are markedly elevated due to tissue trauma, but CK-MB is highly specific. After cardiac surgery, however, CK-MB levels (like other cardiac enzymes) are almost always elevated as a result of manipulation and involvement of the myocardium, and thus the assay is not a reliable diagnostic index. The following guidelines are suggested as criteria for the diagnosis of myocardial infarction:

- Successively higher levels of plasma CK-MB in serial samples (a change of 25% or more between any two values), followed by a decrease to baseline levels.
- An increase in plasma CK-MB activity of at least 50% between two samples drawn at least 4 hours (but not more than 12 hours) apart.
- Preferably, the diagnosis is based on at least two samples drawn 4 hours apart within a 24-hour period.
- If only a single sample is available, diagnosis must be based on an elevation of plasma CK-MB of at least twofold above normal.
- For patients admitted 72 hours after the onset of infarction, LDH isoenzyme analysis is the preferred diagnostic test, because CK-MB levels may have returned to normal.

In our own laboratory, the upper limit of normal plasma CK-MB levels is 13 IU/L in the glass bead assay, 40 µg/L in the radioimmunoassay, and 120 IU/L for total plasma CK activity. However, values for the upper limit of normal vary among laboratories and must be established for each laboratory. About 15% of the total CK activity of the average normal myocardium is due to CK-MB, and the remainder is due to creatine kinase isoenzyme

MM (CK-MM). Other sources of CK-MB, such as certain skeletal muscles or the small intestine, provide only trace amounts of 1% to 2%. Massive skeletal muscle injury is associated with the release of significant amounts of CK-MB, although it seldom accounts for more than 1% to 2% of the total plasma CK activity. Thus, for confirming myocardial infarction, it is generally stated that CK-MB activity must exceed 5% of total activity. At the time of peak activity following myocardial injury, the CK-MB level usually represents 10% to 15% of total plasma CK activity.

Release of LDH is significantly delayed and does not reach a peak plasma level until about 48 to 72 hours after the onset of myocardial infarction and remains elevated for 10 to 14 days. It is recommended that samples be analyzed for isoenzyme LDH_1 activity, which is relatively specific for the myocardium, because skeletal muscle and the liver are rich in isoenzymes LDH_4 and LDH_5, rendering total LDH activity nonspecific. A popular test-tube assay for measuring LDH_1 activity is the so-called hydroxybutyric dehydrogenase, in which 2-oxybuterate is used for the enzyme substrate instead of pyruvate. However, the electrophoretic technique is recommended for determining LDH_1 activity.

Creatine Kinase Subforms

The specificity of plasma CK-MB levels for the diagnosis of myocardial infarction is based on data showing that CK is present predominantly in organs with muscular activity: skeletal muscle, cardiac muscle, and to a lesser extent smooth muscle. Creatine kinase is present in essentially all tissues, but such organs as the liver, spleen, kidney, and brain have minimal activity compared with that of skeletal or cardiac muscle. Tissues are known to contain four CK isoenzymes, of which three are present in the cytosol: CK-MM, CK-MB, and CK-BB.

The CK molecule consists of two monomers, each of which is either an M or a B subunit. In muscle, the predominant isoenzyme is CK-MM, which is composed of two M subunits; the predominant isoenzyme in the brain is CK-BB, which is composed of two B subunits. An exception to this tissue distribution is seen in patients with muscular dystrophy, in which the gene for the B monomer is expressed to such an extent that up to 3% of the total CK activity of muscle may be CK-MB, in contrast to the normal trace amount. Therefore, the specificity of elevations of CK-MB levels for myocardial injury is relative. The fourth CK isoenzyme is found in mitochondria and is restricted to the outer aspect of the inner membrane of the mitochondria. Currently, the mitochondrial CK isoenzyme is not used in the diagnosis of myocardial infarction.

Upon release of CK into the circulation, the plasma enzyme carboxypeptidase-N cleaves lysine from the carboxyl-terminus of the M subunit, resulting in a more negatively charged molecule. As a result, CK-MM is separated into three forms on high-resolution agarose or polyacrylamide gel electrophoresis: MM-3 is the unmodified form newly released from tissue, MM-2 has lysine removed from one subunit, and MM-1 (the most negatively charged) has lysine removed from both subunits (Figure 51). Upon release of CK-MB into the circulation, it is acted upon by carboxypeptidase-N, which cleaves the terminal lysine from the M subunit, but the B subunit remains unchanged. This gives rise to two forms of CK-MB (Figure 52), the unmodified form (MB-2) and the CK-MB with a lysine removed from the M subunit (MB-1).

In a healthy person, MM-1 predominates (55% to 75% of total CK-MM), but the profile changes rapidly after the onset of myocardial infarction, with MM-3 becoming the predominant form of

Figure 51
Schematic representation of the CK-MM isoforms

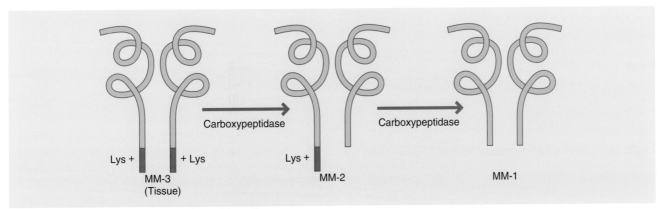

MM-3 is the unmodified form newly released from tissue.
Cleavage of the terminal lysine (Lys) from one of the two MM-3
polypeptides yields MM-2. Removal of the remaining terminal
lysine produces MM-1.

Figure 52
CK-MB subform conversion

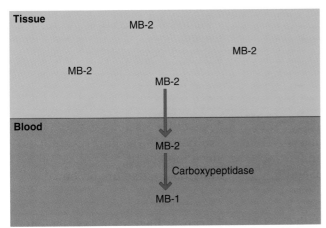

The unmodified tissue form of CK-MB (MB-2) is released into
the blood where it is transformed into MB-1 by the action of
carboxypeptidase-N.

CK-MM. In a similar fashion, MB-1 is normally the predominant form of CK-MB, but MB-2 rapidly becomes the predominant form after myocardial infarction. These observations are significant in the diagnosis of myocardial infarction: even when total plasma CK activity is within the normal range, a change in the relative distribution of subforms can provide an early diagnosis of infarction even earlier than measurement of CK-MB or total CK activity. In addition, by determining the temporal profile of MM-3 (the tissue form) or more specifically MB-2 (the tissue form) as a percentage of the total activity of CK-MM or CK-MB, the onset of infarction can be pinpointed within hours. Any increase in the proportion of MM-3 or MB-2 signifies new tissue necrosis or continuing tissue necrosis. Increases in MB-2 activity specifically signify injury to the myocardium. Assays have been developed that provide rapid analysis of both CK-MB and CK-MM subforms, thus facilitating an earlier diagnosis of myocardial infarction.

Detection of Reperfusion
The rapid increase in the tissue forms of CK-MB or CK-MM (ie, MB-2 or MM-3) and their rapid disappearance after successful thrombolytic therapy offer a means of determining whether reperfusion was successful. The MB-2 assay can also serve as a highly sensitive and early marker of myocardial infarction, which may be important in deciding whether to use invasive techniques, such as angioplasty, if thrombolysis is unsuccessful. The MB-2 assay may also aid in the early diagnosis of patients with possible myocardial infarction. In the United States, only about 30% of patients admitted to a coronary care unit are subsequently shown to have documented myocardial infarction. A marker that can reliably detect infarction within

the first 1 to 2 hours after onset would significantly help to identify patients with myocardial infarction in the emergency room. This early diagnosis is particularly important today in view of the increasingly widespread use of thrombolytic therapy for suspected myocardial infarction. There remains a significant, albeit infrequent, risk of bleeding with thrombolytic therapy, and early exclusion of infarction and subsequent discontinuation of thrombolytic therapy, heparin, and other anticoagulants are desirable.

The marked elevation of plasma myoglobin that occurs within 2 to 3 hours after the onset of myocardial infarction has been well documented. Myoglobin, however, lacks specificity as a diagnostic marker, and for that reason it has not been used on a routine basis for diagnosing myocardial infarction. Because it is released into the plasma within 2 to 3 hours after onset of symptoms, reaches a peak early, and is rapidly cleared through the kidneys, myoglobin is a potential marker for the early detection of reperfusion following thrombolytic therapy. Studies showing that myoglobin is elevated within 30 to 60 minutes following reperfusion suggest it may be a good indicator for detecting whether lysis has occurred. However, myoglobin is measured by a radioimmunoassay that requires considerable time, a limiting factor in determining whether angioplasty or surgery is urgently needed. Similar studies are being conducted with a more rapid assay for the analysis of increased levels of the plasma CK-MB-2 subform. It remains to be determined which of these indices (if either) will be useful in determining the course of additional therapy.

Radionuclide and Echocardiographic Assessment
Myocardial infarction is generally suspected on the basis of the patient's symptoms, which are predominantly that of chest discomfort, and the diagnosis is confirmed either by the appearance of Q waves on the ECG tracing or by isoenzyme analysis of either CK or LDH. In the absence of the availability of these techniques or if the patient comes to the hospital several days or weeks after the onset of symptoms, radionuclide

techniques offer considerable sensitivity and specificity for identifying myocardial infarction. The most widely studied of the radionuclide techniques for the diagnosis of infarction uses technetium Tc 99m stannous pyrophosphate, which is rapidly taken up by the damaged myocardium. This method, however, is less sensitive and less specific than the CK-MB assay.

Damaged myocardium is visible on ^{99m}Tc pyrophosphate scan within 24 to 48 hours after the onset of symptoms and remains visible for at least several weeks and, in about 50% of myocardial infarction patients, for as long as 6 months. The use of ^{99m}Tc pyrophosphate is probably most appropriate in the diagnosis of infarction after cardiac surgery, because plasma CK-MB and LDH levels are markedly elevated as a result of trauma to other tissues, as well as to the heart. Although ECG findings in Q-wave infarction are specific, ECG is insensitive for diagnosing non–Q-wave infarctions, which account for most myocardial infarctions after cardiac surgery. Therefore, preoperative and postoperative ^{99m}Tc pyrophosphate scintigraphy is recommended for patients at high risk of myocardial infarction.

Thallium-201, which is taken up by normal myocardium but not by abnormal myocardium, is also helpful in the diagnosis of infarction. Thallium-201 is particularly useful in patients presenting several months or years after myocardial infarction, because the thallium scan exhibits no uptake by scar tissue and may be the only means of confirming a remote infarction that occurred years previously.

Technetium pyrophosphate radionuclide scans for assessing regional and global function may also be helpful in detecting myocardial infarction in difficult cases. However, ^{99m}Tc pyrophosphate

scans do not differentiate between old and new injury and are not specific for infarction. In patients suspected of having a right ventricular infarction, usually the only means of confirmation is with radionuclide ventriculography, echocardiography, or pyrophosphate scintigraphy.

The technique of echocardiography is now widely used in the noninvasive assessment of myocardial infarction, and it is likely to become more popular as sensitivity and specificity improve. Echocardiography, which has been around for some time, is now markedly improved as a result of the two-dimensional application of Doppler techniques for the evaluation of coronary flow. The recent introduction of contrast echocardiography for visualization of coronary arteries has added a new dimension to this technique. Echocardiography offers the advantage of being rapid, simple, and noninvasive and provides visualization of the anatomy and assessment of ventricular function. This technology also makes it possible to assess other concomitant abnormalities, such as valvular insufficiency, and detect postinfarction complications, such as ventricular septal defects, pericardial tamponade, or aortic dissection. In addition, Doppler echocardiography makes it possible to assess cardiac output serially. Echocardiography is also being pursued as a potential emergency room technique for the early diagnosis and assessment of myocardial infarction. Although the technology as a screening tool for myocardial infarction is in its infancy, Doppler echocardiography offers an additional advantage over other techniques. Flow across the valves can be assessed, as can cardiac output and ventricular shunts. The sensitivity and specificity of echocardiography for detecting myocardial infarction are now being evaluated.

Right ventricular infarction, which almost always occurs as a result of obstruction of the right coronary artery, is difficult to diagnose in the presence of concomitant injury to the left ventricle. Radionuclide ventriculography, which shows impaired regional performance of the right ventricle, is a better technique for diagnosing this type of infarction than echocardiography. Right ventricular infarction may also be diagnosed by ECG. Although less sensitive, the detection of an elevated ST segment in the right precordial leads suggests right ventricular infarction. In the appropriate clinical setting, echocardiography (although somewhat nonspecific) may be helpful in assessing inferior infarction and right ventricular failure and for determining not only whether the right ventricle is involved but also the extent of involvement.

Estimation of Infarct Size

The extent of myocardial damage is the most important determinant of the risks of mortality and morbidity for patients with myocardial infarction. The importance of the extent of myocardial damage was documented in postmortem studies in 1969, when it was shown that death is inevitable when 40% or more of the left ventricle is destroyed. Subsequent studies with enzymatic estimates of infarct size have shown that when 20% to 25% of the ventricle is destroyed, survivors usually have significant disability and recurrent cardiac failure. In contrast, patients with only 5% to 15% destruction of the ventricle usually do well upon recovery and continue with routine activities, including strenuous work, without significant impairment.

In an attempt to obtain a noninvasive in vivo method for assessing infarct size, a technique was developed based on the amount of CK-MB released into the blood. Circulating CK-MB levels correlate closely with postmortem morphologic estimates of infarct size and with parameters reflecting ventricular function, such as the incidence of cardiac failure and cardiac arrhythmias. Blood levels of CK-MB also correlate with short- and long-term survival rates.

To measure circulating CK-MB, plasma samples are collected every 4 to 6 hours for 48 to 72 hours and analyzed, preferably by glass bead absorption or radioimmunoassay. By comparing the total amount of CK-MB released into the circulation with the amount of CK-MB present per gram of normal human myocardium (determined from postmortem studies), the number of grams of myocardium that underwent necrosis can be calculated. The amount of infarcted tissue calculated in this way is referred to as the CK-MB gram equivalents (CK-MB g/Eq).

Enzymatic estimation is regarded as the most reliable technique for calculating infarct size, and it is used extensively in clinical practice. Other methods for determining infarct size have used radionuclide techniques. These techniques include assessing the infarct size with ^{99m}Tc pyrophosphate, thallium-201 scintigraphy with single-photon emission tomography, and short-lived positron emitters.

Enzymatic estimates of infarct size were developed before thrombolytic therapy became available and have been used primarily for research in assessing the effect of various forms of therapy. In both clinical and experimental studies, enzymatic estimates of infarct size have demonstrated that infarct size evolves over time. The introduction of thrombolytic therapy, however, has stimulated a greater interest in assessing infarct size with radionuclide rather than enzymatic techniques. Enzymatic estimates of infarct size from sustained coronary occlusion are based on an experimentally determined ratio of the amount of CK that appears in peripheral blood to the amount released from the tissue, because not all of the CK activity lost from the myocardium appears in the blood. With early restoration of coronary flow by thrombolysis, more of the CK from the infarcted myocardial tissue is released into the circulation rather than being destroyed locally. Under these circumstances, a new ratio has to be validated for enzymatic estimates of infarct size during early reperfusion. Rather than obtain these new data, techniques such as positron tomography and single-photon thallium tomography are being pursued as ways to reliably estimate infarct size despite early reperfusion.

Management of Myocardial Infarction

In the United States, an estimated 1.5 million people have myocardial infarctions each year. About 500 000 of these people die, and about 350 000 of these deaths occur outside the hospital, within 1 to 2 hours of the onset of symptoms. In the 1950s and early 1960s, before the establishment of coronary care units (CCUs), the in-hospital acute mortality rate from myocardial infarction was approximately 40%. Hospital care for patients with myocardial infarction has gone through two phases: the bedridden phase in the 1940s and 1950s and, with the introduction of CCUs, the more aggressive management phase of the 1960s and 1970s. By the mid-1960s, CCUs had reduced the in-hospital acute mortality rate to about 20%. This reduction in mortality was due primarily to appropriate treatment of ventricular arrhythmias, but it also was partly the result of increased awareness of myocardial infarction and its sequelae.

Patients with myocardial infarction are now routinely admitted to CCUs, and several standard treatment protocols have emerged. Routine treatment of ventricular arrhythmias and constant ECG monitoring are now well developed and are standard parts of therapy. In the 1970s, it became apparent that a major barrier to further reduction of mortality was the lack of appropriate therapy for limiting the extent of myocardial damage (ie, limiting infarct size). Cardioprotection to preserve ischemic myocardium became a major thrust of cardiac research in the 1970s and was successful in treating experimentally induced infarction, but clinical application was less successful.

These early attempts to limit infarct size failed, in part, because interventions were designed to decrease myocardial oxygen demand and were implemented too late. The results of these studies indicated that the critical time interval after the onset of symptoms was extremely short (4 to 6 hours) and that restoring blood flow was likely to be more effective than decreasing myocardial oxygen demand. With the introduction of thrombolytic therapy, efforts have focused on increasing coronary blood flow.

Thrombolytic therapy for myocardial infarction emphasizes the need to treat patients earlier and to provide therapy at the site and time of initial patient contact. In the 1970s, mobile CCUs were shown to be effective in reducing mortality in Seattle, Washington and Columbus, Ohio in the United States, and in Belfast, Northern Ireland. Subsequently, the mobile CCU concept was revised to include salvaging damaged myocardial tissue with early thrombolytic therapy, in addition to treating arrhythmias. Thrombolytic therapy presumably also decreases the incidence of arrhythmias and sudden death. With well-trained personnel, portable defibrillators and monitors, and the necessary cardiac drugs, mortality during transport can be markedly reduced.

At the present time, immediate thrombolysis is administered at community hospitals. This therapy is followed by transporting the patient in a specially equipped helicopter to a larger medical center for assessment and more definitive medical or invasive treatment. Results of recent studies indicate that it is safe and appropriate to administer thrombolytic therapy and delay transporting the patient for 24 to 48 hours (if necessary) to a large medical center for possible angioplasty or surgery. In prospective studies, in-hospital mortality was only 5% in patients treated with early thrombolytic therapy. Thus, it appears that treatment of myocardial infarction has entered the third phase, namely, limitation of infarct size by early restoration of coronary blood flow.

The patient with myocardial infarction is most vulnerable to tachycardia and ventricular fibrillation during the initial 36 to 48 hours postinfarction. Patients are moved from the CCU usually after 2 to 3 days, in contrast to 5 to 7 days, which was common in the 1960s and 1970s. These patients should be cared for with continuous monitoring for arrhythmias in an intermediate or stepdown CCU. To suggest that mortality or morbidity is decreased by these units cannot be verified; nevertheless, the added advantage of additional observation by trained personnel, together with the educational benefits they offer in the form of lectures and videotapes, have made these units an attractive concept to both physicians and patients. Patients are generally discharged after about 10 to 14 days. Whether the widespread use of thrombolytic therapy, angioplasty, and newer agents, such as calcium channel blockers, will provide adequate protection (while permitting earlier discharge) remains to be determined. Most patients return to work after about 8 to 10 weeks.

Initial Assessment

The initial contact with a patient suspected of experiencing myocardial infarction requires a careful, rapid assessment of the vital signs to be sure that the patient is not having life-threatening arrhythmia and does not require immediate endotracheal intubation or cardiac resuscitation. After assessment of the vital signs, it is important that an intravenous infusion be set up so that therapy can be administered rapidly and effectively, particularly if ventricular arrhythmias are present. Lidocaine is given routinely for ventricular arrhythmias, along with routine administration of nasal oxygen and morphine. An ECG tracing should be obtained and, if at all possible, the patient's rhythm should be monitored continuously.

After these initial steps, it must be immediately ascertained whether the patient is a candidate for thrombolytic therapy. In view of present understanding of the evolution of myocardial damage, time is crucial; delaying thrombolytic treatment by even 30 minutes may cause considerable residual myocardial dysfunction that could otherwise be avoided. If a physician is present for the initial assessment, thrombolytic therapy should be administered as soon as is deemed appropriate. If a physician is not present, the patient should be transported rapidly to the nearest medical facility where thrombolytic therapy can be administered.

Morphine remains the analgesic drug of choice and is extremely effective, not only in relieving pain, but also in relieving anxiety. It is also a vasodilator that causes venous pooling and decreases afterload. Morphine should be given intravenously in small doses of 2 to 4 mg, repeated every 5 minutes until the pain is relieved. The possibility that morphine may induce hypotension and bradycardia must be kept in mind, particularly in patients with an inferior infarction. Venous pooling and hypotension can be reversed by simply elevating the patient's legs, and bradycardia responds readily to atropine (0.4 mg IV). Other analgesics, such as meperidine hydrochloride, may be substituted for morphine, but they tend to be less effective in reducing pain and are equally likely to produce side effects. Sublingual nitroglycerin may be given if the patient is normotensive, although in the early hours of myocardial infarction it is relatively ineffective as an analgesic. β-Blockade therapy is also safe and effective in the relief of pain from myocardial infarction. In the acute care setting, intravenous administration of a short-acting β-blocker, such as esmolol, is preferred. Nitrous oxide in concentrations of 20% to 50% combined with oxygen is also an effective analgesic.

If the patient is particularly emotionally disturbed or hypertensive, a mild tranquilizer such as diazepam should be given 2 to 5 mg orally four times a day in addition to morphine to allay the anxiety. Because the chest pain of myocardial infarction is frightening and often conjures doom for the patient, the physician and paramedical personnel should make every effort to comfort the patient and to exhibit compassion and confidence in their overall handling of the situation. At this time, the patient needs reassurance, perhaps more than anything else.

Oxygen is routinely given by nasal prong, unless there is severe hypoxia requiring endotracheal intubation. The benefit of routine oxygen administration by nasal prongs for all patients has not been documented. Nevertheless, it has become

Table 24
Large-scale multicenter randomized trial of thrombolytic
therapy in acute myocardial infarction

Time from symptom onset to treatment	In-hospital (21-day) mortality (percent)			P
	Number of patients	Intravenous streptokinase	Control	
< 1 hour	1277	8.2	15.4	< 0.0001
≤ 3 hours	6094	9.2	12.0	< 0.0005
3-6 hours	3649	11.7	14.1	< 0.03
6-9 hours	1352	12.6	14.1	NS
9-12 hours	594	15.8	13.6	NS

Abbreviation: NS, not significant.

Source: Gruppo Italiano per lo Studio della Streptochinasi nell'Infarto
Miocardio (GISSI). Effectiveness of intravenous thrombolytic treatment in
acute myocardial infarction. *Lancet.* 1986;1:397-401.

standard practice. Once the patient's blood gases have been determined and the PO_2 is found to be normal, oxygen therapy may be discontinued.

Thrombolytic Therapy
Several studies have documented that thrombolytic therapy initiated early, preferably within the first 2 to 4 hours of the onset of myocardial infarction, is associated with improved ventricular function and a significant decrease in infarct size and acute mortality. Several thrombolytic agents have been evaluated and shown to be effective. These include streptokinase, urokinase, recombinant tissue plasminogen activator (r-TPA), and single-chain urokinase.

In the initial studies of thrombolytic therapy, streptokinase given by the intracoronary route was shown to be safe and was associated with successful reperfusion in 75% of the patients with acute myocardial infarction. However, performing cardiac catheterization delayed therapy, and the potential for salvaging ischemic myocardium was

decreased. Administration of intracoronary streptokinase will probably be restricted to special situations, such as the development of a thrombus during cardiac catheterization or during surgery.

Intravenous streptokinase given in high doses for short intervals improves ventricular function, decreases infarct size, and reduces acute mortality when administered within the initial 4 to 6 hours postinfarction. In the Group for Intravenous Streptokinase Study (GISSI), 11 712 patients were randomly assigned to treatment with 1.5 million units of streptokinase or to conventional therapy (a thrombolytic agent was not used). The in-hospital mortality rate at 21 days postinfarction was 10.7% among the streptokinase-treated group, compared with 13% in the control group. However, the mortality rate was reduced nearly 50% in patients treated within 1 hour of developing symptoms. There was a significant reduction in the mortality rate of all patients treated within the first 6 hours but no difference thereafter (Table 24). The International Study of Infarct Size (ISIS) showed an in-hospital mortality rate of 12% in the placebo group, compared with 8% in patients treated with intravenous streptokinase. In a study of 1741 patients treated within 3 hours, infarct size averaged 1633 CK units in the intravenous streptokinase group, compared with 1953 CK units in the conventionally treated group.

Tissue plasminogen activator, developed from recombinant DNA technology, has been shown to be more effective in restoring coronary patency than intravenous streptokinase. Tissue plasminogen activator (TPA) is normally produced by the endothelial cells and is part of the hematologic mechanism for preventing clots in the circulation. TPA exhibits little lytic activity, unless it is bound to fibrin. Therefore, TPA has relative clot specificity and produces much less systemic fibrinogenolysis than does streptokinase.

The Phase II Thrombolysis in Myocardial Infarction (TIMI) trial compared intravenous streptokinase (1.5 million units) with intravenous r-TPA (80 mg). Cardiac catheterization before and after treatment showed that two thirds of the subjects receiving r-TPA experienced successful reperfusion compared with only about one third of those treated with streptokinase. Only 27% of patients receiving r-TPA had fibrinogen levels less than 100 mg/dL compared with 57% of those receiving streptokinase.

Thrombolysis is effective only during the acute hospital phase, and the long-term effects are yet to be determined. However, there is a high incidence of rethrombosis (approximately 20%), despite heparinization and administration of aspirin, in the days to weeks after thrombolytic therapy. There is no known therapy to prevent rethrombosis, but evidence suggests that 2 to 3 days of heparin followed by aspirin on a permanent basis is a reasonable therapy. Rethrombosis is more likely to occur in patients with underlying plaques producing 60% to 80% obstruction.

In the Phase II TIMI study, 3262 patients received r-TPA within the first 4 hours after onset of pain. Of these, 1636 patients received invasive therapy consisting of coronary arteriography 18 to 48 hours after administration of r-TPA followed by prophylactic percutaneous transluminal coronary angioplasty (PTCA), if arteriography demonstrated suitable anatomy. The other 1626 patients were treated with a conservative strategy in which arteriography and PTCA were performed only if spontaneous or exercise-induced ischemia occurred. In the group assigned to the conservative strategy, 216 (13.3%) patients were candidates for PTCA within 14 days. Death or reinfarction occurred within 42 days in 10.9% of the group assigned to the invasive strategy and in 9.7% assigned to the conservative strategy. There were no differences between the two groups in the ventricular ejection fraction at rest or during exercise, at hospital discharge, or at 6 weeks after treatment.

In a subset of this study, whether angioplasty should be performed immediately after thrombolysis or after 18 to 48 hours was assessed. In agreement with other studies, the TIMI trial showed that angioplasty should be performed after 24 hours. Thus, if necessary after thrombolysis, angioplasty is likely to give better results when performed electively within days rather than within hours. The overall mortality at the end of 1 year was 7% in both groups. These results indicate that angioplasty is necessary after thrombolytic therapy only if the patient has symptoms of myocardial ischemia (pain) or exhibits ischemia during stress testing.

The question of who should receive thrombolytic therapy has been only partially answered. The trials performed to date have been restricted to patients with acute myocardial infarction presenting within 6 hours of onset of symptoms and showing ST-segment elevation. This combination of conditions may represent less than one half of the patients with acute myocardial infarction. In addition, the trials exclude patients who have a bleeding tendency, prior stroke, hypertension, or peptic ulcer, who have had recent surgery, or who are older than age 76. In light of recent trials showing no benefit in patients treated more than 6 hours after the onset of symptoms, it seems appropriate to restrict thrombolytic therapy to the interval of 4 to 6 hours. Patients with non–Q-wave infarction associated with ST-segment depression should not routinely receive thrombolytic therapy, unless clinical trials show such therapy to be effective.

Angioplasty performed immediately without thrombolytic therapy restores patency in 80% to 90% of patients, although this is not recommended, because the 90 to 150 minutes required to perform angioplasty jeopardize the potential for salvaging the myocardium. However, thrombolytic therapy is unsuccessful in approximately 20% to 30% of patients. If there were some way to identify those patients within minutes, they would be good candidates for immediate angioplasty. Unfortunately, at present there is no rapid, objective means of detecting successful reperfusion. CK isoforms and myoglobin measurements are being evaluated to determine their usefulness for this purpose. For patients with a contraindication to thrombolytic therapy, immediate angioplasty is recommended.

In the future, it is likely that all patients seen within the first 4 to 6 hours after acute myocardial infarction will undergo intravenous thrombolytic therapy with r-TPA, streptokinase, or some other thrombolytic agent. Intravenous r-TPA should be administered as a 6-mg bolus followed by an infusion of 54 mg in the first hour, 20 mg in the second hour, and 5 mg/hr over the next 4 hours. Streptokinase should be administered as an intravenous infusion of 1.5 million units over 60 minutes. Both agents should be followed by full heparinization to maintain the partial thromboplastin time at 1.5 to 2.0 times above normal for 3 to 5 days.

There is some controversy as to whether all patients receiving thrombolysis should undergo cardiac catheterization. The results of the Phase II TIMI study indicate that cardiac catheterization is necessary only if there is evidence of myocardial ischemia. Patients who have coronary obstruction of 80% or more of the infarcted vessel should be considered for angioplasty. The indications for surgery are the same as in any patient.

Pharmacologic Therapy for Limiting Infarct Size
Many laboratory studies have been conducted to evaluate the effect of a variety of pharmacologic agents on limiting infarct size. The principal agents assessed in clinical trials have been β-blockers, calcium channel blockers, nitroprusside, and, to a lesser extent, nitroglycerin.

β-Blockers: Of the five major trials with β-blockers, all except the timolol study showed that β-blockers were well tolerated, safe, and effective in relieving chest pain but were not effective in limiting infarct size. The Norwegian timolol study involved 144 patients who received timolol an average of 3 hours after the onset of symptoms. Infarct size, as measured by plasma CK-MB levels, was 28% less in the group receiving timolol than in the placebo group. The other four trials enrolled over 20 000 patients and no effect was observed on infarct size. Because only one study has shown a beneficial effect, β-blockers are not recommended for reducing infarct size. It is even less likely that β-blockers will be used for this purpose in the future, because most patients presenting within 4 hours after onset of symptoms will be candidates for thrombolytic therapy.

Calcium channel blockers: When used as the sole treatment for patients with unstable angina, Nifedipine did not decrease the incidence of infarction, and in one study it was associated with a significant increase. In the patients who did develop infarction, infarct size was similar to that seen in placebo-treated patients. In four other trials involving over 8000 patients who received treatment within 3 hours after the onset of symptoms, the effects of nifedipine were no different from those of the placebo group. Nifedipine has been shown to have no effect on mortality in over 7000 postmyocardial infarction patients. Thus, nifedipine is not recommended for limiting infarct size or for preventing reinfarction.

Verapamil has been assessed in only one study of more than 1446 postmyocardial infarction patients. Verapamil did not significantly decrease the incidence of reinfarction or death. Diltiazem has not yet been assessed clinically for limiting infarct size. Thus, the routine use of calcium channel blockers at the present time is not recommended for this purpose.

However, diltiazem has been shown to be effective for preventing reinfarction in patients recovering from non–Q-wave infarction (see page 189). Ongoing studies are assessing the effectiveness of the combination of calcium antagonists and thrombolytic therapy. The results of treating experimentally induced infarction with diltiazem appear promising.

Nitroglycerin: The results of studies on the efficacy of using intravenous nitroglycerin to limit infarct size have been inconclusive. In the only randomized study (which involved 120 patients), intravenous nitroglycerin showed no overall effect on infarct size or ventricular arrhythmias. However, there was a 38% reduction in infarct size in a subgroup of patients with inferior or subendocardial (non–Q-wave) infarction when compared with the placebo-treated group, but there was no effect on patients with anterior infarction. In a nonrandomized study, intravenous administration of nitroglycerin was also associated with a significant reduction of infarct size. In another study of 104 patients, intravenous nitroglycerin was given within 10 hours after the onset of symptoms and showed no reduction in infarct size, based on peak CK values. However, the total number of adverse outcomes (extension of infarction, hospital death, or development of new episodes of heart failure) was reduced in patients

receiving nitroglycerin. This effect was most marked in patients with inferior infarction. ST mapping was used in one study to measure infarct size, and nitroglycerin therapy was associated with a smaller ST-segment elevation. In a recent randomized study involving more than 300 patients, intravenous nitroglycerin therapy was associated with reduced infarct size and a lower mortality rate.

Two large, randomized studies of nitroprusside therapy have been performed. One study demonstrated a significant limitation of infarct size and the other demonstrated opposite results; the investigators concluded that nitroprusside therapy was contraindicated in the first 12 hours after acute myocardial infarction. Neither nitroglycerin nor nitroprusside is recommended for reduction of infarct size. However, in patients with myocardial infarction and cardiac failure, nitroglycerin is preferable to nitroprusside as a vasodilator.

Recommendations for limiting infarct size: Despite the lack of a specific effective agent, several recommendations emerged from these cardioprotection studies. Every effort is now made to maintain the lowest heart rate possible (eg, pacemakers are set at the lowest rate possible for adequate cardiac output). An increase in heart rate is avoided by refraining from the unnecessary use of drugs, such as atropine, and blood pressure is kept within the normal range. The liberal use of morphine and β-blockers to control pain and minimize the work of the heart is strongly recommended. However, it appears more likely that limiting infarct size may be effected by increasing coronary perfusion with thrombolytic therapy.

Physical Activity

Patients with uncomplicated myocardial infarction should be confined to bed for the first 24 hours after the onset of symptoms, but during that time they may use a bedside commode. On the second day, the patient may be permitted out of bed for a total of 1 hour and on the third day for up to 2 hours. It is now common practice to transfer the patient out of the CCU after about 3 days, provided that the patient can be moved to a stepdown unit or a regular cardiac ward where telemetry or some form of continuous cardiac monitoring is available. By the fifth or sixth day, patients are permitted to walk in the room, and they are usually allowed to shower by themselves by the eighth or ninth day. Early use of a bedside commode combined with an appropriate diet helps to promote normal bowel movement and avoid constipation, which may in itself cause straining and precipitate arrhythmias.

Patients are usually discharged after 10 to 14 days and are encouraged to walk daily at home for the next 3 to 6 weeks. They should be evaluated carefully and frequently by their physician and usually can return to work in 8 to 10 weeks. Submaximal exercise testing before discharge restores the patient's confidence and provides information for further stratification (see Postinfarction Stratification and Investigation on page 186).

Diet
As mentioned previously, an intravenous catheter should be inserted at initial assessment so that all forms of therapy can be administered intravenously. A soft diet is recommended for the first 2 days postinfarction. The customary recommendation of a diet low in cholesterol, saturated fat, and caffeine during the first 2 to 3 days is probably without a scientific basis and should not be routinely prescribed. A stool softener is usually given to prevent constipation and straining.

Treatment of Arrhythmias
Improved treatment of arrhythmias both before and during hospitalization has been a major factor in reducing the mortality rate associated with acute myocardial infarction. The primary culprits are ventricular arrhythmias, which usually can be treated quickly with intravenous lidocaine. Thus, it has become routine when assessing patients for suspected myocardial infarction to quickly ascertain whether they have ventricular arrhythmias. If

they do, the initial treatment of choice is intravenous lidocaine given as a bolus, followed by intravenous lidocaine infusion for at least 24 to 48 hours. Ventricular tachycardia or multiple premature ventricular contractions (PVCs) or couplets that may lead to ventricular tachycardia should be reduced to a minimum. Nevertheless, a significant number of patients die before reaching the hospital, presumably due to arrhythmias. If patients could be reached in time to receive lidocaine treatment, many of these deaths might be prevented.

The use of prophylactic lidocaine has been proposed. However, clinical studies performed to date do not show a significant reduction in the incidence of mortality, although there is a decreased incidence of ventricular tachycardia and fibrillation. In the patient with a so-called warning arrhythmia, lidocaine is used for treatment rather than for prophylaxis. Because ventricular fibrillation or tachycardia often develops de novo, prophylaxis may be wise. It is generally accepted that prophylactic lidocaine should be given when patients with acute myocardial infarction are transported to the hospital. Similarly, in smaller hospitals where the nursing personnel is less well-trained or where 24-hour coverage by house staff is not available, prophylactic lidocaine for all patients with myocardial infarction may also be appropriate. In the CCU, lidocaine can be administered when arrhythmias appear, such as five or more isolated ectopic ventricular beats per minute, multifocal ventricular extrasystoles, ventricular beats superimposed on the T wave, or runs of three or more ectopic ventricular beats.

Intravenous lidocaine should be given in a bolus of 1 mg/kg followed by an infusion of 2 to 4 mg/min. The ventricular arrhythmias, whether they are isolated PVCs or runs of ventricular tachycardia, usually subside within 36 to 48 hours. If ventricular ectopy increases during the infusion, the physician should proceed with an additional bolus of lidocaine, which can be repeated. However, the physician should keep in mind that patients with cardiac failure, hypotension, or hepatic disease require about half the dose of lidocaine, because the elimination rate of the drug is slowed. The side effects of lidocaine, although reversible, are markedly accentuated in these patients and also in elderly patients. In patients receiving thrombolytic therapy, lidocaine is routinely given prophylactically. Because many patients are likely to receive thrombolytic therapy in the future, the controversy concerning whether prophylactic lidocaine should be administered will become somewhat academic, because most patients will be receiving prophylactic lidocaine while they are receiving thrombolytic therapy.

The development of ventricular tachycardia unresponsive to lidocaine should be dealt with promptly by electrical defibrillation. Patients developing ventricular fibrillation should undergo immediate electroconversion, as should patients with ventricular tachycardia and hemodynamic deterioration. If ventricular fibrillation cannot be immediately cardioverted, then it may be necessary to initiate cardiac resuscitation for improved oxygenation before attempting further electroconversion. If ventricular tachycardia or fibrillation persists or recurs despite lidocaine and electrocardioversion, a second antiarrhythmic agent must be used. This additional therapy usually starts with intravenous procainamide in a bolus of 1 to 2 mg/kg given over 5 to 10 minutes, followed by an intravenous infusion of 20 to 80 µg/kg/min. If this is ineffective, the lidocaine is continued and other agents may be substituted for procainamide, such as incainide, flecainide, ethmozine, or dilantin. For patients with ventricular premature beats associated with hemodynamic compromise that persists despite treatment with lidocaine, the physician should consider using procainamide or a β-blocker.

When treating arrhythmias, it is also important to remember that the patient may have hypoxemia, electrolyte imbalance, acidosis, or hypokalemia and hypomagnesemia. In cases of ventricular fibrillation resistant to repeated electroshock, lidocaine, or other antiarrhythmics, administration of intravenous bretylium tosylate (5 mg/kg) should be considered and can be repeated every 10 to 20 minutes if necessary. If this is effective, then an intravenous infusion of bretylium tosylate at 2 mg/min can be initiated if the arrhythmia recurs. Electroshock is often more effective after a bolus of bretylium. The other therapy for resistant ventricular fibrillation is administration of epinephrine, which often converts the fine ventricular fibrillation to a more coarse pattern that may then be more responsive to drugs and electroshock.

A small percentage of patients have a form of ventricular tachycardia that has a slow rate of 60 to 100 beats per minute. This form of tachycardia has been referred to as an accelerated idioventricular rhythm ("accelerated" because beats originating from the ventricle would normally have a rate of about 40 per minute). This entity occurs most commonly after inferior myocardial infarction, is usually transient and benign, and generally does not require any treatment. Accelerated idioventricular rhythm has been observed with increasing frequency after thrombolytic therapy. If treatment is required, administration of atropine can increase the sinus rate, although the ventricular tachycardia can also be treated with lidocaine.

Supraventricular arrhythmias may also occur with acute myocardial infarction and may include sinus bradycardia, atrial ectopic beats, flutter, or fibrillation. Atrial fibrillation occurs in about 9% of patients with myocardial infarction, is usually transient, and seldom requires treatment. However, if an atrial tachycardia (whether fibrillation or flutter) is associated with a rapid ventricular response and is not immediately abated by β-blockade, then electroshock should be instituted immediately to minimize the demands on the ischemic myocardium.

Sinus tachycardia occurs in 20% to 30% of patients with myocardial infarction. If sinus tachycardia is due to ventricular failure, it should be managed by treatment of the underlying failure. However, the tachycardia may reflect anxiety and should be treated with sedation, or if it is due to recurring pain, with analgesics. If the sinus tachycardia is secondary to pericarditis, treatment with aspirin or some other anti-inflammatory agent is indicated. Sinus bradycardia not associated with hypotension or other symptoms does not require treatment. It is rare that a temporary intravenous pacemaker is needed for sinus bradycardia. However, as with ventricular arrhythmias, other causes (eg, digitalis toxicity and electrolyte or acid-base imbalance) must be excluded. Persistent sinus tachycardia for 12 to 24 hours generally reflects severe pump failure and is an indication for hemodynamic monitoring and further intensive therapy for cardiac failure.

Indications for Hemodynamic Monitoring

The direct monitoring of intracardiac hemodynamics became feasible in the early 1970s with the introduction of the Swan-Ganz flotation catheter. This catheter, which can be inserted percutaneously at the bedside, is a safe and valuable means to aid in the overall treatment of acute myocardial infarction. One well-documented, consistent hemodynamic consequence of myocardial ischemia and infarction is decreased ventricular compliance, which results in increased end-diastolic pressure and an increase in overall systemic vascular resistance. Use of the Swan-Ganz flotation catheter provides important data about cardiac output, the pressures in the chambers, and capillary wedge pressure and provides a means of calculating overall systemic vascular resistance. The Swan-Ganz catheter is probably indicated in fewer than one third of patients with myocardial infarction. However, whether it should be used depends on the experience of the CCU personnel, the nurses, and the physicians. The following conditions in patients with acute myocardial infarction are indications for Swan-Ganz catheterization:

- Cardiogenic shock;
- Hypotension;
- Acute myocardial infarction occurring during or after surgery;
- Cardiac failure unresponsive to therapy;
- Persistent sinus tachycardia;
- Vasodilator therapy in patients with systolic blood pressures less than 120 mm Hg;
- Severe lung disease and suspected left ventricular failure;
- Right ventricular failure from suspected or confirmed right ventricular infarction;
- Development of mitral regurgitation or ventricular septal defect; and
- Unexplained coma, restlessness, hypoxia, acidosis, or oliguria without cardiac failure.

There are considerably less data about which patients should have intra-arterial catheter monitoring of blood pressure. The primary reason for monitoring blood pressure is to assess the response to therapy during hypotension. The automatic devices that inflate, deflate, record, and transmit data to a central station have the advantages of being noninvasive, safer, and not requiring the presence of a nurse or physician. In cases of severe hypotension and vasoconstriction, the cuff pressure may be 5% to 10% lower than pressure measured by an arterial catheter. However, the primary interest is in the change in pressure, which has been shown to be correctly reflected by the cuff or automatic devices. In general, careful monitoring of the vital signs, repeated auscultation of the lung fields, viewing chest roentgenograms, measuring urine output, and measuring the usual laboratory parameters (PO_2, PCO_2, pH, and electrolytes) are sufficient for most patients with uncomplicated myocardial infarction. It is absolutely essential in using the Swan-Ganz catheter or intraarterial catheter that the need for hemodynamic monitoring be reassessed on a 24-hour basis. In most cases, these catheters can be removed within hours, or certainly within 1 to 2 days, after the hemodynamic response to therapy has been established.

Heparin and Anticoagulation

As discussed, patients undergoing early thrombolytic therapy also must receive full heparinization for at least 2 to 3 days. They should then be given aspirin, which should be continued after the patient is discharged from the hospital. Subcutaneous administration of heparin, 5000 to 8000 units every 12 hours, is recommended for patients who do not undergo thrombolytic therapy and do not have a contraindication to heparin. There is an increasing tendency to fully heparinize patients with anterior infarction who do not receive thrombolytic therapy; however, no data support the efficacy of this treatment. Patients at high risk for thrombosis, such as those who are obese or in shock, should also be considered for full-dose heparin therapy for the first 2 to 3 days. The initial intravenous dose should be 5000 to 10 000 units, followed by 1000 to 2000 units per hour to maintain the partial thromboplastin time at 1.5 to 2.5 times above normal. Use of oral anticoagulants in the early treatment of myocardial infarction is not customary.

Complications of Myocardial Infarction

Cardiac Failure

Cardiac failure following acute infarction is due to impaired contractility and is more correctly termed myocardial failure. A brief review of the historical background of cardiac failure and its treatment may be helpful. By the early 1900s, it was established that as the stretch on the myocardium increased as a result of increased ventricular volume, ventricular pressure, or both, the muscle augmented its force of contraction. This relationship is referred to as "the law of the heart" or "the ascending limb of Starling's curve."

Starling's experiments were performed in 1914 in a heart-lung preparation in which fluid was infused into the right atrium through the superior vena cava. Pressure was then determined from the right side of the heart, and cardiac output was determined from the aorta. As the rate of infusion was increased, cardiac output increased until the heart-lung preparation became overdistended and cardiac output decreased precipitously. The decrease in cardiac output as a result of overdistension was referred to incorrectly by subsequent investigators as "the descending limb of Starling's curve" and was thought to correlate with the clinical entity of cardiac failure.

With the development of Huxley's sliding filament theory, it was thought that overstretching of the sarcomeres beyond their optimal length of 2.2 μm corresponded to the descending limb and correlated with the onset of cardiac failure. Physiologists and physicians assumed diuretics would decrease the cardiac volume and thus improve cardiac performance.

Rapid fixation of cardiac tissue in diastole in experimental animals demonstrated that the sarcomeres in the endocardium normally average 2.0 to 2.2 μm, and as the volume or pressure increases, sarcomeres are recruited from the midcardial and epicardial layers. However, the sarcomeres in the midcardium or epicardium do not stretch beyond about 2.3 μm. It was observed that the descending limb of Starling exists neither at the sarcomere level nor hemodynamically in isolated hearts, intact experimental animals, or humans. In cardiac failure the myocardium is depressed, and contractility is depressed throughout the pressure–cardiac output curve.

The use of diuretics might be assumed to decrease cardiac volume and improve cardiac function. However, the administration of diuretics, even in patients with chronic failure and hypervolemia, is not associated with increased cardiac output; in patients with acute myocardial infarction, such therapy is usually associated with a decrease in cardiac output. The effect of diuretics is to relieve systemic and pulmonary congestion, but they have no direct effect on cardiac performance. Occasionally, a slight increase in cardiac output is seen with the administration of diuretics in patients who are normovolemic or hypervolemic, but this is due to decreased afterload rather than decreased preload.

Clinically, cardiac failure after acute myocardial infarction develops when 20% to 25% or more of the left ventricle is involved, a condition that occurs in up to 50% of patients. The decrease in ventricular function is partly reversible, because most patients experiencing failure for the first time return to more normal function in 24 to 48 hours. The decreased contractility results in an increase in end-diastolic volume that, together with decreased compliance from changes in the myocardium or the pericardium, contributes to increased diastolic pressure and pulmonary congestion. In most cases, heart failure is compensated by adrenergic stimulation that increases the heart rate and by the force of contraction of the remaining nonischemic myocardium. Heart size usually remains normal, as does cardiac output.

Because patients are usually normovolemic before infarction, the sudden development of cardiac failure and loss of fluid into the lungs is associated with a decreased vascular volume and relative hypovolemia, which are partly compensated by increased vascular resistance. In the initial days of cardiac failure associated with acute myocardial infarction, patients do not retain significant amounts of salt and water, particularly those with an anterior infarction. Thus, the loss of fluid into the lungs at the expense of the vascular volume may precipitate hypotension that could jeopardize coronary perfusion.

The conventional therapy of using digoxin and diuretics for cardiac failure was developed from clinical observations that most cases of chronic cardiac failure and hypervolemia were due to either valvular or congenital heart disease. Patients with acute myocardial infarction are usually operating on the ascending limb of Starling's curve due to decreased compliance, and thus higher filling pressures are required to maintain an adequate cardiac output. With the administration of diuretics, there is a prompt decrease in venomotor tone that results in pooling of the blood, decreased ventricular filling pressure, and decreased cardiac output. This response occurs independently of the diuresis, which usually peaks sometime later. In addition, depending on the pressure-volume relationship of the ventricle, the diuresis may precipitate a further decrease in cardiac output and produce hypotension. In patients with inferior infarction, particularly with significant right ventricular involvement, the effects of administering a diuretic may be catastrophic and simulate cardiogenic shock.

Until the fluid status of patients with inferior infarction is known, diuretics should be withheld, particularly if the patient has pulmonary edema and borderline hypotension (100 to 110 mm Hg systolic). In such patients, monitoring with a Swan-Ganz catheter is indicated to assess right ventricular function, particularly the end-diastolic pressure. If the patient exhibits hypovolemia, fluids should be administered, and if cardiac output does not increase, administration of dobutamine is indicated. If the jugular venous pressure is not elevated, diuretics and vasodilators should be avoided and a rapid-acting intravenous inotropic agent, such as dobutamine (2 to 5 µg/kg/min), should be started. The heart rate should not be permitted to increase more than 10%. Patients with mild failure, specifically those with a third heart sound with or without basal rales or symptoms of dyspnea, need only morphine for pain, along with oxygen and the usual supportive measures.

For patients who have more significant rales and are experiencing some hypoxemia or dyspnea, a vasodilator is appropriate and achieves the same result as a diuretic without the loss of vascular volume. The vasodilator preferred is intravenous nitroglycerin initiated at 5 to 10 mg/min and increased so that there is no more than a 10% decrease in blood pressure or 10% increase in heart rate.

Patients who have borderline hypotension (systolic pressure of 100 to 110 mm Hg) and are in moderate to severe failure should receive an inotropic agent immediately without a vasodilator. If needed, a vasodilator may be added later. The addition or initiation of vasodilator therapy in this setting may precipitate hypotension that can be deleterious to coronary perfusion. Dobutamine is preferred, because it decreases the ventricular filling pressure, which in turn reduces pulmonary congestion and its corresponding symptoms. Dobutamine induces mild peripheral vasodilation that has been shown to increase coronary flow. If the administration of dobutamine causes no more than a 10% increase in heart rate, infarct size does not increase.

Dopamine, in contrast, does not decrease the ventricular filling pressure, and in moderate to high doses, it causes vasoconstriction and increased ventricular filling pressure. Dopamine may be combined with a vasodilator or with dobutamine. Patients who are in failure with hypotension or cardiogenic shock should receive a vasoconstricting agent, such as dopamine. If a diuretic is used in the treatment of cardiac failure, a low dose is recommended, such as 20 mg of furosemide. Vasodilator therapy or inotropic therapy should be given if this is not adequate.

Digoxin has a minimal inotropic effect compared with the effect of catecholamines, has a long half-life of 31 hours, and achieves maximal effect after a loading dose is administered (preferably over a 24-hour period). Because most episodes of cardiac failure are transient, it is preferable to use an agent that is rapid acting and has a short half-life; if cardiac failure persists, patients should be started on oral digoxin. Amrinone (a new inotropic agent) inhibits phosphodiesterase activity, indirectly elevates cellular levels of cyclic AMP, and increases the availability of calcium. Amrinone is given only intravenously with a loading dose of 1.5 mg/kg followed by infusion at a rate of 10 to 20 µg/kg/min. Amrinone's onset of action is rapid and its half-life is 1 to 2 hours in patients with cardiac failure. Like dobutamine, amrinone increases contractility (although less than dobutamine), lowers left ventricular filling pressure and systemic vascular resistance, and has a minimal effect on systemic arterial pressure and heart rate. The overall objective of amrinone administration is to relieve pulmonary congestion and maintain an adequate cardiac output with as low a ventricular filling pressure as possible.

Cardiogenic Shock
Cardiogenic shock occurs in about 5% to 10% of hospitalized patients with acute myocardial infarction and is the most common cause of death in these patients. The mortality rate from cardiogenic shock is 80% to 100%. Therefore, the only effective treatment is prevention. Postmortem studies show

myocardial necrosis involves 40% or more of the ventricular mass in areas of old and new infarction. Occasionally, patients with an initial episode of myocardial infarction may develop shock followed by an early extension of the area of infarction. However, it is rare for patients with no history of ischemic heart disease to develop cardiogenic shock within hours of their first admission. Despite the gloomy prognosis for patients who develop cardiogenic shock, some patients have reversible injury, and with support, they can recover and lead normal lives. Thus, every step must be taken to maintain the systemic circulation until a definitive diagnosis is made and all treatable lesions are excluded.

Cardiogenic shock consists of circulatory failure and cardiac failure and is manifested by impaired perfusion to multiple organs. The following clinical criteria have been proposed for diagnosing cardiogenic shock:

- Primary cardiac abnormality;
- A sustained drop in systolic blood pressure below 85 mm Hg;
- A ventricular filling pressure of 16 mm Hg or more; and
- Peripheral organ involvement as shown by two or more of the following manifestations: oliguria (urine output less than 20 mL/hr), impaired mentation, cold clammy skin, or a cardiac index less than 1.5 L/min/m^2.

In addition to having the obvious findings listed above, the patient is usually drowsy, restless, and exhibits pulmonary congestion, tachycardia, tachypnea, and peripheral vasoconstriction. Before making the diagnosis of cardiac shock, the physician must exclude hypovolemia that may occur from morphine, diuretics, vasodilators, or dehydration; occasionally cardiac shock may occur from sustained ventricular or supraventricular arrhythmias. Three other diagnoses to be excluded are right ventricular infarction, pulmonary embolus, and tamponade. Complications associated with cardiogenic shock include rupture of the ventricular septum or mitral valve (see Ventricular Septal Rupture and Papillary Muscle Rupture on pages 180 and 181, respectively). Occasionally, hypotension associated with severe cardiac failure may

be precipitated by the use of intravenous antiarrhythmic agents in the presence of moderate to severe left ventricular dysfunction, particularly with the use of procainamide, quinidine, and flecainide.

If adequate oxygen cannot be delivered by nasal prongs, the patient must be intubated. Every effort must be made to restore the blood pressure. Discontinue vasodilators and drugs that have a negative inotropic effect, relieve pain, and monitor hemodynamics. Dopamine should be initiated as an intravenous infusion at 2 to 5 µg/kg/min and increased as needed by increments of 2 µg/kg/min up to 60 µg/kg/min, if necessary. In addition, cardiac output, blood pressure, and overall organ perfusion (for example, as measured by urine output) should be assessed.

An attempt should be made to improve perfusion with the least possible increase in heart rate and arrhythmias. If the blood pressure can be maintained around 90 mm Hg, dobutamine should be used, because it tends to achieve better myocardial perfusion with less increase in systemic vascular resistance. In addition, by decreasing the pulmonary wedge pressure, dobutamine relieves the symptoms of pulmonary congestion. Dobutamine, unlike dopamine, increases coronary flow as a result of a direct coronary vasodilatory effect. Dobutamine should be initiated as an intravenous infusion at 5 µg/kg/min and increased by increments of 2 µg up to 40 µg/kg/min.

Because the basic defect in cardiogenic shock is impaired contractility, mechanical assist devices should be considered. The device that has been used most is the percutaneous aortic balloon. The balloon does not necessarily improve survival but, in the case of correctable lesions, will help to maintain the myocardium and keep the patient viable until therapy that improves survival is available. The percutaneous aortic balloon is particularly useful for temporary management of ventricular septal or papillary muscle rupture until surgery is performed. It is possible that cardiac transplantation may be undertaken in the future for patients in cardiogenic shock. Artificial devices, such as the left ventricular assist device, may be used until a heart is available. Cardiac surgery, consisting of aneurysmectomy and bypass, has not been helpful for patients with cardiogenic shock. Anecdotal information suggests that in selected cases, if thrombolytic therapy is not effective in the first 2 to 3 hours, angioplasty may be attempted; however, at present this approach is not recommended.

Postinfarction Angina

Chest pain associated with acute myocardial infarction usually subsides within 12 to 24 hours. However, its persistence or recurrence after 24 to 48 hours is an important prognostic symptom reflecting viable myocardium that is vulnerable to ischemia. It also indicates that the patient is at increased immediate and long-term risk of recurring pain, reinfarction, and death. Reinfarction must be diagnosed quickly, and the patient must be treated immediately.

The incidence of postinfarction angina varies from 10% to 60% and is most common after non–Q-wave infarction. One recent prospective study of 576 patients with non–Q-wave infarction reported a 43% incidence of postinfarction angina, and in two large retrospective studies the incidence was 46% and 50%. Thus, the incidence of angina after non–Q-wave infarction is about 40% to 50% during the 2-week hospital stay, compared with only about 10% to 15% after Q-wave infarction. However, after thrombolytic therapy the incidence without angioplasty is about 30%.

The incidence of early reinfarction and death in patients with postinfarction angina is threefold to fourfold greater than in patients without angina, and if angina is accompanied by changes in the ECG pattern, it is fivefold to sixfold greater. Reinfarction in patients who have had angina accompanied by ECG changes is associated with more extensive damage than reinfarction in patients who do not develop angina. Numerous studies have reported that over 90% of patients with postinfarction angina and ECG changes have multivessel disease as shown by coronary angiography, and about 10% of these patients have left main artery disease.

Patients should be stabilized with nitrates, β-blockers, or calcium channel blockers and should be considered for coronary angiography (see Postinfarction Stratification and Investigation on page 186). Patients refractory to oral therapy should receive a continuous intravenous infusion of nitroglycerin. If patients are refractory to medical therapy, coronary angiography should be performed to evaluate the desirability of surgical treatment or angioplasty. Although no control studies are available to determine their efficacy, heparin and aspirin should be considered as additional therapies. In the future, treatment of these patients will probably include thrombolytic therapy.

There is some evidence that platelet aggregation may play a role in resting angina. One postulated mechanism for the high incidence of reinfarction is progressive thrombosis over days or weeks, resulting in complete occlusion and reinfarction.

Postinfarction angina is best treated by prevention, and perhaps all patients should receive nitrate therapy in addition to morphine. Available results suggest that patients admitted with non–Q-wave infarction should be treated with nitrates and diltiazem, 240 to 360 mg/day, shortly after admission if no contraindications are present. Results of a prospective double-blind trial in patients with non–Q-wave infarction showed that diltiazem reduced the incidence of reinfarction and refractory angina by 50% (Figure 53). This salutary effect of diltiazem was additive to any benefit obtained from nitrates or β-blockers. Diltiazem was also shown to be effective in the treatment of postinfarction angina occurring in patients after Q-wave infarction; however, a controlled study has not been performed.

Early Reinfarction

Early reinfarction (also referred to as extension of infarction) is relatively common and is of great prognostic significance, requiring intense treatment and follow-up. Early reinfarction is recognized clinically as recurrence of chest pain, but until recently, confirmation of new necrosis was difficult to obtain because of the insensitivity of detecting changes in the Q wave, the nonspecificity of changes in the ST-T segment, and the prolonged elevation of LDH activity. Sensitive and specific recognition of early reinfarction was made possible with the development of assays for the quantitative determination of plasma CK-MB.

Changes in the ECG pattern lack specificity in detecting early reinfarction as illustrated in a report showing a reinfarction incidence of 86% based on serial ECG mapping. The overall incidence of reinfarction as defined by a secondary elevation in plasma CK-MB is about 10%, occurring primarily after non–Q-wave infarction. The incidence after Q-wave infarction is estimated to be less than 5%, unless there has been successful thrombolytic therapy, in which case the incidence is increased to 8% to 10%. The incidence of early reinfarction has decreased significantly over the past 5 years, in part, because patients are discharged earlier and, consequently, early reinfarction may go unrecognized, and, in part, because of presumably more effective preventive therapy. Several studies in which reinfarction was confirmed by a secondary elevation in the level of plasma CK-MB showed that reinfarction is associated with impaired ventricular function and increased morbidity and mortality. Recurrent post-

Figure 53
Reduction of reinfarction and refractory angina in patients with non–Q-wave infarction who were treated with diltiazem

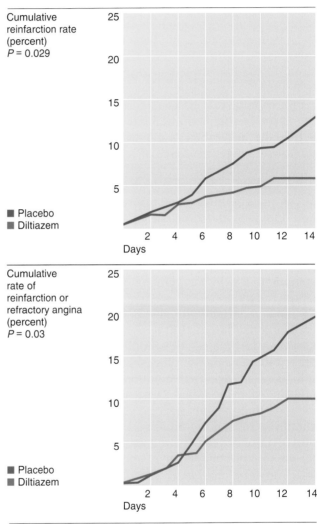

(**A**) Life-table cumulative reinfarction rates according to treatment group.
(**B**) Life-table cumulative rates of reinfarction or refractory angina according to treatment group.

infarction angina, particularly if associated with ECG pattern changes, is highly predictive of reinfarction (see Postinfarction Angina on page 178).

Patients recovering from non–Q-wave infarction should undergo routine plasma CK-MB analysis every 12 hours throughout their hospital stay. Patients recovering from Q-wave or non–Q-wave infarction who develop postinfarction angina should have CK-MB levels analyzed every 12 hours for the remainder of the hospital stay. Early reinfarction should be considered an indication for coronary angiography. Several studies have shown that patients who experience early reinfarction have a high incidence of left main artery and multivessel disease.

Because an estimated 75% of patients who develop early reinfarction are recovering from non–Q-wave infarction, early preventive therapy is recommended. In a prospective, double-blind study of 576 patients with non–Q-wave infarction, patients receiving diltiazem (360 mg/day) in combination with conventional therapy exhibited a 50% reduction in early reinfarction and severe angina compared with patients receiving only conventional therapy (80% received nitrates and 60% received β-blockers). Studies to date with other calcium channel blockers (verapamil, nifedipine) and β-blockers (timolol) have failed to show efficacy. After the initial 24 hours, it is recommended that patients with non–Q-wave infarction should receive, if not otherwise contraindicated, nitroglycerin, diltiazem, and aspirin (80 to 160 mg) throughout the hospital stay and after discharge. In a long-term, double-blind study involving nearly 2500 patients, of whom 634 had non–Q-wave infarction, the rate of mortality or reinfarction was 40% less after the first year in patients receiving diltiazem, compared with the placebo group. A beneficial effect on the rate of mortality or reinfarction was observed even after 4 years of administration of diltiazem. Thus, after recovery from non–Q-wave infarction, patients should continue to receive diltiazem and aspirin after they leave the hospital.

Patients developing reinfarction should be treated with nitroglycerin, diltiazem, and possibly thrombolytic therapy, and after they are stabilized should undergo coronary angiography. Patients with left main artery disease or triple-vessel disease should be considered for surgical treatment. It remains to be determined whether the other patients should have angioplasty or should be treated medically. Despite the increasing use of angioplasty, there are no controlled studies on the efficacy of this treatment followed by nitrates, diltiazem, and aspirin. If pain is refractory to medical therapy, coronary angiography should be performed to determine the suitability of angioplasty or surgical treatment. Both surgical treatment and angioplasty provide effective symptomatic relief for non–Q-wave infarction, although a prospective controlled study has not been performed. The etiology and pathogenesis of non–Q-wave infarction and reinfarction remain to be elucidated. However, studies have demonstrated the beneficial effect of aspirin on reducing the likelihood of reinfarction and death in patients with unstable angina. Therefore, long-term diltiazem and aspirin therapy should be considered for patients with non–Q-wave infarction, regardless of whether they receive angioplasty or surgical treatment.

Ventricular Septal Rupture

Ventricular septal rupture following myocardial infarction probably occurs in fewer than 1% to 2% of patients, but it is a devastating complication associated with a mortality rate between 50% and 90%. Ventricular septal rupture occurs most commonly after an anterior infarction and is associated with a defect in the apical muscular portion of the septum, in contrast to an inferior infarction, which is associated with a defect of the basal portion. Patients experiencing their first Q-wave infarction develop ventricular septal rupture between the first and fifth day of the recovery phase. The rupture initiates a left-to-right shunt, which is always clinically significant and results in biventricular failure, pulmonary edema, and cardiogenic shock with rapid deterioration. In addition to sudden clinical deterioration, the predominant feature of ventricular septal rupture is the abrupt appearance of a harsh holosystolic murmur. In over 50% of patients, the murmur is associated with a palpable parasternal thrill, best felt at the parasternal area. There is usually a hyperdynamic precordium, severe hypotension associated with third and fourth heart sounds, and, if tachycardia is present, a summation gallop.

Rupture of the ventricular septum is more likely to be associated with conduction defects, such as intraventricular or bundle-branch block, than with a ruptured papillary muscle. Right-sided heart failure and elevated jugular venous pressure are also more common in patients with ventricular septal rupture than in patients with ruptured mitral papillary muscle. Confirmation of the diagnosis of ventricular septal rupture can be made at the bedside using a Swan-Ganz catheter to demonstrate an oxygen saturation step-up in the right ventricle. The large V wave observed in the pulmonary wedge pressure tracing with mitral valve rupture is rare with ventricular septal rupture, although a large rupture associated with significant pulmonary hypertension may produce a large V wave. Patients who develop ventricular septal rupture almost always undergo surgical correction, because the untreated defect leads to cardiogenic shock and death. Until recently the results of surgical treatment have been disappointing, because the infarcted tissue did not maintain closure of the defect. The recent use of pledgets and Dacron patches has greatly alleviated this problem and has vastly improved the possibility of survival.

Papillary Muscle Rupture

Papillary muscle rupture following myocardial infarction almost always causes dysfunction of the mitral valve and, as with a ventricular septal rupture, is a catastrophic event. The postero-medial papillary muscle of the mitral valve is most commonly involved. This rupture occurs in association with an inferior infarction, whereas rupture of the anterolateral papillary muscle occurs with an anterior infarction. Posteromedial papillary muscle rupture is more common, because this muscle has a single source of blood supply (the right coronary artery), in contrast to the anterior papillary muscle, which has a dual supply from both the left anterior descending and left circumflex coronary arteries.

The clinical severity of papillary muscle rupture depends, in part, on the extent of the injury from myocardial infarction and on whether both heads of the papillary muscle are ruptured. The rupture usually occurs suddenly, within 2 to 7 days after onset of infarction, and is heralded by pulmonary edema secondary to massive pulmonary hypertension and cardiogenic shock. Postmortem examination of patients who died of papillary muscle rupture has shown that the myocardial injury usually involved less than 25% of the left ventricular wall, indicating the importance of an aggressive surgical approach.

The characteristic finding on auscultation of patients with papillary muscle rupture is a low-pitched holosystolic murmur that can be heard all over the precordium and radiates to the axilla with a characteristic decrescendo feature. Because of the high pressure in the noncompliant left atrium, the pressure difference between the left ventricle and the left atrium drops off quickly and, therefore, the murmur decreases in intensity. There is little correlation between the intensity of the murmur and the degree of mitral regurgitation, because the intensity depends on the degree of left ventricular dysfunction, the peripheral systemic resistance, and other factors. The murmur is much less likely to be accompanied by a palpable thrill than the murmur of ventricular septal rupture. The onset of mitral regurgitation may or may not be associated with chest pain. Often a third as well as a fourth heart sound is heard and, if tachycardia is present, a summation gallop. The arterial pulse may have a brisk, rising upstroke and, depending on the degree of the left ventricular dysfunction, a hyperdynamic apical impulse may be present.

The presystolic distension that occurs as a result of the contracting atrium is often palpable. Physical examination may reveal other features, such as a giant Q wave in the jugular venous pulse. This finding is a result of enhanced right atrial contraction arising from pulmonary hypertension and a sustained right ventricular impulse along the left parasternal border. There may be wide splitting of the second heart sound (S_2) from the shortening of left ventricular ejection, because most of the blood is ejected through the mitral valve. Pulmonary hypotension may accentuate P_2 (the pulmonic valve component of S_2), which may be heard best in the pulmonary and aortic areas. Simultaneous palpation with both hands can detect the early systolic apical impulse and the late systolic parasternal impulse, which produce a rocking motion to the chest. Diffuse rales are usually heard on auscultation of the lungs.

Prompt recognition of papillary muscle rupture is extremely important; usually the diagnosis is confirmed by the large V wave in the Swan-Ganz catheter tracing. To exclude the possibility of a ruptured ventricular septum, oxygen saturation should be determined in blood samples obtained from the pulmonary artery to the right atrium with the Swan-Ganz catheter. A lack of increase in oxygenation suggests a ruptured papillary muscle. Patients should be stabilized and maintained on aortic balloon and medical therapy before surgical treatment. The mortality rate is about 90% without repair and about 50% with early surgical treatment.

Rupture of the Myocardium

Rupture of the myocardium after myocardial infarction is a catastrophic event that occurs in fewer than 1% of patients. Rupture of the myocardium is the third most common cause of death in acute myocardial infarction. Typically, the patient has a Q-wave infarction and the rupture involves the free wall of the left ventricle. Myocardial rupture is more common in patients over age 65, in women, in patients with preexisting hypertension, and in patients experiencing myocardial infarction for the first time. The rupture usually occurs within the first 5 days after an acute myocardial infarction.

Myocardial rupture is heralded by prolonged chest pain, dyspnea, hypotension, neck vein distension, tamponade, and ECG evidence of electrical mechanical dissociation. Death usually occurs within minutes. However, the course may be somewhat slowed or become chronic when the ventricle ruptures into the pericardium through a false sac made by pericardial lesions or from a previously organized clot, so that the ventricle is contained within a saccular lumen of the pericardium.

The diagnosis can usually be made by echocardiography or radionuclide ventriculography, but it should be confirmed by cardiac catheterization. A false aneurysm requires surgical treatment, which should be performed soon after the diagnosis. The more typical acute cardiac rupture requires urgent treatment, but there is seldom time to initiate therapy. However, the patient should be taken directly to the operating room, because some patients have been saved with emergency surgical repair of the rupture.

Pericarditis

Pericarditis occurs in 5% to 10% of patients with myocardial infarction. It usually develops more than 48 hours after the onset of myocardial infarction. Pericarditis occurs more commonly in patients with Q-wave infarction and is usually heralded by the appearance of pleural pericardial pain, as well as a pericardial rub. The recommended treatment is aspirin. Not infrequently, pericarditis may be the cause of chest pain recurring 48 to 72 hours after the onset of myocardial infarction. It is important to investigate the possibility of pericarditis when evaluating recurrent pain to avoid inappropriate treatment with nitrates or β-blockers or exacerbating the problem by administering anticoagulants. The widespread use of thrombolytic therapy and heparin has increased the incidence of tamponade from bleeding into the pericardium.

Dressler's Syndrome

Dressler's syndrome is characterized by fever and pleural or pericardial chest pain and usually occurs within 2 to 6 weeks after myocardial infarction. Dressler's syndrome is often associated with pain and stiffness of the left shoulder but rarely with a pleural effusion. Thought to be autoimmune in origin, the incidence of this syndrome has decreased markedly in the past 10 years. Initial treatment consists of salicylates and, if necessary, steroid therapy.

Prognosis of Q-Wave and Non-Q-Wave Infarction

Approximately 10% of the patients with myocardial infarction who are admitted to the hospital die within a few days; another 10% die during the subsequent year, usually during the first 6 to 12 weeks. This 6- to 12-week interval is a period of extreme vulnerability during which the patient requires intensive follow-up. After the first year, the annual mortality rate decreases to about 5%.

This mortality pattern was assumed to be the natural history applicable to all types of acute myocardial infarction until 1981, when it was discovered that 30% to 40% of patients with acute myocardial infarction, specifically those with non-Q-wave infarction, do not exhibit this profile. It had been known for some time that an initial non-Q-wave infarction is associated with a low rate of in-hospital mortality compared with that of patients with Q-wave infarction. However, 2 to 4 years after myocardial infarction the cumulative mortality is similar.

In a prospective study of 350 patients, enzymatic estimates of infarct size in patients with non-Q-wave infarction averaged 12 CK-MB g/Eq compared with 25 CK-MB g/Eq for patients with Q-wave infarction. The in-hospital mortality for patients with non-Q-wave infarction was 5% compared with 18% for patients with Q-wave infarction. In a long-term follow-up, distinct profiles were observed for Q-wave and non-Q-wave infarction (Figure 54). Mortality rate for Q-wave infarction demonstrates the well-recognized, classic profile of a highly vulnerable period of 6 to 12 weeks, whereas patients surviving non-Q-wave infarction exhibit a highly vulnerable period of

Figure 54
Mortality rates of patients with Q-wave versus non-Q-wave infarction

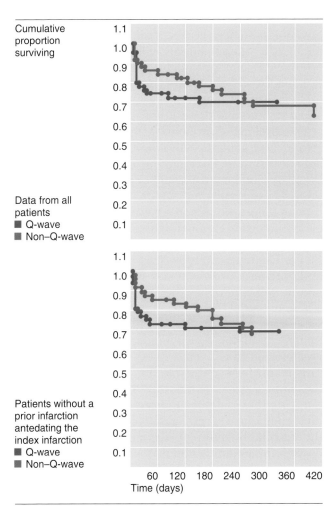

The cumulative mortality rates are similar in Q-wave and non-Q-wave infarction after about 1 year.

Reproduced with permission from Pratt CM, Roberts R. Non-Q-wave myocardial infarction. In: *The Complicated Cardiovascular Patient*. New York, NY: SCP Communications Inc; 1987;1:4-9.

reinfarction and death during most of the first year. The cumulative survival rates for Q-wave and non–Q-wave infarction are similar after about 1 year. Results of subsequent studies have confirmed the distinct profiles of Q-wave and non–Q-wave infarction. The 1-month mortality rate is about 20% among patients with Q-wave infarction and only 8% among patients with non–Q-wave infarction. However, 2 years later the cumulative mortality is 30% for patients with Q-wave infarction and 29% for patients with non–Q-wave infarction.

This prolonged propensity for reinfarction and ischemia in patients with non–Q-wave infarction is believed to be the major factor accounting for the disparity between initial and long-term mortality. These results indicate that although each repeated episode of non–Q-wave infarction is associated with minimal damage, the cumulative myocardial injury after 1 to 2 years is similar to that of Q-wave infarction. This difference in acute and long-term prognosis has important diagnostic and therapeutic implications.

The potential benefit of appropriate prophylactic therapy and the need for close follow-up in patients with non–Q-wave infarction is much greater than in patients with Q-wave infarction. This is in sharp contrast to the previous thinking that non–Q-wave (subendocardial) infarction is a benign entity and does not require therapy. The incidence of early reinfarction or extension during the hospital recovery phase in patients with non–Q-wave infarction is about 15% compared with only 3% to 5% in patients with Q-wave infarction. The propensity for early reinfarction in patients with non–Q-wave infarction who continue to have angina after the initial 48 hours is severalfold greater. Thus, it is important to initiate prophylactic therapy within the first 24 to 48 hours.

The basis for the different profiles of Q-wave and non–Q-wave infarction can be simplified as follows. Direct observations from experimental studies and suggestive evidence from clinical observations indicate that occlusion of one of the major coronary vessels leads to ischemia of 80% to 90% of the myocardium supplied by that vessel. If the occlusion is sustained, necrosis evolves over the next 2 to 4 hours. In the case of Q-wave infarction, the occlusion is sustained and most of the vascular territory undergoes necrosis with only a minimal amount of viable myocardium remaining. In contrast, patients with non–Q-wave infarction appear to abort this process by early, spontaneous reperfusion that limits the extent of damage. Therefore, the patient is left with a large proportion of the vascular territory that is viable but still vulnerable to repeated attacks of coronary occlusion that may produce ischemia, reinfarction, cardiac failure, and sudden death. This early spontaneous reperfusion is suspected to be the cause, but the evidence is indirect and not yet definitive.

Several factors significantly influence the prognosis of both Q-wave and non–Q-wave acute myocardial infarction in survivors. These factors include patient age, infarct size, number of vessels with obstructive disease, site of infarction, residual left ventricular function, and the presence or absence of complex arrhythmias. The most important factors are thought to be left ventricular function and age. Residual left ventricular function is determined by infarct size, site of infarction, and to a lesser extent by the number of diseased coronary vessels.

The risk of dying is severalfold greater with an ejection fraction of less than 40% than with normal ventricular function. The risk of death increases significantly with age, independent of the other factors. In one series, the 3-year mortality rate among patients younger than age 50 was 6% compared with 44% among those aged 70 to 79 years. The prognosis for survival after infarction is also significantly worse for women than for men; however, this may, in part, reflect the occurrence of infarction at a much later age in women. The proportion of patients surviving an inferior infarction, at least during the first 5 years, is twice that of patients surviving an anterior infarction (Figure 55). The effect of infarct size on survival is shown in Figure 56. A recently completed 15-year

Figure 55
Survival curves for patients with inferior versus anterior infarction

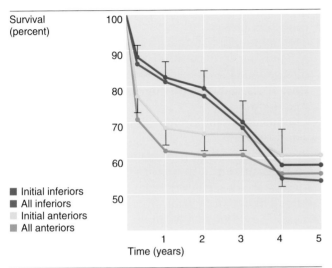

Survival
(percent)

■ Initial inferiors
■ All inferiors
▢ Initial anteriors
■ All anteriors

Time (years)

Separate curves identify patients with initial infarction. The mortality rate for patients with anterior infarction exceeded that for patients with posterior infarction ($P < 0.01$), regardless of initial or previous infarction.

Figure 56
The effect of infarct size on survival

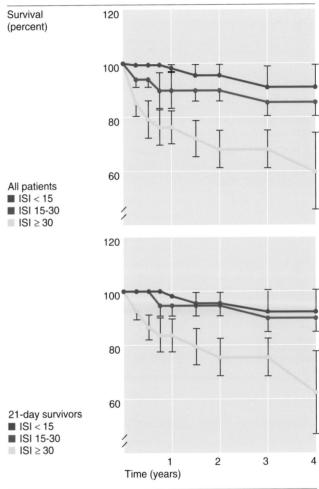

Survival
(percent)

All patients
■ ISI < 15
■ ISI 15-30
▢ ISI ≥ 30

21-day survivors
■ ISI < 15
■ ISI 15-30
▢ ISI ≥ 30

Time (years)

Distinct differences in survival are evident when infarct size was corrected for body surface area (ISI). ISI sizes less than 15 CK g/Eq/m^2 were rated small, those 15 to 30 g/Eq/m^2 were modest, and those over 30 g/Eq/m^2 were considered large. Vertical lines indicate standard error. Survival curves were similar for patients with small and modest-sized infarcts, but were significantly less for patients with larger infarcts, regardless of whether early deaths were excluded.

Reproduced with permission of the American Heart Association, Inc. from Geltman EM, Ehsani AA, Campbell MK, Schectman K, Roberts R, Sobel BE. The influence of location and extent of myocardial infarction on long-term ventricular dysrhythmia and mortality. *Circulation.* 1979;60:805-814.

study demonstrated the importance of the number of involved vessels. For patients with one-vessel, two-vessel, three-vessel, and left main artery disease, the proportion of patients surviving was 48%, 28%, 18%, and 9%, respectively. It is hoped that thrombolytic therapy followed by aspirin and angioplasty or surgery, when appropriate, will alter the natural history and prolong survival.

Postinfarction Stratification and Investigation

Until recently, the assessment and management of patients surviving myocardial infarction consisted only of treating symptoms such as angina or cardiac failure, but today the opportunity exists to prolong and improve the quality of life. Appropriate selection of treatment and secondary preventive measures often requires stress testing and risk stratification. The primary concerns are whether all patients should undergo stress testing and which patients should undergo cardiac catheterization. Precise stratification of patients according to their risks of developing postinfarction sequelae is still not possible, and perhaps this is the reason clinicians have skirted this challenge. Nevertheless, simple noninvasive testing together with cardiac catheterization in selected cases will improve patient management. Should these procedures not be available at the admitting facility, patients surviving myocardial infarction should be referred to an appropriate medical center. It is important to consider the history, physical examination, results of routine laboratory tests, and results of stress testing in order to appropriately devise a comprehensive treatment plan. Optimal management requires that the physician understands which of the following treatment plans should be initiated or whether all should be initiated and to what extent:

- Modification of the person's lifestyle;
- Selective pharmacotherapy for relief of symptoms;
- Selection of medical therapy for prolonging life;
- Treatment of existing high-risk conditions, such as smoking, hypertension, and hypercholesterolemia; and
- Revascularization with angioplasty or surgical treatment.

The necessity for stratification according to risk is emphasized by the recent estimate that only 25% of postinfarction patients are at high risk, yet high-risk patients account for about 50% of postinfarction deaths. High-risk patients are characterized as having an ejection fraction of less than 40%, ECG evidence of ischemia on exercise testing, and frequent or complex ventricular arrhythmias. In contrast, a low-risk group with a risk of 2% mortality in the first year makes up about 25% of the patients who are characterized by a lack of any significant risk factors. The remaining 50% of the patients are at intermediate risk, with about a 10% chance of dying in the first year. The challenge to the physician is to select those patients in the intermediate group who have risk factors that could be modified, either through lifestyle changes or medical intervention, thereby enhancing survival.

Any proposed plan for investigation and treatment is arbitrary and must of necessity be individualized and tailored to each patient's needs, as well as to his or her risk profile (Figure 57). There is agreement that all patients surviving myocardial infarction should have an assessment of left ventricular function prior to discharge from the hospital, either by radionuclide ventriculography or echocardiography. Patients who receive early thrombolysis (within 4 to 6 hours after the onset of myocardial infarction) and who exhibit symptoms of ischemia or show ischemia on stress testing should undergo cardiac catheterization. These symptoms may be evident in 30% to 40% of all patients. In addition, *all* patients should be encouraged to undergo stress testing before being discharged from the hospital.

Figure 57
Protocol for determining which patients should undergo noninvasive testing and/or cardiac catheterization

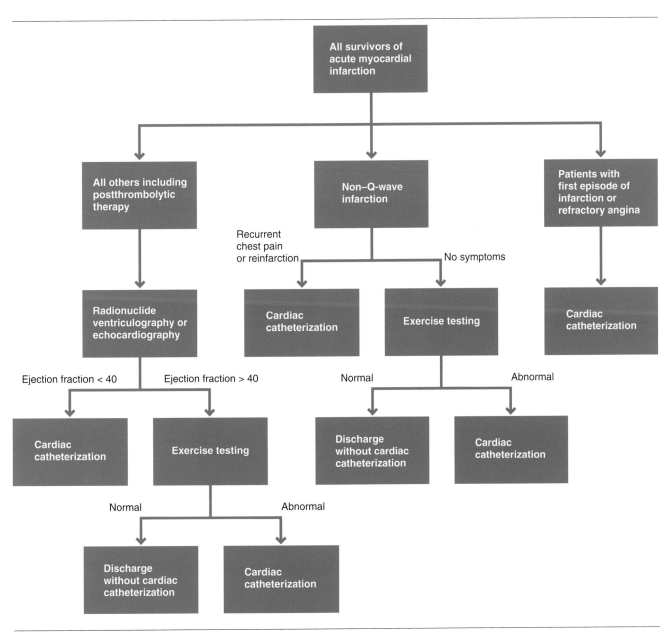

Patients who have experienced their first episode of infarction should have coronary arteriography and a predischarge stress test. Patients who exhibit an ejection fraction of less than 40% to 45% should undergo coronary arteriography, as should all patients who develop refractory pain or early reinfarction. The remaining patients with normal left ventricular function (a large proportion of the total) and one or more risk factors should be considered for exercise testing with thallium-201 scintigraphy, radionuclide ventriculography, or ECG. In the absence of contraindications, it is preferable that all postinfarction patients have some form of noninvasive exercise testing for postinfarction ischemia.

A prospective study that followed 576 patients with non–Q-wave infarction for a minimum of 1 year found that patients with recurrent chest pain or persistent ST-T segment depression are several-fold more likely to develop reinfarction or die during this period than patients who do not have these signs and symptoms. Therefore, cardiac catheterization is recommended for the following patients after non–Q-wave infarction:

- Patients with recurrent chest pain;
- Patients with persistent ST-T changes; and
- Patients with positive findings on exercise testing.

All patients with non–Q-wave infarction who do not have evidence of ischemia should be considered for some form of exercise testing prior to discharge from the hospital.

The preferred noninvasive test is thallium-201 scintigraphy with or without exercise. Thallium is expensive, however, and the newer investigative agent RP-30 is less expensive and may have other advantages. The second test of choice is exercise with radionuclide ventriculography, and the third is exercise echocardiography. If the patient cannot exercise, then scintigraphy before and after intravenous or oral dipyridamole should be considered. There is no uniform recommendation at this time regarding the routine use of Holter monitoring. Patients with arrhythmias continuing beyond the initial 48 hours should have a 24-hour recording. Some clinicians recommend a 24-hour recording on all patients who have had an episode of ventricular fibrillation, cardiac arrest, or pulmonary edema, or patients with an ejection fraction of less than 40%. Patients being considered for antiarrhythmic therapy for whatever reason should have a 24-hour Holter recording and, when appropriate, electrophysiologic testing.

Prophylactic Therapy Postinfarction

β-Blockers

The four β-blockers timolol, propranolol, metoprolol, and atenolol have been assessed in trials involving over 30 000 patients and have been shown to prolong life in postinfarction patients. The side effects of β-blockers, such as lethargy, lack of motivation, and inability to perform maximal physical activity, necessitate discontinuing the drug in some patients. For a variety of reasons, β-blockers are not routinely given to all postinfarction patients. The question of who should receive β-blockers has been and continues to be one of the most lively debated topics in cardiology. It is estimated that of the patients who are at high risk and likely to benefit from β-blockers, about 20% have contraindications, such as heart failure, asthma, conduction disturbances, or Prinzmetal's angina.

There is clearly a group of patients with a low annual mortality of about 2% who do not benefit from prophylactic treatment with β-blockers. The following guidelines are for prescribing β-blockers for patients with Q-wave infarction:

- All patients over age 60;
- All patients with Q-wave infarction who exhibit ischemia during exercise;

- All patients who have 10 or more PVCs during 24-hour Holter monitoring;
- Patients with abnormal left ventricular function (ejection fraction < 45%);
- Patients who require treatment for concomitant symptoms or disease, such as angina or hypertension; and
- Patients who experience an episode of sustained ventricular tachycardia or ventricular fibrillation or who have had cardiac arrest during the hospital stay.

Patients who have no ischemia during exercise do not require β-blockers prophylactically. Patients recovering from non–Q-wave infarction should first be given diltiazem.

Therapy with β-blockers should probably be continued indefinitely, but certainly for at least 3 to 6 years. For patients who do not tolerate β-blockers, an alternative regimen involves decreasing the β-blocker dosage and adding a calcium channel blocker, such as diltiazem or verapamil. This regimen keeps the heart rate low and minimizes the side effects from both β-blockers and calcium antagonists. One of the β-blockers that has been shown to prolong life should be used, and β-blockers with intrinsic sympathomimetic activity that have been shown to be ineffective should be avoided. Therapy can be initiated a few days after infarction, preferably before the patient is discharged from the hospital. In patients recovering from thrombolytic therapy, preliminary studies have shown that metroprolol initiated within the first few hours was more effective than when started after 2 weeks.

In the β-Blocker Heart Attack Trial (BHAT), propranolol was not associated with a reduction in mortality among the patients recovering from non–Q-wave infarction, who represented 23% of a total population of 843 patients. In the timolol study, however, there was improved survival in patients recovering from both Q-wave and non–Q-wave infarction, but the incidence of reinfarction was not significantly reduced in patients recovering from non–Q-wave infarction. Based on these findings and the recent trials demonstrating the effectiveness of diltiazem in reducing reinfarction, it appears reasonable to consider diltiazem as the preferred drug for patients recovering from non–Q-wave infarction.

Calcium Antagonists
Randomized double-blind studies of calcium channel blockers have now been performed with more than 10 000 patients who survived acute myocardial infarction. Diltiazem is the only calcium antagonist that has been shown to be associated with prolonged survival. Results of studies that involved a total of more than 8000 patients and that evaluated nifedipine and verapamil have consistently shown no benefit over placebo.

A long-term study that involved approximately 2500 patients and had a mean follow-up of 2.5 years showed a marked beneficial effect of diltiazem in the subset of 634 patients with non–Q-wave infarction. This difference was significant after the first year and remained significant even up to the end of 4.5 years. In contrast, a dichotomy was noted among patients with Q-wave infarction. In the group as a whole, there was no significant increase in survival. However, when the population was divided into those patients with and those without cardiac failure, both a reduced rate of mortality and a reduced incidence of reinfarction were observed for diltiazem treatment in the 80% of patients who presented without cardiac failure. In contrast, among the 20% of patients with cardiac failure, the mortality rate was increased in the group receiving diltiazem.

Similarly, although there was a marked overall benefit of diltiazem for non–Q-wave infarction, the benefit was restricted to those without cardiac failure. Like the patients with Q-wave infarction, patients with non–Q-wave infarction and with cardiac failure who had been treated with diltiazem had an increased rate of mortality. Patients with non–Q-wave infarction received most of the benefits of diltiazem therapy, but there was also a significant benefit from diltiazem therapy for patients presenting with their first episode of Q-wave inferior infarction. Thus, these results indicate that diltiazem should be considered as prophylactic therapy in patients with non–Q-wave infarction and possibly in patients after inferior Q-wave infarction. For the remainder of patients with Q-wave infarction, the use of β-blockers should be considered.

Unstable Angina

Unstable angina has been called by many different terms, including intermediate syndrome, coronary insufficiency, and reinfarction angina. It is a syndrome of chest pain that may present with one or all of the following profiles:

- Crescendo angina: an increase in the frequency, duration, or severity of pain, or a significant decrease in the pain threshold.
- Angina at rest: pain occurs at rest, either de novo or in a patient who has had chronic, stable angina. At different times the patient may experience angina at rest or during exertion.
- New onset of chest pain: sequential observation is required to determine whether the patient is exhibiting a stable or unstable pattern.

Pathogenesis
It has now been documented that angina at rest is due to an acute or subacute decrease in coronary blood flow. The cause of the obstruction remains unknown, but the obstruction is probably the result of either coronary spasm, aggregates of platelets, or both. Evidence for the role of coronary thrombi is based on morphologic findings at postmortem, observation from coronary angioscopy, and biochemical alterations in the hemostatic mechanisms.

Indirect evidence for the role of platelet aggregation was obtained from two large, randomized studies of patients with unstable angina in which the administration of aspirin was associated with a marked decrease in the incidence of infarction and mortality. Angiographic results from a recent study demonstrated that thrombi were present in patients with angina at rest and that the administration of recombinant tissue plasminogen activator was effective in lysing the clots. There is also mounting experimental evidence that other factors, such as thromboxane and serotonin, may also play a role in the formation of a thrombus.

Thus, it appears that two of the major manifestations of ischemic heart disease, myocardial infarction and angina at rest, relate to the superimposition of coronary thrombi on atherosclerosis. The atheromatous plaque appears to induce certain endothelial dysfunction that alters the local environment in favor of clotting and obstruction of coronary flow. A current hypothesis proposes that the rupture of an atheromatous plaque may be caused by vasoconstriction or other factors that, in turn, cause vasospasm and thrombosis.

Management
Patients with unstable angina, particularly angina occurring at rest, should be admitted to the hospital and treated initially for possible myocardial infarction. However, therapy for unstable angina is undergoing significant change. The mainstays of medical therapy are heparin, aspirin, and nitrates. Upon admission, a patient should receive nitrates. Nitroglycerin can be administered sublingually, orally, intravenously, or percutaneously. If pain is not immediately relieved, a nitroglycerin infusion is recommended, initiated at a rate of 5 to 10 μg/min and, depending on the blood pressure and heart rate, increased as needed for relief of pain. In general, nitroglycerin given intravenously offers the advantage of almost immediate relief of symptoms. The dose of nitroglycerin should be adjusted to lower the arterial pressure by 15 mm Hg or

to 110 mm Hg, whichever represents a smaller reduction. Results of a recent study show that upon arrival at the hospital the patient should also be given heparin. Administration of heparin for 2 to 3 days, followed by aspirin (325 mg/day), was associated with a significant reduction in refractory pain and the incidence of myocardial infarction.

The role of thrombolytic therapy in patients with unstable angina has yet to be determined. Results of seven trials, all of which involved only a few patients, have shown no significant benefit. A large trial evaluating the efficacy of thrombolytic therapy is now under way, but the results will not be available for 2 to 3 years. The National Institutes of Health large, cooperative study performed in the 1970s showed that patients with unstable angina should be stabilized medically before cardiac catheterization or other procedures are performed. The patients should be monitored in a CCU for their heart rhythm, although hemodynamic monitoring usually is not necessary. Plasma CK-MB levels must be determined serially so that myocardial infarction can be excluded. Patients who continue to have pain after 12 to 24 hours of therapy should undergo coronary arteriography to determine the need for possible angioplasty or surgery. These patients represent fewer than 5% of today's patients, the majority of whom are rapidly stabilized with medical therapy. Concomitant factors, such as anemia, thyrotoxicosis, or infection, must be taken into account when considering the initial treatment.

Conclusion

The successful management of myocardial infarction requires early diagnosis followed by aggressive treatment to limit infarct size and restore coronary blood flow. Ideally, thrombolytic therapy is given within 4 to 6 hours of onset of symptoms, and the patient is transferred to a medical center that is equipped to provide further assessment and treatment. During the acute phase, liberal administration of morphine and β-blockers is recommended, because these agents produce the dual benefits of relieving pain and reducing the heart rate. Patients for whom thrombolytic therapy is contraindicated and those with 80% or more obstruction in spite of thrombolytic therapy should undergo immediate angioplasty.

All patients should be continuously monitored by ECG for the initial 48 hours, the period of greatest vulnerability, to detect tachycardias and ventricular fibrillation. Hemodynamic monitoring is indicated for patients with cardiogenic shock, suspected heart failure, hypotension, persistent sinus tachycardia, or other complications. In patients with uncomplicated myocardial infarction, it is usually sufficient to monitor the vital signs and heart sounds at frequent intervals, serially assess the MB-CK levels, and follow with thrombolytic therapy. Heparin should be administered for 2 to 3 days, followed by aspirin thereafter for life.

Successful postinfarction management requires that the physician develop a comprehensive treatment plan based on a careful evaluation of the patient's history and the results of physical examination, laboratory tests, and stress test. A treatment plan tailored to the individual patient may include lifestyle modification (eg, smoking cessation, weight loss, low-fat diet, regular exercise), treatment of existing high-risk conditions (eg, hypertension, hypercholesterolemia), prophylactic pharmacotherapy (eg, β-blockers, calcium channel blockers), and/or revascularization (eg, angioplasty).

Selected Readings

Ambrose JA, Hjemdahl-Monsen C, Borrico S, et al. Quantitative and qualitative effects of intracoronary streptokinase in unstable angina and non-Q wave infarction. **J Am Coll Cardiol.** 1987;9:1156-1165.

Beller GA, Gibson RS. Sensitivity, specificity, and prognostic significance of noninvasive testing for occult or known coronary disease. **Prog Cardiovasc Dis.** 1987;29:241-270.

Boden WE, Krone RJ, Kleiger RE, Miller JP, Hager WD, Moss AJ, and the MDPIT Research Group. Diltiazem reduces long-term cardiac event rate after non-Q wave infarction: Multicenter Diltiazem Post-Infarction Trial (MDPIT). **Circulation.** 1988;78:II-96.

CASS Principal Investigators and their associates. Coronary Artery Surgery Study (CASS): a randomized trial of coronary artery bypass surgery. Survival data. **Circulation.** 1983;68: 939-950.

Chizner MA. Bedside diagnosis of the acute myocardial infarction and its complication. **Curr Probl Cardiol.** 1982;7:1-86.

DeWood MA, Stifter WF, Simpson CS, Spores J, Eugster GS, Judge TP, Hinnen ML. Coronary arteriographic findings soon after non-Q-wave myocardial infarction. **N Engl J Med.** 1986; 315:417-423.

Fuster V, Adams PC, Badimon JJ, Chesebro JH. Platelet-inhibitor drugs' role in coronary artery disease. **Prog Cardiovasc Dis.** 1987;29:325-346.

Gibson RS, Boden WE, Theroux P, et al. Diltiazem and reinfarction in patients with non-Q-wave myocardial infarction: results of a double-blind, randomized, multicenter trial. **N Engl J Med.** 1986;315:423-429.

Gibson RS, Young PM, Boden WE, Schechtman K, Roberts R, and the Diltiazem Reinfarction Study Group. Prognostic significance and beneficial effect of diltiazem on the incidence of early recurrent ischemia after non-Q-wave myocardial infarction: results from the Multicenter Diltiazem Reinfarction Study. **Am J Cardiol.** 1987;60:203-209.

Gold HK, Johns JA, Leinbach RC, et al. A randomized, blinded, placebo-controlled trial of recombinant human tissue-type plasminogen activator in patients with unstable angina pectoris. **Circulation.** 1987;75:1192-1199

Gotoh K, Minamino T, Katoh O, et al. The role of intracoronary thrombus in unstable angina: angiographic assessment and thrombolytic therapy during ongoing anginal attacks. **Circulation.** 1988;77:526-534.

Gruppo Italiano per lo Studio della Streptochinasi nel'Infarto Miocardico (GISSI). Effectiveness of intravenous thrombolytic treatment in acute myocardial infarction. **Lancet.** 1986;1:397-401.

Gutovitz AL, Sobel BE, Roberts R. The progressive nature of myocardial injury in selected patients with cardiogenic shock. **Am J Cardiol.** 1978;41:469-475.

Hackel DB, Reimer KA, Ideker RE, et al. Comparison of enzymatic and anatomic estimates of myocardial infarct size in man. **Circulation.** 1984;70:824-835.

ISIS (International Studies of Infarct Survival) Pilot Studies Investigators. Randomized factorial trial of high-dose intravenous streptokinase, of oral aspirin and of intravenous heparin in acute myocardial infarction. **Eur Heart J.** 1987;8:634-642.

Kelly DT. Clinical decisions in patients following myocardial infarction. **Curr Probl Cardiol.** 1985;10:1-45.

Marmor A, Geltman EM, Schechtman K, Sobel BE, Roberts R. Recurrent myocardial infarction: clinical predictors and prognostic implications. **Circulation.** 1982;66:415-421.

Marmor A, Sobel BE, Roberts R. Factors presaging early recurrent myocardial infarction ("extension"). **Am J Cardiol.** 1981;48:603-610.

Pedersen TR. Six-year follow-up of the Norwegian Multicenter Study on timolol after acute myocardial infarction. **N Engl J Med.** 1985;313:1055-1058.

Proudfit WJ, Bruschke AVG, MacMillan JP, Williams GW, Sones FM Jr. Fifteen year survival study of patients with obstructive coronary artery disease. **Circulation.** 1983;68:986-997.

Puleo PR, Perryman MB, Bresser MA, Rokey R, Pratt CM, Roberts R. Creatine kinase isoform analysis in the detection and assessment of thrombolysis in man. **Circulation.** 1987;75:1162-1169.

Roberts R. Measurement of enzymes in cardiology. In: Linden RJ, ed. **Techniques in the Life Sciences: Techniques in Cardiovascular Physiology.** Vol P3/I, part I. Elsevier Scientific Publishers Ireland Ltd: 1983;P312/1-P312/24.

Roberts R. Recognition, pathogenesis, and management of non–Q-wave infarction. **Mod Conc Cardiovasc Dis**. 1987;56:17-21.

Roberts R. Reperfusion and the plasma isoforms of creatine kinase isoenzymes: a clinical perspective. **J Am Coll Cardiol**. 1987;9:464-466.

Roberts R, Croft C, Gold HK, et al. Effect of propranolol on myocardial-infarct size in a randomized, blinded, Multicenter Trial. **N Engl J Med**. 1984;311:218-225.

Roberts R, Henry PD, Sobel BE. An improved basis for enzymatic estimation of infarct size. **Circulation**. 1975;52:743-754.

Roberts R, Sobel BE. Creatine kinase isoenzymes in the assessment of heart disease. **Am Heart J**. 1978;95:521-528.

Schaer DH, Ross AM, Wasserman AG. Reinfarction, recurrent angina, and reocclusion after thrombolytic therapy. **Circulation**. 1987;76:II-57-II-62.

Smith B, Kennedy JW. Thrombolysis in the treatment of acute transmural myocardial infarction. **Ann Intern Med**. 1987;106: 414-420.

The Multicenter Diltiazem Post-Infarction Trial Research Group. The effect of diltiazem on mortality and reinfarction after myocardial infarction. **N Engl J Med**. 1988;319:385-392.

The TIMI Study Group. Comparison of invasive and conservative strategies after treatment with intravenous tissue plasminogen activator in acute myocardial infarction: results of the Thrombolysis in Myocardial Infarction (TIMI) Phase II Trial. **N Engl J Med**. 1989;320:618-627.

The TIMI Study Group. The Thrombolysis in Myocardial Infarction (TIMI) Trial: Phase I Findings. **N Engl J Med**. 1985;312: 932-936.

Théroux P, Ouimet H, McCans J, et al. Aspirin, heparin, or both to treat acute unstable angina. **N Engl J Med**. 1988;319: 1105-1111.

Willman VL. Percutaneous transluminal coronary angioplasty, a 1985 perspective. **Circulation**. 1985;71:189-192.

Atherosclerotic Occlusive Disease of the Coronary Arteries: Surgical Considerations

Introduction

The primary objective of the surgical treatment of atherosclerotic occlusive disease of the coronary arteries is restoration of normal circulation in the coronary arterial bed distal to the occlusive process. Early attempts to achieve this objective derived largely from the pioneering efforts of Sones in the development of cine-coronary angiography. Endarterectomy, with or without patch-graft angioplasty, was first applied for the purpose of restoring normal circulation in the late 1950s and early 1960s with encouraging results. At the same time, the concept of bypass from a systemic artery or the ascending aorta to the coronary arteries was being investigated experimentally.

In 1954, Murray and associates reported performing resection of a segment of the anterior descending branch of the left coronary artery in dogs, with graft replacement and perfusion of the distal arterial segment from a reservoir of the animal's heparinized blood to prevent infarction during operation. Although they experimented with the use of the internal mammary, axillary, subclavian, and carotid arteries with end-to-side or even end-to-end anastomosis to the coronary artery, they found that best results were obtained by using a free graft of carotid artery as a bypass from the ascending aorta to the coronary artery. In 5 of 17 dogs, the anastomosis was satisfactory with no infarction developing from 2½ hours to 8 days after operation.

Two years later, Absolon and associates reported somewhat similar studies on bypass grafts from the subclavian or internal mammary artery to the circumflex coronary artery in dogs, with a few encouraging results. During the same year, Thal and associates reported similar experiments in dogs, in which the internal mammary artery and end-to-end anastomosis to the circumflex coronary artery were used with successful results in

7 of 17 dogs. The following year, Julian and coworkers reported performance of bypass in one group of 20 dogs, using the internal mammary artery with end-to-end anastomosis to the circumflex coronary artery, and in another group of 7 dogs, using a free homologous graft of the common or external iliac artery from the ascending aorta to the circumflex coronary artery. Results were successful in 9 of the 20 dogs in the first group and in 2 of the 7 dogs in the other group. During the next few years, others performed similar experiments in dogs, with encouraging results.

In 1961, we presented our first report on our experimental studies in dogs, in which we used a bypass graft from the ascending aorta to one or more coronary arteries with end-to-side anastomosis proximally and distally; about 50% of the grafts were patent within a few months after operation. Although these results were encouraging, a higher success rate was considered necessary before clinical application.

In November 1964, however, during an attempted coronary endarterectomy on a patient with severe angina pectoris and arteriographic evidence of severe occlusive disease of the left main coronary artery and the origin of the left anterior descending and circumflex coronary arteries, it was considered preferable to use an autogenous saphenous-vein graft from the ascending aorta to the left anterior descending coronary artery. The patient recovered satisfactorily and became asymptomatic; 7 years later, arteriography showed a well-functioning patent venous bypass graft to the left anterior descending coronary artery. To the best of our knowledge, this became the first successful case of an ascending aorta-to-coronary artery bypass.

This procedure, however, was first performed by Sabiston on April 4, 1962, on a 41-year-old man with severe angina on whom recent coronary endarterectomy had been performed. Symptoms recurred 1 year later, and occlusion of the previously endarterectomized segment was shown by coronary arteriography. The procedure consisted of end-to-side anastomosis of a segment of autogenous saphenous vein to the ascending aorta and end-to-end anastomosis to the right coronary artery distal to the occlusive segment. Unfortunately, a cerebrovascular accident developed in the postoperative period, and the patient died 3 days later.

In 1968, Favaloro reported experience with 55 patients who had interposition autogenous-vein graft replacement by end-to-end anastomosis proximally and distally for segmental occlusive disease of the right coronary artery in order to overcome the unfavorable results after pericardial patch reconstruction. There were only 2 hospital deaths, and postoperative angiographic catheterization showed excellent results.

Two years later, Favaloro and associates reported using the autogenous saphenous vein as a bypass from the ascending aorta to the coronary arteries by end-to-side anastomosis. This was combined with implantation of the internal mammary artery (Vineberg procedure) in about 40% of the cases.

Since then, the bypass principle has become well established and generally accepted for certain forms of coronary artery occlusive disease. There remain, however, some differences of opinion concerning its application in certain forms of the disease, as will be discussed later.

Patterns of Atherosclerosis

The anatomic patterns of atherosclerotic coronary artery disease constitute an important basis for the application of surgical treatment. The introduction of selective cine-coronary arteriography by Sones and associates made possible recognition of these patterns. This diagnostic procedure enables precise delineation of the anatomic site, distribution, and extent of the occlusive disease in the coronary arterial bed. In most patients, atherosclerosis tends to be segmental, with relatively normal proximal and distal beds. Characteristically, the disease assumes one of several patterns of anatomic distribution:

- Involvement of the proximal portion of the arterial bed with little or no significant disease of the distal bed (Figure 58);
- Involvement of the midproximal portion of the arterial bed with a relatively normal distal arterial bed (Figure 59);
- Predominant involvement of the distal arterial bed with insignificant disease of the proximal portion (Figure 60);
- Generalized arteriosclerotic disease throughout the arterial bed.

Involvement of the left main coronary artery with or without significant occlusive disease elsewhere is a particularly important form of proximal disease (Figure 58). An unusual pattern is characterized by segmented aneurysmal and occlusive disease (Figure 61). The first two patterns, which are fortunately the most common, are readily amenable to surgical treatment, but operation is usually not satisfactory for the third and fourth patterns (distal and diffuse disease). Surgical treatment may be applied in some forms of the last pattern (aneurysmal and occlusive disease). Operation is rarely required for aneurysm of the left ventricle, which usually has a good prognosis unless the aneurysm is large and associated with mitral thrombosis and potential embolism.

Rates of Progression

Another significant feature of atherosclerosis is the rate of progression of the disease. On the basis of our experience, we have classified the different rates of progression into three groups:

- Rapid, in which insignificant stenosis (less than 50% narrowing of the lumen) as demonstrated by arteriography becomes significant (producing 70% or greater narrowing of the lumen) within 3 years (Figure 62);
- Moderate, development of significant stenosis within 4 to 8 years using similar criteria (Figure 63);
- Slow, development of significant stenosis after 9 years or longer (Figure 64).

Figure 58

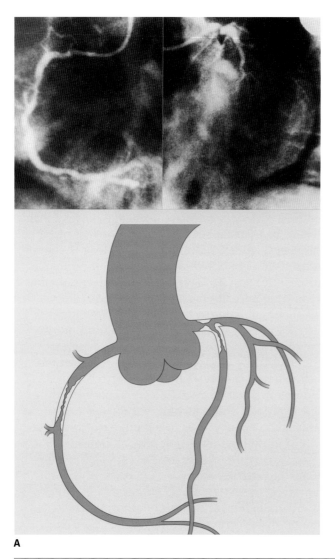

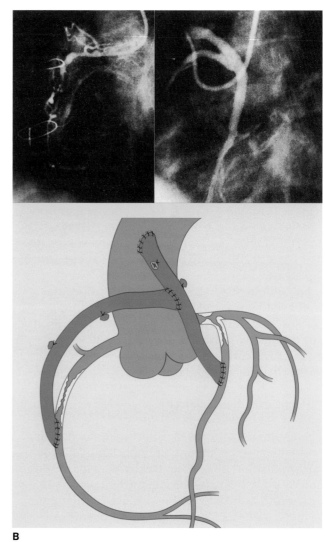

A

B

(**A**) Preoperative coronary arteriograms in a 54-year-old white man with severe angina show severe occlusive disease in the left main coronary artery, the proximal portion of the left anterior descending artery, and the right coronary artery.

(**B**) Surgical treatment consisted in autogenous saphenous-vein bypass grafts from the ascending aorta to the right and left anterior descending coronary arteries. Photograph: coronary arteriograms made 13 years after the operation show patent vein grafts. The patient remains asymptomatic.

Figure 59

Figure 60

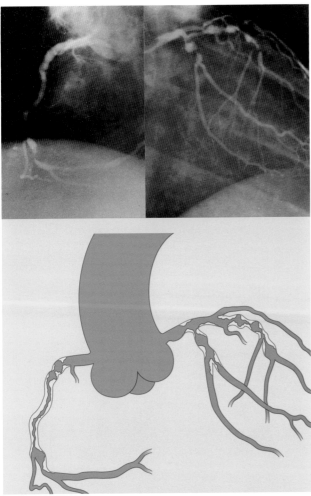

A coronary arteriogram in a 51-year-old white man with angina pectoris shows a typical pattern of severe, well-localized stenotic disease in the midproximal portion of the right and left anterior descending and circumflex coronary arteries.

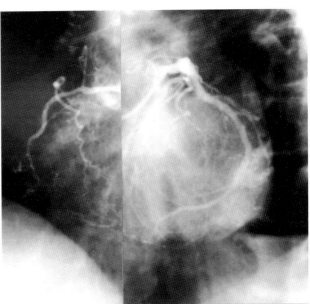

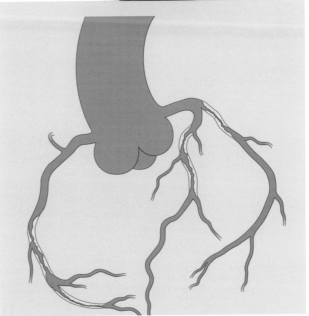

A coronary arteriogram in a 59-year-old white man who complained of angina pectoris shows extensive severe occlusive disease in the distal arterial bed of the right and left anterior descending and circumflex coronary arteries. The patient also had severe hypokinesia and a low ejection fraction. Because of the anatomic pattern of the distal disease, the patient was considered an unsatisfactory surgical candidate and was treated medically. The patient died 5 years later from severe heart failure.

Figure 61

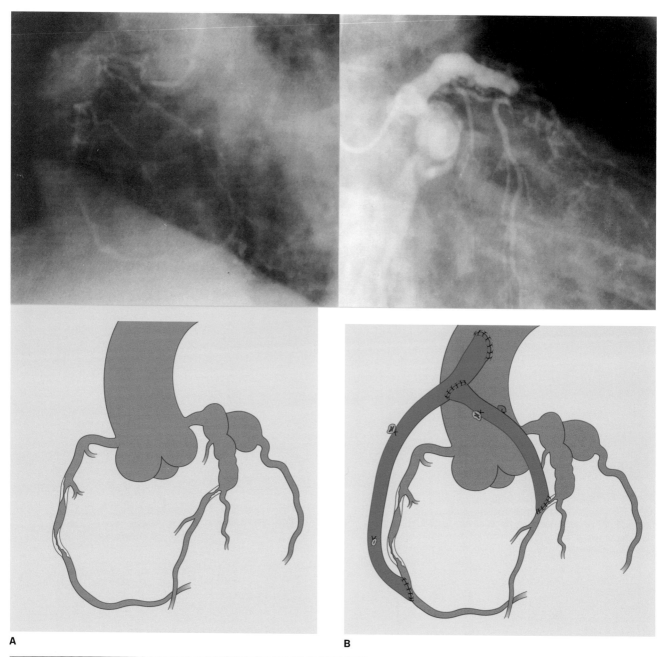

(**A**) Preoperative arteriograms in a 47-year-old white man with severe angina pectoris show combined aneurysmal and occlusive disease involving the right and left anterior descending coronary arteries.

(**B**) Surgical treatment consisted in autogenous saphenous-vein bypass grafts to the right and left anterior descending coronary arteries. The patient has remained well for the past 15 years.

Figure 62

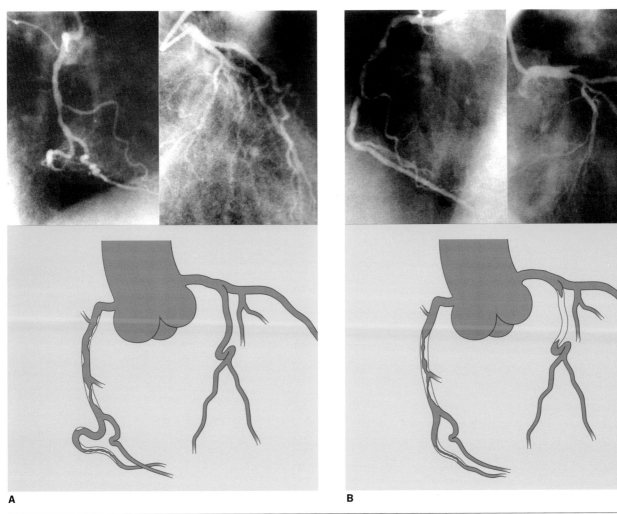

A

B

(**A**) Coronary arteriograms in a 52-year-old white man with mild angina show moderate localized stenosis in the midportion of the right coronary artery and small plaques in the left anterior descending coronary and circumflex coronary arteries.

(**B**) Coronary arteriograms made in the same patient 2½ years later show rapid progression of an occlusive lesion with complete occlusion in the midportion of the right coronary artery and the proximal portion of the left anterior descending coronary artery.

Figure 63

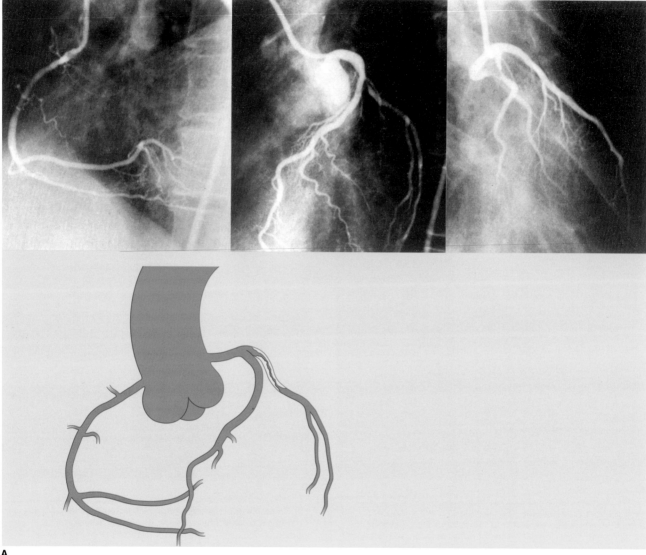

A

(**A**) Preoperative coronary arteriograms in a 61-year-old white man with severe angina show localized occlusive disease in the circumflex coronary artery; the left anterior descending and right coronary arteries have no significant disease. An autogenous saphenous-vein bypass graft was inserted from the ascending aorta to the circumflex coronary artery.

(**B**) Coronary arteriograms in the same patient made 6 years later because of the recurrence of angina show a patent functioning autogenous saphenous-vein graft to the circumflex coronary artery (lower left photograph); severe, well-localized stenotic disease in the midportion of the left anterior descending coronary artery (upper right photograph); and no significant disease in the right coronary artery (upper left photograph). Stenotic disease in the left anterior descending coronary artery was treated by balloon angioplasty, as shown in drawing B, with good results (lower right photograph).

Figure 63 (continued)

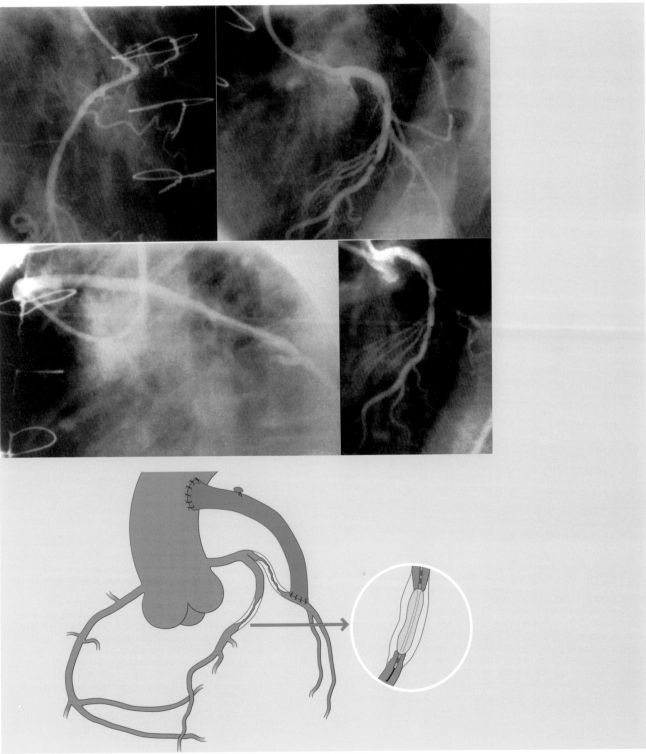

B

Figure 64

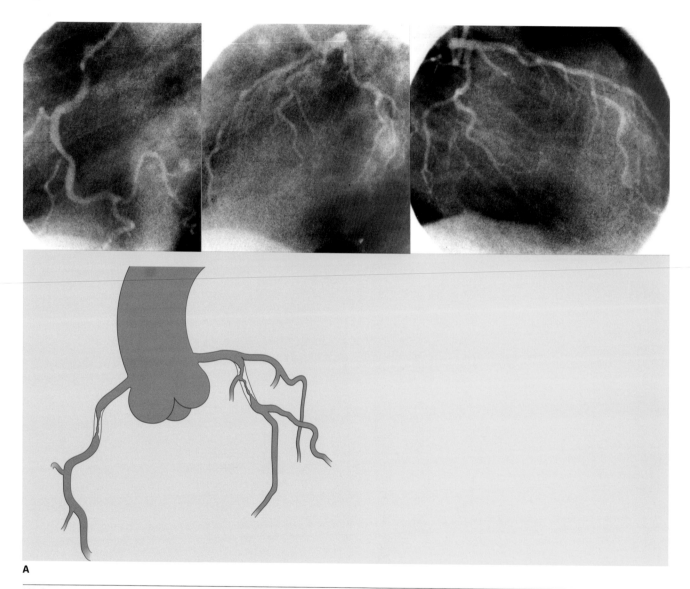

A

(**A**) Coronary arteriograms in a 53-year-old white man with severe angina show well-localized, proximal occlusive disease in the right and left anterior descending coronary arteries.
(**B**) Surgical treatment consisted in an autogenous saphenous-vein bypass from the ascending aorta to the right and left anterior descending coronary arteries. The figures show a patent bypass graft to the right coronary artery, a patent bypass graft to the left anterior descending coronary artery with localized severe stenosis in the distal third of the graft, and localized proximal severe occlusive disease in the obtuse marginal coronary artery. Photographs: coronary arteriograms

made 12 years after the operation because of a recent recurrence of angina.
(**C**) Surgical treatment consisted in removal of a previous left anterior descending coronary artery autogenous saphenous-vein bypass graft with stenotic disease and replacement with a bypass graft to the left anterior descending coronary artery using the left internal mammary artery. Also shown is a bypass graft from the ascending aorta to the obtuse marginal coronary artery using an autogenous saphenous vein. The patient has remained asymptomatic for 3 years since this operation.

Figure 64 (continued)

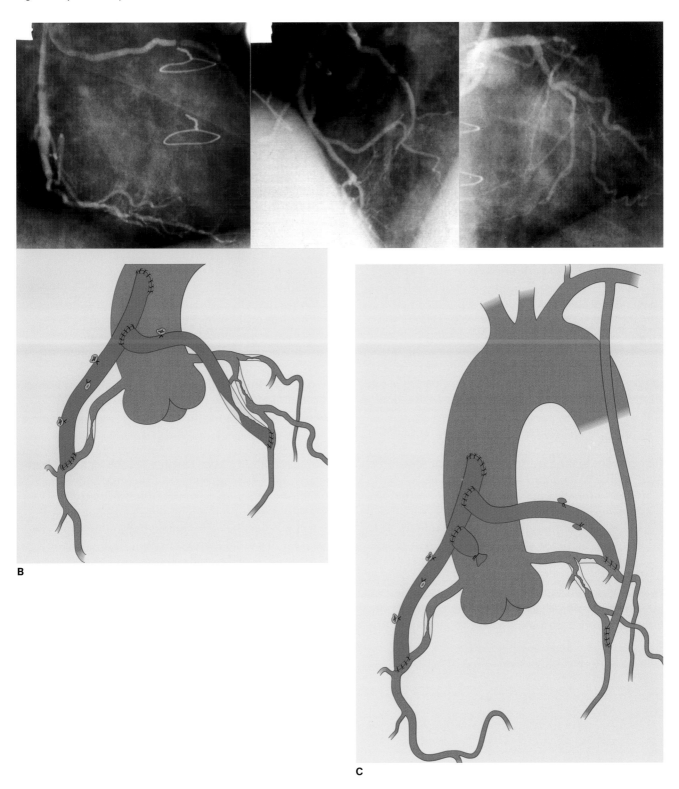

B

C

Indications

Indications for surgical treatment have undergone some changes in recent years as a consequence of the analysis of experience and long-term results and the introduction of more effective medical measures, such as the use of β-blocker agents and calcium channel blocking agents, and percutaneous catheter procedures, such as balloon angioplasty and laser and atherectomy devices.

Angina pectoris remains the most common indication for investigation and possible surgical treatment. Because angina pectoris is a clinical diagnosis based largely on medical history, it is important to obtain precise studies to establish its relation to myocardial ischemia and to determine whether the patient falls into a high-risk category. In mildly symptomatic patients, catheterization is performed if the treadmill exercise test has a strongly positive result, large perfusion defects are observed on thallium scanning, or a fall in ejection fraction occurs during exercise isotope ventriculography. Such studies may also be indicated in asymptomatic patients with a definite history or electrocardiographic evidence of coronary disease requiring major operations, such as valve replacement (Figure 65) or aortic aneurysmal resection (Figure 66).

Surgical treatment may be indicated in patients with:
- Recurrent angina pectoris that interferes with normal activities and does not respond favorably to, or is not adequately controlled by, intensive medical therapy (Figures 67-70);
- Significant left main artery disease (Figure 58);
- Symptomatic three-vessel disease (Figures 71, 72), especially if ventricular function is reduced (Figure 73);
- Two-vessel disease, high-grade proximal left anterior descending disease, and involvement of the circumflex coronary artery (Figures 74, 75).

Other candidates for coronary bypass, based on our experience, are patients with coronary disease and other associated cardiac or vascular disease. For example, in patients requiring valve replacement, coronary bypass to correct coexisting coronary disease should be done at the same time (Figure 65). In other patients with severe coronary disease who require other major noncardiac operations, such as operation to correct aneurysms of the aorta, prior coronary bypass may provide protection against fatal cardiac complications (Figure 66). In light of our experience with patients in this category, we recommend angiography in patients with angina pectoris or other evidence of coronary disease who require major noncardiac operations, such as carotid endarterectomy.

Indications for early operation for acute myocardial infarction remain undetermined despite some reports of excellent results. Although we are pursuing some studies along these lines, we treat most patients in this category with thrombolytic agents rather than immediate operation, if they are seen early enough. In the younger patient whose condition is stable after an infarction, a treadmill exercise test may be performed at the end of the first week after myocardial infarction. If the result of this test is strongly positive, cardiac catheterization is performed, and if severe disease is found, surgical treatment is recommended.

For patients with intractable angina or hemodynamic instability after cardiac catheterization, however, emergency operation is recommended.

Other conditions recommended for surgical treatment include the anatomic complication of coronary disease. Left ventricular aneurysms are resected if associated with angina, congestive heart failure, arrhythmia, or embolic phenomena. Additionally, surgical treatment may be indicated in patients with ventricular septal defects secondary to myocardial infarction or with mitral regurgitation secondary to severe papillary muscle dysfunction accompanied by congestive heart failure. Coronary artery bypass may also be indicated in patients with coronary artery disease and intractable ventricular tachyarrhythmias requiring ablation of arrhythmogenic foci by endocardial resection and cryothermia.

In some patients, reoperation may be indicated because of a recurrence of symptoms resulting from development of stenosis or even occlusion in the vein bypass graft, progression of disease in the coronary arteries, or both of these occurrences (Figure 76).

Percutaneous transluminal coronary angioplasty (PTCA) is another method of restoring circulation in certain forms of atherosclerotic occlusive disease (Figure 63). This procedure may be considered a useful alternative to coronary bypass in selected cases, such as discrete single-vessel or double-vessel disease and persistent angina despite medical treatment. More recently, the procedure has been extended to multivessel disease, but the mortality risk in such cases is comparable to elective bypass surgery.

Although the initial success rate approaches 90%, there is a 25% to 40% chance of restenosis within 6 to 12 months. It is estimated, moreover, that 5% to 10% of patients undergoing PTCA require emergency coronary bypass grafting, which is associated with an operative mortality rate of about 10% and, therefore, is significantly greater than that following elective bypass operation.

Operative Technique

Although the basic principles of the operative technique have remained essentially the same since the first successful procedure performed in 1964, some significant modifications have evolved since then. The median sternotomy exposure and cardiopulmonary bypass remain the same. In the earlier period, intermittent ischemic arrest, ventricular fibrillation, and moderate topical hypothermia were used during the bypass grafting procedure.

We began using cold potassium cardioplegia in 1978, and with further improvement in the composition of cardioplegia solution, along with topical hypothermia and systemic hypothermia using the heart-lung machine, these modifications became routine by 1980.

Increasing emphasis was also placed on completeness of revascularization, with most patients requiring 3 to 4 grafts. Use of one or both internal mammary arteries also became fairly routine during this decade (Figures 64, 70, 77, 78). In some patients, endarterectomy, usually of the right coronary artery, may be possible and, combined with bypass, enhances the revascularization procedure (Figure 78). Some patients with advanced coronary artery disease have been treated by multivessel endarterectomy and bypass as proposed by Brenowitz and associates.

When saphenous-vein grafts are used, they are harvested from the thigh and leg and prepared with a balanced salt solution (Plasma-Lyte, Baxter Healthcare Corporation) at room temperature. Our experimental work demonstrated that normal saline solution, which we used previously, is extremely damaging to the vein-graft endothelium.

During cardioplegic arrest of the heart, distal anastomoses are attached to the coronary arteries with 7-0 polypropylene. The proximal anastomoses are made with 5-0 polypropylene to holes cut in the ascending aorta. One or both internal mammary arteries are mobilized in their pedicles from beneath the sternum. The distal end-to-side anastomosis to the coronary artery is performed with 8-0 polypropylene.

Development of techniques to conserve blood and avoid transfusions has been a major goal over the past decade. More meticulous surgical hemostasis, use of autotransfusion devices, and recognition of the need to control perioperative fibrinolysis with agents, such as epsilon-amino caproic acid and cyclocapron, have led to a drastic reduction in the need for blood transfusion. Indeed, about 70% of patients now receive no blood transfusions during the operation.

Figure 65

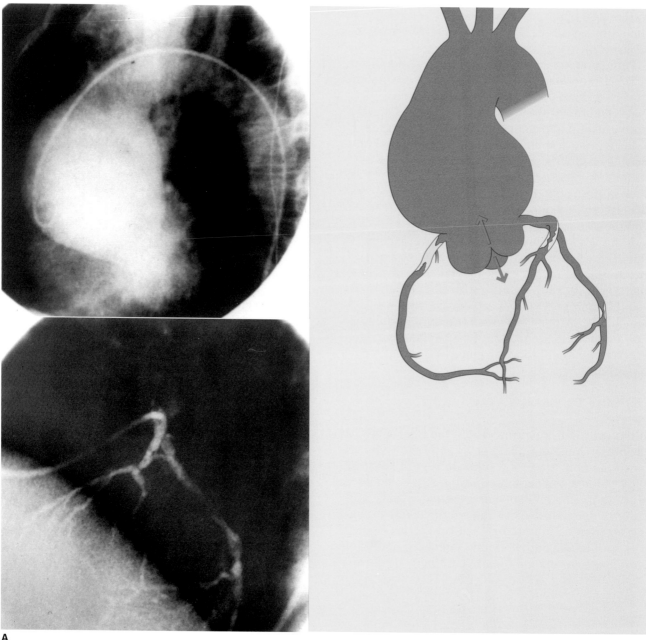

A

(**A**) Preoperative arteriograms in a 55-year-old white man with angina pectoris and aortic insufficiency show an aneurysm of the ascending aorta and well-localized, severe stenotic disease in the proximal portion of the right and left anterior descending coronary arteries.

(**B**) Surgical treatment consisted in a resection of the ascending aorta and aortic valve and replacement with a Dacron tube, St. Jude aortic valve, and an autogenous saphenous-vein bypass graft from the ascending aorta to the right and left anterior descending coronary arteries and with suture anastomosis of the ostia of both coronary arteries to openings in the Dacron graft. The patient has remained asymptomatic for the past 8 years.

Figure 65 (continued)

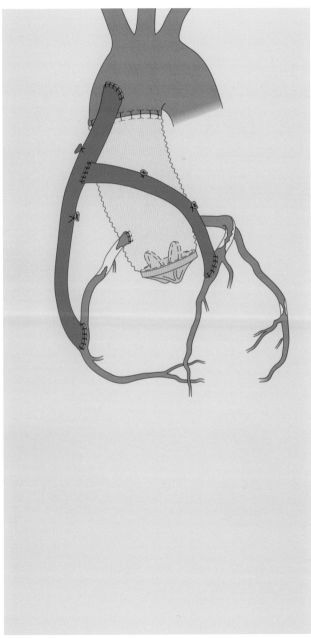

B

Figure 66

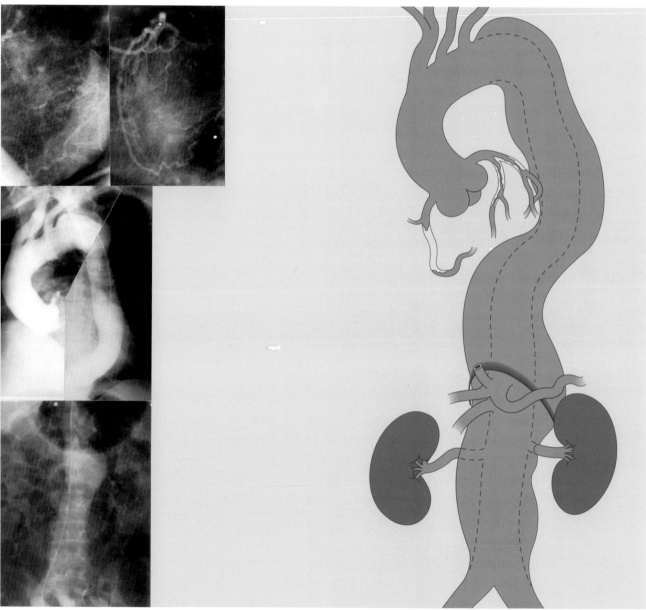

A

(**A**) Preoperative coronary arteriograms and thoracic and abdominal aortograms in a 58-year-old white man with angina show severe, well-localized occlusive disease in the proximal and midportion of the right and left anterior descending coronary and circumflex coronary arteries and a large, extensive thoracoabdominal aneurysm.

(**B**) Surgical treatment consisted in autogenous saphenous-vein bypass grafts from the ascending aorta to the right and left anterior descending coronary and circumflex coronary arteries. About 3 weeks later, the patient had resection of a thoraco-abdominal aneurysm and replacement with a Dacron graft. The arteriogram shows the grafts functioning well. The patient has remained asymptomatic for 7 years since the operation.

Figure 66 (continued)

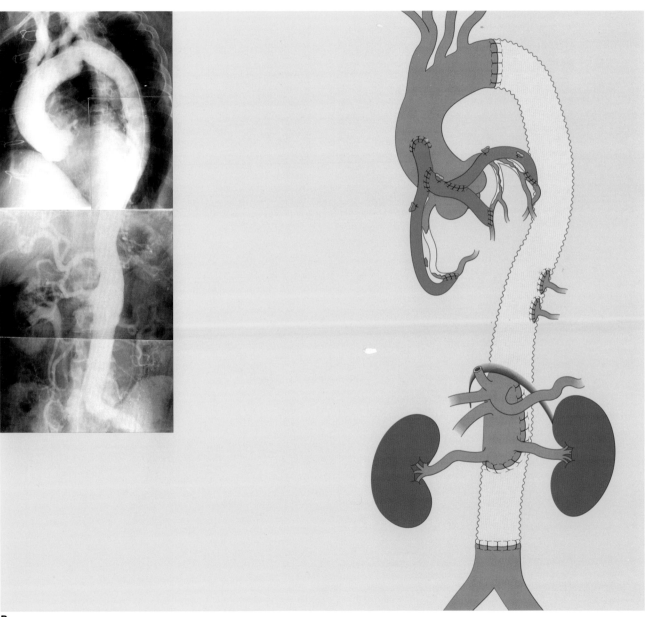

B

Figure 67

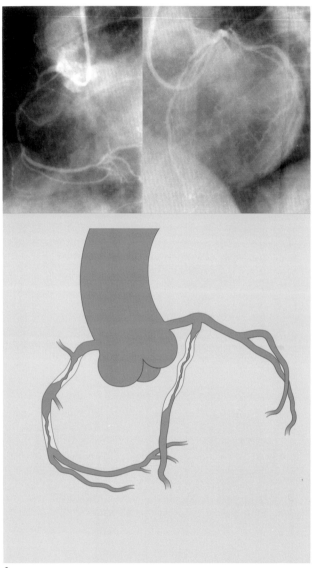

A

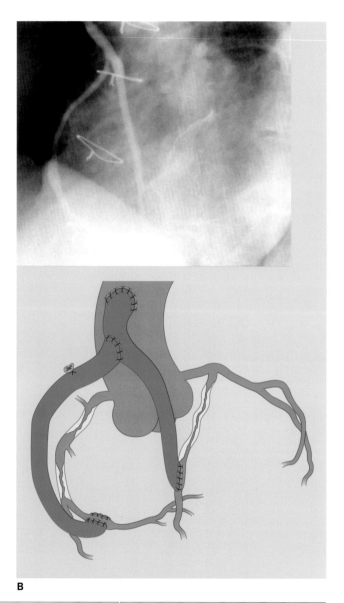

B

(**A**) Preoperative arteriograms in a 53-year-old white man with severe, disabling, recurrent angina pectoris despite intensive medical therapy show severe occlusive disease in the proximal and midproximal portions of the right coronary artery and in the proximal portion of the left anterior descending coronary artery.

(**B**) Surgical treatment consisted in an autogenous saphenous-vein bypass graft from the ascending aorta to the right and left anterior descending coronary arteries. Photograph: a coronary arteriogram made 18 years after the operation shows patent vein grafts. The patient has remained asymptomatic.

Figure 68

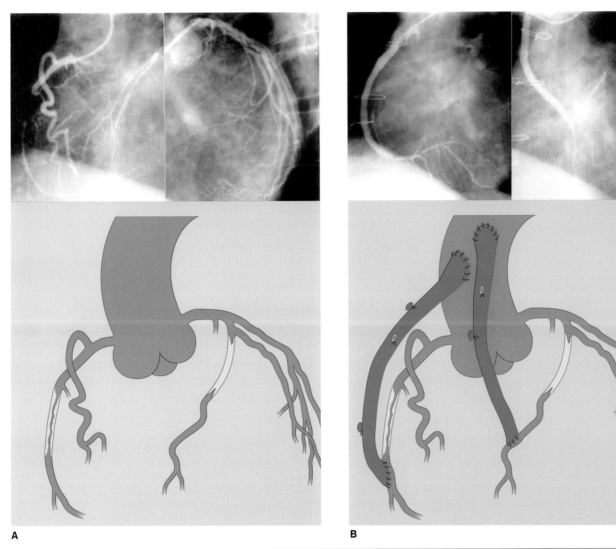

A

B

(**A**) Coronary arteriograms in a 55-year-old white man with severe, disabling, recurrent angina despite adequate medical therapy show well-localized complete occlusive disease in the proximal portion of the left anterior descending coronary artery and in the midproximal portion of the right coronary artery.

(**B**) Surgical treatment consisted in autogenous saphenous-vein bypass graft from the ascending aorta to the right and left anterior descending coronary arteries. Photographs: coronary arteriograms made 16 years after the operation show patent bypass grafts. The patient has remained asymptomatic.

Figure 69

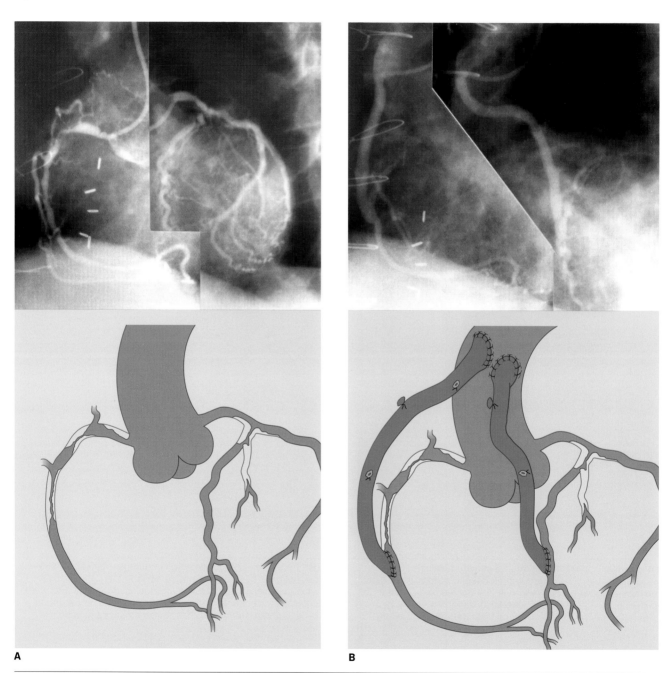

A

B

(**A**) A coronary arteriogram in a 54-year-old white man with severe recurrent angina pectoris despite intensive medical therapy shows severe proximal atherosclerotic occlusion in the left anterior descending and the midproximal portion of the right coronary arteries.

(**B**) Surgical treatment consisted in bypass from the ascending aorta to the right and left anterior descending coronary arteries using an autogenous saphenous vein. Photograph: a coronary arteriogram made 19 years after the operation shows patent bypass grafts. The patient has remained asymptomatic.

Figure 70

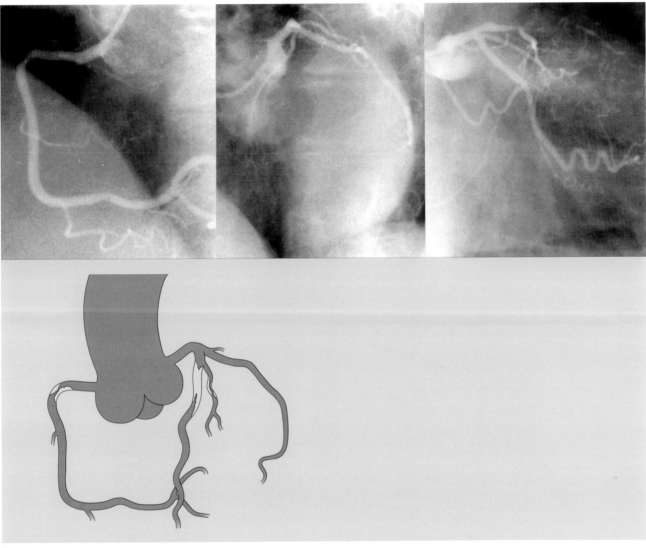

A

(**A**) Preoperative arteriograms in a 57-year-old white woman with severe angina pectoris show severe, well-localized stenotic disease in the proximal portion of the right and left descending coronary arteries.

(**B**) Surgical treatment consisted in an autogenous saphenous-vein bypass graft from the ascending aorta to the right coronary artery and a bypass graft to the left anterior descending coronary artery using the left internal mammary artery. Photographs of coronary arteriograms made 1 year later show patency of both grafts. The patient has remained asymptomatic since the operation. (See following page.)

Figure 70 (continued)

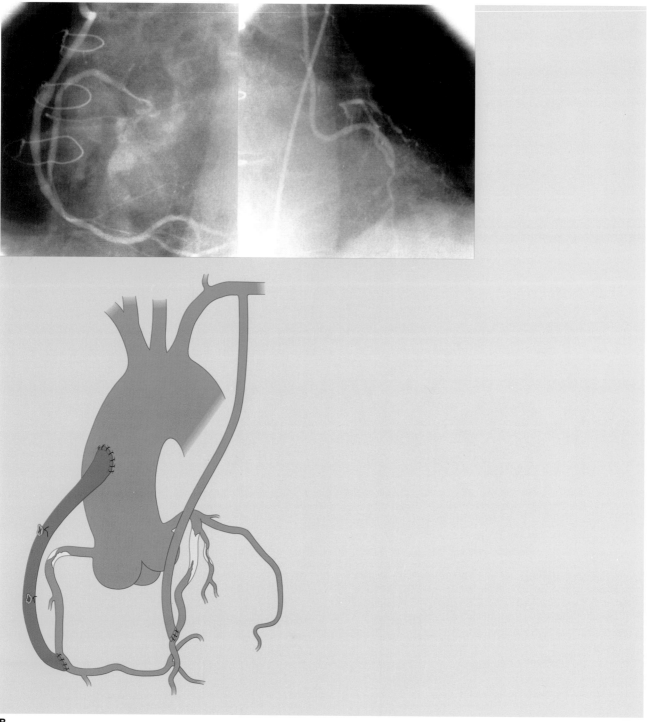

B

See caption on previous page.

Figure 71

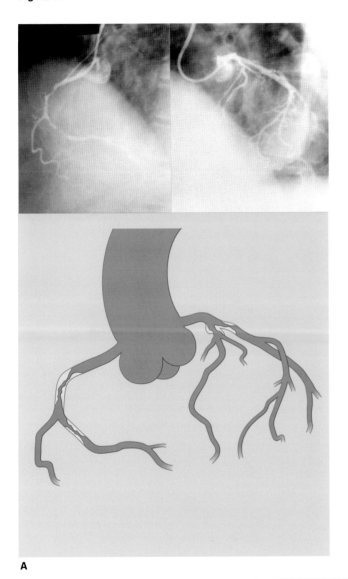

A

B

(**A**) Preoperative coronary arteriograms in a 48-year-old white man with severe, disabling angina pectoris show well-localized, severe occlusive disease in the proximal portion of the left anterior descending and circumflex coronary arteries and in the midproximal segment of the right coronary artery.

(**B**) Surgical treatment consisted in autogenous saphenous-vein bypass grafts from the ascending aorta to the left anterior descending, circumflex, and right coronary arteries. Photograph: a coronary arteriogram made 16 years after the operation shows patency of vein grafts. The patient has remained asymptomatic.

Figure 72

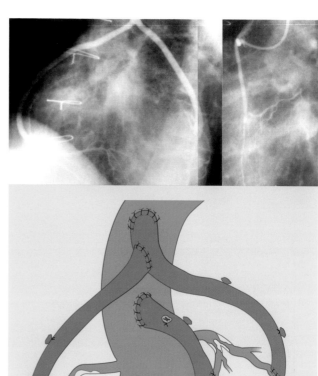

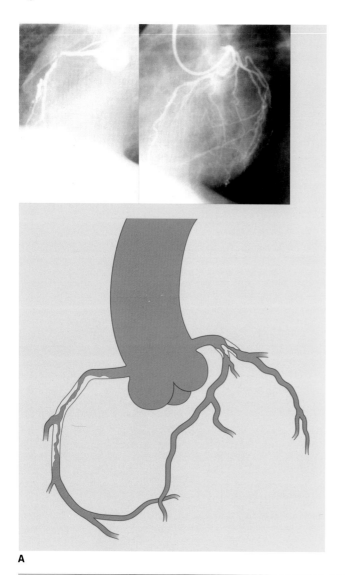

A

B

(**A**) Coronary arteriograms in a 50-year-old white man with severe, disabling angina pectoris. The figures show severe, well-localized atherosclerotic stenosis in the proximal portion of the left anterior descending and circumflex coronary arteries, as well as in the midproximal portion of the right coronary artery.

(**B**) Surgical treatment consisted in an autogenous saphenous-vein bypass graft from the ascending aorta to the right and left anterior descending and circumflex coronary arteries. Photographs: coronary arteriograms made 18 years after the operation show patent bypass grafts. The patient has remained asymptomatic.

Figure 73

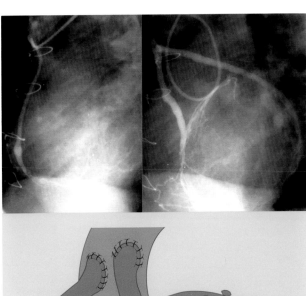

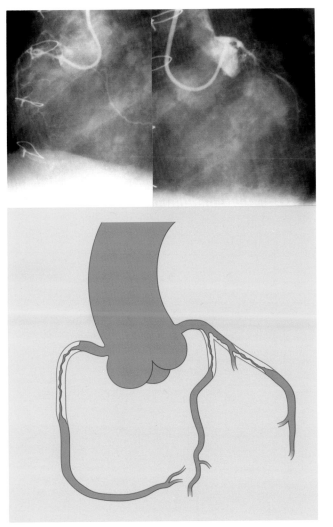

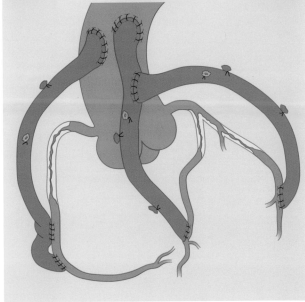

A

B

(**A**) Coronary arteriograms in a 51-year-old white woman with severe angina and exertional dyspnea show severe, well-localized occlusive disease in the proximal portion of the right and left anterior descending and circumflex coronary arteries. The patient also had severe hypokinesia with a low ejection fraction and a high left ventricular end-diastolic pressure.

(**B**) Surgical treatment consisted in autogenous saphenous-vein bypass grafts from the ascending aorta to the right and left anterior descending and circumflex coronary arteries. The patient required assisted circulation for 5 days after the operation but recovered satisfactorily. Photograph of coronary arteriogram made 15 years after the operation shows normally patent bypass grafts. The patient's left ventricular end-diastolic pressure had improved to 18 mm Hg at this time and the ejection fraction had also improved significantly. The patient has remained asymptomatic.

217

Figure 74

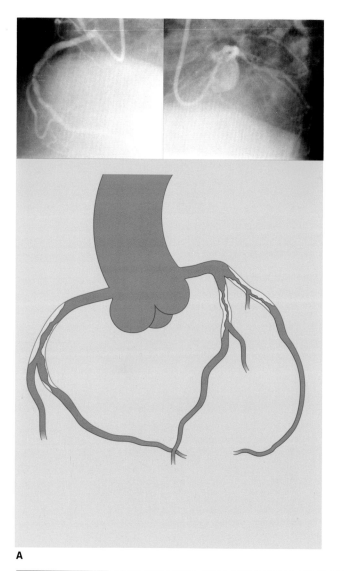

A

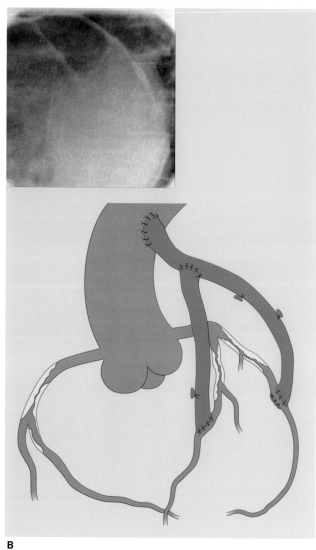

B

(**A**) Preoperative coronary arteriograms in a 55-year-old white man with severe angina and exertional dyspnea show severe, proximal, localized occlusive disease in left anterior descending and circumflex coronary arteries.

(**B**) Surgical treatment consisted in an autogenous saphenous-vein bypass graft from the ascending aorta to the left anterior descending and circumflex coronary arteries. Photograph: a coronary arteriogram made 17 years after the operation shows a patent bypass graft. The patient has remained asymptomatic.

Figure 75

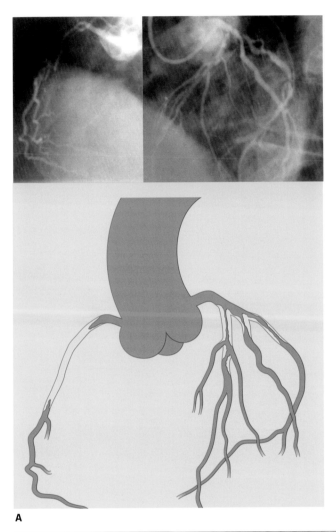

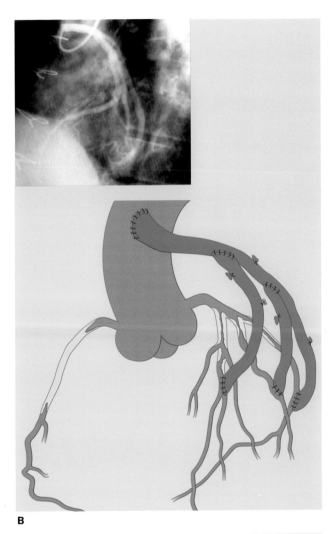

A

B

(**A**) Preoperative coronary arteriograms in a 52-year-old man with severe angina pectoris and exertional dyspnea show well-localized, severe occlusive disease in the proximal portion of the left anterior descending and circumflex coronary arteries. The right coronary artery was completely occluded.

(**B**) Surgical treatment consisted in an autogenous saphenous-vein bypass graft from the ascending aorta to the left anterior descending, obtuse marginal, and posterior descending branch of the circumflex coronary arteries. Photograph: a coronary arteriogram made 16 years after the operation shows patent bypass grafts. The patient has remained in good condition.

Figure 76

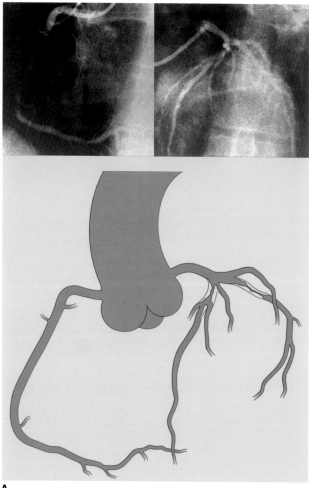

A

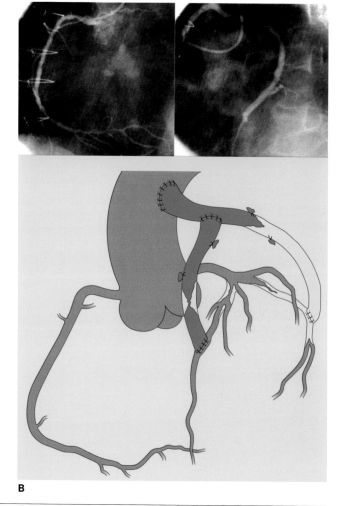

B

(**A**) Preoperative coronary arteriograms in a 39-year-old white man with severe angina pectoris show severe occlusive disease in the proximal portion of the left anterior descending and circumflex coronary arteries.

(**B**) Surgical treatment consisted in an autogenous saphenous-vein bypass graft to the left anterior descending and circumflex coronary arteries. Photographs: coronary arteriograms made 9 years after this operation show complete occlusion of a vein segment of the bypass graft to the circumflex coronary artery and severe stenosis in a vein segment to the left anterior

descending coronary artery. Occlusive disease in the circumflex coronary artery was extensive.

(**C**) The operation consisted in excision of a previously placed autogenous-vein bypass graft and replacement with a new saphenous-vein bypass graft to the left anterior descending coronary artery.

(**D**) Photograph: an open segment of a vein bypass graft to the circumflex coronary artery shows atheromatous-like occlusive disease. The patient has remained asymptomatic during the year since the last operation.

Figure 76 (continued)

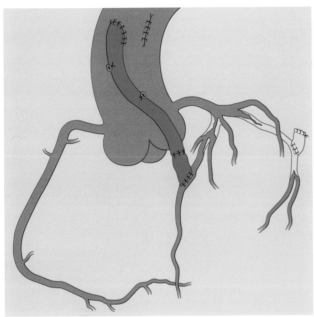

C

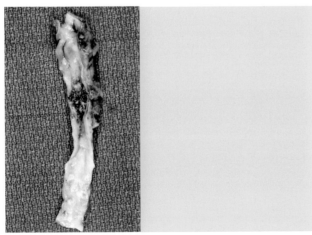

D

Figure 77

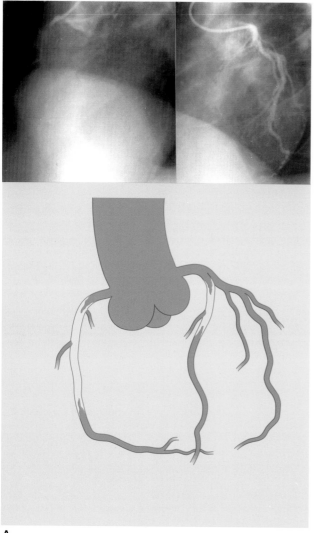

A

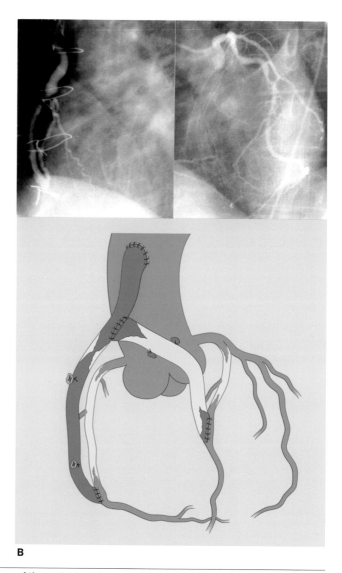

B

(**A**) Preoperative arteriograms in a 33-year-old white man with severe, disabling angina pectoris show complete occlusion of the midproximal segment of the right coronary artery and the proximal segment of the left anterior descending coronary artery.

(**B**) Surgical treatment at original admission to the hospital consisted in autogenous saphenous-vein bypass to the right and left anterior descending coronary arteries. Photographs: coronary arteriograms made 12 years after the original operation following several months of recurring, progressively severe angina pectoris show severe stenosis in the midportion

of the patent saphenous-vein graft to the right coronary artery, complete occlusion of the vein graft to the left anterior descending coronary artery, and development of new occlusive disease in the circumflex coronary artery.

(**C**) Surgical treatment consisted in excision of previous vein grafts and replacement with new bypass autogenous saphenous-vein grafts to the right and circumflex coronary arteries and a bypass to the left anterior descending coronary artery using the left internal mammary artery. The patient has remained completely asymptomatic during the past year since the last operation.

Figure 77 (continued)

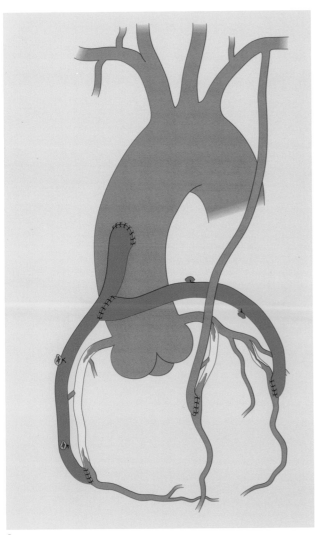

C

Figure 78

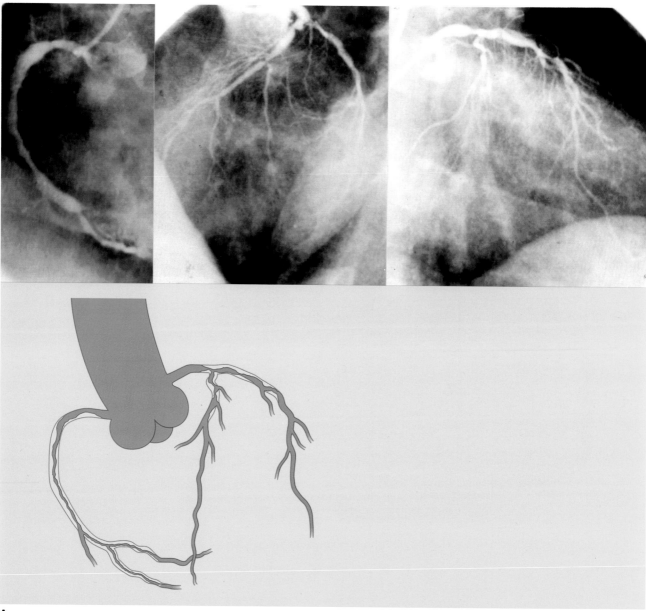

A

(**A**) Preoperative coronary arteriograms in a 64-year-old white man with severe angina pectoris show well-localized, severe stenosis in the proximal and midportion of the left anterior descending coronary and obtuse marginal coronary arteries with extensive occlusion of the right coronary artery.

(**B**) Surgical treatment consisted in bypass graft to the left anterior descending coronary artery using the left internal mammary artery and an autogenous saphenous vein for bypass from the ascending aorta to the obtuse marginal coronary artery and to the right coronary artery after endarterectomy was performed. The photograph shows the atherosclerotic process removed from the right coronary artery by endarterectomy.

Figure 78 (continued)

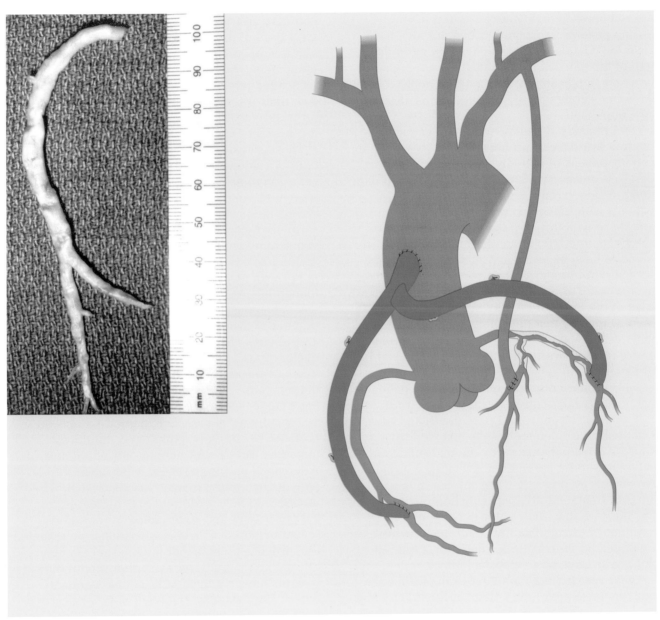

B

Results of Surgical Treatment

It has been generally accepted that coronary artery bypass is highly effective in relieving angina pectoris. Most studies like our own have reported complete relief of angina in more than half of the patients for 5 to 15 years after operation and significant improvement or better control with medical treatment in an additional 25% to 40% of patients.

Until recently, it has been difficult to establish definite evidence of prolongation of life except in certain subsets of patients. The results of randomized prospective studies have confirmed data derived from earlier clinical experience. Thus, patients with left main coronary artery disease and those with three-vessel disease and moderately impaired left ventricular function have been found to have an increased survival expectancy with surgical treatment. In a recent report derived from a study of patients in the observational data base of the Coronary Artery Surgery Study (CASS) registry that does not include randomized patients, the data provide evidence that coronary artery revascularization improves the survival rate of patients with severe angina pectoris and three-vessel coronary disease, including some patients with normal left ventricular function.

In another recent report from the Duke University Medical Center, the results obtained from a study of 5809 patients receiving medical or surgical treatment for coronary artery disease provided persuasive evidence that the survival rate with surgical treatment progressively improved over the study period (1969 to 1984), and surgical treatment was significantly better than medical treatment for most patient subgroups, especially those with adverse prognostic indicators.

These researchers found, for example, that the unadjusted survival rates (Kaplan-Meier) at 5 and 10 years for medical patients were 80% and 65%, respectively, whereas for surgical patients these rates were 88% and 72%, respectively. They also found that the survival benefits derived from coronary artery bypass are greatly influenced by the extent of the disease, the year of operation, and overall medical risks. This is exemplified by the fact that the 1-year and 5-year survival expectancy after surgical treatment has increased from 84% and 76%, respectively, for patients operated on in 1970 to 1971 to 95% and 89%, respectively, for those operated on in 1980 to 1981.

These statistics are particularly significant in light of evidence of a trend in recent years toward selection of more gravely ill patients for surgical treatment. For example, in our own experience, during the past 20 years the mean age of our coronary bypass patients has risen from 54 to 61 years. More women now undergo surgical treatment—20.4% in our more recent experience compared with 14.1% in our initial experience. Although the average preoperative ejection fraction has been constant at about 50%, the preoperative number of diseased vessels has increased from 37% to 50%. There also has been a corresponding decline from 23% to 17% in patients with single-vessel disease selected for operation. Interestingly, the incidence of left main coronary artery stenosis has been constant at about 10% of patients.

The number of vessels bypassed reflects these changes. In our early experience, multivessel bypasses were performed on 66% of patients, whereas in our more recent experience, 91% of patients had multivessel revascularization. The number of grafts performed has increased from 2.0 per patient to 3.4 per patient in our more recent experience. In the early 1980s, we resumed the virtual routine use of the internal mammary artery bypass graft, and since then, about 80% of patients have received at least one mammary bypass graft, usually to the left anterior descending coronary artery (Figures 64, 70, 77, 78). Use of the internal mammary artery has been associated with improved long-term survival rates in previous reports.

Despite these sicker patients, the surgical mortality rate (including elective and emergency procedures) has been stable at about 3% for isolated coronary bypass procedures.

The long-term durability of coronary bypass procedures became a subject of concern after reports of high rates of vein-graft failure in a follow-up study of the early experience from one institution. In fact, although vein-graft deterioration does occur in some patients (Figures 64, 66, 77), particularly those with severe hyperlipidemia, our own long-term experience has been more favorable.

After more than 10 years of follow-up, about 70% of the grafts have been patent in our experience, and some degree of stenosis has been present in about 18% of these grafts. Thus, 86% of the patients surviving at least 10 years have had at least one patent graft, and all grafts were patent in 58% of the patients. The long-term patency of mammary grafts is in excess of 90% at 10 years. Improved function of saphenous-vein grafts also has been achieved by the oral administration of aspirin in the immediate postoperative period. An increase of vein-graft patency by 10% to 15% has been demonstrated in several recent studies. Improved methods of vein-graft preservation are also expected to enhance long-term vein-graft function.

In our entire experience, reoperation has been required for about 1% to 1.5% of patients each year, initially because of a combination of incomplete revascularization, progression of disease, and vein-graft occlusion. More commonly, it is now needed because of graft problems and the progression of disease (Figures 64, 76, 77). In addition to our own patients who have required reoperation, the referral from other centers of patients requiring reoperation has led to the incidence of reoperative cases as a proportion of all cases to rise from 2.3% before 1974 to 17.3% in our recent experience. Although reoperation carries a somewhat higher risk, the long-term relief of symptoms and survival rates are comparable to those achieved by the initial procedure.

The surgical indications in patients with advanced diffuse left ventricular dysfunction (ejection fraction below 35%) have been clarified. If only angina is present, bypass surgery can be performed with a risk of less than 7% and with the expectation of good relief of angina and improved long-term survival (Figure 73). When angina is absent and congestive heart failure is the major symptom, bypass surgery is usually ineffective, and medical treatment, or in advanced cases, cardiac transplantation, should be considered.

Patients in whom sustained ventricular tachycardia develops late after myocardial infarction and is refractory to drugs can be treated by electrophysiologic map-guided surgical ablation and coronary revascularization. In about 90% of our patients, control of the arrhythmia has been achieved by this technique. These critically ill patients often require multiple surgical procedures, such as aneurysmectomy, endocardial resection, cryothermia, and coronary bypass.

Patients with coronary artery disease who experience near sudden cardiac death not associated with acute myocardial infarction or mappable arrhythmias now undergo coronary bypass and implantation of the automatic internal cardioverter defibrillator.

Coronary artery disease is a common cause of end-stage cardiomyopathy. Cardiac transplantation is recommended to patients with severe congestive heart failure and no discrete resectable aneurysm. Cardiac transplantation is effective, producing good results in about 80% of patients at 3 to 5 years of follow-up.

Despite the progressive nature of atherosclerotic occlusive disease and the susceptibility of some vein grafts to deterioration, a certain proportion of patients obtain excellent long-term results with maintenance of graft patency for more than 15 to 20 years (Figures 61, 67, 68, 71-75). Analysis of our data and other investigations are being pursued in an effort to identify the variables that determine such good long-term results.

Selected Readings

Absolon KB, Aust JB, Varco RL, Lillehei CW. Surgical treatment of occlusive coronary artery disease by endarterectomy or anastomotic replacement. **Surg Gynec Obstet**. 1956;103:180-185.

Califf RM, Harrell FE Jr, Lee KL, et al. The evolution of medical and surgical therapy for coronary artery disease: a 15-year perspective. **JAMA**. 1989;261:2077-2086.

Cameron A, Kemp HG Jr, Green GE. Reoperation for coronary artery disease: 10 years of clinical follow-up. **Circulation**. 1988;78(suppl 1, part 1):I-158–I-162.

DeBakey ME, Henly WS. Surgical treatment of angina pectoris. **Circulation**. 1961;23:111-120.

DeBakey ME, Lawrie GM. Bypass surgery: which patient is the ideal candidate – the surgical viewpoint. **Illus Med**. 1986;1:11-16.

DeBakey ME, Lawrie GM. Combined coronary artery and peripheral vascular disease: recognition and treatment. **J Vasc Surg**. 1984;1:606-607.

DeBakey ME, Lawrie GM. Coronary bypass surgery: the total experience at Baylor College of Medicine. In: Hurst JW, ed. **Clinical Essays on The Heart**. Vol 2. New York, NY: McGraw-Hill Book Company; 1984:219-230.

DeBakey ME, Lawrie GM, Glaeser DH. Patterns of atherosclerosis and their surgical significance. **Ann Surg**. 1985;201:115-131.

Favoloro RG, Effler DB, Groves LK, Sheldon WC, Shirey EK, Sones FM Jr. Severe segmental obstruction of the left main coronary artery and its divisions: surgical treatment by the saphenous vein graft technique. **J Thorac Cardiovasc Surg**. 1970;60:469-482.

Garrett HE, Dennis EW, DeBakey ME. Aortocoronary bypass with saphenous vein graft: seven-year follow-up. **JAMA**. 1973;223:792-794.

Green GE. Use of internal thoracic artery for coronary artery grafting. **Circulation**. 1989;79(suppl I):I-30–I-33.

Grüntzig AR, Senning A, Siegenthaler WE. Nonoperative dilatation of coronary-artery stenosis: percutaneous transluminal coronary angioplasty. **N Engl J Med**. 1979;301:61-68.

Hochberg MS, Gielchinsky I, Parsonnet V, Hussain SM, Mirsky E, Fisch D. Coronary angioplasty versus coronary bypass: three-year follow-up of a matched series of 250 patients. **J Thorac Cardiovasc Surg**. 1989;97:496-503.

Julian OC, Lopez-Belio M, Moorehead D, Lima A. Direct surgical procedures on the coronary arteries: experimental studies. **J Thorac Surg**. 1957;34:654-660.

Lawrie GM, Lin H, Wyndham CRC, DeBakey ME. Surgical treatment of supraventricular arrhythmias: results in 67 patients. **Ann Surg**. 1987;205:700-711.

Lawrie GM, Morris GC Jr, Earle N. Long-term results of coronary bypass surgery: analysis of 1698 patients followed 15 to 20 years. **Ann Surg**. 1991;213:377-387.

Lawrie GM, Wyndham CR, Krafchek J, Luck JC, Roberts R, DeBakey ME. Progress in the surgical treatment of cardiac arrhythmias: initial experience of 90 patients. **JAMA**. 1985;254:1464-1468.

McCollum CH, Garcia-Rinaldi R, Graham JM, DeBakey ME. Myocardial revascularization prior to subsequent major surgery in patients with coronary artery disease. **Surgery**. 1977;81:302-304.

Murray G, Porcheron R, Hilario J, Roschlau W. Anastomosis of a systemic artery to the coronary. **Can Med Assoc J**. 1954;71:594-597.

Myers WO, Schaff HV, Gersh BJ, et al, and CASS Investigators. Improved survival of surgically treated patients with triple vessel coronary artery disease and severe angina pectoris: a report from the Coronary Artery Surgery Study (CASS) registry. **J Thorac Cardiovasc Surg**. 1989;97:487-495.

Phillips SJ, Zeff RH, Kongtahworn C, et al. Surgery for evolving myocardial infarction. **JAMA**. 1982;248:1325-1328.

Sabiston DC Jr. Coronary endarterectomy. **Am Surg**. 1960;26:217-226.

Sabiston DC Jr. The William Reinhoff, Jr. Lecture: The coronary circulation. **Johns Hopkins Med J**. 1974;134:314-329.

Sones FM Jr, Shirey EK. Cine coronary arteriography. **Mod Concepts Cardiovasc Dis**. 1962;31:735-738.

Thal A, Perry JF Jr, Miller FA, Wangensteen OH. Direct suture anastomosis of the coronary arteries in the dog. **Surgery**. 1956;40:1023-1029.

Index

A

Abetalipoproteinemia, 19,20

Accelerated idioventricular rhythm, 172

Acetyl LDL receptor, 82

Acute myocardial infarction. *See* Myocardial infarction

Acyl:cholesterol acyltransferase (ACAT)
  activation, 21
  dietary cholesterol and, 37

Adrenergic agents and vascular tone, 40

Adrenergic stimulation and endothelial injury, 71

Alanine aminotransferase (ALT) measurement, 157

Alcohol, 26, 28, 45

Aldose reductase inhibitors, 42

Alpha$_2$-macroglobulin receptor, 22

Ambulatory ECG monitoring, 105, 188

American Heart Association diets, 36-37

Amphipathic helical structures, 11, 13

Amrinone in cardiac failure, 176

Analgesics in myocardial infarction, 166

Androgens and HDL levels, 25

Aneurysm
  atherosclerotic plaque, 51
  radiographic imaging, 107

Aneurysmal atherosclerotic disease, 195, 198

Aneurysmectomy, 227

Angina pectoris
  at rest, 91, 190
  classification, 92-93
  clinical features, 90-91
  crescendo, 190
  ECG during, 102
  management, 190-191
  medical treatment, 130-151
  pain, 90-91
  pharmacologic therapy, 137-147
  platelet aggregation, 178
  postinfarction, 178, 179, 190-191
  prophylaxis, 138
  reinfarction and, 179-180
  surgical therapy, 204
  unstable, 152-193

Anginal equivalent, 91

Angiogenesis growth factor, 43, 65, 66

Angiography
  coronary artery disease, 107-112
  plaque regression, 36

Angioplasty and thrombolytic therapy, 168, 169

Angiotensin II and endothelial injury, 64

Angiotensin converting enzyme (ACE) inhibitors
  hypertension, 41
  nitrate tolerance, 140

Anorexia nervosa and hyperlipoproteinemia, 28

Anterior myocardial infarction
  anticoagulation therapy, 174
  clinical features, 155-156
  complications, 180, 181
  Q-wave patterns, 97, 100
  survival rate, 184-185

Anterolateral myocardial infarction, 97, 101

Anteroseptal myocardial infarction, 125

Antiarrhythmic agents
  cardiogenic shock from, 177
  myocardial infarction, 172

Anticoagulation therapy in myocardial infarction, 174

Antigen-antibody complexes and endothelial injury, 64

Antihypertensive therapy and coronary heart disease risk, 40-41

Antimyosin antibody isotope, 120

Antioxidants, 23

Anxiety and tachycardia, 173

Aortic aneurysm
  detection, 115
  resection, 204, 206-209

Aortic dissection, 163

Aortic stenosis
  angina, 92
  detection, 115

Aortic valve replacement, 204, 206-207

Apo[a], 13

Apolipoproteins
  atherogenesis, 60
  cholesterol transport, 22-25

defects, 17-20, 58
  plasma distribution, 12
  structure and function, 11

Apolipoprotein A (apo A)
  disease associations, 15
  functions, 13-14, 15
  gene mutations, 13-14, 17-18
  HDL content, 24

Apolipoprotein A-II (apo A-II) deficiency, 18

Apolipoprotein B (apo B)
  atherogenesis, 56, 60
  disease associations, 15, 26
  functions, 14-17
  LDL receptor binding, 21
  mutations, 19-20, 26
  structure, 14

Apolipoprotein C (apo C)
  disease associations, 15
  functions, 12

Apolipoprotein C-II (apo C-II) deficiency
  chylomicronemia, 33
  classification, 28

Apolipoprotein C-III (apo C-III) deficiency, 18

Apolipoprotein D (apo D), 12

Apolipoprotein E (apo E)
  atherogenesis, 59, 65, 66
  disease associations, 15
  E_2/E_2 phenotype, 17, 20
  function, 15
  LDL receptor binding, 21

Arrythmias
  coronary heart disease risk, 40
  myocardial infarction, 156
  treatment, 171-173

Arterial injury. *See* Endothelial injury

Artery wall structure, 51-53

Aspartate aminotransferase (AST) measurement, 157

Aspirin
  thrombolytic therapy, 168
  unstable angina, 190-191

Atenolol, postinfarction, 188

Atherectomy devices, 149

Atheroarteritis, 71

Atheroma, 54

Atherosclerotic plaques
  anatomic patterns, 195
  calcification, 106-107
  composition, 51, 54-56
  eccentric and concentric, 71, 72
  progression rates, 195
  regression, 83-84
  thrombus formation, 152-153

Atrial ectopic beats, 172

Atrial fibrillation, 172-173

Atrial flutter, 172

Atrial infarction, 154, 157

Atrial tachycardia, 172

Atropine, 166, 172

Autocrine stimulation, 81

Automatic internal cardioverter defibrillator, 227

B

Bacterial infection and endothelial injury, 64

Balloon angioplasty, 148-149

Bassen Kornzweig syndrome, 19

Bayes' theorem, 95-96

B:E receptor. *See* Low-density lipoprotein receptor

Benign vasoconstriction, 139, 141

Beta-blocking agents
  acute myocardial infarction, 166
  angina, 140-142, 146, 178
  combination therapy, 142, 144-147
  coronary heart disease risk, 40-41
  HDL levels, 26
  infarct size, 169
  mechanism of action, 141
  postinfarction, 178, 188-189
  PVCs, 172
  side effects, 140
  vascular tone, 40

Beta-carotene as antioxidant, 23

Beta-VLDL, 22, 37

Bile acid sequestrants
  familial hypercholesterolemia, 38
  LDL receptors, 30
  niacin and, 83

Blood flow at carotid bifurcation, 74

Blood pool imaging, 115-117

Blood pressure. *See also* Hypertension
  atherogenesis, 78-79
  monitoring after myocardial infarction, 173

Bradycardia in acute myocardial infarction, 172-173

Bretylium tosylate, 172

Bundle-branch block and ventricular septal rupture, 181

Bypass grafts. *See* Coronary artery bypass

C

Calcium, cellular
  atherosclerosis, 56
  myocardial infarction, 120

Calcium channel blockers
  angina, 142-147
  atherosclerotic plaques, 39
  combination therapy, 144-147
  early reinfarction, 180
  hypertension, 41
  infarct size, 169-170
  mechanism of action, 143, 145
  postinfarction, 178, 189-190
  side effects, 144, 145

Canadian Cardiovascular Society grading scale of angina, 93

Capillary wedge pressure, 173

Captopril and nitrate tolerance, 140

Carbon 11 in emission tomography, 121

Carbon monoxide and smoking, 42, 64

Cardiac catheterization
  coronary heart disease, 107-112
  myocardial rupture, 182
  postinfarction, 186-188
  thrombolytic therapy, 169

Cardiac failure
  cardiogenic shock, 177
  hemodynamic monitoring, 173
  postinfarction, 174-176

Cardiac function, evaluation, 115-118

Cardiac output assessment, 163, 173

Cardiac rupture, 113

Cardiac transplantation, 227

Cardiogenic shock,
  clinical features, 94
  hemodynamic monitoring, 173
  papillary muscle rupture, 181
  postinfarction, 176-178
  ventricular septal rupture, 181

Cardiomyopathy and cardiac transplantation, 227

Cardioplegia, 205

Cardioversion, 172

Carotid bifurcation, blood flow, 74

Catecholamines and endothelial injury, 64

Catheter injury, 64

Cell necrosis in advanced atherosclerosis, 69

Chamber pressures, 173

Chest roentgenography, 105-107, 174

Cholesterol, 9-26
  dietary. *See also* Dietary cholesterol
  endogenous, 23-26
  intracellular, 21
  measurement, 33-34
  NCEP guidelines, 33-35
  transport, 22-26

Cholesteryl ester transfer protein (CETP), 25

Chylomicronemia, 20, 26, 33

Chylomicrons
  atherogenesis, 60
  cholesterol transport, 22
  structure, 11-12
  synthesis, 15

Cigarette smoking
  antihypertensive therapy, 40
  exercise capacity, 137
  lipid levels, 26
  pathogenetic effects, 64, 71, 79
  risk factor, 36, 42

Circulating immune complexes. *See* Immune complexes

Circulatory failure, 177

CK-MB enzymes
  early reinfarction, 179-180
  infarct size, 164
  myocardial infarction, 157-162
  unstable angina, 191

Classic angina pectoris, 91

"Clenched fist" sign, 90

Coconut oil in athero-genesis, 76

Coffee and coronary heart disease mortality, 45

Cold-induced angina, 136

Collagen secretion, 82

Collagenase, preventive function, 65

Collateral coronary vessels
  beta-blockers, 141
  myocardial oxygen supply and demand, 154
  nitroglycerin, 138

Compactin, 30

Computed tomography, 122-123

Concentric plaques, 71, 72, 76

Conduction and calcium antagonists, 143, 145

Conduction defects and septal rupture, 181

Congestive heart failure and calcium antagonists, 145

Connective tissue synthesis, 66-69

Contractile smooth muscle cell, 68

Contrast echocardiography, 163

Copper deficiency, 45

Coronary angiography, 107-110

Coronary anteriography
  pre- and postoperative, 196-203, 206-225
  postinfarction, 178, 188
  unstable angina, 191

Coronary artery bypass
  history, 194-195
  reoperation, 205, 220-221
  tomographic evaluation, 122-123
  vs. transcatheter recanali-zation, 150

Coronary artery disease. *See* Coronary heart disease

Coronary blood flow, regulation, 131

Coronary calcifications, 106-107

Coronary care units (CCUs), 165-166

Coronary flow reserve, 110

Coronary heart disease (CHD)
  diagnosis, 89-129
  dietary cholesterol, 37
  risk factors, 35, 36

Coronary insufficiency, 190

Coronary sinus catheteriza-tion, 112

Coronary stenosis, 110

Coronary thrombosis. *See* Thrombosis

Costochondritis, 92

Creatine kinase isoenzymes. *See* CK-MB enzymes

Crescendo angina, 190

Cryothermia, indications, 227

Cushing's syndrome and hypertension, 41

Cytokines and atherogenesis, 80

Cytolysis and atherosclerosis, 66

Cytostatic factors in atherogenesis, 81

D

Defective anginal warning system, 136

Defibrillation, 172

Definite angina, 92

Delayed hypersensitivity and endothelial injury, 71

Dependence on nitrates, 140

Diabetes mellitus
  coronary heart disease risk, 42-43
  endothelial injury, 64, 79
  hyperlipidemia, 73
  hyperlipoproteinemia, 28
  obesity and, 43
  silent ischemia, 93
  triglyceride measurement, 38

Diagnostic tests, predictive values, 96-97

Diastolic function, evaluation, 115

Diastolic murmur in myocardial infarction, 156

Diazepam in acute infarction, 166

Dietary cholesterol
  LDL receptors, 23-24, 37
  recommendations, 37
  transport, 22-23

Dietary fiber, 38

Dietary therapy
  familial hypercholester-
    olemia, 30
  hypercholesterolemia,
    36-38
  postinfarction, 171
  weight loss and, 43
Diffuse atherosclerotic
  disease, 195
Digital angiography, 112
Digitalis and angina, 141, 147
Digoxin, 175-176
Dilantin, 172
Diltiazem
  angina, 143-145, 178-180
  infarct size and, 170
  mechanism of action, 143
  postinfarction, 178-180,
    189-190
  side effects, 144, 145
Dipyridamole with
  scintigraphy, 119, 188
Directional atherectomy, 149
Dissecting aortic aneurysm,
  115
Distal atherosclerotic
  disease, 195
Diuretic agents
  beta-blockers and, 141
  cardiac failure, 175-176
  coronary heart disease
    risk, 40-41
  left ventricular failure, 147
Dobutamine, 176, 177
Docosahexaenoic acid
  (DHA), 37
Dopamine, 176, 177
Doppler echocardiography,
  112-114, 163
Dressler's syndrome, 183
Drug tolerance and
  dependence, 140
Dynamic obstruction, 132,
  135, 146
Dysglobulinemia and
  hyperlipoproteinemia, 28
Dyslipidemia, 9-38
Dyslipidemic hypertension,
  26, 40

E

Early reinfarction, 179-180
Early spontaneous
  reperfusion, 184
Eccentric plaques, 71, 72
Eccentric stenosis and
  nitrates, 138, 139
Echocardiography
  coronary heart disease,
    112-115
  myocardial infarction,
    163-164
  myocardial rupture, 182
  postinfarction, 186, 188
Ectopic beats, 156, 171
Education on myocardial
  infarction risk, 44
Eicosapentaenoic acid
  (EPA), 37
Ejection fraction
  blood pool scans, 115-118
  calculation, 111
Elastase, 65
Electrocardiogram (ECG)
  ambulatory ECG, 105, 118
  coronary heart disease,
    97-105
  during angina, 102
  exercise ECG, 102-105
  myocardial infarction,
    156-157
  resting ECG, 97, 102
Electrophysiologic testing
  postinfarction, 188
Emission computed
  tomography, 120-122
Emotional stress and
  myocardial infarction, 44
Enalapril and nitrate
  tolerance, 140
Encrustation theory, 152
Endarterectomy, history,
  194-195
Endocardial resection,
  indication, 227
Endocytosis, 61, 62
Endothelial cells, secretory
  products, 81-82
Endothelial-derived relaxing
  factor (EDRF), 132, 134, 153
Endothelial injury
  atherogenesis, 61, 63-64,
    152-153
  cigarette smoking, 42
  hypertension, 39
  mechanisms, 79
  monocyte sticking, 65
  oxidized LDL, 57-58

Endothelial leukocyte
  adhesion molecules
  (ELAMs), 65
Endothelium and large-
  vessel construction, 132, 134
Endotoxins and endothelial
  injury, 64, 78
Epinephrine, 172
Esmolol, 166
Esophogeal disorders and
  chest pain, 92
Estrogen
  coronary heart disease
    risk, 45
  hyperlipoproteinemia, 28
  lipid levels, 25
  postmenopausal, 45
Ethanol. See Alcohol
Ethmozine, 172
Exercise
  HDL levels, 26
  hypertension, 41
  risk reduction, 43-44
Exercise capacity
  drug therapy and, 144-145
  ischemia, 135
  physical conditioning, 147
Exercise-induced angina,
  132-134, 136, 146
Exercise testing
  ECG, 102-105
  scintigraphy, 118-119
Extension of infarction, 179

F

False aneurysm, 182
Familial combined hyper-
  lipidemia
  apo B$_{100}$ defect, 26
  classification, 28
  clinical features, 30
  dietary therapy, 38
  triglyceride measurement,
    38
Familial combined
  hypertriglyceridemia, 38
Familial defective apo B$_{100}$, 19
Familial dysbetalipoproteinemia
  apo E deficiency, 20
  clinical features, 28, 32
Familial fasting chylomicronemia syndrome, 28

Familial hypercholester-
  olemia
  clinical features, 27-28
  gene mutations, 27, 29
  treatment, 30, 38
Familial hypertriglyceridemia, 28, 38-39
Familial LCAT deficiency, 19
Familial lipoprotein lipase
  deficiency, 28, 33
Familial mixed (type V)
  hyperlipidemia
  clinical features, 33
  diabetic ketoacidosis, 42
Fat, recommended dietary
  levels, 36-37
Fat distribution and coronary
  heart disease, 43
Fatty streaks, early
  development, 66
Fiber, dietary, 38
Fiberoptic catheter systems,
  112
Fibric acid derivatives, 26,
  38, 39
Fibroelastic artery, structure,
  53
Fish, omega-3 fatty acid
  contents, 37
Fish-eye disease, 19
Fish oil, 36-37, 40, 78
Fixed obstruction, 131-132,
  135, 146-147
Fixed threshold angina, 146
Flecainide, 172, 177
Fluorine 18 in emission
  tomography, 121
Fluvastatin, 30, 31
Foam cells
  formation, 65, 66-69
  oxidized/modified LDL, 43
Food fats and atherogenesis,
  76, 78
Friedewald formula, 34
Furosemide in cardiac
  failure, 176

G

Gallbladder disease and
  chest pain, 92
Gastrointestinal disorders
  and chest pain, 92
Gemfibrozil, 22, 29, 30
Gender differences
  coronary heart disease,
    45
  HDL levels, 25
  survival postinfarction, 184

Gene mutations
   apolipoproteins, 13, 20
   LDL receptors, 27, 29

Genetic defects and atherosclerosis, 58-59

Global function evaluation, 115-118

Glucose levels and atherosclerosis, 42

Glycogen storage disease, 28

Glycosaminoglycans, 82, 153

Growth factors and atherogenesis, 81-82

Guar gum, 38

H

HDL. See High-density lipoprotein

Heart murmurs in myocardial infarction, 156

Heart sounds
   coronary heart disease, 94
   myocardial infarction, 156

Hemodynamic assessment
   during cardiac catheterization, 111-112
   postinfarction, 173-174

Hemodynamic forces and atherosclerosis, 64, 73-75

Hemodynamic sequelae in myocardial infarction, 154

Heparin
   postinfarction, 174
   thrombolytic therapy and, 168
   unstable angina, 190-191

Hepatic LDL receptors. See LDL receptors

Hepatic triglyceride lipase
   activation, 14, 15
   function, 23, 25

High-density lipoprotein (HDL)
   cellular interactions, 59
   cholesterol transport, 24-26
   deficiency, 18, 19
   diabetes mellitus, 42-43
   exercise, 44
   fractions, 56
   hypertriglyceridemia, 32, 38-39
   measurement, 34
   postprandial lipemia, 26
   receptor, 25
   structure, 11-13
   triglyceride levels, 26, 38-39

History in diagnosing coronary heart disease, 89-94

HMG-CoA reductase, 21

HMG-CoA reductase inhibitors, 30, 31, 38

Holosystolic murmur, 181

Holter monitoring. See Ambulatory ECG monitoring

Homocystinemia and atherosclerosis, 64, 78

Hostility and coronary heart disease risk, 44

Huxley's sliding filament theory, 174

Hydrolases, preventive function, 65

Hydroxybutyric dehydrogenase (HBD) measurement, 157

Hyperadrenalism and hypertension, 41

Hyperaldosteronism and hypertension, 41

Hyperapobetalipoproteinemia (hyper-apo B)
   clinical features, 26
   triglyceride measurement, 39

Hypercalcemia
   coronary heart disease, 45
   hyperlipoproteinemia, 28

Hypercholesterolemia
   dietary therapy, 36-38
   drug therapy, 38
   endothelial injury, 79
   hypertension and, 40
   primary, 27-32
   screening and treatment, 33-38
   secondary, 28, 32

Hyperinsulinemia, 26, 42

Hyperlipidemia, 27-33
   immune complexes, 71, 72

Hyperlipoproteinemia, 27, 28

Hyperresponders, 75

Hypertension
   angina, 136-137
   artery wall, 71, 75
   atherosclerosis, 39-41
   diabetes mellitus, 42
   endothelial injury, 64, 79
   exercise, 43-44
   hypercholesterolemia, 40
   insulin, 42
   nonpharmacologic therapy, 41
   obesity, 43
   primary, 41
   triglyceride measurements, 38

Hyperthyroidism and hypertension, 41

Hypertriglyceridemia
   coronary heart disease, 32-33
   defect in, 26
   obesity, 43
   screening, 38-39
   treatment, 39

Hypertrophic cardiomyopathy
   angina, 92
   detection, 115

Hypobetalipoproteinemia, 19

Hyporesponders, 75

Hypotension
   angina, 137
   calcium antagonists, 145
   postinfarction, 173

Hypothyroidism
   endothelial injury, 64
   hyperlipoproteinemia and, 28

I

Immune complex diseases, 64

Immune complexes
   atherogenesis, 75-76
   hyperlipidemia, 71, 72

Immunologic defects and endothelial injury, 64

Incainide, 172

Infarct patterns, 97

Infarct size
   estimates, 164
   Q-wave vs. non-Q-wave infarction, 183
   survival and, 184-185
   therapy to limit, 165-166, 169-170

Inferior myocardial infarction
   arrhythmias, 172
   cardiac failure, 175-176
   clinical features, 155-156
   complications, 180
   ECG pattern, 97, 99, 157
   hypotension, 166
   nitroglycerin, 170
   survival rate, 184-185

Inflammation and endothelial injury, 61, 63

Inotropic agents, 176

Insulin
   measurement, 42
   resistance, 26, 43

Insudation theory, 152

Interferon gamma (IFN-γ) and smooth muscle cells, 82

Interleukins
   atherogenesis, 80-82
   probucol and, 43

Intermediate-density lipoprotein (IDL)
   clearance, 23
   structure, 11-12

Intermediate syndrome, 190

Internal mammary artery bypass graft, 226

Intervention spectrum, 84-86

Interventional cardiology, 108

Intra-arterial catheter blood pressure monitoring, 173

Intramural coronary artery constriction, 134-135

Intraventricular block, 181

Ischemia. See also Angina pectoris; Myocardial ischemia; Stenosis
   necrosis and, 154
   transient global, 94

Ischemic heart disease, 152-155

Isolated systolic hypertension, 41

J

Jugular venous pressure, 156

K

Ketoacidosis and hyperlipidemia, 42

Keys and Hegsted equations, 36

Kussmaul's sign, 156

L

Laboratory tests for myocardial infarction, 157-162, 174

Lactic acid measurement, 112

Lactic dehydrogenase (LDH) isoenzymes, 156, 160

Large-vessel constriction, 132-134

Laser ablation of atheroma, 149

Lateral infarction, ECG pattern, 157

Law of the heart, 174

LDL. See Low-density lipoprotein

Lecithin:cholesterol acyl-transferase (LCAT)
  apolipoprotein activation, 13, 17
  deficiency, 19
Left main artery disease, 178, 186
Left ventricular aneurysm, 113, 114, 195
Left ventricular angiography, 111
Left ventricular assist device, 178
Left ventricular dysfunction
  chest x-ray patterns, 107
  surgical indications, 227
Left ventricular failure, 147
Left ventricular function, 107, 116, 117
  assessment, 111, 186
  cardiac failure, 175
  hemodynamic monitoring, 173
  postinfarction, 186
Left ventricular infarction, 94-95
Levine sign, 155
Lidocaine, 166, 171-172
Linoleic acid and platelet aggregation, 39
Lipid
  components, 9
  lipoproteins and, 12
  transport, 22-26
Lipid transport disorders, 26
Lipophages, 66. See also Foam cells
Lipoprotein lipase
  apo C-II activation, 17
  atherogenesis, 65, 66
  cholesterol transport, 22
  fibric-acid derivatives and, 39
  insulin, 42
Lipoprotein receptors, 20-22
Lipoproteins. See also individual lipoprotein classes
  atherogenesis, 60
  classes, 11-13
  defects, 17-20
  structure and function, 9-13
Lovastatin, 30, 31

Low-density lipoprotein (LDL)
  atherogenesis, 56, 60, 68
  cholesterol transport, 23
  fibric-acid derivatives, 39
  hypertriglyceridemia, 32-33, 39
  measurement, 34, 38-39
  oxidation, 23. See also Oxidized LDL
  structure, 11-12, 16
Low-density lipoprotein receptor (LDL receptor)
  apo B_{100} and, 14
  defects, 27, 29
  dietary cholesterol, 37
  structure and function, 20-22
Low-density lipoprotein receptor-related protein (LRP), 22
Lp[a]
  peripheral vascular disease, 59, 61
  structure, 13
Lp A-I:LI A-II, 24
Lp[x], 13
LRP receptor, 22
Lung disease and hemodynamic monitoring, 173
Lysozyme, preventive function, 65

M

Macrophage-derived growth factor, 65, 66
Macrophage functions, 65-66
Macrophage scavenger receptor, 23-24
Male-pattern obesity, 43
Marine oils, 36-37, 40, 78
Maximum predicted heart rate, 105
MB-2 assay, 162
Mechanical assist devices, 177-178
Menopause and coronary heart disease risk, 39, 45
Meperidine hydrochloride, 166
Metoprolol, 188, 189
Microthrombi in atherosclerosis, 69-71
Microvascular angina, 135, 137
Minor risk factors for coronary artery disease, 45

Mitogenic factors, 81
Mitral valve dysfunction postinfarction, 173, 181
Mitral valve prolapse, 115
Mitral valve regurgitation, 111, 113
Mixed angina, 147
MM isoforms, 160-162
Modified LDL, 23, 73. See also Oxidized LDL
Monoclonal gammopathy and hyperlipoproteinemia, 28
Monoclonal hypothesis, 67
Monocyte sticking, 65-66
Monocyte/macrophage lipid accumulation, 23
Monosaturated fat, 36-37
Morphine in acute infarction, 166
Mortality rate from coronary heart disease, 45
Multivessel disease
  postinfarction angina, 178
  surgical indications, 204, 215-219
  survival postinfarction, 186
Muscular artery, 52
M$\dot{V}o_2$. See Myocardial oxygen supply and demand
Myocardial infarction
  cholesterol levels and, 34
  classification, 155-156
  complications, 174-183
  diagnosis, 156-167
  exercise and, 43-44
  management, 165-174, 186-190
  mortality, 183-186
  nitrate workers and, 140
  pathogenesis, 152-155
  previous, assessment, 94
  radionuclide scans, 119-120
  risk stratification, 186-188
  surgical treatment, 204
Myocardial ischemia. See also Angina pectoris
  mechanisms, 130-131, 133, 135
  silent, 135-136

Mitral valve dysfunction

Myocardial necrosis, 154
Myocardial oxygen supply and demand, 130-131, 133, 135, 136
  angina, 91
  beta blockers, 141
  calcium antagonists, 143-145
  myocardial necrosis, 154
  nitrates, 138
Myocardial perfusion, assessment, 118-119
Myocardial rupture, 182
Myocarditis, 92
Myocardium, glucose uptake, 121
Myoglobin assay, 162

N

National Cholesterol Education Program (NCEP) guidelines, 33-35
Necrosis, myocardial, 154
Necrotic plaques, 54
Nephrosis
  endothelial injury, 64
  hyperlipoproteinemia, 28
Niacin and bile acid sequestrants, 83
Nicotine, cardiovascular effects, 42. See also Cigarette smoking
Nicotinic acid, 38
Nifedipine
  angina, 143-145
  infarct size, 169-170
NIH Consensus Development Conference on Triglyceride, High-Density Lipoprotein, and Coronary Heart Disease, 38-39
Nitrates, 137-140, 146
  combination therapy, 142, 144-147
  dependence and tolerance, 140
  mechanisms of action, 138-140
  postinfarction angina, 178
  side effects, 140
  unstable angina, 190
Nitric oxide. See Endothelial-derived relaxing factor
Nitrogen 13 in emission tomography, 121

Nitroglycerin, 137-140. *See also* Nitrates
  cardiac failure, 176
  early reinfarction, 180
  infarct size, 170
  myocardial infarction, 166
  postinfarction angina, 178
  unstable angina, 190-191

Nitroprusside and infarct size, 170

Nitrous oxide in myocardial infarction, 166

Nocturnal angina, 138

Nonanginal chest pain, 91

Non–insulin-dependent diabetes mellitus, 42

Non–Q-wave infarction
  cardiac catheterization, 188
  classification, 155
  diltiazem, 170
  early reinfarction, 179-180
  infarct size, 183
  mortality rates, 155, 183
  nitroglycerin, 170
  postinfarction angina, 178, 179
  postinfarction therapy, 189-190
  prognosis, 183-186
  reinfarction, 184

Nontransmural infarction, 155

Normotriglyceridemic abetalipoproteinemia, 20

Nuclear magnetic resonance (NMR) imaging, 124-126

Nutritional imbalance and endothelial injury, 64

O

Oat bran, 38

Obesity
  coronary heart disease, 36, 43
  endothelial injury, 79
  triglyceride measurement, 38

Occlusive atherosclerotic disease, 195, 197, 198

Omega-3 fatty acids, 36-37, 40, 78

Operative techniques, 205

Oral contraceptives and lipids, 45

Oxidized LDL
  arterial cells, 82-83
  atherogenesis, 43, 56-58
  cell necrosis, 69
  diabetes mellitus, 43
  mechanisms of cell damage, 23

Oxygen 15 in emission tomography, 121

Oxygen administration, 166-167

Oxygen supply and demand. *See* Myocardial oxygen supply and demand

Oxyhemoglobin dissociation curve and angina, 137

P

Pancreatitis
  familial mixed hyperlipidemia, 33
  hyperlipoproteinemia, 28
  triglyceride measurement, 38

Papillary muscle dysfunction, 204

Papillary muscle rupture, 113, 181-182

Paracrine stimulation, 81

Partial ileal bypass and blood cholesterol, 30

Pathogenesis of atherosclerosis, 51-88

Peanut oil and atherosclerosis, 76

Peptic ulcer disease and chest pain, 92

Percent diameter stenosis estimates, 108-109

Percutaneous aortic balloon, 177-178

Percutaneous transluminal coronary angioplasty (PTCA), 148-149, 150-151
  thrombolytic therapy and, 168
  vs. coronary bypass, 205

Perfusion imaging, 118-119

Pericardial tamponade, 163, 182

Pericarditis
  clinical features, 92
  postinfarction, 182

Peripheral vascular disease
  cigarette smoking, 42
  triglyceride measurement, 38

Personality type and coronary heart disease risk, 44

Phagocytosis in atherosclerosis, 66

Pharmacologic therapy. *See also* specific agents
  angina, 137-147
  limiting infarct size, 169-170

Pharmacologic vasodilation in assessing myocardial perfusion, 119

Pheochromocytoma and hypertension, 41

Phospholipids, 9

Physical activity
  coronary heart disease risk, 44
  endothelial injury, 79
  postinfarction, 170-171

Physical conditioning and angina, 147-148

Physical examination in diagnosis
  coronary artery disease, 94-95
  myocardial infarction, 155-156

Plaques. *See* Atherosclerotic plaques

Plasminogen activator, secretion, 82

Platelet aggregation
  cigarette smoking, 42
  omega-3 fatty acids, 37
  resting angina, 178
  unstable angina, 112, 190

Platelet-derived growth factor (PDGF), 69, 81, 152

Platelet factors, 153

Pollution and endothelial injury, 64

Polyclonal proliferation, 67

Polygenic hypercholesterolemia
  clinical features, 27, 28
  dietary therapy, 38

Polyunsaturated fats, 36-37

Porphyria and hyperlipoproteinemia, 28

Positron emission tomography (PET)
  diagnosing infarction, 120-121
  estimating infarct size, 164

Posterior infarction, 157

Postinfarction angina, 178, 179

Postinfarction prophylaxis, 188-190

Postinfarction risk stratification, 186-188

Postmenopausal status as risk factor, 45

Postprandial lipemia
  cholesterol transport, 23
  clinical features, 33
  HDL levels, 26

Postprandial lipids, 80

Posttest probabilities, 96-97

"Potbelly" obesity, 43

PQ-segment changes in myocardial infarction, 157

Pravastatin, 24, 30, 31

Precordial pulsation abnormalities, 156

Predictive values of tests, 96-97, 102, 104-105

Pregnancy and hyperlipoproteinemia, 28

Premature ventricular contractions (PVCs), 171, 172

Premenopausal status and coronary heart disease, 44-45

Pressure-volume curve, 174-175

Pressure-volume loop measurements, 112

Prevalence estimates, 96-97

Primary moderate hypercholesterolemia, 27, 28

Prinzmetal's (variant) angina, 91
  endothelial dysfunction, 132

Probable angina, 92

Probucol
  antioxidant properties, 23, 43
  cholesterol transport, 25
  familial hypercholesterolemia, 38

Procainamide, 172, 177

Progestin and lipid levels, 45

Propranolol
  mortality and, 40
  nitroglycerin and, 142
  postinfarction, 188

Prostacyclin, secretion, 82

Prostaglandins
  omega-3 fatty acids, 78
  thrombosis, 80

Protein C, 153

Proto-oncogenes in plaques, 67

Proximal atherosclerotic disease, 195, 196, 202

Pseudoaneurysm, 113

Psychosocial aspects of angina, 151

Psychosocial risk factors, 44

Pulmonary hypertension postinfarction, 181

Pulse rate as risk factor, 78-79

Q

Q-wave infarction
classification, 155
complications, 180, 182
diurnal variation, 154
drug therapy, 188-190
early reinfarction, 179-180
infarct size, 183
mortality rate, 155, 183
pericarditis, 182
postinfarction angina, 178
prognosis, 183-186

Q-wave patterns, 97, 99-102, 157

Quantitative angiography, 108-109

Quinidine and cardiogenic shock, 177

R

Radiographic techniques, 105-112

Radionuclide techniques, 115-122

Radionuclide ventriculography
infarct size estimates, 164
myocardial infarction, 162-164
postinfarction, 186, 188

Recombinant tissue plasminogen activator (r-TPA)
myocardial infarction, 168, 169
unstable angina, 190

Redistribution images, 118-119

Refractory angina postinfarction, 178, 179

Regional wall function
abnormalities, 113
evaluation, 115-118

Reinfarction, 179-180, 184

Reinfarction angina, 190

Relaxation techniques for hypertension, 41

Renal diseases
hyperlipoproteinemia, 28
triglyceride measurement, 38

Renovascular hypertension, 41

Reoperation, incidence, 227

Reperfusion
CK-MB analysis, 159, 162
early spontaneous, 184

Response to injury theory, 152

Rest angina, 134
platelet aggregation, 178

Restenosis
after PTCA, 148-149, 205
omega-3 fatty acids, 37

Restriction fragment length polymorphism (RFLP) mapping, 13

Rethrombosis, 168

Retinalis, triglyceride measurement, 38

Reverse transport of cholesterol, 25

Right-sided heart failure and septal rupture, 181

Right ventricular failure, 173

Right ventricular infarction, 154
assessment, 118, 163-164
ECG pattern, 157
jugular venous pressure, 95

Risk factors
cholesterol levels, 34-36
hypertriglyceridemia, 32
hypothesis, 9
minor factors, 45
pathogenetic processes, 71-73
secondary factors, 42-45

Risk stratification postinfarction, 186

RP-30 scintigraphy, 188

r-TPA. *See* Recombinant tissue plasminogen activator

Rubidium 82 emission tomography, 121-122

S

Salt restriction, 41

Saphenous-vein bypass graft, 194-195, 227

Sarcomeres, 174

Saturated fat, 36-37

Scavenger cells, 65

Scavenger receptor, 23-24
oxidized LDL, 43, 82
structure, 24

Scintigraphy, 163, 164

Sensitivity of tests, 96-97, 102, 104

Serotonin, 153, 190

Serum sickness
endothelial injury, 64
hyperlipidemia, 75

SGOT. *See* Aspartate aminotransferase

SGPT. *See* Alanine aminotransferase

Silent ischemia, 93, 135-136

Simvastatin, 30, 31

Single photon emission computed tomography (SPECT)
coronary heart disease diagnosis, 120
infarct size estimates, 164

Sinking pre-β lipoprotein, 13

Sinoatrial node and calcium antagonists, 143, 145

Sinus bradycardia in acute infarction, 172-173

Sinus tachycardia in acute infarction, 173

Sites of predilection, 73-74

SLE. *See* Systemic lupus erythematosus

Small, dense LDL particles, 25
disease associations, 26
hyperinsulinemia and, 42

Small-vessel constriction, 134-135

Smooth muscle cells
contractile vs. synthetic forms, 67-68
hypertension, 40
lipid accumulation, 65
mitogenic and cytostatic factors, 81
phenotypic modulation, 51, 56, 66-69
proliferation, 61, 63, 152-153

Socioeconomic level as risk factor, 44

Sodium-lithium abnormalities, 39

Somatic mutation, 67

Specificity of tests, 96-97, 102, 104

SPECT. *See* Single photon emission computed tomography

ST and ST-T segment
acute infarction, 157
angina, 102-104
nitroglycerin, 170
postinfarction assessment, 188

Starling's curve, 174-175

Stents, 149

Step One and Step Two Diets, 36-37

Streptokinase, 167-169

Stress echocardiography, 113

Stress modification, 41

Stress test postinfarction, 186-188. *See also* Exercise test**??**

Subendocardial infarction, 155

Sudden cardiac death and exercise, 44

Summation gallop, 181

Superoxides in atherogenesis, 80-83

Supraventricular arrhythmia cardiogenic shock treatment, 172-173

Surface receptors in atherogenesis, 66

Surgical treatment of coronary heart disease, 194-228
history, 194-195
indications, 204-205
survival rates, 226-227

Swan-Ganz catheter, 173, 175, 181, 182

Syndrome X
cholesterol transport, 25
clinical features, 26, 42
hyperinsulinemia, 42

Synthetic smooth muscle cell, 68

Systemic lupus erythematosus (SLE)
atherogenesis, 71, 76, 77
endothelial injury, 64
hyperlipoproteinemia, 28

Systemic vascular resistance, postinfarction calculations, 173

Systolic murmur in myocardial infarction, 156

T

T-wave abnormalities, 102

T1 and T2 relaxation times, 124

Tachycardia
    calcium antagonists and, 145
    postinfarction, 171-173

Tamponade, 163, 182

Tangier disease
    HDL deficiency, 19
    lipoprotein defects, 58

Technetium Tc 99m pyrophosphate scintigraphy
    cardiac function, 115-117
    infarct size estimates, 164
    myocardial infarction, 120, 163

Tests, predictive values, 96-97

Thallium-201 scintigraphy
    infarct size estimate, 164
    myocardial perfusion, 118-119, 163
    postinfarction assessment, 188

Thrombi, small mural, 69-71

Thrombolytic therapy, 167-169
    anticoagulation and, 174
    CK-MC analysis, 159, 162
    early reinfarction, 180
    infarct size, 165
    tachycardia, 172
    unstable angina, 190-191

Thrombomodulin, 82, 153

Thrombosis
    atherosclerotic plaques, 51, 55
    diagnosis, 111, 113, 114
    myocardial infarction, 153
    unstable angina, 190

Thrombospondin, 82

Thromboxane, 80, 153, 190

Tietze's syndrome, 92

Timolol, 169, 188, 189

Tissue factor, 82

Tissue plasminogen activator (TPA), 153, 168

Tolerance to nitrates, 140

Trace metals and coronary heart disease risk, 45

Tranquilizers in acute infarction, 166

Transcatheter coronary artery recanalization, 148-151

Transcytosis, 62

Transesophageal imaging, 113

Transmural infarction, 155

Transplant rejection and endothelial injury, 64

Transport vesicles, 61, 62

Triglyceride. *See also* Hypertriglyceridemia
    HDL levels and, 26, 38
    hyperinsulinemia, 42
    measurement, 34, 38-39
    transport, 23

Two-out-of-three criteria for myocardial infarction, 156

Type A and type B behavior, 44

Type I-type V hyperlipoproteinemias, 28

Type V hyperlipidemia and diabetes, 43

U

Unstable angina, 93, 112

Uremia, 64, 78

Urokinase, 167

V

Variable threshold angina, 135, 146

Variant angina. *See* Prinzmetal's angina

Vascular spasm, 132

Vascular tone and atherosclerosis, 40

Vasoconstricting agents in cardiac failure, 176

Vasoconstricting factors, 153

Vasodilating agents in cardiac failure, 176

Vasodilating factors, 153

Ventricular arrhythmia, 166, 171-172, 177

Ventricular fibrillation, 172

Ventricular septal defects
    diagnosis, 111, 113, 163, 173
    surgical treatment, 204

Ventricular septal rupture, 180-181

Ventricular shunts
    diagnosis, 163
    surgical treatment, 204, 227

Ventriculography, 111, 182

Verapamil, 143-145, 170

Very-low-density lipoproteins (VLDL)
    atherogenesis, 56, 60
    hyperinsulinemia, 42
    hypertriglyceridemia, 32-33
    lipid transport, 23
    structure, 11-12

Vineberg procedure, 195

Viremias and endothelial injury, 64

Viruses in atherosclerotic plaques, 67, 78

Vital signs in acute infarction, 173-174

von Bejold-Jarish reflex, 156

von Willebrand factor, 82

von Willebrand's disease, 79-80

W

Wall motion abnormalities, 113

Warning arrhythmia, 171

Watanabe heritable hyperlipidemic (WHHL) rabbit, 82

Weight reduction, 41, 43

WHO classification of myocardial infarction, 156

X

Xanthomas, triglyceride measurement, 38

Z

Zinc excess and coronary heart disease risk, 45